ARMINIUS

Qui nunc per altas aurei cæli domos
Regnat beatus, et suo junctus Deo
Humana celsus spernit ac nescit simul.
Sic, Hospes, ora magnus ARMINIUS tulit.
Cælare mores atque dotes ingeni,
Doctumque pectus quod fuit (sed heu Fuit)
Manus nequivit artifex, et quid manus ?
Efferre cum non lingua non stylus queant.

L. REAEL.

Jacobus Arminius. Posthumous engraving by J. G. Schmidt, with poem
by Laurens Laurensz. Reael.

*Reproduced by permission of the Academisch Historisch Museum, University of
Leiden*

ARMINIUS

A Study in the Dutch Reformation

CARL BANGS

Nashville—ABINGDON PRESS—New York

ARMINIUS

ISBN 0-687-01744-0

Library of Congress Catalog Card Number: 78-148078

The author's quotations from Scripture are, unless otherwise
noted, from the Revised Standard Version of the Bible.

SET UP, PRINTED, AND BOUND BY THE
PARTHENON PRESS, AT NASHVILLE,
TENNESSEE, UNITED STATES OF AMERICA

To Marjorie

ACKNOWLEDGMENTS

Many institutions and individuals have provided valuable resources for this study, including the University of Chicago, the University of Illinois, Yale University, the Newberry Library, the Huntington Library, the Bethel College Historical Library, the Library of the British Museum, the Bodleian Library at Oxford, Cambridge University, Glasgow University, Edinburgh University, the Bibliothèque Nationale, and the University of Geneva. In the Netherlands extensive use was made of resources at the University of Leiden, with valuable assistance received also from the University of Amsterdam, the City Library of Rotterdam, the Royal Library in The Hague, the Central Bureau for Genealogy, the Iconographical Bureau, the National Archives in The Hague and in Utrecht, and the Municipal Archives in Amsterdam, Leiden, Utrecht, Oudewater, and Dordrecht. These institutions have generously permitted photo-duplication of books and manuscripts when requested. Mr. W. F. van Limborch van der Meersch and Mr. Menso Pynappel have made their family archives available to me.

The late President H. Orton Wiley of Pasadena College introduced me to the writings of Jacobus Arminius in the academic year 1942-43, and in many ways this book is an extension of his interests. Professor Jaroslav J. Pelikan encouraged and guided me in the writing of a Ph.D. thesis on Arminius at the University of Chicago. Professor G. J. Hoenderdaal, Remonstrant Professor of Theology at the University of Leiden, has now for many years generously shared with me his books and his knowledge of Arminius. His professional courtesy and personal friendship are highly appreciated. Mr. B. N. Leverland and his colleagues at the Leiden archives and Dr. S. Hart, Dr. W. J. van Hoboken, and Mr. S. A. C. Dudok van Heel of the Amsterdam archives and their colleagues have been especially helpful. Mr. J. H. van den Hoek Ostende, also of the Amsterdam archives, has graciously read portions of the manuscript for this book and has made valuable corrections and suggestions. Mr. J. G. Kam of Amsterdam took it upon himself to discover Arminius' place of residence in Amsterdam, no small task. Dr. R. B. Evenhuis made the geographical setting of Amsterdam come alive as he guided me to sites of historical importance. No one knows Amsterdam church history better than he. Mr. Johan Schouten knows Oudewater, and he put his time and knowledge at my disposal most generously. My son, Jeremy D. Bangs, has assisted me with archival research and with the collecting and identifying of engravings from the period under study. To all these scholars I offer thanks, imputing to them none of the defects of the book.

The Remonstrant Brotherhood must be mentioned. The late Professor G. J. Heering corresponded with me when I hardly knew what questions to ask, and the Reverend W. R. M. Noordhoff also sent me information in those early years. Professor L. J. van Holk and Dr. Jan van Goudoever arranged for me to find needed materials on my first visit to Holland in 1956. The Remonstrants brought me to Amsterdam in 1960 to participate in the Arminius Symposium, and they have often been "the people of God" for me in Holland. I shall long remember their kindness at their 350th anniversary ministers' conference in the Loevestein Castle in 1969.

Financial assistance has come from several quarters. A church school class in Chicago, Illinois, led by Dr. F. M. Whitsell, with assistance from Dr. P. R. Carlson and the late Mr. Ernest R. Friesen, provided the grant which first enabled me to do research in Europe. The late Mrs. Elva Needles was most helpful during the early stages of the research. More recent research has been greatly facilitated by the generous sabbatical policies and secretarial services of Saint Paul School of Theology Methodist under President Don W. Holter. The Kansas City Regional Council for Higher Education provided two grants, one for the purchase of a microfilm reader, the other for the purchase of books. I am especially grateful to the United States Educational Foundation in the Netherlands, Mrs. M. S. van Doorne, Director, for a Fulbright grant in 1968-69, and to the University of Leiden and its Theological Faculty with Dr. H. J. Heering as Dean, who invited me to serve as Guest Professor of Theology that year. There was no small personal gratification in serving in the same institution, of walking through the same doors, where Arminius served and walked.

Mrs. Mary Jo Kingsbury has faithfully typed the manuscript for the book. Her skill, patience, and cheerfulness have made my task lighter.

Finally, my own family has underwritten the task with long-suffering love and loyalty. My sons, Carl and Jeremy; my daughter, Jeanne; and my wife, Marjorie, have contributed more than they can know.

CONTENTS

Part III. Professor

Illustrations

Front endpaper: Map of the Dutch Republic, showing the synodical boundaries of the Dutch Reformed Church, by W. A. Bachiene, Amsterdam, 1768. Reproduced by permission of the Library of the University of Leiden.

Back endpaper: Jacob van Werven's copy (1644) of the map of Leiden by Liefrinck (1574-76). Reproduced by permission of the City Archives, Leiden.

ABBREVIATIONS

ACA	*Acta Classis Amsterdam*
APPS	Reitsma and van Veen, *Acta der Provinciale en Particuliere Synoden*
BWPGN	*Biographisch Woordenboek van Protestantsche Godgeleerden in Nederland*
DTB	*Doop-, Trouw- en Begraafregisters,* Amsterdam
Ep. Ecc.	*Praestantium ac eruditorum virorum epistolae ecclesiasticae et theologicae*
GA	J. ter Gouw, *Geschiedenis van Amsterdam*
GPCH	H. de Vries [de Heekelingen], *Genève: Pépinière du Calvinisme Hollandaise*
HRN	Gerard Brandt, *Historie der Reformatie*
KH	Johannes Uitenbogaert, *De Kerckelicke Historie*
LA	Caspar Brandt, *The Life of James Arminius, D.D.* American edition, 1857
ODWA	R. B. Evenhuis, *Ook Dat Was Amsterdam*
Opera	Arminius, *Opera theologica.* 2nd edition, 1631
Prot	*Protocollen der Kerkeraad Amsterdam*
VA	J. E. Elias, *De Vroedschap van Amsterdam*
VOC	Dutch East India Company
WA	*The Works of James Arminius, D.D.* London edition of 1825, 1828, and 1875
Writings	*The Works of James Arminius, D.D.* American edition of 1956

CHRONOLOGY

1520 Sacramentist activity begins in Holland.

1530 The Edict of Blood. Anabaptism reaches Amsterdam.

1535 Fall of the radical Kingdom of Münster.

1536 Menno Simons becomes an Anabaptist. Death of Erasmus. Calvin's *Institutes*.

1540 Non-Anabaptist Protestant activity begins to appear.

1546 Death of Luther.

1549 Allegiance given to Philip II. The Pragmatic Sanction.

1550 ff. Schoutists and Dirkists in controversy in Amsterdam. Reformed activity in Antwerp. Dutch refugees hold Reformed worship at Austin Friars, London. Mennonites weakened through persecution and internal division.

c. 1559 Birth of Arminius and death of his father.

1559 Margaret of Parma becomes regent.

1560 Death of Melanchthon.

1561 Colloquy of Poissy. Underground Reformed activity in southern provinces. Belgic Confession first printed.

1563 Heidelberg Catechism. Thirty-nine Articles.

1564 Schoutists present protest (*doleantie*) at Brussels. Death of Calvin.

1566 Local nobility resist Spain, are termed "Beggars." Popular uprisings, iconoclastic riots. Field preaching outside Amsterdam. First Protestant Communion service in Amsterdam.

1567 Duke of Alva attempts to suppress dissent. Amsterdam merchant-reformers flee to Emden. William of Orange draws closer to Protestants.

1568 Synod of Wesel.

1571 Synod of Emden.

1572 Sea Beggars capture Brielle and inland towns, including Oudewater and Leiden. Insurgent States of Holland meet at Dordrecht.

Preaching against predestination at Rotterdam and Hoorn. Coornhert attacks it. Arminius begins studies at Utrecht about this time.

1573   Alva flees Amsterdam, is replaced by Don Luis Requesens. Sea Beggars defeat Spanish fleet under Boisot.

1574   Synod of Dordrecht sets up Reformed churches in all Protestant towns. The siege and relief of Leiden.

1575   Rudolphus Snellius takes Arminius to Marburg. University of Leiden established. Arminius' family killed in massacre of Oudewater. He travels to Oudewater, returns to Marburg.

1576   Arminius goes to Rotterdam, then enrolls at Leiden. Requesens replaced by Don Juan. The Pacification of Ghent.

1578   The Alteration of Amsterdam. Don Juan dies, replaced by Alexander of Parma.

1579   Union of Utrecht.

1581   Synod of Middelburg, views of Coolhaes condemned. Merchants' Guild of Amsterdam underwrites Arminius' studies at Geneva.

1582   Arminius matriculates at Geneva.

1583   Arminius goes to Basel.

1584   Arminius returns to Geneva. Assassination of William of Orange.

1585   Arminius makes trip to Zurich. Earl of Leicester made Governor-General.

1586   Arminius leaves Geneva, makes trip to Italy. Synod at The Hague, dominated by Leicester, adopts Genevan church polity.

1587   Arminius reports to Amsterdam for pastoral service.

1588   Arminius ordained. Defeat of Spanish Armada. Leicester resigns. Maurice made Stadtholder. Magistrates set aside Leicester's church polity.

1590   Seminary [*Statencollege*] founded at Leiden to combat Jesuits. Arminius marries Lijsbet Reael. Differences between Arminius and the consistory.

1591   Arminius member of commission to draw up new church order.

1592   Amsterdam burgomasters intervene in dispute between Arminius and the consistory. States General publish Plancius' map of the world. Plancius and three merchants lay plans for East Indian trade.

1593   Further disputes in Amsterdam consistory come to an end.

1594   Arminius draws up new model for Amsterdam schools. Moucheron attempts northern route to the Indies.

1595   Dutch ships under Houtman set out around Africa for the Indies.

1596   Snecanus issues his introduction to Romans 9.

1597   Houtman's expedition returns. C. P. Hooft gives speeches on toleration.

1598   Vogelsangh banished. Oliver van Noort launches first Dutch expedition around the world.

1599   Arminius assigned the writing of a refutation of the Anabaptists.

1601   Death of Laurens Jacobsz. Reael at Middelburg. The plague strikes Holland.

1602   Charter of the Dutch East India Company signed. First expedition sets out. Deaths of Trelcatius and Junius at Leiden.

1603   Arminius appointed professor of theology at Leiden and made doctor of theology. Second VOC expedition sails.

1604   Arminius presents theses on predestination. Gomarus counterattacks.

1605   Arminius is *Rector Magnificus* of university. Leiden theological teachers disclaim any fundamental disagreements. Arminius issues answers to "Nine Questions." Third VOC expedition sails.

1606   Arminius' rectoral address on reconciling religious dissentions. States General call for a national synod "to revise the Confession and Catechism." Fourth VOC expedition sails, second expedition returns.

1607   Stealthy beginnings of truce negotiations. Proposed truce condemned in Amsterdam. Jacob van Heemskerck destroys Spanish fleet off Gibraltar, just after eight-months' truce is signed. First VOC expedition returns. Preparatory Convention (for national synod) meets at The Hague. Gouda Catechism published.

1608   Spanish envoys arrive to negotiate new truce. Popular hysteria over truce, Arminius accused of Roman Catholic sympathies. Arminius and Gomarus are summoned to present views before the High Court. Arminius writes two apologies and delivers his *Declaration of Sentiments* before the States of Holland and West Friesland. The States ask the clergy to submit their objections to the Confession and Catechism. Gomarus addresses the States.

1609   Arminius seriously ill in February. Twelve years' truce signed. Conference at The Hague between Arminius, Gomarus, and their deputies. Arminius leaves because of illness. Death of Arminius, October 19.

PREFACE

JACOBUS ARMINIUS was a Dutch Reformed minister and theological professor in the late sixteenth and early seventeenth centuries. His career was not unlike many others of his time—student years under the principal theologians of the time, service as a pastor, the final years as a teacher of young ministers. He could have passed unnoticed and have been soon forgotten. Tranquillity, however, was not his lot in life, nor obscurity his lot in death. During his last six years he became the focal point of Dutch national life. Around him raged not only the debates of the theologians but also the national issues of foreign policy, war and peace, world trade, and the relation of church and state. After his death, for some three centuries, it often seemed that all non-Lutheran Protestantism was divided between Arminians and Calvinists. In England they were the "prelatists" and the "puritans." Early Methodism came in both Arminian and Calvinist styles. American church history saw prolonged and bitter debates between the two parties. In Holland itself the Remonstrants carried on an Arminian tradition of religious toleration in the face of traditional Calvinism.

Today, even where the labels are forgotten, these divisions of the past can be detected in subtle habits of the theological mind. Twentieth-century debates between Anglo-Catholic and Evangelical, between Methodist and Baptist, or between Liberal and Neo-orthodox have not been without echoes of the early seventeenth century, when Arminius and Gomarus debated the issues of grace, free will, and predestination along the Rapenburg in Leiden. The revival of Reformation theology after World War I explicitly raised many of the old issues, with some of the old language. The historical research which accompanied that movement rediscovered Luther and Calvin and their friends, and a later wave of research brought the Radicals to light. Arminius, who was also one of the Reformers, has not been made available to us. This book is an attempt to bring balance to

17

Reformation research by presenting him again to the modern theological world which has so often felt his influence.

It can be expected that estimates of Arminius and his followers have varied with the sympathies of the observers. One nineteenth-centry writer saw him as the greatest of the church's three great theologians. Athanasius understood God, he said; Augustine understood man; Arminius understood the relationship between God and man. But such Hegelian omniscience is not without its challengers. An English Calvinist who knew-how to make it hurt put it succinctly: Arminianism is the religion of common sense; Calvinism is the religion of St. Paul.

We may expect the truth not to be so neat. Getting at the truth has not been easy. The last edition of the collected *Opera* was in 1635. In Dutch the situation is worse: only a small part of his works ever appeared in Dutch, and none since 1617, except his *Declaration of Sentiments,* reissued in the old Dutch in 1960. He has been more accessible in English, especially since an old edition of the *Works* was reprinted in 1956. So far as I know, there is nothing in German, nothing in French.

To many who have read him in any of the three languages, however, he is an enigma. Some Calvinists, finding that his writings do not produce the heresies they expected, have charged him with teaching secret heresy, unpublished. Many Arminians, finding him too Calvinistic, have written him off as a transitional thinker, a "forerunner" of somebody or other—Simon Episcopius, Philip van Limborch, or John Wesley.

The problem for the English-speaking world is the difficulty of entering into that Dutch world in which Arminius lived. It is not readily available to us. Where can we turn to find an accurate, comprehensive account of the Dutch Reformation? Or, for that matter, a biography of Arminius?

There have been only two full-scale attempts to tell the history of Arminius. The first was by the Dutch Remonstrant writer Caspar Brandt. He finished it at about the beginning of the eighteeth century, but it was not published until 1724 and 1725, in Latin. An English translation appeared in England in 1854 and in the United States in 1857. It is very difficult to obtain. Almost all articles on Arminius in English are heavily dependent on the solid but very incomplete work of Caspar Brandt.

The second biography of Arminius was written by J. H. Maronier in 1905. It adds very little to Brandt's sparse coverage of Arminius' early life up to 1603, when he became a professor at Leiden, but it has some excellent material on his professorial years. Maronier draws heavily on letters of Arminius published late in the seventeenth century. But his book is in Dutch, shut off, like so much Dutch scholarship, from the English-speaking public.

Arminius has remained, then, a shadowy figure, or a digit: something which must be placed in the equation, but not the object of separate attention. This book accepts the task of focusing on Arminius, not as a hero, not as a heretic, and not as a forerunner. And not as a digit. That has been a problem: to discover the *man*. Arminius too often comes through as a theological machine, the producer of ideas, with almost nothing about his youth, his father and mother, his brothers and sisters, his intimate friends and associates, his wife and his children. How did he understand himself? What were his values, his failures, his frustrations, his joys?

Arminius himself is partly to blame for this. The greater part of the extant letters consists of theological treatises, with maybe a word of personal greetings at the end. One seizes on every personal word. Only toward the last, when illness and trouble pile up, does he allow himself to talk rather extensively about his feelings. He is not like Luther, telling everything. It has been necessary, then, to study the setting, the circumstances, his friends—anything to get a clue as to what was going on. This effort has been made with particular vigor for his early life, where so little has been known. For his later life there is much more evidence. The early part of the book, then, may appear inflated as it grasps at every straw of evidence, attempting in many cases reasonable conjectures where hard evidence is lacking. For his later life, the situation is relatively different, and the reader is begged to believe that a great deal of condensation has taken place.

It is not a biography in any narrow sense. Amsterdam was too intriguing; there is really a short history of Amsterdam in this book. I started out to study Arminius and fell in love with his *alma mater*. That may be admitted but also defended. Arminius was the first Dutch pastor of the Dutch Reformed Church of the greatest Dutch city, just when it was emerging out of its medieval past and bursting into its Golden Age. His relationship to Amsterdam began only three years after its Reformation. How can one understand Arminius without understanding the Dutch Reformation and without understanding Amsterdam? And where, in English, can one learn about Amsterdam? So Amsterdam is here, the Venice of the North, New Antwerp, the city on pilings, with its story of pride and persecution, faith and fanaticism, intrigue, dreams, and heroism. Beware lest you too fall in love with the simple, crusty, doughty Old Beggars of 1566. They contributed a great deal to Arminius: money for his studies, counsel, a place to preach, political protection, and, not least, Lijsbet.

For Arminius, however, Leiden was really there first. Amsterdam runs wide open, brash, vigorous, growing. Leiden runs deep. It had suffered and endured in the terrible siege of 1574. The legend is that citizens of Leiden might have had as reward exemption from taxes, and they chose a university. So Leiden is in the book, and its university, now almost four hundred years old. Arminius was the twelfth student, the second doctor, a professor. He died there, just across the parking lot from the Pieterskerk, only it was the churchyard then. When it comes to cities, one may be permitted to love more than one. Leiden is beloved.

To include all these things has created technical difficulties of the first order. Many Dutch words cannot be translated into English, for they refer to a way of life and an organization of society unique to that country. That is why they are sometimes retained in Dutch. The reader will come to feel their meaning. The problem of names is enormous. The story covers just that period when the old patronymics began to disappear, to be replaced by surnames. Spelling was a chancy thing. Some people spelled their own names several different ways. So there is no "correct" spelling, sometimes not any one correct name. Lijsbet is known in some English texts as Elizabeth Real. She signed her name Lijsbet Louwerensdoch.

What system of nomenclature is adopted here? Very little. Some names, well known in English, are anglicized. For Amsterdam names, the spellings used by J. E. Elias in his great study of the Amsterdam city council are adopted. The reader might as well learn the Dutch spellings, or he will not know how to look up these names in the indexes of books in Dutch. And since for the vast majority of the persons in this book there is no standard English spelling, as we have for Calvin and Beza, for example, there will be no loss.

It was hard to begin the story. An early draft started with the fourteenth century. The story of the Reformation is deeply grounded in the "forerunners," as Professor Heiko Oberman has shown. The story in the Low Countries is difficult to condense, for many of the forerunners were there—Gerard Groot and the Brethren of the Common Life, Florentius Radewijns and the Canons of Windesheim, Thomas à Kempis, and the humanists. Rudolph Agricola, Alexander Hegius, and Wessel Gansfoort introduced classical learning into the land, and it often merged with the biblical piety of the Brethren and Canons. Desiderius Erasmus "of Rotterdam" was there, looming large on the Dutch spiritual and intellectual landscape in spite of his frequent disdain for the land of his birth. This book attempts no theories about Erasmus' influence in Holland, or on Arminius, not because the matter hasn't been studied but because evidence is hard to come by.

The Reformation itself came to the northern Netherlands in three stages. Around 1520 there were the Sacramentarians (so-called because they said that the Lord's Supper is "only a sacrament"). It is a loose designation for a lot of people who preached against abuses in the church. Some of them had heard of Luther; others simply objected to what they saw around them. There was Wouter, in Utrecht, and John Sartorius, Cornelius Hoen, John Pistorius, and William Gnapheus (I am spelling in English now), and they had followers, who suffered with them, for it was a dangerous business. Pistorius taught that the decrees and canons of the church are not to be taken lightly; they are to be honored "so far as they agree with the word of God." Arminius was in this sturdy tradition. Hinne Rode was one of them, who taught Zwingli to say "this signifies." When a Sacramentist disciple, the widow Weynken Claesdochter, was offered the oil of unction before her execution, her refusal was curt: "Oil is good for salad or for oiling your shoes."

The Sacramentists gave way to the Anabaptists—probably many of them became Anabaptists in the 1530s. Their "heresy" had come down out of Zurich, where Zwingli finally rejected their radicalism, with a vengeance. But the common people and some of the magistrates in Holland heard them gladly. They radicalized in 1535, trying to set up a kingdom in Münster by force, and the force overwhelmed them. A Frisian priest, Menno Simons, became their shepherd, teaching them the old Dutch biblical piety and the ways of peace. But peace they would not know, for they were hunted by the Catholics and harried by the Protestants. Then they hunted and harried each other, shunning, banning, and excommunicating, until they fractured themselves into impotence by mid-century.

That is where the Reformed come in, but no one knows yet just how that happened. There are all kinds of theories: the organizational genius of the Calvinists, the wedding of a sense of divine destiny with a sense of national destiny. Here the history books tend to jump: Calvinism came in, Arminius nearly ruined it, the Synod of Dort restored it. This book is dedicated to the proposition that it isn't as simple as that.

The earliest Dutch Reformed leaders don't seem to be Calvinists at all. They rise out of the soil, here and there, nurtured by the old Dutch biblical piety, not seized by dogmatic insights but steadily pressing toward a purified life of faith according to Scripture. A priest in Garderen, in the Veluwe, began preaching the Reformation in his church. He was pressured into recanting and sent to Louvain. He fled again to Marburg, but the Protestants there were not sure that they could trust him. He wrote his confession, Melanchthon liked it, it was published as *The Layman's Guide,* and along with Bullinger's *Housebook* it became one

21

of the chief means of instructing the Dutch people in the new faith. That was in 1555, before Arminius was born.

In the *Guide* Anastasius Veluanus rejected the predestination theory that was already blowing down off the Alps. Specifically, he denied any distinction between God's secret will and God's revealed will. When God says he wants all men to be saved, he means it, both secretly and openly. Veluanus also affirmed that God's promise of salvation is coextensive with his command to repent and believe. When God calls a man, it is a "serious call." God means it seriously. Arminius would make precisely these two points forty years later, and be accused of being an innovator! When it came to predestination Veluanus said, "Here we must hold with the primitive Christians, that God has eternally decreed within himself to help and save by his Holy Spirit such persons who use all possible means to be instructed, and continue obedient when they are called, and in like manner to strengthen and confirm others in the way of salvation who earnestly beg it of him." Arminius would find this wording a bit sloppy, and he would express himself much more carefully, but there is a firm line of continuity between Veluanus and Arminius.

Veluanus was not alone. The Dutch people read his book, and Bullinger's, and learned their lessons well. Already, every Dutchman was a theologian. Through their magistrates they provided firm support for the others—Gerard Blokhoven and Tako Sybrants in Utrecht, Cornelis Wiggerts in Hoorn, Gellius Snecanus in Friesland, Hermannus Herberts in Gouda, Jan Ysbrandts in Rotterdam, and Caspar Coolhaes in Leiden. H. C. Rogge has called Coolhaes the "forerunner of Arminius." Arminius had many others. He himself regarded the Dutch church itself as his forerunner.

The plot thickens when Calvinist clergy, and their people, fled north from the southern provinces, driven out by Spain and the Catholics. They brought with them their energy, their money, their talents, their trade connections, and a new brand of Calvinism, precise and intolerant. Then, as the Remonstrant historian Gerard Brandt put it, the term "Reformed" came to have two meanings, one for the old Hollanders, another for the new preachers. But that is getting ahead of the story for now.

In this draft of the story, then, the reader will not have to go back to the fourteenth century. He may begin where Arminius began, in the town of Oudewater, and see how it looked from there.

PART I
STUDENT

1

BIRTH AND BOYHOOD

BEFORE RESULTS of research into the birth and family of Arminius are presented, it will be useful to review the traditional reports. He was born, so it is usually said, on October 10, 1560, in Oudewater, a town on the river IJssel in Holland about twelve miles toward Rotterdam from Utrecht. His name was Jacob Harmensz., the patronymic being the customary foreshortening of Harmenszoon, or Herman's son. His father, a cutler named Harmen Jacobsz., of whose ancestry nothing is reported, is said to have died when Arminius was very young. Arminius' mother was Engeltje (latinizers put it "Angelica") Jacobsdr. from Dordrecht. Her patronymic is the short form of Jacobsdochter, or Jacob's daughter. His parents are described as being "of the middle rank of life." Upon the death of Harmen Jacobsz., Engeltje was left in reduced circumstances and with the care of several children. She and all the siblings of Arminius were murdered in the massacre of Oudewater in 1575. Arminius himself was under the care and tutelage of a series of friends. Later, according to the custom of scholars of that time, he latinized his name Jacob Harmensz. to Jacobus Arminius, Arminius being the name of a first-century Germanic chieftain remembered for having resisted the Romans.

The literary sources for this traditional account are the funeral oration delivered after the burial of Arminius by a Leiden teacher, Petrus Bertius (the younger), in 1609,[1] and a biography of Arminius, heavily dependent on Bertius, written in the late seventeenth century by the Remonstrant Caspar Brandt.[2] These are almost the sole sources for what has subsequently been written about the origins and early life of Arminius, and, for that matter, about his later life as well. It is necessary to call this tradition in question and to attempt to supplement its meager content.

The place of birth, the name of Arminius' father, and the death of

---

[1] *Petri Bertii Liick-Oratie over de Dood vanden Heere Iacobus Arminius.* The English translation of Bertius' oration by James Nichols in *WA*, I, 13-47, will be cited throughout this book.

[2] *Historia vita I. Arminii.* The English translation by John Guthrie, *LA*, will be cited from the American edition.

remaining members of his family in the massacre of Oudewater in 1575 seem to be accurate. As for the rest, either verification is difficult or contrary evidence exists. Arminius' father appears in a number of archival remains from Oudewater. It is a common name, but it is never duplicated in any one document and it is identifiable often enough so that it may be safely concluded that the same person is designated in the several occurrences of his name. On the night watch list for 1542, for instance, he appears in the seventeenth position in section A.[3] He is listed in the Tenth Penny tax records for 1547 and again in 1553, where it appears that he owns a house which is separate from the place of business where he probably also lived.[4] In 1558, however, he does not appear in the Tenth Penny records. Instead, there is the name of "Elborch Harmen Jacobss wed.*" or Elborch the widow of Harmen Jacobsz.[5] Her name appears also in the tax records of 1561 and 1562.[6]

From this it must be concluded that the death of Arminius' father occurred between 1553 and 1558, and that Arminius could not have been born later than 1559. The date of 1559 is probable on two counts. First, it is nearest the popularly reported date of 1560, and, second, there is a tradition in records kept by certain descendants of Arminius that he was born in 1559.[7] As for the day of October 10, I find no justification for holding to it. It appears only in late secondary sources, for what reason I know not.

Arminius' mother appears in the archives as Elborch. Why do all other accounts list her as Engeltje? Perhaps it was supposed that Arminius' oldest daughter, Engeltje, had been named for his mother. Indeed, she could have been, but with a change to a name similar to Elborch, similar but not identical, for the name Elborch had gone into disuse with the advent of Protestantism. The evidence seems clear, in any case, that Arminius' mother was Elborch, and there is no reason to question the patronymic of Jacobsdr. No evidence has been found in the archives of either Oudewater or Dordrecht to confirm or deny the latter as her birthplace. Of her ancestry nothing is known.

It is misleading to speak of Arminius' father as a cutler. The old Dutch term in the Oudewater archives is *messemaker,* or knifemaker, but even that must be understood in the broader sense of *wapensmid,* or

---

[3] Archief Gemeente Oudewater.

[4] Oudewater tax records, Staatsarchief, The Hague, I, 340, fol. iii; I, 743, fol. ix verse, fol. x.

[5] *Ibid.,* I, 1070, fol. x verso.

[6] *Ibid.,* I, 1521, fol. xviii verso; I, 1393, fol. xxvii.

[7] There is such evidence in a letter of March 15, 1939, from Abraham van der Hoeven to Rudolf Mees, a copy of which is in the possession of Mr. Menso Pynappel (a descendant of Arminius) of Englewood, New Jersey.

armorer, a smith who makes swords and armor and possibly guns. The *wapensmid* was an important person in a town of that era, especially a town of the stature and military significance of Oudewater, which had enjoyed the privileges of town status since 1265 and which was often involved in border wars during the period of the struggle for independence from Spain. The armorer usually had a *meesterknecht,* or foreman, and in the case of Harmen Jacobsz. it is possible that it was Willem Huichsz. (or Huijgensz.), a man prominent in Oudewater life. Huichsz. was one of those who went with a contingent from nearby Gouda to raise the Spanish siege of Haarlem in 1574.[8] The night watch list of 1542 lists in section M a *Huijch die messemaker,* who could have been the father of Willem Huichsz.[9] It is also possible, as van der Capellen portrays it, that Huichsz. carried on the family business after the death of Arminius' father. These are conjectures, but within the range of possibility.

What of Arminius' father's ancestry? There are some clues. From memoirs written by Arminius' son Daniel Arminius (the latinized patronymic became a surname with his generation) we know that Arminius had a great-uncle called the "Heer Jan Claesz. van Leiden." This great-uncle was buried in the church in Oudewater under a gravestone bearing his coat of arms of three post horns.[10] This clue is especially important in view of the fact that Arminius also used the coat of arms of three post horns. His signet ring may still be seen in the Historical Museum in Rotterdam.

But who was Heer Jan Claesz. van Leiden, and what were the family connections? The title *heer* could indicate membership in a noble family, it could designate a Roman Catholic priest, or it could mean both. There was such a priest, a Heer Jan Claesz. van Leiden in Amsterdam in the middle of the sixteenth century, but his identity as a great-uncle of Arminius cannot be established.[11] The name also occurs in the Oudewater archives in a list of those who had made advance payments of their

---

[8] The story is told by Pieter Bor Christiansz., *Oorsprongk, Begin en Vervolgh der Nederlandsche Oorlogen, 1555-1600,* I, 644-47. The speculation that Willem Huichsz. might have been Harmen Jacobsz.'s foreman is put forth in a nineteenth-century romantic novel about the massacre of Oudewater: J. van der Capellen, *Het Beleg en de Moord van Oudewater.*

[9] Archief Gemeente Oudewater.

[10] The memoirs of Daniel Arminius (1606-1649), the eleventh child of Arminius, were reported by a great-grandson of Arminius, Henrick Sorgh (or Sorch) (1666-1720), and included in an article by D. W. van Dam van Hekendorp, "Familie-aanteekeningen Rombouts, Arminius, Reael, e. a.." The reference to Heer Jan Claesz. van Leiden is on p. 310.

[11] He was buried in the Old Church on August 20, 1574, when Amsterdam was still Roman Catholic. DTB 1040/88.

death duties in 1556. The list includes "Heer Jan Claesz., pater van Sint Pauwels tot Amsterdam," [12] probably the same person who was buried in the Old Church there.

The name van Leiden itself is suggestive. In the case of Arminius' great-uncle it may mean nothing more than a place designation; that is, it may not be a family designation at all. On the other hand, there was an ancient and large family by that name, evidently the descendants of the burggraves (viscounts) of Leiden, the holders of the partly extant twelfth-century Leiden stronghold, Den Burcht. The family provided numerous priests and members of the town government, including a Jan Claesz. van Leiden who was a *schepen,* or judge, in 1495. It was a wealthy family, at least in its noble branches, and it established numerous vicaries in Leiden and in other parts of Holland. A vicary was an ecclesiastical endowment for the saying of Masses or for other pious works. At the Reformation they were often devoted to the education of future clergy or other public purposes, or in some cases they remained in the control of the heirs of the donors.

Arminius received the proceeds of one such vicary in Amsterdam to apply to the costs of his theological education; that story will be told later. But another curious scrap of evidence ties him to an inherited vicary. Daniel Arminius, in the aforementioned memoirs, tells more about his father's family. Arminius' father had two sisters, Geertje and Neeltje, and a brother, Jan. Jan Jacobsz. was a *tinnegieter,* or worker in pewter, in Dordrecht, and he had a son who was called Jacob de Wilde. Daniel Arminius reports that "Jacob de Wilde, now presently still living [the memoirs were written most likely around 1640], is a former Captain [of the Militia]." "This Jacob de Wilde," continues Daniel, "took a certain vicary away from my father with force, indeed, at knife point [*met geweld, ja met het mesjen afgedwongen*]." [13] The language might be literal, or it might be figurative. What is important is that a vicary was at stake. What was the source of the vicary? Was it an inheritance through some line of the van Leidens? Apart from further evidence, one can only speculate.

There is yet another clue, although it in itself leads to no certain conclusions. Arminius used a coat of arms of three post horns, and this may be assumed to have been inherited through his father's side. That coat of arms does not occur in the van Leiden family, at least in its main branches (and there is considerable confusion as to the limits and extent of that family). There was a noted sculptor, Nicolaas (Claes) Geertsoen

---

[12] The list is printed in A. C. van Aelst, *Schets der Stad Oudewater,* p. 265.
[13] *van Dam van Hekendorp,* p. 310.

(Gerhaert) van Leiden, who was born in Leiden and did important work in Trier, Strassburg, and Constance in the 1460s.[14] He died around 1473. His coat of arms was three post horns.[15] It is not known that he was from the noble van Leiden family, although such a connection is possible. His coat of arms does provide a presumptive link with the Heer Jan Claesz. van Leiden who was the great-uncle of Arminius, and with Arminius, too, who used the same insignia.

From our modern point of view, these questions seem scarcely worth exploring, but in the sixteenth century they were matters of considerable importance. It seems quite possible that Arminius did not come from an obscure family, and that may be one reason that he came to the attention of a series of benefactors who made sure that he had access to the best education available.

Some further information is available about the family of Arminius. His father's sister, Geertje Jacobsdr., married a stonecutter named Govert Dircksz. Steencop, and after his death she became, in 1596, the fifth and last wife of the Leiden theologian Johannes Cuchlinus. She thereby became the step-mother-in-law of the younger Petrus Bertius, who had married a daughter of Cuchlinus by an earlier marriage. Geertje outlived both her second husband and her nephew Arminius and spent her last years back in her native Oudewater, where she was named on the annual list of the survivors of the massacre of 1575 until 1621, when her death was reported.[16]

Arminius had older siblings, all of whom died in the Oudewater massacre. Bertius speaks first in his funeral oration of "three fatherless children" (including Arminius); later he says that Arminius mourned the loss of his mother, his sister, and his brother.[17] Gerard Brandt, who could have had independent access to sources, mentions the death of Arminius' sister, two brothers, "and other blood relatives." [18] Johannes Uitenbogaert, who knew Arminius intimately, speaks of "sisters and brothers." [19] These accounts cannot be harmonized by means of available evidence. In the Tenth Penny records for 1553, there is a "Jan Harmenss messemaecker," and in 1558 there is a "Dirck Harmenss" living in a house owned by Willem Huichsz.[20] These seem the likeliest names for older brothers of Arminius. No credence can be given at all to the names Andries and Reinera proposed by van der Capellen in his novel.

[14] van Gelder and Duverger, *Kunstgeschiedenis der Nederlanden,* I, 251.
[15] Index of coats of arms, Centraal Bureau voor Genealogie, The Hague.
[16] "Kuchlinus," *BWPGN,* V, 293; Archief Gemeente Oudewater, 97, 98.
[17] *WA,* I, 17, 19.
[18] *HRN,* I, 560.
[19] *KH,* Part III, p. 102.
[20] Oudewater tax records, Staatsarchief, The Hague, I, 1070, fol. x, verso.

There are very few direct reports of the boyhood of Arminius. Bertius reports that his father died when he was but an infant. From the Tenth Penny tax records it appears highly possible that his father died before he was born. According to the custom of the times there would have been a family celebration, the *kraammaal*, or lying-in feast. At the birth there would have been some female relatives present, and perhaps some neighbor women. Included would be the midwife, who also had the responsibility of bringing the child to baptism. Baptism would occur within a day or two after the birth. The first few months of life were spent wrapped to the chin in blankets and lying in a heavy wooden cradle. Early physical development was with the threefold aid of mother's apron strings, a toddler or go-car, and a *valhoed*, or padded cap for protection in falling. Later toys included hobby horses, longbows, dolls, toy instruments, miniature guns and cannons, and tops. There were numerous street games common among the children of the time—rolling hoops, blindman's buff, something called goat-goat-hold-still, and others.[21]

Oudewater was a typical Dutch town, and we may assume that its customs were similar to the general customs of the time. The death of Arminius' father left the family in some degree of hardship, however, and perhaps Arminius never knew a normal and carefree childhood. His mother was hard pressed to support her family. She and her children remained in the same house where Arminius was born and where his father had operated his smithy. In such cases it was customary for the foreman or *meesterknecht* to carry on the business for the widow; indeed, it was not uncommon for the foreman to marry the widow, although in this case that did not happen. It is likely, however, that there was a large household which included the foreman and perhaps some other relatives or laborers.

The town of Oudewater was an oblong diked and walled eminence along a bend of the IJssel, rising above the depressed fields like a fortified island. Its origin is lost in the dim past. The first historical records of its existence are from the first half of the thirteenth century. The meaning of the name is in doubt. It was long assumed that it meant what its spelling implies literally, *Oude Water*, or Old Water, referring to the river on which it is built. More recent writers find warrant for seeing the name as a popular corruption of *Oude Waerdt*, or Old Ward (district, polder). In earliest historical times it was politically a part of the Bishopric of Utrecht. Later it became a part of the lands of the Counts of Holland, a border post, by the way, which made it the scene of violence more than once. It is now in the province of South Holland.

[21] van Aelst, p. 512.

Along the river IJssel, on the west side of the town and towering over it, was the church with a tower and three parallel aisles or bays of equal height. The tower was built around 1300; the bays were completed in the fifteenth century. As with most Dutch churches, it had no crypt. The sandy floor was the town burial ground, and by the sixteenth century flat burial stones constituted the floor of the church.

It was in this church that Arminius was undoubtedly baptized, and here his relatives were buried. As late as the seventeenth century the gravestone of his great-uncle, the Heer Jan Claesz. van Leiden, was extant with its arms of three post horns. The stone is lost, but many of the ancient gravestones are scattered throughout present-day Oudewater, incorporated into stone walls of houses or turned upside down as door stoops. The church still stands, scarred by time and neglect but beautifully restored in the 1960s. Although none of the gravestones of Arminius' immediate family remain to be seen, the visitor will find in the choir the stone of Dirck (Theodorus) Willemsz. Tromper and his wife Margarita Arminia, who died in 1673 and 1676 respectively. Tromper was from an old Oudewater family and was the town secretary. His wife was the granddaughter of Arminius.

There were five town gates, a town hall, a hostel, three or four monastic houses, male and female, a jail in one of the gate towers, and a weigh house. In 1557 there were 352 houses occupied by their owners and 60 houses occupied by renters. It was a period of rapid growth, for by 1561-62 there were already 517 dwelling houses and 34 barns. The population would be somewhere near 2,000.[22]

A map of Oudewater from the middle of the sixteenth century can still be used for finding one's way in the center of the present town. The town was divided in four parts, the Leeuweringerdeel (*deel*=part or section), the Capellerdeel, the Wijdstraaterdeel, and the Gommigerdeel. The house in which Arminius was born (according to a very old local tradition) was in the Leeuweringerdeel, roughly the northeastern quarter of the town. The house faced the bridge called the Hallebrugge, where a part of the market was held, and was on the corner of the canalside street called the Hallebrugge Oostzijde (east side) and a small street or alley called the Gasthuisstraat (hostel street). The house was destroyed, at least partially, by the Spaniards in 1575 and rebuilt in 1601. It was restored in the 1960s, with a statue of Fortune, long kept in the Rijksmuseum in Amsterdam, brought back to its original place. It is a fine early example of the architecture of Holland's Golden Age. It is not the same building in which Arminius lived, but it probably maintains

[22] This and the following description of Oudewater is from van Aelst, p. 320 *et passim.*

considerable continuity of style and size with its predecessor. It would have been one of the principal houses in Oudewater. The smithy could have been on the first floor, with the family living on the upper floors, an arrangement still found in many small businesses in Holland. Behind the present house there is a sizable outbuilding of uncertain age. The building survived the destruction of Oudewater in 1575, and exists today quite unspoiled by renovation. It too could have housed the family business.

Across the Gasthuisstraat from Arminius' house was the weigh house, an important feature of Oudewater life in the sixteenth century. Its great pan scales were the scene of the weighing not only of all kinds of produce but also of people. In the great sixteenth-century witchcraft hysteria the Oudewater weigh house, for reasons which are unclear, became a place where persons accused of witchcraft were weighed. If an accused person weighed an appropriate amount for his age and size, it was adjudged that he was innocent of witchcraft. If his weight was supernatural, that is, abnormal, he was obviously in league with the evil powers. There were no standard weight tables; the judgment was the weigh master's, with concurrence of several other town officials. Money changed hands, of course, and many people were found innocent. By the time the fees had been paid to the town council, the secretary, the weigh master, the collector, and the midwife (*vroedvrouw*), the supplicant was relieved of six guilders and ten stuivers.

Why should Oudewater get all this traffic? One reasonable hypothesis is that the weigh master had a reputation for honesty. The Oudewater scales were, for instance, the standard by which the Gouda scales were to be tested. But where witchcraft is concerned, reasonable hypotheses are unnecessary.

Oudewater had received permission in 1394 to establish a school. The schoolmaster, or rector, as he was called, often performed a multiple role, sometimes serving also as *koster*, clerk, or town secretary. It was basically a Latin school, but a great deal of attention was given also to singing, the schoolboys serving in the church choir. There is in Oudewater a small one-room building on the Rootstraat, a few doors from the Donkeregaard, which is identified as the old Latin school. It could well be the school which existed when Arminius was a boy. Bertius says nothing of this school, giving the impression that Arminius received his instruction from Aemilius. It is possible, however, that Aemilius made it possible for Arminius to study in the school. The rector was Arien Cornelisz., about whom little is known except that he was trained in law. After the Spanish attack on Oudewater in 1575, the name of Dirck Tromper appears as rector. The Dirck (Theodorus) Willemsz. Tromper

32

who married a granddaughter of Arminius in 1655 was probably his grandson or great-grandson.

There was a town government with the usual officials—councilmen, burgomasters, bailiffs, secretary, weigh master, and others. There was a militia, whose duties included standing watch on the walls at night. The night watch lists reveal the fact that one person from each household must be provided for watch duty. When a husband died, his widow took his place on the watch. There were markets, annual and weekly, with appointed times and places. The weekly market was opened at 9 A.M. by the ringing of the bell in the Gasthuis; no sales were permitted before the sound of the bell. The town was the market center for the animals and crops of the farms in the surrounding polders. The farmers lived in the town. There were businesses: rope and thread manufacturing, draperies, breweries, grain mills, bakeries, oil mills, and the *wapensmederij*, or armament smithy, of Arminius' father. There was a surgeon, or *heelmeester* (literally, health master), whose duties included dentistry and barbering. There were a hostel master, a stable master, and shippers. There was a town brothel, to which housewives, transients, and Jews were denied entrance. Antisemitism has many faces.

In 1559 Oudewater was still under Spanish control and of Roman Catholic faith. The stirrings of independence and of Protestantism were already being felt, however, and when Arminius' father died, a local priest of Protestant sympathies acted *in loco parentis* to the young boy. Of this priest, Theodore Aemilius, nothing is known but what is told by Bertius, who as usual embellishes a hard core of fact with the trappings of pious rhetoric. Undoubtedly Aemilius played an important part in Arminius' early development. What Bertius says will be repeated here, and the reader will have to make his own judgment about the "historical Aemilius." Says Bertius:

His name was Theodore Aemilius, and, on account of his singular erudition and holiness, his memory is to this day cherished by the living with the greatest veneration. When this good man had conceived a taste for religious doctrines of a superior kind and of greater purity than those in which he had been educated, he determined at once never again to celebrate that abominable sacrifice of the Mass; and, for this reason, at various times he changed the place of his abode, and occasionally resided at Paris, Louvain, Cologne, and Utrecht. Finding young Arminius without a father, this excellent clergyman charged himself with his education; and as soon as his tender age was thought capable of receiving the elements of learning, he had him carefully instructed in the rudiments of the Latin and Greek languages, and his mind imbued with principles of religion and virtue.[23]

[23] Funeral Oration, *WA*, I, 17.

The passage continues with a florid description of Arminius' abilities and Aemilius' good advice, neither of which is precise enough to add to one's knowledge of the situation.

From this one cannot know whether Aemilius was at this time the parish priest in Oudewater. Bertius says that he lived in Oudewater at the time of the death of Arminius' father. His wanderings to other cities must have taken place earlier, and perhaps he was now inactive as a priest if not openly a Protestant. Oudewater was not yet a Protestant town and did not become so until 1574, although there was evidently a private circle of Protestants under the care of a Reformed pastor in nearby Gouda. At least one list of Reformed clergy names Aemilius as the *pastoor* (the Dutch word meaning a Roman Catholic parish priest) of Oudewater in 1566, evidently as a forerunner of the first Reformed *predikant* (the Dutch word indicating a Protestant clergyman), Huyg Dircksz., whose date is given as 1575.[24]

Bertius does give another clue. In speaking of the death of Aemilius, he says, "After he [Arminius] had thus, for some years, in a most exemplary manner, advanced in his studies and in personal piety, and had resided at Utrecht, in the house of Aemilius, his opening prospects were suddenly beclouded by an unexpected calamity in the death of that excellent and religious old clergyman, his patron [Aemilius]." [25] Nothing is known of the date of Arminius' removal to Utrecht, although the death of Aemilius was probably in 1574 or 1575. It is safe to assume that Arminius spent his early teen-age years in Utrecht. It is certain that he was getting a solid education, for shortly after the death of Aemilius he was to be admitted to university studies. This has led some writers to suppose, with good reason, that in Utrecht he attended the famous *Hieronymusschool*, or St. Jerome School.

The *Hieronymusschool* was a result of the upsurge of biblical piety and humanistic learning which had appeared in the Low Countries in the fifteenth century. Houses of the Brethren of the Common Life sprang up in many cities and towns, and these houses were usually for the purpose of the instruction of young men of leading families. They often took the names of one of their two patron saints, Jerome and Gregory. The school in Utrecht had been established a century before Arminius' time by brothers from the house in Delft. The most famous rector had been Hinne Rode, who had had to leave Utrecht in 1522 because of his Protestant opinions. One of the early students was Jan de Bakker, later martyred. The rectors during Arminius' possible term of study there

[24] Martinus Soermans, *Kerkelyk Register . . . van Zuyd-Holland*, p. 66.
[25] *WA*, I, 18.

were Cornelis Lauerman, who served from 1554 to 1573, and Theodorus Cornelius Berg, 1573 to 1575.[26] Lauerman was famous for his Latin poems. From the statutes adopted in 1565 one may see a program of studies in dialectic, rhetoric, mathematics, and physics, with exercises in the composition of Latin prose and poetry and in oral expression. Greek studies centered in the *Dialogues* of Plato and especially in the *Oeconomica* of Xenophon. One sees also the names of Cicero, Aristotle, Homer, Plutarch, and Terence, but the biblical and Christian sources were not neglected, for there were studies in the Hebrew language, in the Gospels in Greek and Latin, and in St. John Chrysostom, Basil the Great, and the Athanasian Creed. One more name should be mentioned: Erasmus.[27]

Studies were long, from early morning until seven in the evening. Latin and Greek were taught from the best grammars of the time, those of Macropedius and of Valerius. On Sundays and holy days the lessons were devoted to the Bible or to a church father. In the tradition of Gerard Groot, the Gospel lessons were for the ethical study of the life of Christ.[28]

There are no lists of students from this period, but one student is known, Johannes Uitenbogaert, who was to become a lifelong, intimate friend of Arminius. Uitenbogaert was born on February 11, 1557, in Utrecht, the son of Augustijn Pietersz. Uitenbogaert (of the family Van de Bogaerden or Wtenbogaerden) and Helena (or Heylwich) Hamel, of Heusden. Both his parents came from substantial old families which had begun their rise to eminence in the thirteenth and fourteenth centuries. Three of his five older siblings had died of the plague in the year he was born. The immediate family was an impoverished branch of the old family. Uitenbogaert's father had to support his family by teaching school and singing in the choir at the Cathedral of St. Peter in Utrecht. Uitenbogaert was placed in the *Hieronymusschool* in his tenth year, about 1566, and he probably studied there for the next eight years. Of his teacher Lauerman, Uitenbogaert later said, "I still remember that the teacher often said to me and my fellow students that the root of study is very bitter to bite into but that the fruit is very sweet." [29]

Uitenbogaert's parents were Roman Catholic, but like many others they were increasingly under the Protestant influence. Another Protestant influence on Uitenbogaert was his godfather, for whom he was named,

[26] A. Ekker, "Theodorus Cornelius Berg, Rector der Hieronymus School te Utrecht van 1573-1575."

[27] The statutes are printed in A. Ekker, *Berigt omtrent de Latijnsche Scholen te Utrecht*, pp. 57-58.

[28] H. C. Rogge, *Johannes Wtenbogaert en Zijn Tijd*, I, 10.

[29] *Ibid.*

the canon of the Utrecht cathedral, Johan Block. They were all later to be influenced by the married and Protestant-minded priest of the St. James Church in Utrecht, Hubert Duifhuis.

There is no direct evidence that Arminius studied at the *Hieronymus-school* or that he became acquainted with Uitenbogaert there. He and Uitenbogaert could have met for the first time as theological students at Geneva. Nevertheless, Arminius was in Utrecht at the time that his future friend was studying there, he learned the very subjects being taught in the *Hieronymusschool,* he was known in the community of scholars (by Rudolphus Snellius, for example), and he was ready to undertake university studies. It is more reasonable to believe that he studied in the Latin school and was acquainted with Uitenbogaert than not.

Arminius' studies in Utrecht ended with the death of Aemilius, which was probably in late 1574 or early 1575. This was to be the end of his Oudewater-Utrecht days; from now on he would be in the larger world of universities and of Amsterdam.

2

RUDOLPHUS SNELLIUS;
THE DESTRUCTION OF OUDEWATER

For the next events of Arminius' life we are dependent on Bertius, who reports that the death of Aemilius left Arminius stranded in Utrecht. Before long, however, he came under the protection of a new benefactor, Rudolphus Snellius, a linguist and mathematician from the University of Marburg, who was visiting Utrecht. Snellius, himself a native of Oudewater who had fled Holland under Spanish persecution, was attracted to the bright and needy Oudewater teen-age boy, and he took him back to Marburg to place him in the university there. Bertius gives the time as 1575. The journey probably took place in June or July, for Bertius reports that Arminius had scarcely become settled in Marburg when the news of the massacre of Oudewater arrived. The massacre was in August. After about two weeks of "weeping and lamentation, almost without intermission," Arminius left Marburg and returned to Holland "to look once more upon his native town, though in ruins, or to meet death in the attempt." After determining the fate of his family and the town, he returned to Marburg, making the entire journey on foot, a distance on modern roads of some 400 kilometers or 250 miles. Then hearing of the founding of a university at Leiden, he returned to Holland in order to study there. Those are the bare facts reported by Bertius.[1]

Rudolphus Snellius van Roijen (Rudolf Snel) was born to wealthy, upper-class parents in Oudewater on October 5, 1547. He studied at Cologne and Heidelberg, evidently also giving instruction in those places, because it is reported that at Cologne he taught Aristotelian logic for three years. Marburg was his next location, and there he became enamored with the logic of Petrus Ramus (Pierre de la Ramée), forsaking with some vehemence his earlier Aristotelianism. He traveled to Italy and lived in Pisa, probably between 1575 and 1578. In 1578 he returned to Oudewater to live but was soon called to be professor of Hebrew and mathematics at Leiden. He married a survivor of the massacre of Oude-

---

[1] Funeral Oration, *WA*, I, 19-20.

water, Machteld Cornelisdr., in the summer of 1578. He taught at Leiden until his death in 1613, and he is buried in the church at Oudewater, where there is a monument in his memory.[2]

He was thus a wealthy, well-educated, single scholar about twenty-eight years of age when he befriended Arminius. Their acquaintance at this point was scarcely a year at the most. Later, when Snellius taught at Leiden, Arminius again became his pupil for a very short time. It was undoubtedly through Snellius that Arminius became interested in Ramus. About Ramus more will be said in connection with Arminius' studies in Leiden.

What about Marburg? This first university to be established without papal sanction had been founded in 1527 by Philip of Hesse as a means for promoting Protestantism in his territories. Philip Melanchthon was the guiding spirit in the founding of the university, although he never accepted Philip's invitation to join its faculty. In 1529 it was the scene of the famous Marburg Colloquy. Whether the Melanchthonian influence extended down to 1575 to be felt by Arminius cannot be determined, for nothing is known of Arminius' brief time there.

For Arminius, the destruction of Oudewater was the coincidence of national struggle and personal tragedy. It was while Arminius had been studying at Utrecht that Oudewater had gone over to the side of William of Orange, national independence, and Protestantism. On April 1, 1572, William of Orange, having earlier assumed the role of leader of the resistance, was able to launch an offensive in the north by the use of violent and hardy fishermen-patriots, the Sea Beggars. They had come by sea to capture Brielle on that day. The reaction within Holland and Zeeland was mixed. Many continued to sympathize with the Catholic cause and the Spanish regent, the Duke of Alva, and his stadt-holder (*stadhouder,* lieutenant, or *locum tenens,* a subregent) Bossu (Maximilian de Hennin, Count of Bossu). Some brutality on Bossu's part in Rotterdam and other factors, however, along with the long-growing anti-Catholic sentiment of the century, combined to make for an increasing receptivity on the part of the population to the Prince and his Sea Beggars. A three-pronged campaign began from Brielle. The first was directed southward toward Zeeland and its important coastal towns, Vlissingen (Flushing), Middelburg, Veere, Goes, and Zierikzee. The second was by sea around from the north, invading at Enkhuizen and proceeding to Hoorn, Medemblik, Alkmaar, Edam, Purmerend, and Haarlem. Amsterdam was still holding out for the Catholic and Spanish

---

[2] Van Aelst, pp. 548-50; *WA,* I, 55; *LA,* 40. Often underlying early accounts of persons connected with the University of Leiden is Johannes Meursius, *Athenae Batavae.*

side. The third was from Brielle directly inward, to Dordrecht and then, with some wandering northward, finally to Schoonhoven, Oudewater, Gouda, Leiden, and north to Haarlem. Oudewater was thus the point of first deep penetration inland by the forces of Orange.

The attack was led by nine daredevils, four of whom were from Oudewater. They were under the command of the Leiden nobleman Adriaen van Swieten, a deputy of Orange. Spanish troops had been momentarily withdrawn from the area, and by a variety of stratagems the Sea Beggars were able to reach Oudewater by June 18. They success-fully entered the city and took over the town hall in the name of William of Orange from the unsuspecting burgomaster, Dirk Dirksz. A new town government was installed, the parish priest was set aside and allowed to take refuge in the cloister of the Cellezusters, and Protestant worship was instituted in the church. Catholics remained in the town, but they no longer controlled the government nor held public worship. Van Swieten's forces now turned their attention to Gouda and with the gleeful help of Oudewater partisans, who took some pride in their newly won primacy over Gouda, liberated that town on June 20.[3]

No details are known about the progress of the Protestantization of Oudewater, except that by 1574 there was a Reformed preacher in the church, Huyg Dircksz. In 1575 he removed to the church at Gouda and was replaced by Johannes Gelasius (Jan Jansz.), about whom more will be said.

Now that the liberation and the Protestant cause were taking such a decisive turn in the north, Orange felt it wise to assert his authority in a new way. At the summons of the Leiden *pensionaris,* or pensionary, Paulus Buys, representatives of the liberated towns (Dordrecht, Haarlem, Leiden, Gouda, Gorinchem, Alkmaar, Oudewater, Hoorn, Enkhuizen, Medemblik, Edam, and Monnickendam) met at Dordrecht on July 19, 1572, under the chairmanship of Marnix St. Aldegonde. Orange was unanimously recognized as stadtholder of Philip II in his former terri-tories and in his absence. This gave to the north a new juridical basis, and Oudewater played an integral role in this new development. For that reason, the future fortunes of Arminius' birthplace were to be of greatest interest to everyone in the north.

In these stormy events religious and civic passions were raised to a frenzy. Neither the loyalist nor the rebel leaders could keep their troops under control. In January, 1573, William of Orange had to discharge the leader of the Sea Beggars at Brielle, Lumey (Guillaume Count de

---

[3] J. Walvis, *Beschrijving van Gouda,* quoted in van Aelst, pp. 162 ff. Much of this material is summarized in a recent book by A. W. den Boer and Johan Schouten, *Oud-Oudewater.*

la Marck, Baron of Lumey), who had allowed Brielle to become little more than a pirate den and who had violated agreements with town governments to respect the private rights of Catholics. Lumey, incidentally, retired to Germany and returned to the Roman Catholic Church. William, who himself did not leave the Catholic for the Reformed fold until April, saw himself as the protector of all oppressed persons, Protestant or Catholic, and envisaged a new order of religious peace and toleration. Not all his followers shared that vision.

I think that it is not simply prejudice to say that the greater atrocities came from the Spanish side, and certainly Oudewater was to be an example unparalleled even in those bloody days. Alva retired from his duties in the Low Countries in 1573 and was replaced by Don Luis de Requesens. Orange had personally appeared in the north and had made great strides in bringing order out of the chaos created by his own overzealous troops. Yet he could not expect to hold the two rebel provinces of Zeeland and Holland against the might of Spain without outside assistance. He tried to get aid from France and England, and his brother, Louis of Nassau, raised a mercenary army in Germany to join Orange in Holland. The Spaniards responded by gathering all their troops in the north to meet the invaders. Louis and another brother of Orange's were killed, and the invading army defeated. The Spanish could not press the victory, however, for their troops began to mutiny over unpaid wages. It was increasingly difficult for Spain to sustain a war and maintain its power among subject people who fought for their own liberty on their own soil. In 1574 Requesens laid siege to Leiden, but that town had also been reorganized on Reformed lines in 1572 and offered a spirited, self-sacrificing resistance which, with help from Orange, resulted in the lifting of the siege on October 3, 1574.

The political aims of the resistance movement were as yet unclear. The north was still willing to accept the authority of the King of Spain provided its privileges were restored, occupation troops withdrawn, and religious liberty respected. There were unsuccessful attempts at negotiation. In 1575 the Spanish forces made yet another vigorous military effort against the north. By borrowing money at high interest, Requesens had been able to make a three-pronged campaign—an invasion of North Holland which came to nothing, an attack on Holland, Zeeland, and Utrecht, and an attack on the islands of Schouwen and Duiveland in the west.

The campaign in the center was led by the new stadtholder of Holland, Zeeland, and Utrecht, Hierges (Gilles de Berlaymont, Baron of Hierges), who had replaced Bossu. Starting from Utrecht, Hierges captured Buren,

Oudewater, Schoonhoven, and the fortifications near Krimpen on the Lek. He attacked Woerden, but there he was stopped.

The attack on Oudewater, dramatic and tragic, became a *cause célèbre* throughout the north. The primary sources of information are Pieter Bor (Christiaensz.), *Oorsprongk, Begin en Vervolgh der Nederlandsche Oorlogen, 1555-1600,* and Arnoldus van Duyn, *Oudewaterse Moord.* Both writers had access to eyewitness accounts, for Bor had a relative, possibly a brother-in-law (the Dutch *zwager* could also mean "friend"), who lived through the event, and van Duyn lived in Oudewater in the seventeenth century when he could have heard eyewitness accounts directly or at second hand. Van Duyn tends to dramatize the events with a possible exaggeration of numbers. Nevertheless, the basic outline of what happened can be discerned from these sources. Some supplementation and verification is possible from archival sources and one or two early pamphlets. A fairly reliable summary of what happened can thus be reconstructed.[4]

Hierges divided his troops in three groups, one to go to Zaltbommel, another to Woudrichem, while he himself led the third contingent toward Schoonhoven. These were all feints, and suddenly all three turned toward Oudewater, their real target. He had 11,000 foot soldiers, 15 companies of *pioniers,* or advance infantry, and 1,000 cavalry. There were 28 cannon, including four that could fire 65-pound iron shot. The greater part of the soldiers were Sicilians, Piedmontese, and Spaniards. The rendezvous at Oudewater was effected on July 19, 1575. The alarm was sounded in the town, and the defenders organized their forces for its defense.

The example of Leiden's long and costly siege was before both the defenders and the attackers. Inside the city, heroic and sometimes foolish measures were taken, bravery often mingled with cupidity. Outside, Hierges hesitated, fearing that Orange would come again and cut the dikes in order to drown the attacking army, as he had done at Leiden. Messages passed clandestinely between Oudewater and Gouda and the Prince. Outside help did not come, and Hierges made preparations for the attack. On Friday night, August 6, he was ready to bombard the town. The next morning he sent a messenger with white flag and trumpeter to seek the peaceful surrender of the city. The conditions were unacceptable to the town government, and the attack began.

Some 300 citizens, mostly women and children, took refuge in a large farmhouse in the town. The cannonballs began to rain on the roofs. The church was the prime target, because the defenders used the tower both for observation and for shooting at the besiegers. Fortunately, the

---

[4] I follow especially van Aelst and den Boer and Schouten.

tower was not hit, and it stands today. Breaches were made in the town walls, however, and although they were repaired in the night, the artillery of the attacking army kept up its work of destruction faster than repairs could be maintained. The Spanish troops then entered the city itself, and a new phase of the attack began.

It is not a nice story. First the defending soldiers on the walls were shot or stabbed to death. Those who fled into the town were pursued and killed. Then the massacre spread to noncombatants. Mothers were killed in front of their children; children in front of their mothers. Girls and women were raped in view of fathers and husbands, and then all were killed. No place, no person, was exempt from the pillaging invaders. When nuns in the cloisters were discovered, they pleaded that they were faithful Roman Catholics. "So much the better for your souls," said the soldiers as they raped and murdered them.

Dramatic but not untypical was the case of the Reformed preacher, Johannes Gelasius, a story oft recited by early Dutch historians. Gelasius was put in prison, but upon payment of 500 guilders his captors, not knowing his identity, released him. He was then seen by a *beguine* (nun), who denounced him to the Spanish authorities as a Protestant preacher. He was seized again and his recantation demanded. He refused to abjure his Reformed faith. Thereupon the Spaniards brought his small son before him, killed the boy before the father's eyes, and hanged the preacher on the gallows in the marketplace.

It was in this massacre that Arminius lost his mother, his siblings, and according to earliest accounts, all his other relatives. According to van der Capellen, it was the whole household which was murdered, including the *meesterknecht* Willem Huichsz. It cannot be known whether this detail is based on oral tradition, for van der Capellen was an Oudewater man, or purely on the novelist's imagination. It is a possible conjecture. Neither can it be known that there is a source underlying Bor and van Duyn other than Bertius' oration for affirming the death of Arminius' family in the massacre. There is no reason to doubt the story, however, for Arminius did make the trip back to Oudewater and did find that his loss was as sore as the reports in Marburg had indicated.

There was a great destruction of property. The early accounts which indicate that the town was entirely destroyed and burned should not be taken literally. Some buildings, including the church, were relatively unharmed. Others, such as the town hall and the weigh house, were only damaged and were restored in the rebuilding. A great many buildings were destroyed and not replaced; others were completely rebuilt in the new style and more durable and fireproof construction of the seventeenth century. The result is that Oudewater today is one of the most charming

Dutch towns and is filled with fine examples of Golden Age architecture.

The town remained under the control of an occupying garrison until it was liberated again by Dutch troops under van Swieten, probably in December, 1576. That means that when Arminius made his sad pilgrimage back to Oudewater, it was still in the hands of the enemy, which would account for Bertius' saying that Arminius was determined to see his native city again "or die in the attempt."

Not all the inhabitants were killed. Some fled the city during the massacre, swimming through the canals, hiding in haystacks, or passing themselves off as collaborators with the Spanish. A few were released upon payment of ransom from outside sources; the Spanish were always hard pressed to pay their troops. Some probably continued to exist in clandestine ways during the occupation. Some of the priests and monastics were spared because of their religious and political sympathies. It is noteworthy that upon the liberation of Oudewater, these persons, although not restored to their former power in the life of the city, were maintained on pensions at public expense until their natural death. Many of the refugees fled to Rotterdam, among whom was eventually Arminius himself.

Our knowledge of the massacre is derived from eyewitness accounts of the survivors, and many of the stories are precise in details of geography and identification of known persons. Many of the survivors returned to Oudewater, and there they were honored both with financial aid and with veneration and respect. Among them was Arminius' aunt, the sister of his father, Geertje Jacobsdr.

Arminius' second stay in Marburg must have been about a year in length, for about fourteen months later he had enrolled in the University of Leiden. He went first to Rotterdam, where refugees from both Oudewater and Amsterdam, which was also still under Spanish control, were gathered. There he was befriended by Jean Taffin and Petrus Bertius the elder, the father of the Petrus Bertius who later delivered the funeral oration over Arminius.

Jean Taffin was the pastor of the French-speaking or Walloon Reformed congregation in Rotterdam. He was also the chaplain to William of Orange and a member of his council. It was he who later would advise Uitenbogaert to cultivate a friendship with Oldenbarnevelt, and he was to be an older colleague of Arminius when the latter became a Reformed pastor in Amsterdam.

The elder Bertius was born in Beveren, near Brugge, and following his father he embraced the Reformation and became a Reformed leader, although without being ordained to the office of preaching. In 1567 or 1568 he had had to flee to London, where again we find him functioning as an elder and sick-visitor in the Dutch church at Austin Friars. He was called and ordained to the Reformed pastorate at IJselmonde in 1572, and he transferred to Rotterdam in about 1574, where he remained until 1580. He served much of his remaining years in Zeeland, where he died in 1594.[5]

Arminius spent some time in the home of the elder Bertius in Rotterdam until he could make his way to Leiden. In the meantime, Bertius recalled his son, Petrus Bertius the younger, from his studies in England, so that the two young men could proceed to Leiden together. Arminus was about four or five years older than his companion.

---

[5] B. Glasius, ed., *Godgeleerd Nederland,* I, 109; "Bert (Pieter de) ," *BWPGN,* I, 434-35.

3

STUDIES AT LEIDEN

On October 4, 1574, the day after Leiden had been liberated, William of Orange entered the city and began making plans for its future. It seems to have been on his personal initiative or at least certainly with his hearty concurrence that it was decided to establish a university there. On December 28 he addressed a letter to the States of Holland and West Friesland describing the function of the proposed university as that of providing "a firm foundation and support for the freedom and good lawful government of the country, not only in religious matters but also in those pertaining to the general civic welfare, it being particularly necessary that here in our own country there be established a university where the youth can be educated both in the right knowledge of God and in other good and honorable arts and sciences." [1] The letter goes on to state that this would be a bulwark for the entire nation against the enemy's attacks on both true religious worship and the freedom of the country. By "nation" he could mean empirically only Holland and Zeeland, still excluding the as yet Roman Catholic city of Amsterdam but with hopes of including the entire north. By this time it was becoming apparent that the south was to be lost to the cause of Protestantism and independence.

The letter was read to the States, meeting in Delft, on January 2, 1575, and on the next day they had agreed to establish the university. Leiden was chosen because of its steadfastness and heroism in resisting the enemy. Other options might have been Middelburg, which was neither centrally located nor entirely secure from enemy attack, or the commercial city of Amsterdam, which was not available because of its tenacity in holding to the Spanish cause. There was a popular legend that Orange, on the day he had entered Leiden, had been moved to offer the city fathers as a reward for their courage the choice of tax exemption

[1] H. C. Rogge, *Caspar Janszoon Coolhaes,* I, 45-46. West Friesland, the area north of Holland that had been attached to Friesland before the great storm of 1282, which broke the North Sea dunes to form the Zuider Zee, was now politically united to the province of Holland.

for the city or a university. They demonstrated their nobility and love of culture, so the story goes, by choosing the university. The legend is probably not true, a more mundane account being both possible and supported by documentary evidence.[2]

With astonishing haste the plans went forward. Three curators were charged with taking the steps necessary to make the dream a reality. They were the great Leiden leader and patriot, Johan van der Does (Dousa, Dauze, Doeza), Lord of Noordwijk and commissioner of the water authority in the Rijnland (a most important post in a country below sea level, where each man's dike is every man's security); Gerard Amelitz van Hoogeveen, Lord of Hoogeveen and Leiden *pensionary* and council member; and Cornelius de Koninck van Belois, a burgomaster of Delft, where Orange had his temporary (and final) headquarters.

The curators were appointed on January 6. The charter, granted by Orange in the name of Philip II, whose stadtholder he still regarded himself to be, was signed on January 6. It gave as the principal reasons for the founding of the university "the setback to needed education of the youth of Holland and Zeeland which the war had caused, the fear of the inhabitants of the land of the cost and danger of sending their children to other universities in the king's territories, especially with regard to religious controversies, and the lack of good education in those lands, whereby all morality, knowledge, and learning have gone to nothing to the detriment of the common state, police, and government."[3] The universities in question would have been at Louvain, where there was a large and powerful Roman Catholic university founded in 1425, and at Douay, where there had been a new and militant Roman Catholic university since 1562. Neither of these was an option for the Reformed leaders of the north. They had been sending their youth, clergy and lay, to Wittenberg, Heidelberg, Basel, and, in greatest numbers, to Geneva. William saw universities generically as the source of national character, and he envisaged a Dutch university as the necessary condition for good religion and good government in the emerging new nation.

For Orange the cause of religion and the cause of liberty were two sides of the same coin. When the faculties were organized, the theological faculty had the priority as *primus inter pares*. Perhaps this was no more than the medieval tradition of granting theology the queenship of the sciences. To this day the theological faculty at Leiden marches at the head of academic processions, although this status is quite reversed in

[2] *Ibid.,* I, 47-48.

[3] *Ibid.,* I, 48-49. Cf. City Archives, Leiden, Municipal Archives 1575-1581, inventory no. 73.

the budget. For Orange and the curators the gathering of the theological faculty was not the *sine qua non* for beginning operations. The dedication was set for February 8, with no theological faculty in sight.

Two days earlier, on February 6, the curators called on one of the Leiden Reformed preachers, Caspar Jansz. Coolhaes, to give the dedicatory address and to begin the lessons in theology. Thus with great haste the opening of the university took place.

It was a national event, rich in symbolism and powerful in its appeal to a new sense of nationhood. On the appointed day, Tuesday, February 8, 1575, the festivities began even before daylight with a religious service at 7:00 A.M. in the Pieterskerk led by Coolhaes. At 9:00 A.M. there was a great procession from the town hall on the Breestraat to the university building, which was near the north end of the Rapenburg. Leading the procession was a dashing, brightly arrayed military escort. This was followed by a woman dressed in pure white riding in a chariot and accompanied by four attendants. She was the Holy Gospel; the attendants were the Four Evangelists. After her came allegorical figures representing the four faculties: theology, law, medicine, and arts. The procession passed under triumphal arches which spanned the route from the town hall to the university. The inaugural address was then delivered by Coolhaes. Thus was launched Holland's first university, to which Arminius would shortly make his way.

There was some wheel-spinning at the first. By the time that Arminius enrolled on October 23, 1576, as a student of the liberal arts, he was only the twelfth to be registered. This is the first known use of the latinized form of his name, "Jacobus Arminius." [4] Bertius, who was only about twelve years old at the time, tells of these events much later in the funeral oration:

We were therefore sent off in company to Leyden: and from the moment when, together, we first entered within the walls of this University, the greatest unanimity subsisted between us, and we were most intimately connected in our tempers, studies, pursuits and desires. But I will not attempt in this place to relate how pleasantly that important aera in our lives passed along. I will only state, that the contention was so strong between the students in regard to their progress in literature and wisdom, so profound was the reverence which they evinced towards their teachers, and the zeal and impulse of true piety were so great in them, as scarcely to be exceeded. But the only one of our order who meritoriously distinguished himself above the rest of his companions was Arminius. If any of us had a particular theme or essay to compose, or a speech to recite, the first step which we took in it, was, to ask for Arminius. If any friendly discussion arose among us, the decision of which required the

---

[4] "Arminius (Jacobus)," *BWPGN*, I, 209, which cites *Album Stud. Acad. Lugd. Bat.* (The Hague, 1875), col. 1.

The University of Leiden. Early engraving, showing student being punished.
By permission of the City Archives, Leiden

sound judgment of a Palaemon, we went in search of Arminius, who was always consulted. I well recollect the time when Doctor Lambert Danaeus, our learned Professor, paid him a public compliment and eulogized him for the endowments of his genius, and his proficiency in learning and virtue; he also urged us who were Divinity students to imitate the example of Arminius, by the same cheerful and diligent attention to the study of sacred Theology. Why should I here recount his talents for poetry, in which he particularly excelled? Or why should I advert to his skill in Mathematics, and other branches of philosophy in which his attainments were solid and profound? There was no study of that description in which his genius had not penetrated; and he never engaged in any literary undertaking which he did not happily complete.[5]

If there be any accuracy in this florid account, it would indicate that Arminius studied mathematics, logic (the chief of the "other branches of philosophy"), and theology. It is also known that he began his study of Hebrew at once. The incident with Danaeus would have occurred at the very end of Arminius' studies in Leiden, for Danaeus arrived only a few months before Arminius departed.

It is from a more mundane circumstance that we know something of Arminius' personal affairs while he was a student in Leiden. Members of the university, that is, professors and students, were entitled to an annual allotment of tax-free wine and beer, and in 1577 the city council found it necessary to determine the eligible subjects of this exemption. A list was drawn up on November 22. It is the oldest extant roll of members of the university.[6]

"Iacobus Hermannus Oudewater" is listed as living in the home of Hermannus Reynecherus, along with "Johannes Gruterus Brabantus, Joannes Hesychius van Bremen, Georgius Benedictus van Haerlem, [and] Petrus Bertius Flaming." It was customary for professors to augment their incomes by taking in students. Reynecherus, whose professorship had actually terminated before Arminius arrived but who continued to teach until 1578, was Arminius' Hebrew teacher. It is curious that Gruterus and Bertius, along with three other tax-exempt students, do not yet at this date appear on the register of the university.

Money for living expenses must have been a serious problem for Arminius, for there is no reason to believe that he had a personal fortune. His room and board may have cost 250 guilders or more a year, and a grant-in-aid of such a sum would have been no small matter.[7] No records of such a grant are known.

---

[5] *WA*, I, 21-22.

[6] The document is reported by H. J. Witkam, "Een Lijst van Lidmaten der Leidse Universiteit op 22 November 1577," *Jaarboekje voor Geschiedenis en Oudheidkunde van Leiden en Omstreken*, LXI (1970), 101-5.

[7] Christiaan Sepp, *Het Godgeleerd Onderwijs in Nederland Gedurende de 16e en 17e Eeuw*, I, 66.

The names of other teachers are known, and from that much can be inferred about Arminius' education. The famed Johannes Drusius assumed the chair of Hebrew in 1577. Greek was taught by Petrus Tiara, who was the first *Rector Magnificus* of the university, and from 1578 by Bonaventura Vulcanius. Nicolaus Dammius was professor of Latin until he resigned in 1579. The professors of law included Joost de Menijn, Cornelius Grotius (the uncle of Hugo Grotius), Hugo Donellus, and Justus Lipsius, who also taught history.[8] There is, however, no reason to think that Arminius studied law at all. Lipsius, an authority on Tacitus, who had the reputation of being one of the most learned men of his day and whose presence at Leiden brought added fame to the university, did not arrive until April, 1578, and there is no indication that Arminius was under his teaching of history. The point is made because it was Lipsius who created a scandal a few years later by returning to the Roman fold, in which course he was followed many years later by his Leiden student and the self-alleged intimate of Arminius, Petrus Bertius.

Arminius did not study medicine, so no mention of that faculty is pertinent.

The first theology lectures at Leiden were given by Coolhaes, but he was not of professorial rank and he seems only to have filled in until a regular professor could arrive. The first professor of theology was Guilhelmus Feuguereus (Guillaume Feugueray), who came in April, 1575, and taught until May, 1579. He had Johannes Bollius as a colleague for about four months only in the winter of 1577-78. After the departure of Feuguereus, two men assumed duties in theology. Hubertus Sturmius served as lector in theology from November 30, 1579, until May, 1584, and Lambertus Danaeus as professor from March 17, 1581, until May, 1582. Shortly after Arminius' departure from Leiden two more theologians arrived, Johannes Holmannus in 1582 and Adrian Saravia in 1584.

Of these, only Feuguereus and Danaeus are of direct significance for the theological studies of Arminius. Feuguereus[9] was born in Rouen, where he had been strongly influenced by the Protestant pastor, Augustin Marlorat. He was the Protestant pastor at Longueville at the time of the Massacre of St. Bartholomew's Day in 1572. He had to flee to London, where he came across the needy widow and children of Marlorat in the Huguenot community there. There he edited the manuscript of Marlorat's *Scripture Thesaurus*, a vast topical arrangement of the Old and New Testaments of some 800 pages, published in London in 1574.

[8] On Reynecherus and the other Leiden faculty mentioned here, see Martinus Soermans, *Academisch Register . . . Universiteyt tot Leyden.*

[9] Sepp, *Godgeleerd Onderwijs,* I, 34 ff.

It was this publication which led to his appointment in Leiden. A Huguenot in London, Petrus Lozelerius Villerius, who had just fled his Protestant pastorate in Rouen, wrote to a confidant of Orange, Adriaan van der Mijle, calling his attention to the merits of the work of Feuguereus. This circumstance is mentioned because of the light it sheds on the latter's theology, for Villerius was a moderate Calvinist who is described with approval by the Remonstrant historian Gerard Brandt.[10] Orange was not unfamiliar with Feuguereus, for in 1570 Feuguereus had dedicated a book to Orange in which he said that the Prince should cultivate religion, but not by all men nor by all methods, especially "not by such methods as are destructive both to the country and to religion itself," for "men in that case may be led, but not driven." [11]

From these brief glimpses of Feuguereus one sees a mild Reformed orthodoxy consonant with the liberal and tolerant spirit of the early Dutch National Reformation.

Danaeus,[12] whom Arminius knew only briefly, was the first strict Calvinist to teach theology at Leiden. He was born around 1530 in Beaugency-sur-Loire and educated at Orleans, Paris, and Bourges, where he became a Doctor of Law in 1559. Under the influence of Anne of Bourges, and especially in response to her martyrdom, he chose for the Reformation and became one of its foremost leaders. In 1560 he went to Geneva to study under Calvin, and from 1561 to 1572 he was pastor at Gien, near Orleans. The Massacre of St. Bartholomew's Day drove him from his home and all his possessions, including his books. He fled to Geneva, served two congregations nearby as pastor, and in 1574 became pastor and professor in Geneva and a close friend of Theodore Beza, through whose offices he was persuaded to come to Leiden. In Leiden he was appointed professor of theology and pastor of the Walloon congregation. He did not arrive in Leiden until March 13, 1581.

His acquaintance with Arminius lasted less than a year. Mention has been made of Bertius' report of the esteem in which Danaeus held Arminius. It is impossible to draw theological conclusions from this. Of Danaeus' doctrine of predestination nothing is known. It was not the issue in Leiden in the 1580s that it was to become in the 1600s. What was at issue was the question of church order. Danaeus was imbued with the Genevan polity, and in Leiden he came into conflict with another kind of Reformed polity, much less presbyterial. As with many of the early Dutch Reformed churches, the Leiden burgomasters exercised

[10] *HRN,* I, 665-66.
[11] *Ibid.,* p. 558: *KH,* Part III, p. 22.
[12] Sepp, *Godgeleerd Onderwijs,* I, 57 ff.; "Daneau," *BWPGN,* II, 379-83.

the right of passing on nominations for elder and deacon made by the consistory. In Genevan polity the consistory was a law unto itself. Many early Dutch Reformers had rejected this aspect of Genevan polity, fearing the uncontrolled, literally iconoclastic Calvinist zealots. The Genevans, in turn, feared the subjection of the church to the state.

The controversy became bitterly personal, with the Leiden Reformed pastor Coolhaes siding with the burgomasters against Danaeus and his colleague Sturmius. The whole university was caught in the uproar which led before long to the resignation of Danaeus and his departure from Leiden in May, 1582. From this incident, however, we get another glimpse into the development of Arminius' theological sympathies, for in later years he cites Coolhaes as one of the early, non-Genevan Dutch Reformers in whose tradition he saw himself standing. It is appropriate that H. C. Rogge's great study of Coolhaes should describe him as the "forerunner of Arminius."

Rogge says that the whole controversy within the Dutch Church can be reduced to two topics, the relationship between church and state and the relationship between God's foreordination and man's free will.[13] On both these points Coolhaes took essentially the same positions which were later to be known by the name of Arminius. Thus some word about Coolhaes is in order, if an adequate historical context for the understanding of the development of Arminius' ideas is to be given.

Coolhaes (Koolhaes, Coelaes, Coolhaze, etc.)[14] was born in Cologne of Roman Catholic parents on January 24, 1534. He was trained in the Reformation-resisting university there and at Dusseldorf, but at Dusseldorf he came under the influence of a humanistic supporter of the Reformation, the Rector Johannes Monheim. Nevertheless, he went on to become a Carthusian monk in Coblenz, but the monastic life did not satisfy his religious aspirations, and he went over to the Protestants in his twenty-fourth year.

He served in a number of pastoral positions in the Duchy of Zweibrucken, where his sympathies lay with Melanchthon and Zwingli rather than with Luther or Calvin. In 1566 he was called to Deventer. The immediate past history of the Protestant cause in Deventer had a lot to do with forming the views of Coolhaes and helps to illuminate the kind of Protestantism which Arminius was to uphold. In the first place, the moderating influence of the Brethren of the Common Life was still felt, not only as a preparation for the Reformation but also as an influence of the kind of Reformation which would take root. The sharp

---

[13] *Coolhaes*, I, 3.
[14] Rogge, *Coolhaes;* "Koolhaes," *BWPGN*, V, 172-205.

controversies between Lutherans, Mennonites, and Calvinists were relatively unknown there. Then when the Beggar movement was under way, issuing in radical anti-Catholic iconoclastic riots, the town government took affairs under control, determining the form that the Reformed Church would take. They assigned the Lieve-Vrouwenkerk to the Reformed, but only on the threefold condition that they would not damage it, that they would permit the Catholics to celebrate Mass in it, and that they would not call a preacher without the approval of the magistrates. The purpose of this last condition was to prevent the church from falling into the hands of zealots who would break the peace with their uncontrolled intolerance.

The first preacher called under these conditions was Coolhaes. He found a warm reception from all segments of the population, and he threw himself into an intense program of preaching twice daily and thrice on Sundays. This most happy period of his life ended only thirty-four weeks later, when the Spaniards under Alva forced their way northward so that Coolhaes with many other Protestants had to flee to Germany.

Back in Germany he was caught in the cross fire of the several rival religious groups: Lutherans, Melanchthonians, Calvinists, Zwinglians, and Catholics. When conditions were improved in the north, he returned, this time to Gorinchem, in the winter of 1573. In May, 1574, during a lull in the siege of Leiden, the burgomasters there issued him a call to serve the church in Leiden. The call, being issued by the burgomasters, was contrary to the provisions for calls laid down by the recent Synod of Emden of 1571, which had put such matters in the hands of the consistory. For Coolhaes, however, with his moderate Reformed sentiments and his appreciation for the peace of the church as upheld by the burgomasters of Deventer, this was no obstacle, and he set out for Leiden.

In the meantime the siege had resumed intensity, and he was not able to enter the city until October 3, the day of its liberation. There was a great service of thanksgiving in the packed Pieterskerk, and on that day he began his Leiden ministry. When the university opened the next year, it was he who gave the opening addresses and the first lectures in theology.

Leiden was not to be for him another Deventer, however, for although he had the support of the burgomasters, there were those in the church who opposed his doctrine of church and state. Foremost among these was his fellow minister, Pieter Cornelisz. Their first difference arose over the practices of saying evening prayers, preaching funeral sermons, and celebrating Christian festivals which did not fall on Sunday (such as

Christmas and Epiphany). Cornelisz. held, with the Calvinist-minded Provincial Synod of Dordrecht of 1574, that these were vestiges of Roman Catholicism which should be stamped out. The town sided with Coolhaes, the consistory with Cornelisz.

From that point on the controversy became wider and more bitter. In 1578 another pastor was called, Johannes Hallius, who transferred from Warmond and sided with Cornelisz. The result was soon a virtual split in the Leiden church, with Coolhaes and the old Leiden ruling elements on one side and the other two clergy and the increasing number of high Calvinist refugees from the south on the other. The chief issue was the relationship of burgomasters and consistory, but this was soon complicated with charges and countercharges of a personal nature. Not in the forefront of discussion but present nonetheless was a much wider range of issues, for two basic types of Reformed pattern were involved. Coolhaes represented the old North Netherlands indigenous Reformation, with its biblical piety, its irenic spirit, its distaste for extremism in either theology or church renewal, and its urbane, oligarchic exercise of power. Cornelisz. and Hallius represented a confessional and Geneva-oriented dogmatics, high Calvinism with its doctrine of predestination, rigid church discipline, the authority of consistory, classis, and synod, and intolerance of dissent.

It was in the midst of this near-schism in the Leiden church that Arminius pursued his university studies. It was into this unpleasant situation that Danaeus came from Geneva. There is no record that Arminius participated directly in the controversy, but in later years he did express his appreciation for Coolhaes. As for Coolhaes, peace was not to be obtained. Amidst much wrangling and intrigue, the magistrates attempted to suspend Cornelisz., who continued to preach in nearby villages where he drew the Flemings who were pouring into Leiden. Attempts were made to suspend Coolhaes, but he was maintained in office by the power of the magistrates. The magisterial party in Leiden brought in Dirck Volckertsz. Coornhert to write an apology for their position. Coornhert warned against a new papacy of the presbytery. Coolhaes followed by publishing his own defense, in which he advocated toleration of Lutherans and Mennonites. Then, to point out that intolerance is a two-way street, he advocated toleration of high Calvinists! With outside help a superficial reconciliation was effected in 1580, but charges were brought against Coolhaes at the National Synod of Middelburg in 1581, where his views were condemned, and at the Provincial Synod of Haarlem in 1582, where he was deposed from the ministry and excommunicated.

The Leiden burgomasters refused to set him aside, however, and although he could no longer fulfill his pastoral functions, they continued him on a salary of 300 guilders per year with an annual housing allowance of 30 guilders. Coolhaes accepted the stipend only as an interim measure until he could develop other means of support for his family (his wife bore him seventeen children). With the help of his next-door neighbor, a Leiden professor, he learned the art of distilling *aqua vitae* and other liquors. He operated his distillery for many years on the Rapenburg in Leiden, and during this time he continued to be a potent factor in Dutch religious life through his many writings and translations. One of the unique pieces in all theological literature is his 1588 book on the art of distilling, the medicinal uses of the products which he with God's help was producing, and the theological and historical justification for his being a distiller.

The Coolhaes affair was no tempest in a teapot. It was an expression of a fundamental cleavage in the Dutch Reformed Church made at the vital university center of Dutch life. Arminius could not have gone from Leiden to Geneva without being aware of this unresolved antinomy in Dutch Reformed theology and polity. At the same time it should be pointed out emphatically that predestination was not the issue which divided the church at Leiden. At the most, it lay under the surface.

There was yet another major episode or development in the thought and experience of Arminius which took place by the time he had finished his studies at Leiden, namely, his enthusiastic espousal of the logic of Petrus Ramus. There can be little question about the source of his Ramism, for his former protector Snellius was an avid Ramist. Arminius could have gained his knowledge of Ramus before going to Leiden, for his earlier association with Snellius could have been as long as a year, from mid-1575 to mid-1576. There was still a later opportunity, however, for Snellius became a *professor extraordinarius* of mathematics at Leiden on August 2, 1581. That date is so close to Arminius' departure, however, that it is safer to conclude that Arminius began his Ramist studies prior to going to Leiden.

Because of the role that Ramism was to play in the further career of Arminius, it is important to give an account of Ramus in order to understand better the frame of mind with which Arminius undertook his studies with Beza at Geneva.

4

THE INFLUENCE OF PETRUS RAMUS

PETRUS Ramus (Pierre de la Ramée) was born near Soissons in 1515, and he died at Paris during or just after the Massacre of St. Bartholomew's Day in 1572. He was a student of Johannes Sturm at Paris. He joined in the humanist reaction against medieval orthodoxy, especially in logic, and became a critic of Aristotle. There is a popular tale to the effect that his master's thesis in 1536 consisted of one proposition: *Quaecumque ab Aristotele dicta essent, commentitia esse*—all that Aristotle has said is false. His judges, Aristotelians all, were unable to make their customary appeal to Aristotle for fear of committing the (Aristotelian) logical fallacy of begging the question, and hence they were unable to refute him, so the story goes. This *tour de force,* if it occurred, or at least his early vehement attacks on Aristotle, made him one of the leading figures in philosophical discussion by the time he was twenty-one years of age.

Ramus published two works in 1543, a book on dialectic, *Dialecticae partitiones ad Academiam Parisiensem,* and *Aristotelicae animadversiones,* an outright attack on Aristotle. For this he was forbidden by Francis I to teach philosophy, and his books were ordered to be burned. He nevertheless continued to teach mathematics and rhetoric, however, and in 1545 became the head of the Collège de Presles. After the death of Francis I in 1547, he was free to speak and write, and in 1551 he became professor of rhetoric and philosophy at the Royal College. In the meantime, he had stirred up personal and professional enmities among the Aristotelians, particularly with Pierre Galland, who held that all that Aristotle had said was commensurable with Christian truth, and with Jacques Charpentier (Carpentarius), a disciple of Galland. Charpentier became a bitter enemy of Ramus, and there is strong evidence that he murdered Ramus during the confusion of the St. Bartholomew Massacre.[1]

At the Royal College, Ramus broke from traditional methods of teaching and became even more influential and controversial. He combined rhetoric with logic, interspersing the customary series of propositions

---

[1] The evidence for Charpentier's part in the murder of Ramus is presented in Charles Waddington, *Ramus, sa Vie, ses Ecrits et ses Opinions,* pp. 258 ff.

with pertinent quotations and illustrations. His innovations soon involved the total educational system, in all of which he pleaded for practical applications of the subject matter. He began to turn out new textbooks for the various parts of the *trivium,* and later worked on new texts for the *quadrivium.* His innovations spread also to the structure of the university itself. He made recommendations that the practice of retaining as faculty members all who held doctorates be discontinued, that only the most competent doctors be retained, and that tuition be lowered. Finally, he proposed an entire reconstruction of the curriculum, in which a lot of dead weight left over from the medieval system was eliminated. The details of his educational reform have been presented ably by F. P. Graves.[2]

Two aspects of his work which are of particular importance for this study are his logic and his theological teachings. Arminius avowed his approval of the Ramean logic, and it is improbable that he was uninfluenced by Ramus' religious teachings.

Ramus was intemperate in his attack on Aristotle. This seems strange now in that he looks, to the modern abserver, to be so Aristotelian. But, as Waddington points out, this violent attack was in an age of violent academic partisanships, and any modification of Aristotle at all could be expected to take an extreme form.[3]

Ramus tries to get away from the rigidity of Aristotelian logic as propounded at that time. He reduces the number of valid syllogisms, and, above all, he tries to make logic a "practical" science. He starts with the most general statement possible and proceeds to less general and more particular statements. The general statement should be a practical statement involving some practical end; in this way the conclusions will be relevant to some practical purpose. This logical structure can be seen in actual usage in the construction of his grammars. Grammar is defined generally and practically as "the art of talking correctly." [4] Thus a practical result is held in view as the goal of the whole enterprise.

His method from this point can be called that of "dichotomization." The general category is divided into two parts; each part is divided into two parts; and the subparts are divided again. Finally, when the process is complete, one arrives at the particular. Grammar, for instance, is divided into etymology and syntax. Etymology is divided into letters and pronunciation. (At this point Ramus recommended using *j* and *v* to refer to consonant sounds then included in *i* and *u*: hence *j* and *v*

---

[2] Graves, *Peter Ramus and the Educational Reformation of the Sixteenth Century,* pp. 108 ff.

[3] Waddington, p. 365.

[4] Graves, p. 124.

were once known as the "Ramist consonants.") After some five or six levels of dichotomizing, the categories of grammar are exhausted.

This sort of division plays some odd tricks with the problems of grammar, such as separating in theory items which come close together in practice. It was, however, a decided advance over existing grammars, and it represented progress in the humanist endeavor to be free from scholastic subtleties.[5]

Ramus expressed his methods in grandiose charts which elaborated the subdivisions of the general until the multiplicity of the species had been exhausted. Thus in a late edition of his *Training in Dialectic (Dialecticae institutiones)*, written after he had developed his system to a point of a rigidly bifurcating simplicity, there is a chart of his system of logic which begins, from left to right, as follows (but continues several stages further) :[6]

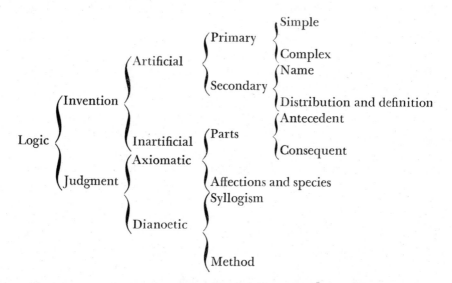

Walter J. Ong sees this method of dichotomization, especially as it is worked out in charts, as an expression of a new kind of vision and communication made possible by printing. It is a "class logic in space," reflecting a metaphysical polarity in being of form and matter, act and potency, but not arising from a metaphysical insight on the part of Ramus. Ramus simply found something of the sort in Agricola's *De inventione dialectica* (1529) and found it attractive for its pedagogical

[5] Cf. Graves's elaboration of this point, pp. 141 ff.

[6] The entire chart is reproduced in Walter J. Ong, *Ramus: Method, and the Decay of Dialogue,* p. 202; cf. Herschel Baker, *The Wars of Truth,* p. 102.

appeal.[7] Thus the question as to its significance for Arminius may not turn at all on some metaphysics hidden beneath the method but rather on the excitement of liberation from old methods and their restricted images. "The relative simplicity of [Ramus'] logic," says one commentator, "must have seemed a godsend to young undergraduates, anxious to learn the art of disputation in the shortest possible time." [8]

Ramus' binary system looks to the modern observer curiously like a computer program, based as it is on a two-digit number system. A student of mine who is a trained computer programmer once reduced Arminius' exposition of Romans 7 to a computer program.

A number of Protestant scholars began to use the conceptual tools of Ramism, including Z. Ursinus, Johannes Piscator, and William Perkins. By the 1590s Ramist exegetical and theological charts were appearing. These were summaries of the argument of a book printed on one page or on a fold-out paper. Piscator may have been the first to provide such a visual aid for his commentaries, and Perkins at Cambridge did the same.[9] Arminius had a number of Piscator's commentaries in his library,[10] and he was an admirer of the early writings, at least, of Perkins.[11] Thus it is no surprise to find Arminius constructing a Ramist chart on the doctrine of predestination in 1598 in a letter to his close friend Uitenbogaert, and the first edition of his *Dissertation on Romans Seven* (Leiden, 1613) contains a Ramist chart of the argument of the exposition, inserted on a large fold-out sheet.

R. Hooykaas sees the thought of Ramus as the ambivalent link between the "New Learning" of the sixteenth century with its revival of classical literature and science and the "New Learning" of the seventeenth century with its new use of experimental scientific method.[12] It stands with one foot in the older humanistic logic and the other in a new empiricism. It moves from scholastic theory (which it has simplified) to practice, and its ultimate concern lies with practice.

It seems certain that Arminius found himself in much the same situation. He was feeling the winds of change, philosophically, and his Ramism contributed to the mood and method if not the content.

The question of content cannot be bypassed, however. Ramus, in

---

[7] Ong, pp. 199-202 *et passim*.

[8] I. Breward, "The Life and Theology of William Perkins, 1558-1602," p. 18.

[9] *Ibid.*, pp. 18, 71.

[10] *Catalogus librorum clarissimi viri D. D. Iacobi Arminii.* This is an auction catalog for the sale of Arminius' library the year after his death. The only copy known to me is in the British Museum.

[11] So he says in the opening lines of his *Examination of Perkins' Pamphlet, WA,* III, 266.

[12] *Humanisme, Science et Réforme, Pierre de la Ramée (1515-1572).*

Aristotelian fashion to be sure, places a great emphasis on causes. "The cause," he says, "is that by whose force the thing is: and therefore this first place of invention is the fountain of all sciences: for that matter is known perfectly whose cause is understood: So that not without good reason, the Poet doth say:

> Happy is the man withouten doubte,
> Of thinges who may the causes well find oute." [13]

He goes on to propose the four Aristotelian causes: efficient, material, formal, and final. But he proceeds to dichotomize until the subcauses are multiplied enormously. Thus Arminius in a typical passage, revealing his Ramist training, in speaking of repentance lists the following causes: the primary efficient, the inly moving, the outwardly moving, the proximate yet less principal, the external, the internal and inly moving, the instrumental, and still other minor causes. But these causes themselves are set over against the form, which in turn is dichotomized. And the cause and form together are set over against the fruit and parts. The parts are two. Then repentance itself is contrasted with impenitence, of which there are of course two kinds. And so on.[14]

But the question of content is approached more closely by examining the theological opinions of Ramus. His intellectual pursuits brought him into increasing contact with the Huguenot Protestants, and in about 1561 he turned from his previously zealous Catholicism to Calvinism. In the field of religion he proved to be as ardent as in his other studies. He had been present at the Colloquy of Poissy (1561) and was impressed not so much by Beza's famous exposition of Calvinism as by the weakness of the argument made by the Cardinal of Lorraine. He began at once to apply his dialectic to religious problems, and his break with Catholicism was complete in perhaps less than a year. He wrote a work entitled *Commentaries on the Christian Religion* which was not published until after his death but which was in print by the time of Arminius' university studies.[15]

His religious views were essentially Calvinistic, but with certain deviations (related to his humanistic sympathies) which brought him into conflict with the Calvinist leader, Beza. The first and broadest point of conflict was over the matter of Aristotelian logic itself. In 1570, during one of the periods when Ramus was in exile from Paris, he appears to have wanted a position as professor at Geneva under Beza. Beza wrote a reply in which Ramus' overture is turned down for an ostensibly financial

[13] *The Logike of the Most Excellent Philosopher P. Ramus Martyr,* p. 18.
[14] Public Disputation 17, in *WA*, II, 238-42.
[15] *Petri Rami Veromandvi, philosophiae et eloqventiae Regii professoris celeberrimi, Commentariorum de Religione Christiana, Libri quatuor, Eivsdem Vita.*

reason, but in which the real philosophical differences are brought to light. The letter reads, in part:

Although I differ greatly with you on certain things concerning our studies, I know how to appreciate your erudition, your eloquence, and so many of the superior qualities with which God has adorned your genius; and my fondest desire would be to favor you entirely in serving the interest of this Academy. Only two things stand in the way. . . . The first obstacle is that there is at the moment no vacancy in the Academy, and our resources are so small that we cannot enlarge the number of professors. . . . The second obstacle lies in our determination to follow the position of Aristotle, without deviating a line, be it in logic or in the rest of our studies. I tell you this frankly, as the old adage advises: "Between men of good will there must be good deeds." [16]

The second reason is undoubtedly the important one, not only for Ramus in his personal situation, but for the understanding of Beza's theology and method generally. The fact that Arminius regarded himself as a disciple of Ramus before he had ever studied under Beza is very important for the interpretation of the development of Arminius' thought.

Ramus came into conflict with Beza at another point—that of the Lord's Supper. Beza persisted in the use of the scholastic term "substance," which had been such a point of controversy between the early Reformers and the Roman Catholics and between the various branches of the Reformation. On one occasion Ramus wrote to Heinrich Bullinger (March 3, 1571) indicating that this was a point of controversy between himself and Beza. It is significant also that in this letter Ramus warns Bullinger to be on guard against "l'ésprit subtil et le caractère dominateur de Théodore de Bèze." [17]

The occasion of the letter itself was an ecclesiastical controversy between Ramus and Beza. Beza was in the process of revising the church constitution to place all power of government at the minimal level of the consistory (to all practical purposes, the clergy), thereby eliminating the lay deacons from exercising control in church affairs. Ramus' humanism led him to an anti-clericalism which saw in Geneva Protestantism some of the same injustices which had caused the earlier

[16] The letter is quoted in Waddington, pp. 229-30.

[17] *Ibid.* On January 14, 1572, Beza had written to Bullinger: "Il y a dix ans déja, comme j'étais en France, apprenant que Ramus s'était rallié à notre cause, j'ai prédit,— que n'ai-je tort!—que l'ésprit de discorde entrerait un jour dans les Eglises françaises avec cet homme. Pense-t-on que celui-là puisse nous être bien agréable, fut-il des nôtres, pour lequel Aristote n'est qu'un sophiste, Cicéron est incapable d'enseigner la rhetorique, Quintillien est un ignorant, Galenus et Euclide lui-même manquent de méthode?" Manuscript in Bibliothèque de Genève, quoted in Charles Borgeaud, *Histoire de l'Université de Genève,* I, 114. Borgeaud discusses in some detail the relationship between Ramus and Beza (pp. 110-15).

Reformers to protest against Rome. This was more than personal animosity; it was a consistent application of the Ramist dialectic to the theory of the church. Perry Miller points out that in England and New England the controversies over church polity between Congregationalists and Presbyterians were concurrent with controversies over logic. Says Miller: "The treatises upon polity were maintained . . . upon Ramist principles; many of the Presbyterians persisted in using Aristotelian methods, and from a reading of the controversies between them and the New Englanders arises an impression which is almost a certainty that the Congregational theory developed hand-in-hand with the application of Ramus' dialectic to the Bible, that there was a deep-seated affinity between the logic and the polity." [18]

If Miller is right, the point is of great significance for understanding Arminius, for Arminius was to be the constant champion of the rights of the layman, in the person of the magistrate, to exercise functions in the church which limit the powers of the consistory.

As for theology itself, Ramus defines it as "the science of living well," going on to say that "the final purpose of the science is not mere acquaintance with matters relating to it, but use and practice." [19] The Scriptures are the rule of faith, but should be studied not merely for knowledge but for truths to put into practice. Scholastic minutiae are to be set aside in favor of a plain theology as a basis for action. The Bible as interpreted by the Reformers is in full accord with the best of classical antiquity. In pre-Christian Greek thought there are prophecies and anticipations of Christ and Christian teaching.

Theology should be reorganized according to the "three laws of content"—nature, system, and practice. It should be divided into doctrine and discipline; doctrine consists of faith and works; works consist of obedience and prayer, on the one hand, and sacraments, on the other; and so on.[20]

As for predestination, which was to become a central issue in Arminius' later career, Ramus repeats with little precision the usual formulas. Predestination is that "wherein God out of his gracious mercy assigns some to eternal salvation and out of his justice relegates others to eternal perdition." [21] There is nothing about the order of the decrees, nothing vigorously Calvinistic. Thus the Calvinist Paul Lobstein complains, "How thirsty and feeble appears this topic compared with the bold and sublime

[18] *The New England Mind*, p. 120.
[19] *Commentariorum de religione Christiana*, chap. 1, sec. 1, pt. 6.
[20] Graves, pp. 189 ff.
[21] *Commentariorum de religione Christiana*, chap. 1, sec. 8, pt. 28,

affirmations of a Zwingli and a Calvin!" [22] Ramus spoke out of another mind-set.

It would be wrong to conclude, however, that Arminius derived his doctrine of predestination either from Ramus' theology or from his logic. Ramism is not the *differentia* between Arminius and Calvinism. Perkins, whom Arminius charged with Calvinistic error on predestination, was no less a Ramist than Arminius.

In fine, Arminius espoused Ramism as a sign of a new spirit, non-dogmatic, open to human values, and concerned with practice. In later years he would insist that our theology is a theology of grace, not of glory, that the Object of theology is not merely to be known but to be worshiped. "For the Theology which belongs to this world, is practical and through faith: Theoretical Theology belongs to the other world, and consists of pure and unclouded vision. . . . For this reason we must clothe the object of our Theology in such a manner as may enable it to incline us to worship God, and fully to persuade and win us over to that practice." [23]

---

[22] *Petrus Ramus als Theologe,* p. 36.
[23] *Oration on the Object of Theology; WA,* I, 264.

5

GENEVA AND THEODORE BEZA

ARMINIUS finished his studies in Leiden in 1581, when he was still only about twenty-two years old. He had established a reputation for brilliant scholarship, and he was too young for pastoral duties. Accordingly, his friends sought for him the means to continue his theological studies, which meant going outside Holland, Leiden then having the only university in the Protestant northern provinces. It was the burgomasters and the clergy of Amsterdam who took an interest in him at this point.[1] They recommended him to the officers of the Merchants' Guild (*Kramersgilde*) of the city for financial aid for further study.

How Arminius became known to the burgomasters and clergy we do not know, but many channels were available: his Leiden professors and fellow students, the clergy in Rotterdam and Leiden, or even trade connections between Amsterdam and Oudewater. Prior to the Alteration of Amsterdam in 1578, just three years earlier, many Amsterdam Protestants had been refugees in Rotterdam and Leiden. Some of these could have been in the circle of Arminius' friends.

The Amsterdam connection was to be fateful for the future career of Arminius, and it will be helpful to give careful attention to the situation there. The Merchants' Guild, or St. Martin's Guild, had separated itself from the older Tailors' Guild (*Kleermakersgilde*) at the beginning of the fifteenth century, and with the growth of trade in Amsterdam it had become a large and wealthy civic power.[2] It had an altar to its patron, St. Martin, in the Old Church, and before the Alteration this altar and the services connected with it were maintained at considerable

[1] This detail we know from the manuscript, " 't Kerck'lijck Amsterdam," a remarkable document by Henricus Selijns, a Dutch Reformed clergyman who had been a pastor in New Amsterdam and had returned to Amsterdam in 1664. He wrote his manuscript after his return, and he evidently had access to documents of the Merchants' Guild which are now lost. That portion of his manuscript dealing with the guild is printed in J. G. van Dillen, *Bronnen tot de Geschiedenis van het Bedrijfsleven en het Gildewezen van Amsterdam*, I, 787-91.

[2] I. H. van Eeghen, *Inventarissen der Archieven van de Gilden en van het Brouwerscollege*, pp. 45-46.

expense. Each year in early July on the first Sunday after St. Martin's Day the guild members attended in a body a High Mass at their altar. This was followed by a sumptuous feast. We have a record for guild expenditures for 1576. There were gold, silver, and velvet appointments to be restored. The Mass for July 8 entailed expenditures for musicians and for the organist (who was the father of the famous Jan Pietersz. Sweelinck), breakfast, four priests, the sextons, cushions for the priests to sit on, the ringing of the church bells, holy water, and many other such items; a total of 48 guilders, 10 stuivers, and 2 pennies—a considerable sum. Then there was the feast, which required a chef, three assistants, and numerous large pots and pans.[3] The Merchants' Guild altar represented one of the important capital funds of Amsterdam.

After the Alteration the traditional uses of this fund were made obsolete. It was decided "by my Lords the town government" (*mijne Heeren van den Gerechte,* i. e., *schout, burgemeesteren, schepenen*), with the advice of the City Council (*Vroedschap*), that the fund would no longer be used "as formerly, in unnecessary superstition, drunkenness, and unbecoming carousing, but for the care and maintenance of old, impoverished, or disabled and needy guild brothers and sisters or for other godly and worthy purposes."[4] What took place was that the silver appointments of the altar were turned over to the burgomasters, the income being administered by the officers of the guild under the advice of the burgomasters.

On September 13, 1581, there was available a sum of 100 guilders. The officers, Walich Sivertsz. and Dirck Clemments, agreed to allot this amount to Arminius. Arminius signed an agreement to devote his life, upon completion of his studies, to the service of the church in Amsterdam. The guild agreed to continue its support of his studies, so far as possible with available income, for three or four years.[5]

Arminius evidently paid a visit to Amsterdam at this time, satisfying the authorities there as to his fitness to receive financial benefits which at one time had gone to the altar of St. Martin. We know no details of this visit, except that he signed an agreement. The document itself is lost. We know little of what he did, whom he met. We may assume that he spoke with the four burgomasters, who that year were Reynier van Neck, Jacob Bas, Wilhem Baerdesen, and Cornelis Florisz. van Teylingen. Baerdesen and van Teylingen were to play an important part in his later life. The clergy were Johannes Cuchlinus, Martinus Lydius, Hillebrandus Cunaeus, Johannes Ambrosius, and Johannes Hallius.

---

[3] " 't Kerck'lijck Amsterdam," in van Dillen, *Bronnen . . . Bedrijfsleven,* I, 787.
[4] *Handvesten . . . der Stad Amsterdam,* Part 5, bk. 1, 3 (p. 1178).
[5] " 't Kerck'lijck Amsterdam," in van Dillen, *Bronnen . . . Bedrijfsleven,* I, 789.

These, too, Cunaeus excepted, were to figure largely in his subsequent career. The membership list of the Merchants' Guild is lost, but undoubtedly the prominent Amsterdam merchant Laurens Jacobsz. Reael was a member. Did Arminius meet him, or his twelve-year-old daughter Lijsbet? We do not know, but this could have been the occasion of Arminius' first acquaintance with his future wife.

Geneva was chosen as the place for study. Since Calvin had established an academy there in 1559, it had attracted increasing numbers of prospective clergy from the Low Countries. By 1565 approximately fifteen Dutch students had matriculated. During the next five years approximately thirty-two Dutch students entered. During the decade extending through 1580 there were sixty-four entering Dutch students, and Arminius was one of seventy-nine Dutch students who entered between 1581 and 1585.[6]

Arminius traveled to Geneva in late 1581. He signed the register at the academy on January 1, 1582.[7] He was now to encounter the head of the academy, Calvin's epigone and successor, Theodore Beza.

Beza was sixty-two years old. A native of Vézelay, he had studied at Orléans under Melchior Volmer and at Paris. After an early career of brilliance and dissipation, he joined forces with the Reformed Church, arriving at Geneva the first time in 1547. From 1549 to 1559 he was at Lausanne as a professor of Greek; in 1559 he became preacher and then professor in Geneva. He became Calvin's heir apparent and then his successor, and by the time Arminius studied under him, Beza was the aged and honored patriarch of the Reformed churches.

In Beza, Arminius was face to face with a derivative Calvinism, not that of the master himself, but that of an epigone who tries to be faithful to his teacher by imposing a strict internal coherence on what had been a free and creative theology. Perhaps everything that Beza says can be found in Calvin, but the emphasis is different. Beza lifts the doctrine of predestination to a prominence which it did not have for Calvin. Predestination, made an end in itself, becomes for Beza an utterly inscrutable mystery of the divine will. It is a decree *preceding* the decree of creation (an "order of the decrees" is not to be found explicitly in Calvin). Predestination, says Beza,

is God's everlasting and unchangeable ordinance, going in order before all the causes of salvation and damnation, whereby God has determined to be glorified,

---

[6] The names, matriculation dates, and brief curricula vitae of Dutch students at Geneva are given in *GPCH*, Vol. I. The figures are approximate because the register of the academy at Geneva does not always give the date of matriculation. The figures given here are from pp. 44 ff.

[7] *Ibid.*, p. 108.

in some by saving them of his own mere grace in Christ, and others by damning them through his rightful justice in Adam and in themselves. And after the custom of scripture we call the former the vessels of glory and the elect or chosen, that is to say, those appointed to salvation from before all worlds through mercy; and the other sort we call reprobates and castaways, and vessels of wrath, that is to say, appointed likewise to rightful damnation from everlasting: both of which God has known severally from time without beginning.[8]

Beza refers here to Romans 9, the prime biblical background for predestinarian controversies, and is taking the position that the *massa* (Vulgate), lump (KJV and RSV), refers to mankind regarded as not yet created, much less fallen. In answering his own rhetorical question, "Do you not by the term 'lump' (which the Apostle Paul uses) understand mankind as created and corrupted, out of which God ordains some to honor and some to dishonor?" Beza replies:

There is no doubt but God takes both sorts out of the same lump, ordaining them to contrary ends. Yet do I say and plainly avow, that Paul in the same similitude mounts up to the said sovereign ordinance to which even the very creation of mankind is submitted in order of causes, and therefore much less does the Apostle put the foreseen corruption of mankind before it. For first, by the term "lump" there is manifestly indicated a substance as yet unshapen and only prepared to work upon afterward. Again, in likening God to a potter and mankind to a lump of clay out of which vessels are afterward to be made, without a doubt the Apostle betokens the first creation of men.[9]

Beza argues that if predestination were to be regarded as referring to mankind as corrupted by sin, Paul would have gladly seized on this reasonable solution to the problem. But Paul is not looking for a reasonable solution, nor does he presume to search God's secrets. "But why then," asks Beza, "should the Apostle mount up to that secret will of God which is rather to be honored than searched, if he has so ready an answer at hand, especially which might carry a likelihood of truth with it even in the reason of man?"[10]

This position is even more extreme than that later called "supralapsarianism." It may be useful to digress a bit to explain some terms which sprang up around the question. The words *supralapsarianism, infralapsarianism,* and *sublapsarianism* do not appear to have come into use before the Synod of Dort (1618-19), but they appear shortly after. Supralapsarianism is the position that the decrees of election and damnation have priority over the decree of permission of the fall. The other two terms, usually interchangeable, indicate that the decrees of election

---

[8] *A Booke of Christian Questions and Answers,* p. 76. This and other old translations used in this book have been revised and modernized.

[9] *Ibid.,* pp. 84-85.

[10] *Ibid.,* p. 85.

and damnation are with respect to man considered as fallen. Beza's position refers the decrees of election and damnation to man not yet considered as created. James Nichols proposes the horrendous term "the Creabilitarian opinion." [11] Fortunately, it has never caught on. In practice, Beza's position has been called supralapsarianism.

Beza's doctrine of predestination is the fountainhead of what is often called "high Calvinism." It was the insistence on the details of his system as essential to Reformed orthodoxy which had a great deal to do with the precipitation of the so-called Arminian controversy.

This extreme insistence on the sovereign and inscrutable decree of predestination to salvation and damnation led to a corresponding insistence that in sinful man there is no free will, no movement toward the good, no desire for holiness, and no striving against sin. The scriptural battleground for this issue was the latter part of Romans 7. It is a description of a man who cannot do what he wants, who does the very thing he hates, who delights in the law of God but cannot perform it, who struggles against sin but fails in the struggle. The theological question was put this way: Is this a picture of an unregenerate man or a regenerate man? Or, can an unregenerate man "delight in the law of God" in his "inmost self" (vs. 22)?

Beza answers categorically, "Except the spirit of adoption . . . were present in us, there should be no striving in us, but sin should reign quietly at his pleasure." The unregenerate man can say only, "I do the evil that I have a mind unto; I do no good, nor have I any desire to do it." The regenerate man, on the other hand, says, "I do the evil that I would not, I do not the good that I would do." This shows that he is elected, "howbeit as yet still wrestling." Only in the other world can the elect man say, "I do the good that I would do, and I do no evil, nor do I wish to do any." [12] The interpretation is in the tradition of Calvin, but Calvin does not put the matter quite so baldly. In speaking of Romans 7:15, Calvin ascribes to the unregenerate man at least "the stings of conscience" and "some taste of bitterness." [13] It is characteristic of Beza to take a position of Calvin's, fasten on a difficult facet of it, and throw it into stark, isolated prominence where it can be only accepted or rejected, but not softened.

So it is with the question of the origin of man's sin. Calvin at least speaks about it with two voices. Adam, says Calvin with one voice, "by free will had the power, if he so willed, to attain eternal life. . . . Adam could have stood if he wished, seeing that he fell solely by his own

[11] *WA,* I, 581.
[12] *Christian Questions and Answers,* pp. 89-90.
[13] *Commentaries on the Epistle of Paul the Apostle to the Romans,* pp. 261-65.

will." [14] With the other voice, however, Calvin says, "Yet no one can deny that God foreknew what end man was to have before he created him, and consequently foreknew because he so ordained by his decree. . . . God not only foresaw the fall of the first man, and in him the ruin of his descendants, but also meted it out in accordance with his own decision." [15]

Beza has only one voice, and it is the voice of rigor. If God decrees the salvation of some and the damnation of others, it becomes then

necessary that man should be so created good that notwithstanding he should be mutable and fall from this degree and that by his own good fault. For if sin had not so entered the world, a god had not found such cause to magnify his mercy in saving those which he has ordained to salvation, nor matter to declare his justice in condemning those which he has ordained to his wrath to the end that he may punish them for their demerits. [16]

Beza does not want to say, nevertheless, that God is the author of sin, and he tries to avoid it by explaining how man sinned willingly and of his own accord but yet not contrary to God's will. "God, whose judgments no man can comprehend [etc.] . . . has determined from before all beginning with himself, to create all things in their time, for his glory, and namely men: whom he has made of two sorts, clean contrary one to the other." [17] Beza insists that God does not create man a sinner, for then he would be the author of sin and could not justly punish it (Beza was concerned about the punishment of sinners and heretics, too). So man sins "willingly and of his own accord." But there is more. "Yet we must confess that this fall came not by chance or fortune, seeing his providence both stretches itself even to the smallest things, neither can we say that anything happens that God does not know or cares not for." What, then, is God's role in man's sin? "For seeing he hath appointed the end [damnation], it is necessary also that he should appoint the causes which lead us to the same end. . . . We cannot think that anything happens contrary to God's will." [18]

There is, then, a determinate class of people born reprobate. Of these, some are cut off as infants, but others are allowed to come to maturity, to whom is reserved "a more sharp judgment." But how are such mature reprobates to regard themselves? Well, they are in ignorance about it, because one difference between election and reprobation is that

[14] *Institutes of the Christian Religion*, 1.25.8.
[15] *Ibid.*, 3.23.7.
[16] *A Briefe and Pithie Summe of the Christian Faith*, p. 5.
[17] *A Briefe Declaration of the Chiefe Poyntes of the Christian Religion*, Chap. 2.
[18] *Ibid.*, chap. 3.

the former is revealed to the individual (but not to anyone else) by the Spirit of God, while reprobation "is ever hidden from man, except it be disclosed by God, contrary to the common course of things." A person whose election is doubted by himself and by others, even for manifestly good cause, should nevertheless not give up hope, "for who can tell, if God has determined to show mercy at the last hour of death to him who has spent all his life past lewdly and wickedly." [19]

[19] *Ibid.,* chap. 8.

6

STUDIES AT GENEVA AND BASEL

It was Beza's form of Calvinism which was promoted in Geneva when Arminius went there to study. It is the position which Arminius is alleged by Bertius and Caspar Brandt to have espoused as a student and held until the early years of his pastoral ministry in Amsterdam. In order to assess this allegation and come to a more complete understanding of Arminius during his Geneva days, it will be necessary to examine all available evidence.

At the outset it becomes apparent that Arminius did not get along smoothly in Geneva. He had come to Geneva enamored with the logic of Ramus. The inevitable conflict developed, but not between Arminius and Beza directly. Arminius is reported to have defended Ramus publicly "in the warmest manner," and a number of students, including Uitenbogaert, asked him to give private lectures on Ramus in his study. This he did, but not without incurring the wrath of the authorities. According to Uitenbogaert, it was a new professor of philosophy, Petrus Galesius (Pierre Galez), a Spaniard and an Aristotelian, who was particulary offended. Because of this, Arminius found it necessary to leave Geneva for a time. He went to Basel to study. There is the suggestion from Bertius that he was not the only one making this academic detour, for Bertius speaks of "those who were the companions of his journey to Basel" who could "bear witness to the great honors which were conferred on the young man in that city." [1]

The time of his departure for Basel is difficult to establish. There is a report that Arminius defended theses in Basel on September 1, 1582, and on November 21, 1583.[2] Galesius, however, did not serve on the Geneva faculty until 1583; hence, at least the first of those dates must be called in question. The September theses must have been in 1583, and his departure for Basel in the summer of 1583.

In Basel, Arminius became the favorite of Johannes Jacobus Grynaeus,

[1] *KH*, Part III, p. 102; Funeral Oration, *WA*, I, 23.
[2] Rudolf Thommen, *Geschichte der Universität Basel, 1532-1632*, cited in *GPCH*, I, 108.

professor of sacred literature and dean of the theological faculty. Grynaeus (1540-1617) was a grandnephew of the more noted Simon Grynaeus. Originally a Lutheran, he had become involved in controversy over the Lord's Supper and had adopted more or less Zwinglian views by the time Arminius studied under him. Not much is known about the specific influence of Grynaeus on Arminius except that it was under Grynaeus that Arminius presented expositions of several chapters of Romans. It was the custom at Basel to permit advanced students to give public lectures during the harvest holidays. Uitenbogaert reports that Arminius expounded a few chapters of Romans, with Grynaeus occasionally in attendance and expressing his approval. It was on Romans that Arminius was to begin his preaching in Amsterdam a few years later, and it was his expositions of chapters 7 and 9 which first brought him under fire from his more Calvinist colleagues.

Grynaeus and Arminius evidently maintained cordial relations for many years, for there is extant a letter of Arminius to Grynaeus dated as late as March 18, 1591.[3] On September 3, 1583, Grynaeus wrote an open letter to Amsterdam commending Arminius for his "piety, moderation, and assiduity in study," and reporting that Arminius had given "the best ground to hope that he was destined ere long—if, he goes on to stir up the gift of God that is to him—to undertake and sustain the function of teaching." Speaking directly to "the church of God in the famous city of Amsterdam," Grynaeus closed with an appeal: "I respectfully entreat that regard may be had to that learned and pious youth, so that he may never be under the necessity of intermitting theological studies which have been thus far so happily prosecuted." [4]

Between the lines we see a plea to Amsterdam to continue its financial support of Arminius. Indeed, the letter most likely is not an "honorable dismissal," as if Arminius were leaving Basel, but rather a plea for financial aid. The income from Amsterdam was by no means regular, and Arminius was at times forced to borrow money in order to survive. In the year 1583 he had received from Amsterdam 30 pounds Flemish, suggesting, possibly, that the authorities did not disapprove of his being in Basel.[5] The response of Amsterdam to the letter of Grynaeus is not known.

Both Bertius and Uitenbogaert report that when Arminius was about to return to Geneva, the theological faculty at Basel offered him the title of Doctor "at the cost of the university." This may have been on the occasion of his defense of theses on November 21, 1583. Arminius is said

[3] The text is in J. H. Maronier, *Jacobus Arminius, een Biografie,* pp. 60-61.
[4] *LA,* p. 50.
[5] *Prot,* May 29, 1586; I, 277.

to have refused, on the grounds that his youth (he was only twenty-four or twenty-five years old at the time) would not bring honor to the title.[6] His departure from Basel must have been in 1584 and not in 1583, as most accounts put it, and it must have been in the summer and not late in the year, as Tideman maintains.[7] Arminius signed the register at the academy in Geneva the second time shortly after October 10, 1584, but he had evidently been in the city since at least August, because he had inscribed in his autograph book or *album amicorum* a Latin poem to his friend Carolus Martinus with the identification of "Genevae 27 Aug. An° a Christo nati 1584."[8] His return could have been even earlier, because on August 19 the burgomasters of Amsterdam addressed a letter to Beza inquiring about Arminius. They wanted to know about his personal development. Is he stubborn and arrogant? Does he obstinately defend his own personal opinions? Is he making proper use of his education?[9] The burgomasters were evidently nervous about the earlier episode of Arminius' defense of Ramus.

Uitenbogaert reports, in fact, that after his return to Geneva, Arminius "did not dispute so much, conducted himself in a milder manner, and was not so enamored with the Ramist philosophy as formerly."[10]

An answer to the burgomasters, written by Beza in the name of the Company of Pastors, was returned shortly after receipt of the inquiry. Some time later, when Beza had the opportunity to communicate with Amsterdam by a confidential carrier and because of the uncertainty of mail delivery, another version was sent. It is this version of June 3, 1585, which is known to us. The matter is further complicated by the fact that Caspar Brandt, the biographer of Arminius, mistook the date for 1583, and this error had been perpetuated in most subsequent accounts, thereby confusing the chronology of Arminius' studies at Geneva and Basel.[11]

Beza says of his Dutch student:

To sum up all, then, in a few words: let it be known to you that from the time Arminius returned to us from Basel, his life and learning both have so approved themselves to us, that we hope the best of him in every respect, if he

---

[6] *KH,* Part III, p. 102; *WA,* I, 23.

[7] Joannes Tideman, "Twee Brieven over den Student Jacobus Arminius," p. 290.

[8] The *album amicorum* is number 407 in the manuscript collection of the Remonstrantse-Gereformeerde Gemeente, Rotterdam. Arminius began the album on October 23, 1583. For a detailed discussion of the chronology of Arminius' studies in Basel, see the article on "Arminius (Jacobus)," *BWPGN,* I, 230-34.

[9] Tideman, pp. 287-88; *GPCH,* I, 235-37.

[10] *KH,* Part III, p. 102.

[11] Tideman, p. 290.

steadily persist in the same course, which, by the blessing of God, we doubt not he will; for, among other endowments, God has gifted him with an apt intellect both as respects the apprehension and the discrimination of things. If this henceforward be regulated by piety, which he appears assiduously to cultivate, it cannot but happen that this power of intellect, when consolidated by mature age and experience, will be productive of the richest fruits. Such is our opinion of Arminius—a young man, unquestionably, so far as we are able to judge, most worthy of your kindness and liberality." [12]

Again reading between the lines we see Beza now making the appeal to Amsterdam to continue its financial support of Arminius. The appeal was successful, for in August, 1585, he received 50 pounds Flemish from the Amsterdam authorities.[13]

The theological issue appears in this letter. Beza, the arch-Calvinist, commends Arminius, the future antagonist of Calvinism. Does this mean that in 1585 Arminius was a Calvinist? Caspar Brandt so concluded, as have almost all writers since. With great rhetorical flourish but with little evidence, Brandt says:

Nothing appeared to Arminius of greater consequence while at Geneva, than to conciliate toward himself Beza's interest and affection, inasmuch as he hoped. by means of his conversations and intercourse, to become not only a more erudite and polished, but also a better and a wiser man. For, with the utmost gravity of manners, this theologian excelled his compeers in persuasiveness of address, and in promptitude and perspicuity of utterance; while his learning and attainments in sacred literature were profound and extraordinary. With ears intent Arminius drank in his words; with eager assiduity he hung on his lips; and with intense admiration he listened to his exposition of the ninth chapter of Paul's Epistle to the Romans.[14]

It is this passage, along with Beza's letter, which has led most subsequent writers to describe Arminius as a believer in Beza's doctrines of grace and predestination.

There is one more piece of direct evidence bearing upon the relationship between Arminius and Beza, a Latin poem about Beza that Arminius wrote in his *album amicorum*. The poem was probably written during Arminius' student days in Geneva. It reads:

> To the Portrait of T. Beza
> Why are you amazed at looking upon the face of the man
> That you are permitted to view only in a picture?
> Never would you be able to imagine it to yourself,
> However intently you viewed it with astonishment, the wonderful
> mind

[12] The autograph is in the Musée de la Reformation, Geneva, and is quoted in *LA*, pp. 48-49.
[13] *Prot*, I, 277.
[14] *LA*, pp. 44-45.

Which the writings of the man so portray,
That you may at the same time see it
And in gazing form your own mind like unto it.

What can be concluded from the direct evidence, namely, the letter
of Beza and the poem of Arminius? Note well that Beza commends
Arminius for his ability and diligence, but not for his theology and not
even for his piety. He expresses hope that continued growth will produce
"richest fruits." Nothing is said about predestination. Arminius likewise
praises Beza for a wonderful mind which is worthy of a student's emula-
tion. Nothing about predestination.

Beza was, in fact, in spite of his reputation for rigidity and even
harshness, not a despot. He tolerated the presence on the faculty of
the more liberal Charles Perrot, and he tolerated among the students
many who disagreed with him on predestination, including especially
Arminius' close friend Uitenbogaert and another liberal Dutch student,
Conrad Vorstius. Beza's friendship for these three primary founders of
Remonstrantism, Arminius, Uitenbogaert, and Vorstius, has led de Vries
to discern in Beza a duality of loyalties. On the one hand, he was the
faithful and forceful defender of Calvin; on the other, having been
delivered from Roman authority, he was not willing simply to impose
his own. There is a sense, then, in which Arminius and his friends were
indeed disciples of Beza, in that they adhered firmly not to ecclesiastical
authority but to the "Word of God," in which they found the basis for
their doctrine of the liberty of conscience. Other students such as Johannes
Bogerman and Gosvinus Geldorpius were disciples of Beza in holding
to the content of his doctrines.[15] It is a mistake to say either that
Arminius followed the content of the doctrines or that Beza did not
know of the difficulties his students were having with these doctrines.
Jacobus Triglandius, the violent critic of the early Remonstrants, has
tried to maintain that Arminius and Uitenbogaert concealed their true
opinions from Beza.[16] There is no need for this hypothesis; indeed, available evidence is against it. Uitenbogaert's views were known during his
stay in Geneva, and as late as 1595 Beza and Vorstius enjoyed cordial
relations.[17]

Charles Perrot has been mentioned. Most accounts of Arminius fail
to explain the importance of this Geneva theologian. Neither Bertius
nor Caspar Brandt mentions Perrot. James Nichols mentions the fact that
Arminius studied under Anthony Faye and Perrot, but he says nothing

[15] *GPCH*, I, 212-20 ("Remonstrants et Contre-Remonstrants: La Dualité en
Théodore de Bèze").
[16] *Kerkelycke Geschiedenissen*, p. 344.
[17] *HRN*, II, 122; *GPCH*, I, 213-15.

about the significance of this for the development of Arminius' views. The importance of Perrot is seen by H. D. Foster and de Vries.[18] Gerard Brandt mentions Perrot more extensively but does not connect him with Arminius.[19]

Perrot, who taught theology and presided over students' discussion of theses, was a liberal force in theology at Geneva. He was critical of Beza's extreme emphasis on grace and is reported to have said respecting it, "Justification by faith only has been preached up too much; it is time to speak of works." [20] Perrot argued for tolerance in theological matters, and, when Uitenbogaert was about to leave Geneva for the Netherlands, Perrot gave him this advice:

Never assist in condemning any for not agreeing in every point of religion with the established church, so long as they adhere to the fundamentals of Christianity, and are disposed to maintain the peace of the Church, and bear with others their brethren who do not reject the fundamentals of religion, though a little differing from them. For this is the way to avoid schisms, and to arrive at the pious union and tranquillity of the Christian Church.[21]

Perrot got into difficulty over his tolerant theological views, and his book, *De extremis in religione vitandis,* was suppressed by the Genevan authorities. In the preface to this book Perrot had said, "I desire and approve beyond all things, that every man should enjoy his own opinion freely and entirely." [22]

To overlook the presence of Perrot on the theological faculty at Geneva and to assume that Beza's influence was all-compelling distorts the situation. Arminius' later statements on religious toleration are certainly closer to Perrot than to Beza.

We have a few more glimpses of Arminius during his Geneva years. We know, for instance, that he was surrounded by many Dutch fellow students there. One of these was his intimate and lifelong friend Johannes Uitenbogaert, whom he may have known earlier in Utrecht. There was Nicolas Cromhout, younger brother of the Amsterdam burgomaster Barthold Cromhout. Nicholas, a medical doctor, was to become the delegate of the States General to the Synod of Dort and one of the

---

[18] H. D. Foster, "Liberal Calvinism; the Remonstrants at the Synod of Dort in 1618," p. 14.; *GPCH,* I, 213-15.

[19] *HRN,* II, 122-24.

[20] Reported by Isaac Casaubon, professor of Greek at Geneva from 1582 to 1596 and himself a liberal Calvinist, in a conversation with Uitenbogaert on April 20, 1610, and quoted from a letter of Uitenbogaert; *ibid.,* II, 122.

[21] *Ibid.* Perrot's theological role at Geneva is described by Borgeaud, pp. 158, 255, *et passim.* Cf. J. E. Cellerier, "Charles Perrot, Pasteur Genevois au XVIᵉ Siècle."

[22] *HRN,* II, 124.

judges who condemned Jan van Oldenbarneveld to death. There were
the jurists Peter Brederode from The Hague and Hermannus Bysius
from Dordrecht. Brederode was later the ambassador of the States General
to Germany. There were also Dominicus Baudius, Paulus Merula, and
Antonius Thysius, later to become important scholars in Leiden. Many
others could be mentioned, but not to be overlooked is Adriaan de
Jonge Cornelisz., or Adrian Junius, from Dordrecht, who in Geneva days
was an intimate companion of Arminius but who in later years was also
one of the judges who condemned Oldenbarneveld.

Even during Arminius' stay in Geneva there were students who dis-
sented from Beza's rigid Calvinism. Uitenbogaert has been mentioned;
there were also Joannes Halsbergius, Cornelis Royenburgh, and the
moderate Calvinists Franciscus Junius, Werner Helmichius, Jeremias
Bastingius, Johannes Becius, Thysius, Adrianus Lymphaius, and Johannes
Polyander. Geneva continued to produce opponents of strict Calvinism
after Arminius had finished his work there, including Jacob de Graeff,
Vorstius, Adriaan van der Mijle, Theophilus Rickwaert, Henricus Leo,
Isaacus Diamantius, Nicolas Grevinchovius, Cornelius Burchvliet, Daniel
Wittius, the later Remonstrant professor Stephanus Curcellaeus (de Cour-
celles), Johannes Arnoldus Corvinus, and Niclaes van Sorgen—all in the
days of Beza himself. De Vries has called Geneva the "seedbed of Dutch
Calvinism." It is almost as fitting to call it the "seedbed of Dutch Armin-
ianism."

After his return to Geneva, Arminius made a trip to Zurich. The date
is uncertain, but it had to be before August 18, 1585, because on that
date he wrote a letter to the Zurich pastor and professor of Hebrew,
Burckhardt Leemann, in which he spoke of his recent trip. The letter
tantalizes us, because it speaks of news which he, Arminius, cannot
write, but which some of his fellow Dutchmen will convey to Leemann
personally.

The next year, 1586, was evidently the last spent by Arminius in regular studies in Geneva. On May 29 the Consistory of Amsterdam considered a letter it had received from Arminius,[23] expressing regret over some
misunderstanding about money and requesting that more be sent him.
If he receives money by autumn, he can stay in Geneva; if not, his
studies must come to an end. It is reported in the meeting that Arminius
had received 30 pounds Flemish in 1583 and another 50 in August, 1585.
It is decided by the burgomasters that he may stay in Geneva until the
autumn *misse,* the market held traditionally at the time of the St. John's
Mass. He will be sent 25 pounds travel money, which will reach him by
way of Strassburg, where monetary exchange can be handled by a friend

[23] *Prot,* I, 277.

77

of Cuchlinus. These arrangements were related to Arminius in a letter written by Cuchlinus on June 1.[24] Cuchlinus expresses the hope that Arminius' doubts will be dispelled by the letter and informs him that the burgomasters want him to return in the autumn "adorned with modesty, humility, and piety."

Arminius did not receive the 25 pounds, at least at that time. On August 17 Cuchlinus reported to the consistory that he had received word from a brother-in-law of the agent in Strassburg that the Geneva merchants who were to deliver the money had found that Arminius had already departed from Geneva to go on a trip to Italy.[25] It is evident that Arminius left for this trip at least by mid-summer of 1586. The consistory looked with approval on this trip and made plans to get the money to Arminius by other means. They evidently regarded this, however, as the termination of their support of Arminius, expecting that he would soon return to Amsterdam to present himself for examination and subsequent duties there. Accordingly, on September 11, 1586, the burgomasters suggested that upon Arminius' return they should send to Geneva the son of the deceased pastor Johannes Nicolai van Wassenaar.[26]

The trip to Italy was to be the occasion for vicious attacks on Arminius back in Amsterdam. He was accused of having kissed the pope's slipper and of having consorted with Cardinal Bellarmine. The rigid Calvinists could not find any innocent motive for visiting the territory of the Antichrist. As late as 1929 an Amsterdam Calvinist was speculating that it was in Italy that Arminius associated with Jesuits and lost his true Calvinist faith. "For Arminius and his country," says F. J. Los, "this trip was a disaster." [27] In passing it should be noted that the modern Calvinist Los agrees that Arminius was no Calvinist when he assumed the pastoral office in Amsterdam.

For what facts there are, we are dependent primarily on Bertius.[28] Neither Uitenbogaert nor Caspar Brandt adds anything, and Arminius himself is characteristically silent about his own personal history. According to Bertius, Arminius found himself deserted by most of his fellow Dutch students at Geneva. Some of them had been called home, and others, "sons of the principal noble and honorable personages" of Holland, had gone on a tour of Italy. At this juncture, Adrian Junius,

[24] The autograph is in the University Library, Leiden, and the text is printed in *GPCH*, II, 31-33.

[25] *Prot*, I, 286.

[26] Resolutiën der Vroedschappen, N° 5 van i Januari 1584 tot 4 Mei 1588, p. 361; manuscript in Gemeente Archief Amsterdam.

[27] *Grepen uit de Geschiedenis van Hervormd Amsterdam*, p. 52.

[28] Funeral Oration, *WA*, I, 25-26.

the law student from Dordrecht, suggested to Arminius that the two of them travel together to Italy themselves. One particular attraction was a renowned professor of philosophy at Padua; in addition, there was the excitement of foreign travel and the fascination of Rome and its church. The two of them set out, armed with a Greek New Testament and the Psalms in Hebrew. They spent some time at Padua, listening to the lectures of the philosophy professor Giacomo Zabarella, during which time Arminius himself gave lessons in logic to some German noblemen. Afterward they made a hasty trip to Rome on the way back to Geneva. They saw the Pope from a great distance in a large crowd; they did not see Bellarmine. Bertius recalls having heard Arminius say that the trip was profitable in many respects, disadvantageous in others.

The disadvantages were chiefly the displeasure incurred in Amsterdam, whose permission he had not sought for the trip. Perhaps he felt secure enough in his relationship to the burgomasters not to feel the need for seeking and gaining permission, a slow process in view of uncertain communication. It seems that the burgomasters themselves would have raised no objections had the enemies of Arminius not used the Italian trip to embarrass them for their support of Arminius. At this point the burgomasters too were irritated, and Arminius had to face some opposition upon his return.

The advantage which Bertius mentions is that of having seen " 'the mystery of iniquity' in a more ugly and detestable form than his imagination could ever have conceived." The Pope was the newly chosen Sixtus V, who had begun his reign with a campaign against lawlessness in Rome. It was a reign of terror. Soon after it began, according to one report, there were more bandits' heads on the Bridge of St. Angelo than there were melons in the market.[29]

What Arminius thought of this we do not know. He never did have a kind word for popes, with the exception of the one Dutch pope, Adrian of Utrecht. A modern observer, however, wants to know more about Zabarella.[30] He was a native of Padua, had studied Greek, philosophy, and mathematics, and had attained the title of Doctor in 1553, at age twenty. In 1564 he had become professor of logic at Padua, and in 1579 he exchanged the chair of logic for that of philosophy. His ideas were a mixture of serious thought and popular fancy. He became a famed astrologer while at the same time making some discriminating

---

[29] Ludwig, Freiherr von Pastor, *The History of the Popes* (37 vols.; St. Louis: B. Herder, 1952), XXI, 83.
[30] "Zabarella (Jacques, comte)," *Grand Dictionnaire Universal du XIX* Siècle* ed. Pierre Larousse (Paris, 1876), XV, 1443; "Zabarella, Giacomo," *Encyclopedia Italiana* (Rome, 1937), XXXV, 858.

judgments about Aristotle. He taught, for instance, that it was impossible on Aristotelian grounds to prove the immortality of the soul and that it was impossible to prove the existence of a first mover without affirming the eternity of the movement. When threatened with church censure, he adroitly asserted that he could hold by faith what reason alone would not support. Why did he attract an international following? Probably it was his critical approach to Aristotle, who reigned supreme not only among Roman Catholics but also among many Protestants. Beyond that we know little. Arminius does not mention him.

After the trip to Italy, Arminius remained in Geneva for several months before returning to Amsterdam. He arrived in Amsterdam in the autumn of 1587. His student days were over, and soon he was in the second phase of his career, the pastoral ministry in Amsterdam.

PART II
PASTOR

7

AMSTERDAM, ARMINIUS'
ALMA MATER

WHEN Arminius made his way to Amsterdam in the autumn of 1587 to take up pastoral duties there, he was moving from the mainstream of Reformed theological life to the burgeoning center of Dutch commercial life. Amsterdam was in the chaotic and exciting transition from its significant but limited commercial past into its Golden Age, when commerce would provide the foundation for an impressive superstructure of political power, urban planning, banking, art, and literature.

Arminius spent the greater part of his professional career as pastor in Amsterdam, fifteen years compared with the six years he spent in Leiden. Furthermore, his theological productivity reached its peak during the Amsterdam years. The academic theses he defended in Leiden were for the most part but the restatement of the longer treatises he composed in Amsterdam.

Amsterdam also provided Arminius with something he had lost as a youth—a family and the social, economic, and political relationships which a family can provide. The family was that of his wife, who was a daughter of one of the leading Amsterdam merchants. Arminius was thus a foster son of Amsterdam in a double sense: a protégé of its church and a son-in-law of one of its town fathers.

For these reasons it is important to know something about the *alma mater* in which Arminius labored and which provided so much of the context which surrounded his life and work.

As European cities go, Amsterdam was not old. It first appears in historical records in the second half of the thirteenth century as a small town already important for its fisheries and its Baltic Sea trade. It was located at the confluence of the river Y and the river Amstel.[1] It lay in the territory of the lords of Amstel, whose seat was at Ouderkerk.

---

[1] For the following account of the history of Amsterdam, I have been dependent on J. Wagenaar, *Amsterdam, in zyne Opkomst, Aanwas, Geschiedenissen, Voorrechten, Koophandel, enz.*, and J. ter Gouw, *Geschiedenis van Amsterdam tot 1578* (hereafter *GA*).

Its future was as yet not apparent. Haarlem, to the west, was already several centuries old, and Utrecht had a history going back to Roman times and had been a Christian bishopric since St. Willibrord had been consecrated there in 696. What "turned the tide" for Amsterdam was literally that: the damming of the Amstel around 1270 by the then Lord of Amstel, Gijsbrecht IV, thereby providing a safe harbor for small ships. The great square opposite the palace in present-day Amsterdam, at the juncture of the Damrak and the Rokin (tourists will think of it in terms of the Hotel Krasnapolsky) is on the site of that ancient dam and is still called the Dam.

On October 27, 1275, Count Floris V of Holland granted to Amsterdam freedom from tolls. It was his policy to strengthen the towns in this way in order to use them to counterbalance the power of his sometimes rebellious liege lords. This gave the city an advantage which contributed to its economic growth. Amsterdam by this time was a bustling collection of wooden buildings lining the diked waterways. The main harbor was the Damrak, and parallel to this on each side ran the Warmoesstraat, to the east, and the Nieuwendijk, to the west. These three arteries, from east to west, extended inland (south) to form the Nes, the Rokin, and the Kalverstraat. The Old Side was originally called the Church Side and the New Side the Windmill Side. Later on the names were Old Church Side and New Church Side. Where the present Old Church stands there was probably its wooden predecessor, the Sinterklaas-kapel. The patron saint of town and chapel was to become the Sinterklaas of Dutch folklore and the Santa Claus of American Christmas festivities.[2]

The future of Amsterdam's trading patterns was in evidence by this time, with her ships moving primarily eastward as far as Lubeck on the *Oost Zee* or Baltic Sea. The cargoes were usually timber and grain, which along with herring were the foundations of Amsterdam economy.

The relations between Gijsbrecht IV and Floris V became complex and strained in the latter part of the thirteenth century, with a final break as the result. Gijsbrecht took part in a conspiracy which led to the murder of Floris and had to flee the country, taking refuge, along Amsterdam trade routes, in Prussia. Amsterdam came into the hands of the Counts of Holland, who in turn gave it further privileges which contributed to its growth. In the early fourteenth century it was raised to the level of a town, and in the fifteenth century it was walled and fortified. It continued to grow, ever pushing at its old boundaries, until in mid-sixteenth century it had grown larger than all other towns in the Low Countries except Antwerp itself.

[2] For a description of Amsterdam at this time, see *GA*, I, 123-25.

In the Historical Museum there is a marvelous painted pictorial map of mid-sixteenth-century Amsterdam. Painted from the assumed perspective of an aerial vantage point over the harbor and looking southward over the town, it shows every waterway, every dike, every street and alley, the fortifications, walls, windmills, churches, bridges, and each individual house and building. The painting was done by Cornelis Anthonijsz. in 1538, and it was also made into a drawing and printed in 1544. The printed map was photographed and reprinted in fourteen colors in 1885 and published as a companion volume to ter Gouw's eight-volume history of Amsterdam.

From this map we see a bustling seaport (the harbor is full of sailing ships and the canals are lined with barges and boats) bounded mainly by the Kloveniersburgwal on the east, the bend of the Amstel on the south, and the Singel on the west, roughly an ellipse with one focus in the harbor itself on the north.

As Amsterdam entered the sixteenth century, it was at least in public life a solidly Roman Catholic town. There were two great churches, the St. Nicholas Church (*Sint Nikolaas* or *Oude Kerk,* the Old Church) on the Old Side and on the New Side the St. Catherine's Church (*Sint Catharina* or *Nieuwe Kerk,* the New Church), but these were not all. There were two chapels, on the Old Side the St. Olofskapel and on the New Side the Heilige Stede, and there were some twenty cloisters. On the Old Side they occupied more than half the available ground.

The chapel called the Heilige Stede (Chapel of the Holy City) was the focal point of civic devotion, for it was on the site of the popularly revered Miracle of Amsterdam. The miracle was said to have taken place on March 15, 1345, when a sick man who feared that he was dying called for a priest to give him the sacred Host. After having received the bread, he vomited. The women caring for him threw the material in the fire without noticing that it contained the sacred Host. The fire was kept high during the night, but in the morning it died down. When a woman went to stir up the coals, she saw the Host unsullied by flame or ash. She picked it up without harm to herself, and finally it was taken as a sign that a chapel should be built there. The relic was displayed in a monstrance, and when the Heilige Stede burned in the great fire of 1452, it was rescued. It became the focus of an annual procession in the city, a practice which has been renewed by some Amsterdam Roman Catholics in modern times. Such celebrations were suppressed when Amsterdam opted for the Reformation; the Heilige Stede was transformed into the New Side Chapel; and in later, more tolerant times, the monstrance and its alleged miracle wafer are once

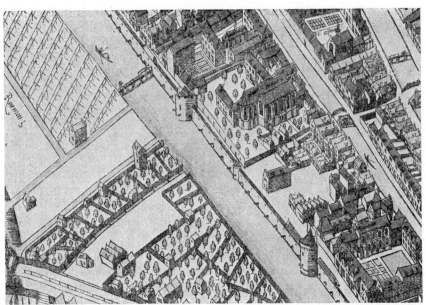

Details from the printed map of Amsterdam by Cornelis Anthonijsz., 1544. Reproduced from the 1885 reprint of J. ter Gouw, *Geschiedenis van Amsterdam*, Vol. 5. Top: This section includes the premises of the St. Ursula Cloister. Arminius's last residence in Amsterdam shows just above the west (right) end of the "Paules Broers" church. Bottom: The Reael family premises—"in den gouden Reael"—are just above the W of "opt Waeter."

again on display, now in the seventeenth-century *schuilkerk* or hidden church in the Begijnhof.

Such was popular Catholic devotion in Amsterdam well into the sixteenth century. The Old Church was also a center of the special devotions of the guilds, who maintained costly altars and Masses in its side chapels. The Merchants' Guild has already been mentioned in this connection.

When the Reformation appeared in neighboring lands and indeed in Amsterdam itself in the 1520s, the Catholic character of the town could no longer be taken for granted. In terms of the public life of the town, which is to say from all outward appearances, Amsterdam could well remain Catholic indefinitely. There was a well-ordered town government, a modest but growing economy, and an accepted form of Catholic church life. Amsterdam was in a position to seal itself off from imported, alien, Lutheran ideas, books, and men. What it discovered, however, when Protestantism first appeared as an external threat from Germany, was that there was within the city a remarkable readiness to espouse new forms of religious life. R. B. Evenhuis in his history of the Reformed Church in Amsterdam correctly observes that Reformation sentiments had always existed in Amsterdam, that the beginnings of Protestantism belong in the fourteenth and fifteenth centuries. He mentions the fact that Gerard Groot did his first preaching in the Dutch language in Amsterdam in the fourteenth century, and that the Franciscan priest Johannes Brugman engaged in reforming activities in Amsterdam in the fifteenth century. And in the early sixteenth century, before Luther's influence had been felt in Amsterdam, a certain Adriaan (called "One-eyed Adriaan") had said to those who were entering the Heilige Stede, "Why do you attend the Sacrament? I regard the cheese and bread in my hand as good as the Sacrament." To one Catholic observer it seemed that he would turn all Amsterdam to his opinions.[3]

Sacramentarians and humanists were much in evidence in Amsterdam in the 1520s. These have been mentioned earlier. Mention should also be made, however, of five reforming priests in Amsterdam who appear in fragments of historical evidence from around 1524. At this time the Old Church tended to hold closely to traditional Catholicism; the New Church showed more openness to new ideas. Simon Pieters, a priest of the New Church, was sentenced to jail by the Court of Holland for his heretical leanings, but the Amsterdam magistrates would not carry out the sentence. Another priest, Claes van der Elst, had heard Luther in Wittenberg and was accused of being "full of errors and mistakes."

[3] Reported in *ODWA*, I, 16-19.

Other names which appear are Joannes Pelt, head of the Franciscan monastery, Willem Ottens, and IJsbrand Dirks Schol.

Evenhuis finds evidence for other indigenous sentiment for reform before Amsterdam's public espousal of the Reformation. The *schutters,* or civic militia, had traditionally been obligated to march in the Catholic religious processions. Some of them withdrew out of disaffection with this kind of devotion. One guild of *schutters* had their group portrait painted, and instead of being clad in their correct bright colors, they were shown as wearing the brown habits of Franciscan monks—in ridicule of the widely hated *Minderbroeders.*[4]

Another evidence of dissent among the general population was the Chamber of Rhetoric, or *Rederijkers.* They wrote and performed allegorical plays which not too subtly poked fun at the established authorities, both civil and ecclesiastical. In one of them, Jesus and "his party" are condemned on placards like those used to condemn Protestants. In another, the patroness of Amsterdam (the Virgin Mary) is portrayed as a very sick woman.[5]

Amsterdam was not a democracy, and the presence of widespread dissent did not necessarily presage a change in the official position of the city. The town government was an oligarchy of old, interconnected families whose positions had been established in earlier centuries. The course of the Reformation was to be tied closely to what happened within the oligarchy. From Evenhuis' excellent report on the period of the 1530s, it appears that the magistrates were not of one religious mind and included in their number both Roman Catholics and critics of Catholicism. It is more appropriate to express their dissent in general terms than to call them "Lutherans" or "Zwinglians," because these latter terms now imply a doctrinal precision which did not apply in Amsterdam at that time. They were, as Evenhuis says, freedom-minded (*vrijheidsgezind*), and they often did *sub rosa* what they could not do officially. There are numerous instances in which they looked the other way in order not to see Sacramentarian and Anabaptist activities that were forbidden by placards from higher authorities. When the first Anabaptists had been taken away from Amsterdam and condemned and executed in The Hague, the magistrates privately resolved to hinder a repetition of the event. Evenhuis sees them following a threefold policy: first, they detested the Inquisition; second, they fought for the historic privileges of the city by which no Amsterdammer could be tried outside the city walls; and third, they put a high priority on the interests of trade, which

[4] *Ibid.,* I, 22.
[5] *Ibid.*

they felt was enhanced by the greatest possible freedom, religious freedom included.[6]

The impetus toward reform was heightened by forces both negative and positive. There were problems in the church, on the one hand, and there were increasing outside Protestant influences by way of trade routes with Protestant centers in Germany and France.

The abuses were the common ones of the time. Priestly concubinage was almost universal, and financial inequities abounded. Amsterdam had only two parish priests, and in a growing trade center they had far too many people, some twenty thousand in their care. At the same time there were in the Old Church alone eighty-two "Mass priests," idlers whose only duty was to say the Masses which had been endowed by or for wealthy departed Amsterdammers. The funds were known as vicaries, and the disposal of these vicaries was a problem requiring new solutions when Amsterdam later embraced the Reformation.

There were also the other corruptions among the clergy which figured commonly in the era of the Reformation. One of the priests of the Old Church, Gerrit Pietersz., would for a price perform marriages outside the church and without publishing the banns, to the circumvention of canon law and the lining of his own pocket. To make matters worse, when the magistrates complained to the Bishop of Utrecht, the supreme spiritual leader of Dutch Catholics replied that the priest had paid a lot of money for his office and he could not be deposed without a costly refund.[7] There were many similar cases. Complaints about these abuses were made by both overt Protestants and loyal Catholics.

The indigenous reforming sentiment in Amsterdam was increasingly strengthened and focused by influences from Protestant centers outside the Low Countries, and the chief avenue for these influences was the trade routes. Of prime importance were the Hanseatic cities, especially Hamburg and Danzig, where Amsterdam trade connections had been strong since the fifteenth century. There was in the Old Church, in fact, an altar for the "Hamburg Choir," the brotherhood of Hamburgers who maintained a priest and buried their dead in the first chapel to the left of the west door of the church. Numbered in this Hamburg-oriented group of traders was the founder of the Pauw family which was to figure largely in Amsterdam Protestantism.[8] The merchants in the Baltic Sea and in the trade routes extending around to France, Portugal, and the Mediterranean were a potent and growing force in Amsterdam affairs. They were not all from the oligarchy; they constituted a class of *nouveau*

[6] *Ibid.*, pp. 23-25.
[7] *Ibid.*, p. 28.
[8] *Ibid.*, p. 31.

riche whose interests would clash with the more conservative financial practices of the late medieval Amsterdam oligarchy. The clash would be compounded of financial, political, and religious factors.

It was largely through these merchants that Bible translations and the tracts and hymns of Martin Luther and other Reformers would appear in Holland. A portion of Luther's Bible was printed in Amsterdam as early as 1523, with other "heretical books" following. The influence of Ulrich Zwingli is a more difficult matter to assess; indeed, the major line of influence was most probably in the other direction, from Hoen to Zwingli. Nevertheless, Zwingli's influence was felt in Amsterdam, especially through the widespread distribution of the *Huysboeck* of his follower Heinrich Bullinger.[9]

It appeared in the 1530s that matters would come to a head in Amsterdam, with the Protestant factions the winners. The very nature of the controversy presaged change, for even the defense of the Roman Church was undertaken by two humanists, with two more humanists leading the attack. The defenders were Alardus Amstelredamus (1494-1544) and Cornelis Crocus, a friend of Erasmus and of Sir Thomas More. Their opponents were Johannes Sartorius and Wouter Deelen. Sartorius gave lessons above the old weigh house on the Dam, in which he was supported by the burgomasters. Deelen, also with the support of the burgomasters, taught in something like a "folk university," providing Amsterdam's first instruction in Greek and Hebrew. He had Anabaptist sympathies, and eventually he had to flee, first to London and the Dutch refugee congregation there, and then to Hamburg and Emden. He finally died of the plague in England in 1563.[10]

Why did not Sartorius and Deelen, who had the support of the burgomasters, prevail? The answer is that the burgomasters themselves were in trouble. The magistrates who hoped to have in Amsterdam a purified church were put under pressure by the national government, and in 1534 the reform-minded *schout,* Jan Huybrechtsz., was deposed.

It was the Anabaptist movement itself which directly or indirectly brought the reform movement to an end. The events of 1534 and 1535, leading to the Münster debacle, included a revolutionary uprising in Amsterdam under Jan van Geelen. There were strange and bloody scenes, including the famous incident of the "naked tramps" (*naaktlopers*), who on the night of February 11, 1535, gathered in the Zoutsteeg, took off their clothes, declared that the day of judgment had arrived, ran through the city crying, "Woe, woe, the wrath of God, the wrath of God," and defended themselves when apprehended by declaring that

[9] *Ibid.,* pp. 32-34.
[10] *Ibid.,* pp. 36-37.

they were "the naked truth." All but one of the dozen or so men and women were summarily executed. The climax came on the following tenth of May, when the militant Anabaptists under their "bishop," Jan van Campen, attacked the city. There were deaths on both sides, with the surviving dozen Anabaptists captured and executed.

The attack on Amsterdam and the Münster episode left the Amsterdam Protestant cause in peril. The popular fear and hatred of Anabaptists which led to their persecution, torture, and death for the next several decades throughout the Low Countries contributed to the decline of the public advance of reform in Amsterdam. For the next forty years the government of Amsterdam was in the hands of Roman Catholic magistrates who suppressed all open dissent and removed from public office all who supported reform.

During the first three decades of this final Roman Catholic period, roughly from 1535 to 1565, reform sentiments continued to flourish underground. The strength of the underground was in the rising group of merchants, those whose new fortunes and new family dynasties were based upon coastal trading from the Baltic Sea to the Mediterranean. Their contact with other lands gave them an opportunity to hear and speak which they did not enjoy at home. In Amsterdam all was conformity and silence. The Sacramentarians had disappeared; the Anabaptists could meet only secretly and at great peril. Lutheranism had no visible presence, perhaps no existence at all, and Zwinglian or Calvinist sentiments could be promoted only at a distance, in the refugee communities in Emden and London. The presence of reform-mindedness in Amsterdam during these decades took the form of a persistent pressure from the merchants and others who continued to worship as Roman Catholics but who found ways to make dissent effective.

It was in the 1540s that this dissent became again a public affair. In 1542, Willem Dircksz. Baerdesen was named *schout,* and by the end of the decade he had become involved in an intense rivalry for a position as burgomaster with an incumbent, Hendrik Dircksz. Although both the Dirckszoons, Baerdesen the *schout* and Dircksz. the burgomaster, were loyal Catholics, religious aspects to their rivalry were in evidence. Baerdesen in his office as *schout* gave secret warnings to Anabaptists about to be apprehended as heretics. Soon the whole town had taken sides, using labels derived from the names of the two Dirckszoons. The followers of the burgomaster became *Dirkisten,* the followers of the *schout, Schoutisten.* Within a few years the *Schoutisten* became the leaders of the uprising which was the prelude to the Protestantizing of Amsterdam's government.

It was on October 2, 1564, that the faction of *Schoutisten* addressed

91

a protest or *doleantie* to the king through the government in Brussels. It took issue with what were regarded as corrupt or unjust practices in the government of the city, especially against the exclusion from the government of those who were not related to the incumbents by blood or marriage.[11] The government consisted of the *schout,* whose functions approximated that of a sheriff; four burgomasters; seven *schepenen,* or judges; the *Vroedschap,* or town council, of thirty-six members; and the *gecommitteerde collegien,* or commissioners—the two treasurers, the three orphanage masters, and the three excise masters. Some of these offices were for life, including membership as a *raad* (councilor) of the town council; others were for one year, as the burgomastership. The offices were held by members of old and wealthy families whose fiscal policies ran more to conservative banking than to risky and innovative overseas trading. The dissidents of the *doleantie* were the enterprising, new-rich merchants. Although they did not sign the document, they were to become famous, for fourteen years later they became the Reformers of Amsterdam and their descendants played major roles in the exciting developments in political, ecclesiastical, and economic history which ushered in Holland's Golden Age of the seventeenth century. Their names, familiar to students of Amsterdam history, bear repeating: Reynier Cant; Dr. (the term indicates a physician) Maarten Jansz. Coster; Wilhem Baerdesen; Dirck Jansz. de Graeff; Jan Claesz. Kat; Egbert Roelofsz.; Reynier Simonsz. van Neck; Jacob Bas; Claes Boelens; Jan Verburg—all of whom later became burgomasters. Others were the future *schepenen* Claes Reijersz., Hendrik Boelens, Windrik Hendriksz., Wybout de Wael, Egbert Pietersz., and Laurens Jacobsz. Reael (Arminius was to marry his daughter). Still others were Jan Bethsz.; Harmen Roodenburg; Jan Jansz. "in 't Hart" and his brother Klaas; Reynier Cant's brother Pieter; Wybout de Wael's brother Frank; Dirck Jansz. de Graeff's brothers Lenaart and Jakob; Andries Boelens; Arent Jansz. Coesvelt; Hendrick Fransz. Oetgens; Clement Volkertsz. Coornhert (the brother of the noted Dutch humanist Dirck Volckertsz. Coornhert) ; Piet Jacobsz. Schaep; Pieter Corver; Jan Muurling; and Hans Sprenkhuizen. In that year Sprenkhuizen built two houses on the Turfmarkt and named them *Vredenburch* (Castle of Peace). The hope thus expressed, as ter Gouw points out, was not to be realized in his time.[12]

Two years later, in 1566, there emerged from this group the beginnings of a new form of Protestant activity which was to lead eventually to overthrow of the Catholic regime in Amsterdam. A resident of the Engelsesteeg, a side alley of the Nieuwendijk, Pieter Gabriel by name, had

[11] *GA,* VI, 42 ff. The text is reproduced on pp. 43-47.
[12] *Ibid.,* pp. 57-58.

been expounding the Heidelberg Catechism to a small group of persons in his home every Sunday. The catechism had been adopted only three years earlier by a synod in Heidelberg. Also active in Amsterdam was Jan Arendsz., a basketmaker from Alkmaar, who had had to flee to Kampen, from which he had spread Protestant teaching throughout the area known as the Veluwe. Reynier Cant invited Arendsz. to come to Amsterdam. The burgomasters were alarmed at this upsurgence of Protestant activity and attempted to suppress it.

On July 8, there was a gathering of merchants of Protestant sympathy outside the St. Antoniespoort in a field of reeds along the river Y between the city wall and the hamlet Outewaal. Present were Reynier Cant, Frank de Wael, Cornelis Jansz. Coster (the brother of Maarten Jansz. Coster), Albert Heyes, Willem Florisz., and Laurens Jacobsz. Reael. Arendsz. began the service with a fiery prayer, "but with a soft voice," according to Reael, who recorded the event in his memoirs (Gabriel was momentarily out of town). The group agreed to institute "hedge preaching" or field preaching throughout Holland.[13]

This secret meeting in the reeds proposed nothing less than an indigenous national Reformation. It was begun by Hollanders; no outside agents were present, no clergy, no theologians, no Anabaptists, no Lutherans, and in the strict sense no Calvinists. The doctrinal basis was a biblical humanism directed against the Roman corruption of the church. The Heidelberg Catechism played no official role but was probably regarded as a useful tool of instruction. It was from this small meeting that events would move to the establishment of a Dutch Reformed Church in Amsterdam. To understand the church to which Arminius was to be called as pastor, the movement from the field of reeds to the Alteration of 1578 must be taken into account, and also the theology of the merchant-reformers of 1566 must be assessed.

The movement was far from smooth. When the group returned to the city they found a placard on the Dam threatening the gallows and confiscation of goods to all who harbored heretics, with a reward of 600 guilders for informers. The six merchants prudently decided that the hedge preaching should begin elsewhere. Jan Arendsz. began the campaign outside Hoorn on July 14. A week later the political character of the movement became evident when the hedge sermon took place on the Overveen estate of Hendrik van Brederode, the supporter of the Stadtholder William of Orange. The Amsterdam authorities tried to prevent the meeting by shutting the town gates, but many people swam out through the canals, escaped through the walls, or forced their way

[13] These details are known from the lost memoirs of Laurens Jacobsz. Reael which had been used by G. Brandt. Cf. *HRN*, I, 316-17.

out the gates in the morning when the milkmaids were being let out into the fields. By 11 o'clock the authorities relented and opened the gates, with the result that over five thousand people gathered to hear Pieter Gabriel preach a four-hour sermon on Ephesians 2:8-10: "For by grace you have been saved through faith, . . . not because of works." By July 31 the preaching was just outside Amsterdam itself, outside the Haarlemerpoort, and on August 21 Jan Arendsz. preached to a great crowd in the city itself, at the Lastage.

Reael saw that more preachers were needed, and he wrote to Cornelis Cooltuyn in Emden asking for preachers to be sent. Cooltuyn had been the reform-minded priest in Alkmaar under whom Jan Arendsz. had become a Protestant. Cooltuyn, now with the Dutch Protestant merchant and refugee community in Emden, sent a number of helpers whose names are not known.

These events in Amsterdam occurred on the heels of events of national importance in Brussels. Anti-Spanish and anti-Catholic agitation had been boiling among the masses and among the lower nobility. In early April, some four hundred nobles appeared at Brussels to present a petition to the Governess, Margaret of Parma, demanding that the King, Philip II, abolish the Inquisition in the Low Countries. Led by Brederode, they made a solemn procession to her palace, upon which her adviser, Charles Count of Berlaymont, contemptuously called them *gueux,* beggars. These noblemen of the League of the Nobility gleefully accepted the title, and the independence movement was provided with a name and a badge, Beggars and beggars' clothing. William of Orange became the leader of the national movement and Brederode returned to his native Holland to solicit funds, where he was supported in Amsterdam by Reael, van Neck, and Cornelis Pietersz. Boom. The nobles took sides, and the stage was set for a war for independence.

Among the masses, however, there was abundant fervor and impetuous action. In August there was a great outbreak in Flanders of *beeldenstormen,* iconoclastic riots, in which mobs of the proletariat, beginning in the west part of Flanders, sacked the churches, destroying the windows, statuary, altars, and organs. Just two days after the first preaching inside Amsterdam, merchants from Antwerp began exciting a crowd with tales of the plunder of Antwerp churches. Reael and his friends immediately warned the Catholic burgomasters of Amsterdam, who in turn ordered the priests, monks, and nuns to flee the city with what church treasure they could carry. At 11 o'clock in the morning they poured out into the streets, just when the workers of the city were going home for lunch. The result was a riot with the plundering of the Old Church, the traditional center of loyalist sentiment. The New Church was less hated, and it was spared for the time.

During all this the merchant-reformers tried to dissuade the mobs from their violence, but with little success. Reael, Cant, de Wael, and Coster appeared with ostentatious calm in the Dam in order to dissociate themselves from the rioters.

The upshot of this and other developments was the capitulation of the magistrates to the demands of the Reformers for permission to hold public worship. An additional preacher was called, Nicolas Scheltius, another protégé of Cooltuyn, and the three preachers assumed regular duties as leaders of the new church life in Amsterdam. Scheltius preached his first sermon on August 26 on the parable of the mustard seed. Deacons and elders, their names now unknown, were chosen. The churches were closed, and a great deal of plundering took place. In September the Franciscan cloister church was assigned for Protestant worship, and chairs and pews were installed.

The term "Protestant" needs qualification. What kind of Protestants were these Reformers of 1566? It is an important point for the understanding of Arminius and his work, because it was this group which determined the character of the Dutch Reformed Church in Amsterdam with which Arminius was to become so intimately involved just fifteen years later. Evenhuis calls them *de gereformeerden,* "the Reformed." The term is ambiguous in Dutch as well as in English. It carries the special connotation of Zwinglian and Calvinist sympathy vis-à-vis the Lutherans, and this meaning applies to the Amsterdam Reformers, but with local qualifications which must be set forth. There are two kinds of evidence, the events of 1566 themselves and documentary evidence of theological opinions from the period between 1566 and 1578.

The Reformers of 1566 found themselves at once in two controversies. The first was with the Lutherans and had to do with the Lord's Supper. When they had applied for the use of the Franciscan cloister church for their services of worship, a small group of Lutherans made application for separate use of the St. Olaf's Chapel, arguing that they differed with the main body of Protestants over the question of the Lord's Supper. The burgomasters sought the advice of the new "Reformed" church council. The reply from Jan Arendsz. and his merchant followers was that the dispute was over a secondary matter and did not warrant a division among the Protestants. This reply reflected both the broad and non-precise nature of the merchants' religious views and their failure to grasp the significance of the Eucharistic controversy for the Lutherans. Arendsz. tried to pacify the Lutherans by reading publicly the 10th and 13th articles of the Augsburg Confession, affirming that he was in agreement with them. The Lutherans correctly mistrusted this well-meaning gesture, undoubtedly feeling that the agreement failed to get at the heart of the matter. The significance of the event for understanding the temper of the Amsterdam Reformed community is twofold: (1) the Reformed leaders wanted a comprehensive church which could include both Reformed (i.e., Zwinglian and Calvinist) and Lutheran Christians; and (2) it was the Lutherans who saw quite correctly that the Eucharistic belief and practice of the new ecclesiastical regime in Amsterdam was non-Lutheran.

The inclusivist position of Jan Arendsz. and the church council was rejected not only by the Lutherans but by stricter Calvinists themselves, and this circumstance leads to a further qualification of the term *gereformeerden,* "Reformed," when applied to the Amsterdam Reformers of 1566. The Calvinists of Antwerp sent Caspar van der Heyden to admonish the Amsterdam community for its lax doctrine. Antwerp Calvinists had been through severe struggles with both the Roman Catholics and the Lutherans; furthermore, like most of the Reformed party in the south of the Netherlands, they were generally much stricter Calvinists than those in the north. Evenhuis is correct in estimating reasons for this when he points out that they had been subjected to greater pressure from the Roman Catholic authorities; they were geographically closer to France and the influence of Calvin and Beza; the north had had less contact with the Huguenots; none of the Amsterdam leaders except Baerdesen had studied in Geneva; the Augsburg Confession was felt in the north; and the influence of the Sacramentarians was still in force.[14]

What became evident from the Eucharistic controversy in Amsterdam was that the "Reformed" church of Amsterdam was in many respects *sui generis,* not to be subsumed under ecclesiastical and dogmatic categories applicable in other Protestant lands. When van der Heyden attempted to scold them for their inclusivism and toleration, it was a foreshadowing of storms to come, in which Arminius would find himself a central figure.

The first Communion service itself was finally held on December 15, 1566, when after the communicants had been examined as to their faith and life by the preachers and a sermon calling the community to repentance and conversion had been preached, some one thousand people gathered in the Franciscan cloister church. According to Laurens Jacobsz. Reael, who recorded the event, the lesson was read by Scheltius, and Arendsz. served the table. He used the formula, "Take, eat, and believe that the body of Jesus Christ was given on the cross for your sins,"

[14] *ODWA,* I, 66.

and "Take, drink, and believe that the blood of Jesus Christ was shed for the forgiveness of your sins." [15]

The congregation gathered at the table in groups of from twelve to twenty. The service lasted all day. At the first table were Hendrick van Marcken, Adriaen Reynertsz. Cromhout, Lubbert Nuts, Philips du Gardyn and his brother Guillaume, Egbert Meynertsz., Egbert Roelofsz., Reynier Cant, Jan Muyen, Albert Heyes, Cornelis Jansz. Coster, and Laurens Jacobsz. Reael. Perhaps these were the elders. Thus was launched what appeared at the time to be the beginning of a new religious era in Amsterdam.

It was a short-lived era, for within four months the tide of political and military affairs was to sweep the Roman Catholic church order back into Amsterdam. William of Orange appeared in the city on December 15 to try to resolve differences in the sharply divided city. The magistrates attempted unsuccessfully to turn him against the Reformed party. An agreement was signed on January 18, 1567, permitting the Reformed the use of the Franciscan church, which had been momentarily closed, the Leper's Chapel, and four warehouses, pending their building a church of their own. The magistrates soon attempted to hinder the exercise of the Reformed religion, and there was the threat of a civil war within Amsterdam. Brederode appeared in the city on February 27, acting as the agent of the now departed Prince and as the defender of the Reformed.

Reynier Cant, Jan Jansz. "in 't Hart," Frank de Wael, and Laurens Jacobsz. Reael presented a petition seeking to have the agreement of January 18 put into effect. There was a sharp exchange between Reael and one of the burgomasters, Simon Kops. The latter observed that Reael had leaned toward "Lutheranism" since before his marriage (which would have been about 1553), which he lamented, for the sake of Reael's wife's mother, after having been good neighbors for so many years. Reael replied that his mother-in-law, being a wise woman, did nothing to hinder his salvation, and that Kop would be better concerned for his own son, who, said Reael, would be better off attending Reformed preaching than running outside the town to drink Delft beer.[16]

This kind of encounter presaged trouble to come, and on April 18 the burgomasters forbade further Reformed preaching. The Reformed party complied on April 25, but they realized also that they must flee. Alva was coming from the south with Spanish troops and an edict of excommunication, and his deputy, Noircarmes, was believed to be approaching the city.

The greater part of the refugees fled to Emden, and for the flight

[15] *HRN*, I, 388.
[16] *Ibid.*, p. 445.

of their leaders we are again indebted to Gerard Brandt's recounting of what he had read in the now lost memoirs of Reael.[17] Reynier Cant fled to Medemblik on the evening of April 29. Reael, who was being sought by the burgomasters, realized that he too must flee, and he boarded a small boat in company with Frank de Wael, Mathijs Jansz., and Adriaen Cromhout. Brandt adds that he also had his wife and fourteen-year-old daughter with him, and James Nichols identifies the "brave daughter" as the future wife of Arminius.[18] This detail is incorrect, for at this time Reael had only two daughters and a son, the oldest being still less than six years old. Reael's entire family will be described later.

These refugees, and possibly their families as well, met in Medemblik on May 2. There they learned that they were being pursued by cavalry from Alkmaar. They hurriedly took to a herring boat which carried them to the island of Wieringen. They were still clinging to the notion that the Amsterdam authorities would give them passes for safe conduct, but they finally realized that their flight must be swift and permanent. When they got as far as the island of Vlieland, they found that refugees going to Emden and Bremen had already engaged all available vessels, and they also learned that the burgomasters had sent a letter to Vlieland ordering their arrest. The now desperate fugitives were driven to hauling up a sunken three-ton crab boat and trying to keep it afloat. The task was so hopeless that they decided to put in at Harlingen, but at Harlingen they saw soldiers, so they landed their traveling sieve on the sandbank to the north known as the Abbot. There they plugged the holes in their boat with the linens they had with them, and they managed to reach Emden by May 22.

Back in Amsterdam all progress toward Protestantism was quickly reversed. The party of the Roman Catholic burgomaster Joost Buyck was in power, the troops of Noircarmes entered the city on May 9, and the great annual Miracle procession was held on the next day. The remaining Protestants were banned and their goods seized. Those who persisted in their dissent were burned, and Amsterdam saw a reign of terror which was to earn for it the nickname *Moorddam,* "Murderdam." One of the victims was Willem Dircksz. Baerdesen, the *schout* mentioned earlier; Egbert Meynertsz., the brother-in-law of Reael, was imprisoned and condemned to death, although he died in prison the night before sentence was carried out. Adriaen Pauw, who had tried to play a mediating role in the earlier course of events, came to realize that his sympathies were with the Reformed, and with his wife and nine children he fled

[17] *Ibid.,* pp. 457-59.
[18] *WA,* I, 124.

to Emden. Amsterdam went into decline. Its merchant leaders were gone, its port was blockaded, its grain supply dwindled, the town treasury was depleted, the Spanish troops mutinied, and Alva had to flee the town at night with his personal debts unpaid. Outside, the independence movement was gaining. An inhabitant of the town complained that the rebels were trading and getting rich while Amsterdam was getting poorer and poorer and seemed threatened with extinction. The reason, it was now felt, was that Amsterdam was sealing its own doom by stubbornly adhering to Roman Catholicism and the King of Spain.[19] Joost Buyck and his circle refused to change their course, even when the end of their road was in sight, an end which was to come in 1578.

In Emden, meanwhile, the refugees continued to trade and to worship, to the strengthening of their purse and faith. The exact number of Amsterdam exiles is unknown, but there are about 170 names known to have been under sentence of confiscation of goods and "eternal banishment." Most of them stayed in Emden; a few went to Danzig and other trade centers. A few Protestants remained in Amsterdam, but in the case of Egbert Meynertsz. it was at fatal risk. Others left wives or children to look after business and property interests. Many took their families with them into exile.

The Amsterdam contingent of 1567 was not the only group to arrive in Emden at that time. There were refugees from other towns and provinces of the Low Countries and from the Palatinate as well. Many of these were absorbed into the Reformed community already established in Emden by still earlier immigrants, but the Amsterdam group was so large that they formed their own congregation in exile with the same three pastors who had served them briefly back home. Scheltius was released shortly to serve the older Emden congregation, but he died soon after.

One finds in the documents from the Emden church of this period names of laymen who would become leaders in the Amsterdam church after its eventual Protestantization. "Laurends Jacobs" (Reael) appears as a deacon in 1573, and "Waelwijck Sywers" in 1575.[20]

Although in one sense the many refugees assembled at Emden constituted a "church of the dispersion," they were at the same time the first gathering of a national church; indeed, the national church preceded the nation itself and contributed to its formation. A particular series of events in Emden meanwhile gathered together the conflicting tendencies in the church and projected them forward into the future. In 1570 there

---

[19] H. Brugmans, *Opkomst en Bloei van Amsterdam,* pp. 83-84.

[20] J. J. van Toorenenbergen, *Stukken Betreffende de Diaconie der Vreemdelingen te Emden, 1560-1576,* p. 7.

were proposed two plans of action. One was to gather from all the refugees a statement of grievances to be presented through William of Orange to the Reichstag in Speier, seeking the help of the German nobility. The other plan was to develop a common fund for the payment of pastors' salaries and the support of the education of future clergy, and to hold a synod for establishing a common church order. The first plan was backed by William and his supporters, who were the *rekkelijken*, the "loose" and comprehensive "libertines," or broad-minded Reformers. The Amsterdam merchants were among their number. The call for a central treasury and a general synod was supported by the refugees from the south and the Palatinate, the *preciezen*, precisionists, stricter Calvinists who mistrusted William's political aims and continued to fight their old doctrinal battles with the Lutherans. The *preciezen* wanted a church that ordered its own affairs without interference from the magistrates, with its members under the discipline of a binding doctrinal confession. The *rekkelijken* wanted to assign to the laity in the persons of the Christian magistrates the function of maintaining good order in the church through the exercise of the right of approval of the call of pastors, thereby protecting the church from what one of their number, Dirck Volckertsz. Coornhert, called "the papacy of the presbytery."

The Prince yielded to the extent of setting in motion the proposed synod, and in 1571 the Synod of Emden was the occasion of at least a partial victory for the *preciezen*. It prescribed the Belgic Confession as the formula of doctrinal unity for the Dutch-speaking churches, and it adopted a plan of church government. There was opposition from the Amsterdam refugees, but either through pressure from the Prince (which I judge unlikely) or through persuasive coercion on the part of the able president of the synod, Caspar van der Heyden, the two Amsterdam pastors, Jan Arendsz. and Pieter Gabriel, joined in the signing of the acts of the synod. Whether or not this action represented the inner feelings of the two pastors, it was to become evident that they were not speaking for the Protestant merchant leaders of Amsterdam, for in subsequent years the church in Amsterdam was among the many Reformed churches in the north which did not accept the Emden decisions in either doctrine or polity.

Because of the precedent and wide influence of the Synod of Emden, however, it is important to survey its decisions. The Belgic Confession had been written in 1559 by a French Protestant, Guido de Brès, as an apology to convince the authorities of the nonseditious character of the French Protestant movement. He was assisted by Adrian Saravia and several other ministers. Saravia took it to Geneva for approval, but the approval was not granted. It was published nonetheless in Rouen in 1561, and in 1563 it appeared in German and Dutch. In 1566 it was published again in slightly shorter form in Dutch and French. Its distribution was hindered by the authorities, and it was only in the nineteenth century that a copy of the early Dutch edition was discovered and published.[21] The text went through various alterations after the Synod of Emden until its final revision at the Synod of Dort in 1619. Thus the modern texts do not represent what was endorsed at Emden, and it is in terms of the original Dutch text presented by van Toorenenbergen that the Emden action must be understood.

The doctrine of the Lord's Supper (Article 35) is neither Roman Catholic nor Lutheran, but Calvinist. "We err not when we say that what is eaten and drunk by us is the proper and natural body . . . of Christ. But the manner of our partaking of the same is not by the mouth, but by the Spirit through faith." [22] On baptism: "We detest the error of the Anabaptists, who are not content with the one only baptism they have once received, and moreover condemn the baptism of infants of believers, who, we believe, ought to be baptized and sealed with the sign of the covenant" (Article 34). On the question of the magistrate, the texts in use in 1571 differ from the revision approved at Dordrecht in 1619. Article 36 in the original French and Dutch texts says that the magistrate's office "is not only to restrain and safeguard the political order, but also the ecclesiastical order." [23] The last phrase was dropped at Dordrecht. The Amsterdam merchants could interpret it to mean that the lay magistrates should have a voice in the call of pastors. Such an interpretation was too Lutheran for the clergy from Antwerp and the Palatinate, but they did not plug the loophole at Emden. Thus there would be continuing controversy about the procedures for the call of pastors.

The paragraph in Article 36 which condemns those who reject all magistracy did not mention the Anabaptists by name, as did later revisions of the Belgic Confession.

The church order prescribed at Emden was less ambiguous than what was stipulated in the Confession. It affirmed at the outset that no church was to have authority over any other church (*Acta*, 1) .[24] In each church

[21] In J. J. van Toorenenbergen, *Eene Bladzijde uit de Geschiedenis der Nederlandsche Geloofsbelijdenis.*

[22] The English text appears in Philip Schaff, *Creeds of Christendom*, and in A. C. Cochrane, ed., *Reformed Confessions of the 16th Century.*

[23] My translation of the French text in van Toorenenbergen, *Eene Bladzijde uit de Geschiedenis*, p. xliv, and of the Dutch text in J. N. Bakhuizen van den Brink, *De Nederlandsche Belijdenisgeschriften*, p. 137.

[24] F. L. Rutgers, *Acta van de Nederlandsche Synoden der Zestiende Eeuw*, pp. 55-56.

there should be a consistory made up of ministers, elders, and deacons who should meet at least once a week (*Acta*, 6). Adjoining churches should send deputies to a classis, which should meet once in three or six months (*Acta*, 7). Every year the scattered churches in Germany and East Friesland should meet together (*Acta*, 8), and every two years there should be a general meeting of all the Dutch churches (*Acta*, 9). Ministers are to be called by the consistory with the concurrence of the classis or of two or three ministers of neighboring churches (*Acta*, 13). No role is ascribed to the magistrate as such in the call of the minister; it is entirely an ecclesiastical matter.

Although in another couple of decades the Dutch Church was to be torn by strife over the doctrine of predestination, and although there were already differences of emphasis at least on this point among the Reformed clergy in 1571, the question was not controverted at Emden. Article 16 of the Belgic Confession put the matter in a form that was both brief and mild:

We believe that all the line of Adam being thus cast into perdition and ruin by the sin of the first man, God showed himself to be such as he is, namely, merciful and just; merciful, in drawing and saving from perdition those whom in his eternal and unchangeable council he has chosen by his pure goodness in Jesus Christ our Lord, apart from consideration of their good works; just, in leaving the others in their ruin and fall in which they are fallen.[25]

The text in modern editions ends with that, but at Emden the text still included another section defending God against injustice and appealing to God's "eternal and immutable decree founded in Jesus Christ before the creation of the world." Even that is an ambiguous phrase, and it did not provide a clear answer to questions which later would be raised about sub-, infra-, and supralapsarianism. But at Emden these questions did not arise; predestination was not a topic in the wind.

During the Emden years, many books were printed in Dutch, books which furthered one or another aspect of the Protestant cause and which were spread from Emden throughout the Low Countries. These included Dutch translations of Melanchthon, a favorite theologian among the Dutch; Bullinger, Calvin, and Beza; and *In Praise of Folly* by Erasmus. Of especial importance was a book written in Emden in 1570 by the Dutch adviser to the Prince of Orange, Philippe de Marnix, Lord of St. Aldegonde, *De Biëncorf*, or *The Beehive of the Romish Church*, a bitterly polemical document of wide effect, inspired by Calvinism, which

---

[25] My translation from the French text in van Toorenenbergen, *Eene Bladzijde uit de Geschiedenis*, pp. xxv-xxvi, and the Dutch text in Bakhuizen van den Brink, p. 89.

Marnix St. Aldegonde had learned in Geneva itself. The book neverthe-less lacked the precise doctrinal content in matters such as predestination on which later Dutch Calvinists were to be so insistent.

It would be a mistake to suppose that Emden marked a complete victory for Calvinism in the Dutch Reformed Church. Its decision to endorse the Belgic Confession did not entail the doctrinal precision that even that mild document would achieve in the revisions which would be made in later years. The polity set forth in the *Acta* was a proposal which did not receive universal implementation, particularly not in Leiden and Amsterdam. There remained in the Dutch churches many who sympathized with the milder theology of the Amsterdam merchants; indeed, the conflict was often along the lines of clergy against laity. Gerard Brandt, the seventeenth-century historian whose sympathies ad-mittedly were with the reforming magistrates, describes the polarity this way:

From hence it proceeded, that the word Reformation, or the Reformed religion [*Gereformeerde Religie*], was understood in one sense by the laity, in another by the clergy; many of the latter meaning nothing else by it but an agreement in all points with their teachers; but the former, a religious worship, purged from grave abuses, and not too much limited with respect to opinions about disputable points. . . . These different views of the old rulers of the country and of the churchmen [clergy] in time led to different outworkings, the church-men aiming for decisions and definitions, and the magistrates aiming for ac-commodation and reasonable toleration in such disputes. The former wanted to make the church narrow by decisions about many disputable points; the latter sought to open the church as wide as possible to all Christians of un-blameable lives.[26]

Among the books published at Emden there is none written by one of these allegedly tolerant laymen. We are not without primary evidence about their religious views, however, for one of their principal leaders, Laurens Jacobsz. Reael himself, wrote a catechism for the instruction of his own children. The manuscript is extant and now has been published, and it is instructive to study it for the light it sheds on the religious sentiments of the Amsterdam merchants generally and on the future father-in-law of Arminius in particular.[27]

Reael's catechism consists of 123 questions and answers plus one more question with only a fragmentary answer. J. C. Breen has shown that Reael often followed closely the catechism which Marten Micron had published in 1558 in London for the Dutch Reformed congregation there. Other catechisms were also available and in use in Emden. Why

[26] *HRN*, I, 551-52.
[27] J. C. Breen, "De 'Kinderlere' van Laurens Jacobszoon Reael."

103

did Reael write one more? Breen accepts, correctly I believe, the obvious answer. Reael needed a simple document which he could use for his own children, five youngsters at the time ranging from ten to one-and-a-half years in age. The little one, Lijsbet, born in Emden, was the future wife of Arminius. What was her religious instruction?

One who is familiar with Reformation catechisms will be startled by the answer to the first question. "What are you?" it asks; the answer: "I am a reasoning man created by God after his image, righteous and holy." It is an important, positive affirmation, too often obscured amid the pessimism of Lutherans and Calvinists. But Reael was not a humanist. In the seventh answer he affirms that man has lost the image of God, is estranged from God, and will be eternally lost without the gracious intervention of the Son of God. The saving deed of Christ is not effective for all men, however, but only for those who believe (Q. 38), whose good works in themselves can only be sinful and unavailing for salvation (Q. 42). Breen and Evenhuis both comment that there is nothing here which would be unacceptable to a "precise" or rigid Calvinist, although such a one might want some expressions strengthened. Granted, but it is equally true that the document expresses the faith of the rekkelijken, and of Arminius a generation later, both in its insistence on the fact of the fall and the necessity of grace and in its silence about theories of how that grace works and its omission of a rigid doctrine of predestination. Reael was another of the many "Arminians before Arminius" who exercised important leadership in the Dutch Church in the formative years of its existence.

The tide of events was soon to turn against the Spanish. In 1572 there was the great Sea Beggar uprising. In 1573 Alva had to flee Amsterdam in the middle of the night in order to get away from his creditors. In 1574 Leiden withstood its siege. In 1576 Alva's successor, Don Luis de Requesens, died and was succeeded by the colorful but ineffective (politically) Don Juan. That year saw also the Pacification of Ghent, by which the Prince of Orange was recognized in his original stadtholderships over Zeeland and Holland. There was also the implicit recognition of the Reformed faith in these provinces. All of this served to make Amsterdam's isolated Roman Catholicism increasingly untenable politically and also disastrous for its commercial interests. The result was that by May, 1578, the Roman Catholic clergy and monastics either left town or were deported, and the Roman Catholic town government was set aside and reconstituted by the now returning refugee merchants. It was a victory for those Reformers of 1566 who had endured and survived.

Reformed church services began on May 11, 1578. The three pastors of 1566 were all dead, and a minister from Delft, Thomas van Til, conducted the service. On May 24 the elders and deacons were chosen. Among the elders were Adriaen Cromhout, Hendrick van Marken, Reynier van Neck, and Reynier Cant; and among the deacons were Cornelis Florisz. van Teylingen, Egbert Roelofsz., Guillaume du Gardyn, and Jan Philipsz. de Bisschop. These are only a few of those who played a large role in both church and commerce in the city which would begin now to become the leading city of Europe. Missing from the list is Laurens Jacobsz. Reael. He had moved from Emden to Hoorn and was evidently not in the city when the new regime was set up. On the list of deacons, however, was his brother-in-law, Johan Pietersz. Reael, another important merchant leader of Amsterdam Protestantism. Laurens appears in Amsterdam as a sergeant in the militia in 1579, and in 1580 he became an elder of the church.

There was the problem of reconstituting the town government of Amsterdam. It was not a question of moving from an oligarchy to a democracy; democracy was not the issue or the option at that time. It was a question of validating a new oligarchy which would reflect the new distribution of power. An old "privilege" of 1477 was interpreted to mean that the new "council of thirty-six," or city council, could be chosen by the militia, and on May 27 this was done.

The new council was made up of three groups.[28] There were thirteen "Old Beggars," the militant Reformers of 1566 who had suffered exile rather than compromise their principles. There were thirteen "mild Reformers," whose sympathies lay with the former but whose actions had been less revolutionary. There were also ten Roman Catholics, not of the most intransigent to be sure, but including members of the old town government and the husband of the granddaughter of the old Dirkist, Hendrik Dircksz., himself. Some of the latter refused to serve, for reasons of conscience. The balance of power shifted to the returned exiles, and the four new burgomasters—Adriaen Cromhout, Maarten Coster, Wilhem Baerdesen, and Dirck Jansz. de Graeff—were all from their number. The greater part of the oligarchy consisted of the merchants who had come to prominence in the recent decades, but not all. Four old patrician families from the fourteenth century were represented in the new government: Bicker, Benningh, Baerdesen, and Boelens. Thus was constituted a new Amsterdam regent-patriciate, which was to form a ruling class in state, church, and commerce for the next two centuries.

Something of the closed society which this group constituted can be seen from the way in which public offices were passed on within families. Of the original thirty-six members of the council, sixteen were succeeded

---

[28] J. E. Elias, *Geschiedenis van het Amsterdamsche Regentenpatriciaat*, pp. 18 ff.

at death by sons, sons-in-law, or in one case a brother-in-law. Of the seventeen burgomasters chosen between 1578 and 1590, there were nine whose sons or sons-in-law were to become burgomasters later, a total of thirteen.[29]

It was this government which, through the administration of the secu-larized vicary of the Merchants' Guild, adopted Arminius as its foster son and future minister in 1581, just three years after the Alteration. Nine years later he would be admitted into the closed family circle itself when he married the daughter of Laurens Jacobsz. Reael, and he would become the favorite preacher of the "Old Beggars" in Amsterdam. In a very real sense he was to become "Arminius of Amsterdam."

An immediate result of the Alteration was the revival of trade and the beginning of rapid population growth. The old regime had allowed Amsterdam to fall into economic stagnation, and it had prohibited the erection of new housing outside the city walls (to protect the property interests of its own members, it is believed), with the result that there were only about 30,000 people in the city in 1578. Trade was now re-sumed, and people began flocking to Amsterdam out of motives both religious and economic. Many of them were fleeing the Spanish regime in the south. It is estimated that the population had doubled by 1610, had reached 145,000 by 1640, and 200,000 by 1660, at the height of the Golden Age.[30] There was no census, and figures must be projected from such partial indicators as marriage and death records.

It is also impossible to know precisely how many members of the Reformed Church there were in Amsterdam in this period. Evenhuis accepts a very low figure—as few as 10 percent in 1578, with perhaps an increase to one third of the population within the next fifteen years. It is important to keep in mind that the increase in percentage would mean a great increase in actual membership in a time of rapid population growth, and that a great part of the population growth would be made up of refugees from the south, where Calvinism was strong. The church would thus grow in numbers and at the same time change in character. Arminius remained in Amsterdam until 1603, long enough to feel the effects of these changes.

The Alteration entailed a new regime in both city and church. In the church, elders and deacons were chosen, and steps were taken to call ministers. One man turned them down for lack of adequate moving expenses. The first two who accepted were Johannes Cuchlinus and Petrus Hardenberg. They were first presented to the congregation on three successive Sundays in August, 1588, and on the last Sunday they

[29] *Ibid.*, p. 26.
[30] *ODWA*, I, 129.

were inducted at the first Communion service since the Alteration. Presiding was Petrus Dathenus, who had been invited to come for the occasion. The service was held in the St. Nicholas Church, which since the Alteration was no longer known by that name but by the "secularized" appellation of "the Old Church." It was on the "Old Side," still the center of Amsterdam life, just off the fashionable Warmoesstraat, still the chief street of Amsterdam.[31]

Hardenberg left for Deventer and Zwolle in 1579, but Cuchlinus remained as a permanent pastor. He was joined in 1580 by Martinus Lydius from Antwerp. In the same year Johannes Nicolai van Wassenaar was called as pastor, but he died before the year was over. It was Cuchlinus who carried the heavy responsibility of bringing order out of chaos in the new Reformed Church in Amsterdam.

Cuchlinus, who was to play an important role in the life of Arminius, was born in 1546 in Hesse and studied at Frankfurt, Mainz, Strassburg, Tübingen, Heidelberg, and Neustad. After serving as pastor in Fackheim and in Hesse, he served in Emden briefly before going to Amsterdam in 1578. He was a sober and mature leader, a strong person in controversy, doctrinally loyal to the Heidelberg Catechism as a statement of Calvinism. With a firm hand he piloted the church through the external and internal storms which raged in and around those early merchant-reformers, whom someone has called *een ongevormde en gistende klomp geuzen,* a seething, shapeless mass of Beggars. The church fathers were seldom of one mind, and they were less concerned for doctrinal and ecclesiastical regularity than was Cuchlinus. There was a large number of Roman Catholics who looked for help from the south. Firm leadership was needed, and Cuchlinus provided it. In dealing with the burgomasters he dispensed with honorific titles and used simple last names. In the meetings of the consistory his fellow ministers became known by their familiar names. Dominee Arminius became Broeder Jacobus.[32]

During the next decade, while Arminius was pursuing his theological studies, several other pastors were called to Amsterdam. Hillebrandus Cunaeus served from 1580 to 1583. Johannes Ambrosius came in 1580, Johannes Hallius in 1581 from Leiden, Everhardus Hermanni in 1583, and Petrus Plancius in 1585. More will be said about Plancius, who was to become the first great antagonist of Arminius. When Arminius reported to Amsterdam in 1587 for examination and induction into the

[31] For a remarkable work of archival research on the ownership of the some 400 premises on the Warmoesstraat from the fourteenth to the eighteenth centuries, see J. G. Kam, *Waar Was dat Huis in de Warmoesstraat.*
[32] *ODWA,* I, 141.

pastoral office, the ministers with whom he had to deal were Cuchlinus, Ambrosius, Hallius, Hermanni, and Plancius.

The interaction between political and ecclesiastical affairs in the north during the 1580s had brought to a head a number of unresolved tensions within the Reformed churches. In 1581 the Synod at Middleburg had condemned Coolhaes. A long controversy in Utrecht was raging between Hubert Duifhuis and the rigid Calvinistic party. Duifhuis died in 1581, but the trouble continued with pressure being brought on his disciple, Tako Sybrants. In Gouda there were Calvinistic pressures on the pastor, Hermannus Herberts. In Franeker, Gellius Snecanus found himself in controversy over the doctrine of predestination. In 1584 William of Orange, who had joined the Reformed Church and who had sided with the Old Beggars whose theology was anti-Roman without being strictly Calvinistic, was assassinated at Delft. The new Council of State was under Maurice of Nassau, who was primarily a military man. Help was sought from England, and the Earl of Leicester was sent with troops to aid the north. Leicester established his headquarters at Utrecht and immediately began to show his sympathy for the extreme Calvinist party. Under his aegis there was a so-called National Synod held at The Hague in 1586. It eliminated any function of the magistrates (burgomasters) in the calling of pastors, a victory of the precise Calvinists over the so-called Libertines. It soon became apparent that there were two kinds of patriotism in the north. One wanted to establish a federal regime of toleration with power exercised by the provincial States. The other wanted a religious war against Spain with power centralized in the Stadtholder. Maurice was appointed Stadtholder in 1585. Jan van Oldenbarnevelt, the pensionary of the States of Holland and West Friesland, became the leader of the civil branch of goverment, which tended to be federalist, oligarchic, and libertarian. Maurice became the military leader who gained the support of the Protestant religious zealots among the clergy and the new urban lower middle class which consisted increasingly of immigrants from the Calvinistic south. Leicester, partly through his own ineptness, partly due to the duplicity of Queen Elizabeth (who was negotiating with Parma), was forced to resign in 1588. The split between north and south was now complete, and apart from the shifting of borders in military action would become permanent. What emerged in the north was what Pieter Geyl has called "the oligarchic, erastian, decentralized Republic of the Seven United Provinces." [33] Holland was the dominant force in the republic.

It was beginning to be apparent that there was a polarity within the

---

[33] Geyl, *The Revolt of the Netherlands*, p. 215.

north between the old *preciezen* and the *rekkelijken*. The disputes now turned on the role of the magistrate in maintaining the welfare of the church, the autonomy of the consistory and the classis, the manner in which the Confession and the Catechism were to be used, the republican nature of the national government, the prosecution of the war with Spain, and the relative positions of the civil and the military arms of the government. It was not yet a controversy over predestination. The polarity at the end of the decade represented still only divergent tendencies and not yet mutually exclusive and openly discernible parties.

In Amsterdam there was outward unity between the Libertine magistrates, who were also the elders and deacons in the consistory, and the more orthodox clergy. Only in subtle ways was their different orientation visible in public affairs. One of these had to do with the organ in the Old Church. It had been played for years for the Roman Catholic Masses by Pieter Sweelinck until his death in 1573. After his death his son, Jan Pietersz. Sweelinck, was sent by the city to study organ at the city's expense in Venice. Upon his return in 1580 the new order had been established. Not only was there no Mass which required organ music, but organ music itself was banned from the Reformed service, along with the candles, statuary, stained-glass windows, private altars, funeral sermons, and the host of things now forbidden under the firm Calvinistic hand of Cuchlinus. The town fathers were not to be denied their music, however, and Jan Pietersz. was employed not by the consistory but by the city government, and not for music at divine worship but for recitals on Sunday afternoon. The Old Church became the fashionable *wandelplaats*, promenade, of the wealthy patricians of the adjoining Warmoesstraat and adjacent fashionable streets, where the merchants and their wives and offspring could stroll in their finest clothes while Sweelinck played his compositions for their enjoyment. Sweelinck remained in the employ of the city in this manner for the remaining forty-one years of his life, including, of course, the fifteen years that Arminius served as minister in Amsterdam. It is said that he never left the city in all those years.

What were his religious views? He did not commit himself at this point, and thus neither he nor the clergy made an issue of it. He did continue to compose Masses (which he himself could never play), and it is possible that he was another one of the hidden Roman Catholics in Amsterdam who managed to function right under the noses of the Calvinists with the tacit acceptance of the more tolerant magistrates.[34]

---

[34] On the career of J. P. Sweelinck in Amsterdam, cf. J. W. Enschedé, "Jan Pietersz. Sweelinck."

8

ADMISSION TO THE MINISTRY

ARMINIUS arrived in Holland in the autumn of 1587,[1] and he reported to the Classis of Amsterdam on October 5. A classis in the Dutch Church corresponds to the presbytery of British and American Presbyterian churches and is made up of ministerial and lay delegates from each of a group of churches in a district. In practice, the lay elders were usually not present, so that the classis was in effect a company of ministers. It was charged with the examination of *proponenten,* ministerial candidates, who were to be questioned on the chief points of doctrine. The candidates were also to be required to sign the Belgic Confession according to actions taken by the National Synod of Dordrecht (1578) and the National Synod of Middelburg (1581).[2] This, as will be seen, was not uniformly observed. The classis had the oversight of the calls of ministers, including the transfers of ministers from one town to another. It was not to concern itself with the affairs of civil government or with the internal affairs of other classes.

The Classis of Amsterdam included ministers from Weesp, Loenen, Loosdrecht, Naarden, Muiden, Saerdam, and Amsterdam. Amsterdam's greater size caused it to be charged with half the costs of the classis, and it may be assumed that Amsterdam's ministers, of whom three were required to be present at each session, dominated the proceedings.

The classis, in view of the expectation that Arminius would be given a call from Amsterdam, gave him the preparatory examination which would admit him as a *proponent,* or candidate for the ministry. They received his letter of commendation from Beza "and other pious professors" (Grynaeus would be one; the other letters are unknown), and they voted unanimously that he be admitted to the ministry as soon as he should receive a proper call from Amsterdam and should pass the full examination yet to be given by the classis.[3]

---

[1] At the time of the Frankfurt autumn fair, according to Los, p. 52.

[2] Rutgers, pp. 237, 390.

[3] *Prot,* I, 34 (October 5, 1587), but there is a problem of dating here. Here I follow Los, who gives the date of October 5 (p. 52). From the manuscript entry, however, it is possible to interpret this entry as that of February 1, 1588, which would be the final and not the preparatory examination.

Arminius next appeared before the Consistory (*Kerkeraad*) of Amsterdam on November 12. According to the minutes of that meeting, "Jacobus Arminius, an alumnus of this city, having come from Geneva, appeared in the consistory and delivered his testimonial from the school in Geneva, which was signed by Beza." The minutes go on to say that he was given a friendly reception. He declared his readiness to serve the church of God in Amsterdam whenever the call be extended. He reported that he was requesting of the burgomasters permission to make a trip to South Holland to take care of some personal affairs and to visit some friends, and that he was requesting funds for the cost of the trip. He also mentioned his trip to Italy, taken without the consent and knowledge of the authorities in Geneva, and "he gave the brethren some reasons and excuses for it." The consistory was pleased with his report and proposal and ordered two elders, Hendrik Olfertsz. and Gerrit Jacobsz., to convey their approval to the burgomasters.[4]

The burgomasters granted the request and Arminius made his trip, evidently during the following weeks of 1587 and perhaps into the first weeks of 1588. The details of the trip are unknown, but undoubtedly it included Leiden, and possibly Oudewater. It is also likely that it included The Hague, where Arminius' close friend, Uitenbogaert, was now the court preacher to Prince Maurice of Nassau.

The minutes of the consistory for February 4 continue the story. "Hallius informed the brethren that the classis had met on Monday [which would be February 1]. Accordingly, he announced that Arminius had been examined at that time [the full or final examination] and is well qualified to be admitted to the ministry." The consistory examined him and ordered that he proceed immediately to preach a trial sermon to prove himself before the church on the next Sunday. The burgomasters were to be informed of this, and the next day he was to meet with them in order to obtain their approval.[5] In Amsterdam the specifications of the synods of Emden and The Hague for the calling of pastors without any participation by the magistrates was not observed. The call was to proceed "provided the burgomasters made no objections." No objection was made.

This is the story as derived from the minutes of the consistory. Is it the whole story? There is another tradition, cherished by Calvinist partisans, which stems from the seventeenth century. Jacobus Triglandius (1583-1654), who became a minister in Amsterdam in 1610 and a professor at Leiden in 1634, was a bitter foe of the Remonstrants. When Uitenbogaert's *De Kerckelicke Historie* appeared in 1646 with its pro-

---

[4] *Prot*, I, 361.
[5] *Ibid.*, I, 370.

Remonstrant account of the controversies in the Dutch Church, Triglandius responded in 1650 with his own *Kerckelycke Geschiedenissen,* a chapter-by-chapter attack on Uitenbogaert. In his account of the call of Arminius, he draws on two sources whose veracity has been called in serious question. The first is an entry in the minutes of the Consistory of Amsterdam for 1617. At that time, when the antagonism between Remonstrants and Contra-Remonstrants was approaching its bitterest stage, an Amsterdam Contra-Remonstrant minister, Adrianus Georgy Smout, asked in the consistory "what really happened" when Arminius had been called to Amsterdam thirty years earlier. The consistory assigned the task of providing an answer to four ministers, Plancius, Hallius, Johannes Ursinus, and Joannes le Maire, Contra-Remonstrants all. The latter two had come to the ministry in Amsterdam in 1600 and 1601 respectively and had not been witnesses of the matter in question. The drafting of the report is generally credited to Plancius. It contains matters which the Contra-Remonstrants regarded as prejudicial to Arminius. This entry has been attacked by many historians on obvious grounds. It was drawn up by enemies of Arminius, and it purports to relate sermons and conversations from thirty years earlier, events lacking in documentation and conspicuously missing from the minutes of the consistory. The entry, in short, was born in malice and served the political interests of its authors.

Triglandius, still another thirty years later, drew on these minutes of 1617, but he claimed now to have documentary support for their veracity. He has in hand, he says, another set of consistory minutes from 1587 and 1588. The consistory had two secretaries. One was a minister, who kept a written record of the actions of the consistory. The other was an elder, who wrote these acts in another book. The first book was lost, he says, and what is known as the *Protocollen* (extant both in Triglandius' time and now) is the transcript made by the elder. What he has in hand is an extract from the minister's minutes, signed by both the president and secretary (*praeses en scriba*) of the consistory. No one other than Triglandius is known to have claimed to have seen this document.

It is on the basis of this mysterious document that Triglandius elaborates the story of Arminius' call. Arminius had conducted an evening service, so the story goes, during which he had said

that there were many groups which men called sects, but that in the eyes of God and of God's people this was not so, because if one holds to the foundation, which is to acknowledge that Jesus Christ is God and man and the Savior, he is then no sectarian in God's sight; and that those in the Roman Church who

112

receive the sacrament of the Holy Oil (as it is called) [Extreme Unction], for the sake of Christ and with a good conscience are not condemned.

The bewildered consistory sent two ministers to remonstrate with him, and under the pressure of their questioning Arminius was "very disturbed and unsettled, and great drops of sweat broke out all over him in spite of the fact that it was a very bitter and cold day." Arminius remained stubborn for several weeks, so the story goes, and was not permitted to teach the congregation. Finally he abandoned his opinion, and after some time was given a call.[6]

Is it a likely story? Yes, in the sense that Arminius *might* have entertained such a view (which would disturb very few Protestants today as such tolerance disturbed the vehement Triglandius). And had Arminius said such a thing, it is quite possible that the Amsterdam consistory, especially the ministers, would have remonstrated with him. On historical grounds, however, the story is unlikely. It is true that minutes were taken in the meeting by a minister-secretary and afterward written in the permanent book by an elder-secretary, but there is no evidence to substantiate Triglandius' claim to having seen the rough-draft minutes. It is possible—indeed, highly probable—that the zealous Triglandius fabricated the story and the document out of his own fervent, fervid imagination. It is not the only fabrication in his book. He is the one who alleges that Arminius, on his trip to Italy, associated with Bellarmine and other noted Jesuits and kissed the pope's toe. These stories have been accepted at face value by the extremely partisan writers Vos and Los.[7] The modern reader will understand them to be typical products of the bitter controversies of the times. A bird in hand is worth two in the bush, and the bird in hand in this case is the *Protocollen* of the Consistory of Amsterdam, safely kept in the City Archives of Amsterdam.

Arminius began conducting the evening service in the Old Church on Sunday, February 7, 1588, as a *proponent,* a preacher on trial. His duties consisted of offering the prayers and preaching a sermon. According to Bertius, "as soon as he was seen in the pulpit, it is impossible to describe the extraordinary grace and favour which he obtained from men of all ranks, who were eager to hear him and to profit by his discourses." [8] Bertius, in delivering the funeral oration to the university community in which Arminius had worked, described Arminius' preaching:

[6] Triglandius, *Kerckelycke Geschiedenissen,* p. 282. G. Brandt attacks Triglandius in *HRN,* II, 48. Triglandius is defended at length by ter Haar, *Jacobus Triglanduis,* pp. 159 ff. Cf. *Prot,* IV, 193-97, for the minutes of 1617.

[7] G. J. Vos Az., *Voor den Spiegel der Historie,* p. 36; Los, pp. 54-55.

[8] Funeral Oration; *WA,* I, 28.

This flattering reception ought to excite no wonder; for—I speak before those who knew him well,—there was in him a certain incredible gravity softened down by a cheerful amenity; his voice was rather weak, yet sweet, harmonious, and piercing. . . . He disdained to employ any rhetorical flourishes, and made no use of the honeyed sweets collected for this purpose from the Greeks.[9]

The preaching at the evening service evidently continued through the spring and summer. In July the processing of his call and ordination was resumed. One problem that had to be cleared up was a personal debt which he had incurred. It seems that the Merchants' Guild funds promised by the burgomasters for the support of Arminius in Geneva had not in fact all been paid from the specified fund, for reasons that are unknown. Instead, an Amsterdam moneylender, Pieter Jacobsz. Bolwerk, had advanced funds in the amount of 637 guilders, 5 shillings, and 4 pennies, a considerable amount at that time, when an annual salary might be 100 guilders. The loan had been given on the security of the burgomasters' promise to pay, so that it was not an obligation to the discredit of Arminius. Nevertheless, it was felt that the matter should be settled before a call could be extended to Arminius.

In a meeting of the consistory on July 14, an elder, Hendrik Olfertsz., reported that he had spoken with the burgomasters about the problem and that they had taken care of the debt and had in their possession the paper held by Bolwerk. Thereupon the consistory agreed to meet with the deacons on the following Tuesday, July 19, to handle the call of Arminius.[10] The call was evidently approved, although the matter is not recorded in the minutes, because on Thursday, July 21, it was unanimously agreed that the call of Arminius, who now for a long time had been heard as a preacher, should be be presented to the city, subject to the approval of the burgomasters.[11] His difficulties with Bolwerk were now cleared up, he had received the assent of the deacons, and all was in order.

At the meeting of the consistory on July 28, Ambrosius reported that the burgomasters had given their consent. It was agreed that Arminius, who was momentarily out of the city, should be invited to the meeting on the following Thursday, when the call would be given.[12]

The next Thursday was August 4, but Arminius was not called on that day. There is in the minutes a strange anomaly, two blank spaces, each sufficient for the minutes of a meeting and dated August 2 and August 4. Why there should be a space for August 2 is unclear. The

[9] *Ibid.*
[10] *Prot,* I, 404 (July 14, 1588).
[11] *Ibid.* (July 21, 1588).
[12] *Ibid.* (July 28, 1588).

regular meeting of August 4 may not have been held, and the scheduled business actually took place one week later, on August 11. The minutes report as follows:

The deacons being invited to the meeting of the elders, Arminius was in the presence of all presented with the call of this city [*gemeente*]. Whereupon it was impressed upon him that he should help carry the burden of the city just as did the other ministers, in visiting the sick as well as in other things. Also that in nonessential matters [*middelmatige dingen,* the Dutch term for *adiaphora*] concerning the administration of the church [the word is longer and indistinct; it could be *kerckeraet,* church council or consistory], he should not casually seek to change anything or introduce something new except that which upon common advice is deemed good for the establishment of this community [*gemeente.*]. All of which he promised to fulfill, so the community was invited to come together on the coming Sunday since he has been called to be a minister here. The legal hindrances concerning him now being overcome, he is to be confirmed in the service of the church in the presence of the congregation [*gemeente*] at the Saturday evening before the communion service.[13]

Communion services were held on the last Sunday of every second month. For each Communion celebration there was a service of preparation on the Saturday night preceding. That means that Arminius was ordained on Saturday evening, August 27, 1588, in the Old Church, which was the center of church life in Amsterdam. Hands were laid on him, but in the Reformed churches this was not regarded as imparting sacramental grace or implying a theory of succession. The long process of preparation was now at an end, and he was about to enter into the full exercise of his pastoral ministry in Amsterdam, a ministry which would run for fifteen years.

Two questions regarding this process remain. First, does the lacuna in the minutes of the consistory for August 4 imply some sinister problem? Second, what doctrinal agreements were made by Arminius at the time of his examination and calling?

Los, ever expecting to find something amiss in Arminius, speculates that the consistory did indeed meet on that day and that someone brought a charge against Arminius. Either the charge was not accepted, or, as Los puts it, the consistory tolerantly overlooked it. The secretary, at home writing up the minutes, was not sure that this should be recorded. The consistory, in order to protect the reputation of their prospective young colleague, ordered him to leave it blank.[14]

It is pure speculation, born of no little malice. There is no documentary evidence for solving the problem. If one must speculate, a simpler

[13] *Ibid.,* I, 409 (August 11, 1588).
[14] Los, p. 55.

hypothesis lies at hand. On July 28 Arminius had been out of the city. On that day and in his absence, the consistory had decided to invite him to be present one week later, on August 4. He had not received the message and was hindered in his travels. The consistory simply held the matter over for another week.

The second question is raised in a querulous way by Los,[15] which in itself is not very important, but the question does open up an interesting insight into the church in Amsterdam. Did Arminius sign the Belgic Confession? Of the nine ministers called to Amsterdam before Arminius, only one, Johannes Hallius, signed the Confession. Hallius had come in 1581, just after the Synod of Middelburg, and the consistory requested this of him not because of any doubts about his orthodoxy but in a desire for "peace and unity in the church and in the government of the church." [16]

All the earlier ministers in Amsterdam had been ordained elsewhere; Arminius was the first *proponent* in that city. One would expect that the signing of the Confession would be put to him, but there is no evidence for it. The practice had evidently been dropped and possibly forgotten in Amsterdam. One must concede to Los that this synodical provision was omitted, but neither sinister motives nor dark subterfuges need be deduced. Neither ministers nor elders nor deacons had raised the question. That in itself is significant.

The Ministers

Cuchlinus has already been mentioned. He was the first pastor from the time of the Alteration, and he was the only German minister. Three of his wives had died, and in 1587 he had married an Amsterdam widow. In another nine years he would marry his fifth and last wife, the sister of Arminius' father, thus becoming Arminius' uncle by marriage. He was a Calvinist, but not of the new sort who would make so much trouble in the church in later decades. The Belgic Confession and Heidelberg Catechism defined his faith, and he was not one to speculate on the order of the decrees. He was only forty-two years old, but in that time forty-two was a ripe old age, and Cuchlinus functioned as the unofficial senior minister of Amsterdam.

Johannes Ambrosius was the only incumbent out of four who had been called to Amsterdam in 1580, and he was the last ex-priest to serve the Amsterdam church. He had been a Reformed preacher in North

---

[15] *Ibid.*, p. 67.
[16] *Prot*, I, 89; cf. *ODWA*, I, 155, and Los, pp. 67-68.

Holland since 1573, and he had a great influence in the North Holland provincial synod. He was a moderate Calvinist.

Johannes Hallius had been called in 1581 from Leiden, where he had resisted Coolhaes. In spite of that, it would not be correct to call him a rigid Calvinist. He was probably another moderate Calvinist with views and temperament similar to Cuchlinus.

Everhardus Hermanni had a unique and somewhat secondary position among the Amsterdam ministers. He was the *gasthuispredikant,* the chaplain of the almshouse, where he preached and visited the sick but did not serve the Lord's Supper. He had been called in 1583 over the objections of the consistory and at the insistence of the burgomasters, who had observed that as a pastor in Maasland he had been a popular preacher. They hoped that he would attract people who would not listen to the other pastors, to the improvement of the collections! Those burgomasters knew how to find the relevance of spiritual matters to material. Evenhuis reports that the consistory objected to his youth, fearing that he would fraternize too freely with the young people of Amsterdam. He evidently allayed the fears of the consistory and met the expectations of the burgomasters, for he served until his death in 1589. He too was a mild Calvinist.

The last minister to be mentioned is Petrus Plancius, who was decidedly not a mild Calvinist. He was, in fact, the first of the new sort of rigid Calvinists to be called to Amsterdam. Born in 1552 in Danoutre, in West Flanders, he had been through the bitter experiences of the South Netherlanders under Spanish and Roman Catholic tyranny, and he had been under the influence of the strict Calvinism of nearby France. His father, a relatively wealthy man, had gone over to Calvinism, and Plancius was sent to Germany and England for his education. He served as pastor of various Reformed churches in West Flanders under difficult circumstances and often with narrow and heroic escapes from death. After the Pacification of Ghent in 1576, he was one of some thirteen Reformed ministers who were able to work openly in Brussels itself until 1585. Pressures on the Protestants were becoming severe at the end of that period, and Plancius wrote to the church in Amsterdam imploring help. When Parma captured Brussels in 1585, Plancius fled to Bergen-op-Zoom, and at the insistence of many church members in Amsterdam, also refugees from West Flanders, he was called to be a minister in Amsterdam. He had hoped to return soon to the south, but the political breach became permanent, and Plancius served the Amsterdam church for nearly forty years.

In addition to his training in theology Plancius had been trained in astronomy and had achieved his first fame in that study. He had dis-

Petrus Plancius. Engraving by W. Delff five years after the death of Plancius.
By permission of the City Archives, Amsterdam

covered a constellation called the Dove, and he had invented a marine range finder. He was also making maps, and soon he would play an important and dramatic role in Dutch exploration and trade. About that, much more must be said. And much more must be said about his later, bitter enmity toward Arminius. At this point it is sufficient to say that in 1588 he was thirty-six years old, some seven years older than Arminius, a bearded, hunchbacked, fighting Calvinist who wore a tight skull cap. He was forceful, and many were to feel his force. He was perhaps the first to try to propagate the doctrine of predestination in the Dutch Reformed Church in Holland. His biographer, J. Keuning, says that until Plancius went north, the preaching there was based more on Bible than dogma, more on piety than theology, with no trace of the doctrine of predestination to be found.[17]

And thereupon will hang an important part of this tale.

Officials of Church and City

Arminius was now tested and accepted by the leaders of both church and state in Amsterdam, and his life was to be closely bound to the affairs of official Amsterdam. One would be left in the dark about an important aspect of Arminius' life without some knowledge of these men, but bare lists of names would be relatively unilluminating. A more extended answer is offered as being more adequate for putting flesh on the bones of the historical account of Amsterdam affairs.

The organization of the consistory on May 24, 1578, had been followed in the next few days by the organization of the city government. While the city government had a broader base than the church government, at the core the two were interlocked. Each was for the most part a self-perpetuating oligarchy, and the two oligarchies were for the most part the same.

The two governments were each constituted basically by two groups or boards, individual offices usually being filled by members of these governing groups. In the church there were twelve elders and twelve deacons. It became the practice to replace half of each board each year, so that in effect the term of office was often two years. Many members came back into office after a year's required absence. In the city there were four burgomasters and thirty-six city council members. The burgomasters were elected for one-year terms by all current and former burgomasters. Each year there was one holdover, the other three being either former or new burgomasters but not incumbents. Most burgomas-

---

[17] Keuning, *Petrus Plancius: Theoloog en Geograaf*, p. 7; cf. *ODWA*, I, 157-62.

ters were already members of the city council or soon became such, holding the offices concurrently. The city council members were elected for life (or until they should move away from the city) from and by the burghers, or what was in effect the financial leadership of the city. The council was to be chosen from among "the richest and most distinguished" burghers. Elections in both church and city were held at the beginning of February. The structure and philosophy of the city government, which included many other functional offices (such as *schout* or sheriff, the *schepenen* or judges, treasurer, and others), was precisely that which had been established in earlier centuries. What happened at the Alteration was a revolution only in the sense that the old regency was replaced by a new one which included the new power of the merchant-reformers.

If there was any precedence of status among these four groups, whose memberships overlapped, the burgomasters would be first, followed by the city council, the elders, and the deacons. A case in point would be the brother-in-law of Laurens Jacobsz. Reael, Johan Pietersz. Reael, who was a deacon in 1578, an elder in 1581, a *raad* or member of the city council in 1603, and a burgomaster in 1604. There were exceptions to this rule, but they became less common as time passed. It was not usual for a man to become burgomaster before being chosen to the city council, although it did occur. Deacons often became elders, but elders did not become deacons. Furthermore, the social distance between city leaders and church leaders increased as time went on. Three of the elders of 1578 became burgomasters and three more were in the city council. Others were progenitors of first families. In 1588 there were among the elders no burgomasters, only one council member, and two whose sons became council members. Of the deacons of 1578 six became council members, three of whom became burgomasters. Of the deacons of 1588 not one name appears even in the index to Elias' *De Vroedschap van Amsterdam,* the exhaustive genealogical study of Protestant Amsterdam's early city council.

The Elders

In 1588, when Arminius was admitted as a minister in Amsterdam, there was one elder, Hendrik Olfertsz. Fuyck, who had been among the original elders of 1578 and had been on the city council since the same year.[18] He was a ropemaker, which is to say that he owned a rope walk,

---

[18] The elders, deacons, deaconesses, and churchwardens (*kerkmeesteren*) for this period are listed in Vos, pp. 410-23. Information about these persons is obtained primarily from *VA* and *ODWA.*

and was thus an important local merchant. He was often charged by the consistory with the responsibility of conveying messages to and from the burgomasters. He had not been among the exiles of 1567-78. Two other elders were among the leading families. Theunis Jansz. Schelling-wou, a cloth merchant, was married to the daughter of one of the original burgomasters, Adriaen Cromhout, who had died on July 6, 1588. Cornelis Cornelisz. Schellinger the Elder was the *kerkmeester* or church warden of the Old Church and lived to see his son become a city council member and a director of the Dutch East India Company. Another elder was well enough known, both for his business and for his religious opinions. Walich Sivertsz. was an apothecary on the Wijde Kerksteeg, the short access from the Warmoesstraat to the west front of the Old Church. Here he compounded the medicines of that time, and here he purveyed his own brand of Protestantism, which was compounded primarily out of hatred of all things Roman Catholic. Born in 1549, he remembered the Roman Catholic days in Amsterdam before the Alteration, and he could be counted on to keep alive the grievances he had felt in those years. Later, he was to write the *Roomsche Mysterien Ontdekt, Romish Mysteries Exposed* (1604), a one-sided but historically not unuseful description of Amsterdam before the Alteration, although the Roman Catholics who accused him of lying were probably right, too. Sivertsz. the heresy-hunter argued for using the power of the magistrates to suppress not only the Catholics but also the Lutherans.[19]

Of the other elders in 1588, less is known. Baptista Oyens achieved local notoriety by defending dancing against the rest of the consistory, and by going bankrupt. Undoubtedly it was felt by some that he received his just deserts. Cornelis Jansz. was an engraver; Hans Verlaen was a lacquerer; Barent Gerritsz. was a basketmaker. The other elders were Francois de Raet, Jan Thomasz., Stoffel Jansz., and Willem Barentsz. Whether the last-named elder is the Willem Barentsz. who discovered Spitzbergen and Novaya Zemblya I cannot determine; the name was common at that time.

The Deacons

The deacons were merchants, often members of rising merchant families, including new arrivals from the south. They were Hans Martensz., a grocer; Pieter van Pulle, from Antwerp; Bartholomeus Claesz., from Delft; Willem Gerritsz., a cooper; Hendrick Cock; Adriaen Jansz. Carel, a dairy products merchant who had purchased Amsterdam citizenship

---

[19] *ODWA*, II, 54, 117.

only in 1583 (his brother, Jan Jansz. Carel, was to become a major shareholder in the Dutch East India Company) ;[20] Onno Lievensz. van Stamhart; Kaerel Leenaertsz., a grocer; Willem Theunisz., a painter; Tobias Wirtsz.; Jan Kerstensz.; and Cornelis Cornelisz. Helfertsz.

The Burgomasters

In speaking of the burgomasters, it will be useful in each first reference to indicate in parentheses the serial number in the city council (*Vroedschap*), which is the number in order of election beginning with the Alteration of 1578. The first thirty-six were elected in 1578; for higher numbers the date will be given. Indication will also be given of the years in which a burgomaster held that office. This will provide ready reference to Elias' *De Vroedschap van Amsterdam*, from which the information is gathered.

In 1587, the year in which Arminius reported to Amsterdam, the burgomasters were:

Egbert Roelofsz. (No. 13; Burg. 1579, 1580, 1582, 1583, 1585, 1587) ;

Pieter Cornelisz. Boom, (No. 42, 1582; Burg. 1583, 1585, 1587, 1588, 1590, 1591, 1593, 1594, 1597, 1598, 1600, 1602, 1603, 1605, 1606, 1608) ;

Cornelis Florisz. van Teylingen (No. 54, 1589; Burg. 1579, 1581, 1583, 1584, 1586, 1587, 1589, 1590, 1592, 1593, 1597, 1602, 1604;

Jan Claesz. Boelens (No. 72, 1597; Burg. 1587, 1589, 1593, 1596, 1599, 1600).

In 1588, the year in which Arminius was approved, the burgomasters were:

Pieter Cornelisz. Boom;

Reynier Cant (No. 26; Burg. 1580, 1581, 1583, 1585, 1586, 1588, 1591, 1592, 1594, 1595) ;

Cornelis Pietersz. Hooft (No. 49, 1584; Burg. 1588, 1591, 1594, 1596, 1597, 1601, 1602, 1604, 1605, 1607, 1608, 1610) ;

Claes Fransz. Oetgens (whose name often appears as Nicolas Franssen; No. 51, 1585; Burg. 1586, 1588, 1590, 1592, 1598, 1602, 1608, 1609).

It should be mentioned that in 1589 there was re-elected one of the original burgomasters of 1578, Wilhem Baerdesen (No. 17), who served thirteen times from 1578 to 1601.

Still predominant among the burgomasters were the *Oude Geuzen*, the Old Beggars from before the exile of 1567. Egbert Roelofsz., Reynier Cant, and Wilhem Baerdesen had been among the *doleanten*, or petitioners, of 1564; all three were in the new government of 1578 (Baerde-

[20] J. G. van Dillen, *Het Oudste Aandeelhoudersregister van de Kamer Amsterdam der Oost-Indische Compagnie*, pp. 107, 240.

sen was one of the first four burgomasters) ; and Cant had been an elder and Roelofsz. a deacon in that year. Cant had worked closely with Laurens Jacobsz. Reael in setting up Protestant preaching in 1566. Baerdesen had fled the city with Reael in 1567. Cornelis van Teylingen and Cornelis Pietersz. Hooft had also been refugees. Pieter Boom was the son of a refugee, as was Jan Claesz. Boelens, and Claes Fransz. Oetgens was the younger brother of a refugee who had died in exile. They were all merchants, but Baerdesen also represented the old Amsterdam patriciate. His father was the *Schoutist* Willem Dircksz. Baerdesen, and his great-great-great-grandfather had been burgomaster in 1426. Boom, too, was descended from the old regime, being the grandson of a burgomaster of 1496. These men, with the later exception of Claes Fransz. Oetgens, were to be firm in support of Arminius. Baerdesen, in fact, had been one of the burgomasters who had granted him study funds from the Merchants' Guild in 1581.

The City Council

The city council was in transition. Twenty-two of the original members still served. Many of these had been refugees, and several other former refugees were among the newer members of the council. There were still a few Roman Catholics on the council. Among those on the council, in addition to the burgomasters just mentioned, was Laurens Jacobsz. Reael, about whom even more will be said.

The religious temper of the council was still predominantly Old Beggar—that is, the mild reforming spirit of 1566 and 1578, neither dogmatic nor vindictive, broad in its sympathies. The wife and sister of Baerdesen were Anabaptists, and he had protected Anabaptists in 1578, as his father had done before him. Cornelis Pietersz. Hooft's wife, Anna Jacobsdr. Blaeu, was an Anabaptist, and their children were not baptized. It is also a question whether or not he was a communicant in the Reformed Church. He was a strong defender of liberty of conscience; of that he has left abundant literary evidence. How he exercised his own conscience with respect to specific religious doctrines is less clear. He became a strong defender of Arminius in later years and resisted those who attempted to impose narrow doctrinal standards on the Dutch Church.

Granted the difficulty of summing up the religious temper of the Amsterdam regents, it is possible to point to one piece of concrete evidence, their action respecting Dr. Maarten Jansz. Coster. Coster was a native of Amsterdam who had studied law under the humanist Cornelis Crocus and had studied medicine at Paris and Bologna. He had been one of the *doleanten* in 1564 and went into exile in 1567. Exile for him was not such a bad period, for he served as the court physician to the King of Denmark. Through political intervention he was able to return to Amsterdam two years before the other refugees. When they returned in 1578, he was the second man chosen burgomaster. He differed from the other Old Beggars, however, by becoming one of what Evenhuis calls *de harde gereformeerden,* "the hard Calvinists." The issue was joined when Leicester was brought to Holland. The Amsterdam leaders were hostile both to Leicester's militaristic politics and to his Calvinism, and when Leicester came to Amsterdam in 1585, they were offended by Coster's fraternizing with the Englishman. Coster was serving his fifth term as burgomaster, but after the Leicester incident he never again sat *op het kussen,* "on the cushion," as incumbency in that high office was termed. He continued on the council and continued to function as a medical doctor, however, until his death in 1592. But in the 1580s, "hard Calvinism" was not palatable in Amsterdam.[21]

What about the future? The balance of power in the city government was indeed going to change, and already in 1588 there was one new member of the council who would become a part of a "hard Calvinist" triumvirate that would dominate Amsterdam. He was Claes Fransz. Oetgens, but his departure from the broad principles of the old order and his hostility to Arminius either had not developed or were not yet apparent in 1588.

This was the situation in the leadership of church and state as Arminius entered into his fifteen years of pastoral duties. For seven years he had been the foster son of the city. Now, at twenty-nine years of age, he was one of the ministers of the city, accepted by the Old Beggars of the city council as a kindred spirit and respected by his brother ministers for his scholarship and training.

[21] *ODWA,* II, 274-75.

9

EARLY DUTIES; MARRIAGE

THERE is no record of a formal enrollment of Arminius into the ministry, but he appears in the minutes of the classis as active in the session of September 5, 1588 (having to do with the deposed minister of Ouderkerk aan den Amstel, Gerardus Pauli).[1] He appears in the minutes of the consistory for September 22, where he and deacon Cornelis Jansz. are assigned the task of visiting a woman communicant, Mayken Bresmans, suspected of having gone over to the Mennonites (the term used is *Wederdopers,* or "Anabaptists").[2] A week later he reports back that the call had been made, that the woman had just given birth to a child on September 21, so that they had not examined her about her faith, that she said she was not in contact with the Anabaptists at the moment but was sympathetic with them, that she was at rest in her soul, and that she had kindly requested the two visitors to stay out of her house.[3]

Both these entries are typical of the business affairs of the church at that time and serve simply to indicate that Arminius was now involved in the everyday work of both classis and consistory.

There was, of course, the work on Sunday. Arminius soon began taking his turn at conducting Sunday services. The principal services were held in the two great churches, the Old Church and the New Church. The churches had been purged of many decorations and furnishings reminiscent of Roman Catholic days, and new features for accommodating the new order had been provided.[4] Gone was the distance between priest at the high altar in the east end and the faithful far removed in the nave. Now the congregation was gathered around the pulpit. In the Old Church, where Arminius served probably most often, the old pulpit was still in use in his time. Around it were benches for the consistory, including the deacons and also the ministers who were attending but not preaching. The church officials thus both set an

[1] *ACA,* I, 38.
[2] *Prot,* I, 420.
[3] *Ibid.,* I, 421.
[4] *ODWA,* II, 12 ff.

example to the congregation and kept an eye on the proceedings, lest something unacceptable should happen. Not the least of their functions was that of passing judgment on the sermons. A deviation from sound doctrine would become an item for business the next Thursday when the consistory had its weekly meeting. Also admitted to this special area were the children to be baptized, with their parents and witnesses.

Around the pillars opposite the pulpit were benches for the city officials. At first, these were for the burgomasters only; later, the number was broadened. Early in 1590 a special place was built for the Stadtholder to use when he was in the city. Wives of the officials also had permanent seats. Most of the officials attended regularly, many of them both mornings and evenings.

The rest of the congregation sat on benches and stools gathered around the permanent reserved seats, or they stood. Church attendance was high, and often the churches were full, especially if the preacher was popular. By all accounts, Arminius was such a popular preacher and was favored especially by the group which constituted the ruling element in Amsterdam, the merchant-regents who were the burgomasters and council members.

The Old Church, Amsterdam, an early engraving.
By permission of the City Archives, Amsterdam

The Sunday morning service was preceded and followed by an hour of organ music, although the earlier music had to end a half hour before the service began. Provincial and national synods in 1574, 1578, and 1581 had all condemned the use of organs for services, citing I Corinthians 14:19 and linking organ playing with papacy, Judaism, heathenism, and superstition.[5] The Old Church and the New Church each had a small and a large organ. The small organ in the Old Church, which was often played by Sweelinck, is still in use. The Reformed churches rejected organs also in order to involve the whole congregation in singing. The organ music on Sundays was mostly psalms with some other music permitted, but with the explicit exclusion of Mass music.

Thirty minutes before the service was to begin, the organ music stopped and the clerk took his place near the pulpit. The half hour was spent in reading from the Bible. At the time for the service itself, the minister, dressed in the scholar's garb of tabard with a ruff, ascended into the pulpit, took his cap off, and pronounced the *votum*. The cap was the symbol of freedom, and the minister was a free man who doffed his cap only in the presence of God. The *votum,* which still begins all Reformed services in Holland, was Psalm 124:8: "Our help is in the name of the Lord, who made heaven and earth." This was followed by the Scripture lesson, the morning prayer, the sermon, the closing prayer, and the benediction. There could also be interspersed the singing of psalms, a confession of sin, and the announcement of gracious forgiveness. The prayers were written out in advance. There was an offering, not for the expenses of the church, which were provided by the magistrates, but for the relief of the poor, specifically those in the almshouse and the orphanage. There was also a collection plate at the door for offerings for special purposes.

Although there had been earlier instances of sermons lasting as long as four hours, in Arminius' time the service itself lasted only an hour and a half. On this the burgomasters were insistent, because they often met at the close of the service. The sermon, then, lasted only about an hour. There were several systems of organizing the preaching schedule. Sometimes the sermons followed the course of a certain biblical book, with the various ministers taking turns in the series. Another plan was for a certain minister himself to follow the course of a biblical book. In neither case did the congregation know in advance which minister would be preaching in which church on a given Sunday.

These arrangements were made by the ministers themselves, and permission had to be given for any one minister to preach on a certain

<hr />

[5] Rutgers, pp. 174, 253, 409, 422; *ODWA,* II, 16.

biblical book. Caspar Brandt reports that Arminius began preaching alternately on Romans and Malachi on November 6, 1588.[6] None of these sermons is extant, nor do any of the other sermons from this period survive. Why did Arminius choose these two books? From his later expositions of chapters 7 and 9 of Romans, published after his death, there is a clue. Arminius was fascinated by Romans 9, especially verses 10-13: "Rebecca . . . was told, 'The elder will serve the younger.' As it is written, 'Jacob I loved, but Esau I hated.'" This story of Jacob and Esau is in Genesis 25, but Paul is quoting Malachi 1:2-3. This is to say that Arminius, from the outset of his ministry in Amsterdam, was dealing with the problems of grace and predestination. This series of sermons on Romans lasted until September 30, 1601. It was not until 1591, when he had reached chapter 7, that his preaching aroused controversy.

For the time being, Arminius apparently had a normal round of duties in the church. On April 17, 1589, he was elected secretary of the classis.[7] On June 25, 1590, he was received as a delegate from the classis to the Particular Synod of North Holland meeting at Hoorn.[8]

He was busy enough on a nonecclesiastical matter. He was addressing his attentions to a daughter of Laurens Jacobsz. Reael, Lijsbet by name. Unlike Luther, who often wrote of his Katie, Arminius has left us nothing about his Lizzie. His marriage to Lijsbet, however, was a matter of the utmost significance, not only for the personal meanings it entailed but also for the fact that Arminius was now linked to the *Vroedschap* of Amsterdam, the city council whose members were drawn from the closed circle of regents who had ruled Amsterdam, both city and church, since the Alteration. Arminius for the first time since his boyhood had a family circle. This circle tied him to the Old Beggars of the 1560s, to the upper levels of Amsterdam society, to the merchant traders who had brought Amsterdam its new wealth, and to the rising merchant adventurers who would forge trade routes around the world and usher in Holland's Golden Age. The Reael family in its various branches was in the center of the action.

There are interesting backgrounds for both of Lijsbet's parents. On her father's side, the family can be traced back to a certain Laurens, probably in Amsterdam, who had a son, Jacob Laurensz., a sea captain. He married Imme (or Emme) Willemsdr., and in 1536 they had a son, Laurens Jacobsz., who took the surname Reael and was the father of Lijsbet. Jacob Laurensz. and his family were living next door to Gerrit

[6] *LA*, p. 58.
[7] *ACA*, I, 34.
[8] *APPS*, I, 154.

Ildsen (alias Holft) on the Nes (an Amsterdam street) in 1548.[9] He was killed at sea by English privateers, his widow died in 1563, and the house on the Nes became the property of the son, Laurens Jacobsz. Reael, although he was living elsewhere.[10]

Behind the name Reael itself there lies another story, and it is on the side of Lijsbet's mother.

There was in the fifteenth century a Meeus Pietersz. who was married to a Lijsbet Pietersdr. Velserman. They had a son, Pieter Meeusz., born around 1500 in Ransdorp, a village northeast of Amsterdam. He married Lijsbet Jansdr. Pauw, the daughter of Jan Martsz. Pauw and Diewer Hendricksdr. Leydecker, and they had six children. Their oldest child was a daughter, Geerte Pietersdr., and their fourth child was a son, Johan Pietersz. Pieter Meeusz. was a goldsmith and later a grain merchant. He lived on the west side of the Amstel, in the long row of houses designated "op 't Water." The street is now called the Damrak, and the house was on the location of the present number 53. Outside his goldsmith's shop, which occupied the front of the ground floor of the house, was an *uithangbord,* a signboard which hung out over the street to indicate the nature of the business. It was in the shape of a Spanish gold coin, a "real." Hence, the house was known as "in den Gouden Reael."

Geerte Pieterdsdr., the daughter of Pieter Meeusz., married Laurens Jacobsz., and Laurens took over the premises and the business when his father-in-law died in 1558. He also adopted as a surname the Reael which was the identifying mark of the premises. He became a grain merchant, which meant that he ventured in sending ships to Baltic ports. Johan Pietersz., the son of Pieter Meeusz., another grain merchant engaged in shipping, also took Reael as a surname. Sister and brother thus both became progenitors of Reael families.

Laurens, as has been indicated, had been a leading merchant-reformer. A man of many talents, he had been active in the circles of the *Rederijkers,* the Chambers of Rhetoric, centers of libertarian sentiment— indeed, of "Libertine" sentiment—which produced poetry and drama in the Dutch language, a body of literature which fanned the flames of national self-consciousness and independence in both politics and religion. The Amsterdam chamber, *De Egelantier* (The Sweetbrier), which had as its motto *In Liefde Bloeyende* ("Growing in Love"), met after the Alteration in a room over the Small Meat Market on the Nes.[11] It is probably not coincidental that the motto of Laurens Reael, *Liefde*

[9] *VA,* I, 137; *Rooyboek,* 70 verso.
[10] *Weeskamer Inbrengregister,* 5, 241 verso.
[11] A. E. d'Ailly, *Historische Gids van Amsterdam,* p. 20.

vermacht all ("Love conquers all"), was similar to that of the Amsterdam Chamber of Rhetoric.[12] Laurens was a prolific author himself. His catechism has been discussed. He also wrote many poems and Beggar songs. The manuscripts of these poems are in the Library of the University of Ghent. It was Reael who translated Luther's "A Mighty Fortress" into Dutch.

Of even more importance to the historian are his memoirs. The manuscript is lost, but it was used extensively by Gerard Brandt,[13] D. P. Pers,[14] and P. C. Hooft.[15] From these, with the addition of a manuscript passed down through the Hooft family and believed to be copied from the original, it is possible to reconstruct with a significant degree of reliability Reael's original text. It is the primary and often the only source of information for the events in Amsterdam in 1566 and 1567.[16]

Reael held many public offices. In 1580 he became a lieutenant in the militia; in 1589, a colonel. In 1581 he was a commissioner for the Prince of Orange in a matter concerning convoys in Friesland. In 1582 he was a *schepen,* or judge. In 1583 he was elected to the city council and became a regent of the orphanage. On March 14, 1599, he became a receiver of the *Lommerd,* the Lombard or Capital Loan (*de Capitale Leening te Amsterdam*). In 1600 he was appointed to the Admiralty of Zeeland. He died in Middelburg the next year.

He had thirteen children: Pietertje, stillborn in 1559; Magteld, born in 1561; Dieuwertje, born in 1562; Jacob, stillborn in 1564; and another Jacob, born in 1565. These were all born in Amsterdam. The family then fled to Emden, where four children were born: Pieter in 1567; Lijsbet on August 22, 1569; Immetje in 1572; and Maritje in 1573. During these years Reael is reported to have lived also in Bremen and Danzig, but his next two children were born in Hoorn: Aefjen in 1576, and Bartholomeus in 1577. At the time of the Alteration or soon after, the family was back in Amsterdam, and two more children were born: a still born child in 1581, Laurens in 1583.[17]

Lijsbet was thus the middle child, born in exile, and about ten years younger than Arminius. The story told by James Nichols, that

---

[12] On the Chambers of Rhetoric, cf. G. D. J. Schotel, *De Invloed der Rederijkers op de Hervorming,* and L. M. van Dis, *Reformatorische Rederijkersspelen uit de Eerste Helft der Zestiende Eeuw.*

[13] *HRN.* Brandt cites page numbers in the Reael manuscript.

[14] *d'Ontstelde Leeuw, of Springhader der Nederlandscher Beroerten.*

[15] *Neederlandsche Histoorien.*

[16] The texts in G. Brandt, Pers, and Hooft are collated with an additional piece of manuscript evidence in J. C. Breen, "Uittreksel uit de Amsterdamsche Gedenkschriften van Laurens Jacobsz. Reael, 1542-1567."

[17] van Dam van Hekendorp, p. 310.

she was fourteen years old when her father fled Amsterdam in 1567, is in error. The brothers and sisters of Lijsbet are worthy of notice. Magteld married Hendrick van Marken, and their descendants formed an important branch of that family.[18] Dieuwertje married Andries Prippelnagel, and they became the progenitors of that important family.[19] Jacob became the secretary of the Amsterdam Admiralty. Immetje married Jacobus Bruno, minister in Arnhem. Maritje married a de Vries, and they had a son in the Amsterdam government. Bartholomeus became the treasurer of the Amsterdam Admiralty. Laurens played an important role in the organization of the Dutch East India Company and became the third Governor General of Indonesia. Pieter did not marry and died in the East Indies. Aefjen did not marry.

Lijsbet's uncle, Johan Pietersz. Reael, who was born in 1548, and who had probably accompanied his widowed mother into exile in 1567, was also important in the new order in Amsterdam. His wife, Hillegond, was the daughter of the eminent Warmoesstraat merchant Reynier Simonsz. van Neck, one of the refugees of 1567 who had helped form the new government at the Alteration and had been on the city council since 1578, and in other important posts, including that of burgomaster. Van Neck died in 1581. J. P. Reael, like his brother-in-law, was a grain merchant with ships ranging from the Baltic Sea to France. His business took him to Rouen, where he came in touch with the Protestants there, and there he arranged for an underground printer, Abel Clemence, to print Petrus Dathenus' Dutch translation of the Psalms. On the title page is a printer's mark, a print of a merchant ship in full sail. H. de la Fontaine Verwey had noticed the almost identical nature of this ship to that in an engraving of a drawing by Pieter Brueghel the Elder, published shortly before the Psalm book. There is little doubt that it is the same ship; furthermore, a close inspection of Brueghel's engraving reveals something that de la Verwey did not notice, that Brueghel's engraving carries a banner with three arrows—the coat of arms of J. P. Reael! Brueghel had drawn one of Reael's ships, and Reael had used it for the printer's mark on the book of Dathenus' psalms.[20]

J. P. Reael served in many capacities in both church and city—deacon, elder, council member, and burgomaster. In 1581 he succeeded his father-in-law as collector of taxes (*Ontvanger van de Gemenelands-middelen*) for Amsterdam and vicinity. In his latter years he was a

---

[18] *Familie-archief Backer,* 44.
[19] *Ibid.*
[20] H. de la Fontaine Verwey, "De Geschiedenis van een Drukkersmerk."

supporter of Arminius and of the Remonstrants. He had six children, and they married within the regent circle of Amsterdam. Jacob was a council member (No. 112, 1623) and a *schepen*. Reynier was also a *schepen* and a wealthy merchant who developed much of the section of Amsterdam known as Reaeleneiland.[21] Various members of both Reael families owned many properties in Amsterdam, and the family was heavily involved in the planning of the famous concentric canals which were developed in the early seventeenth century. The Reael name disappeared in the seventeenth century, but descendants by other names were in the city government into the nineteenth.

Lijsbet's forebears had a number of collateral relationships of importance. On the side of her uncle, Johan Pietersz. Reael, the lines extended to the families van Neck, Oetgens, Uitenbogaert, and van Beuningen, to name a few. More remotely, her uncle's wife was the sister of the husband of a niece of the celebrated humanist Dirck Volckertsz. Coornhert. Her father's sister, Dieuwer Jacobsdr., was married first to Egbert Meynertsz., the Old Beggar who died in prison on the eve of his scheduled execution in Amsterdam, in 1568. Their son (and Lijsbet's cousin), Dr. Sebastian Egbertsz., was council member (No. 78, 1602) and burgomaster (1606, 1608), and a close friend of Arminius when the latter was under fire. A medical doctor, he appears in an "anatomy lesson" painting by Aert Pietersz. (1603), and again by Thomas de Keyser (1619). Dieuwer remarried the next-door neighbor of her brother Laurens (Lijsbet's father), Pieter Jansz. Pauw, a soap manufacturer "in den Blinden Ezel" (the Blind Ass, now Damrak 54-55), one of whose sons by a previous marriage was Dr. Pieter Pauw, who later became professor of medicine at the University of Leiden. There he founded the Anatomical Theater, was a close friend of Arminius, and was in attendance at the final illness of Arminius. He was the teacher of Dr. Nicholas Tulp, who appears in Rembrandt's "Anatomy Lesson of Dr. Nicholas Tulp" (1632).

Such details on the surface may seem tedious, but they serve to establish and make precise an important point. By 1590 Arminius, the orphan from Oudewater, was no longer an isolated individual lacking in supportive relationships and dependent on charity. By his call to the Amsterdam ministry and by his marriage to Lijsbet, he was caught up in an extended network of professional, political, economic, and family relationships which extended into every corner of the leading families of Amsterdam. More than once these relationships were to function in his favor in the turbulent years which lay ahead.

[21] I. H. van Eeghen, "De Zandhoek."

The marriage of Jacobus and Lijsbet took place in September, 1590, according to the laws and customs which prevailed. Permission to marry had to be granted by the city through its Commission on Matrimony, where the couple would be asked the questions specified by law. Although the commission's functions were purely civil, it met in the sacristy of the Old Church, the former St. Sebastian's chapel of the *Handboogschutters,* or Handbow Militia. The room was entered from outside the church through a large red wooden door, over which was the inscription *Tis haest Getrout, Dat Lange Rouwt* ("A hasty marriage is long regretted"). The Amsterdam idiom for getting married was *Gaan door de Roo-deur,* "to go through the Red Door." Jacobus and Lijsbet went through the Red Door on August 25, 1590. All Amsterdam couples, high or low, entered matrimony through this door. Forty-four years later, Rembrandt Harmensz. van Rijn and Saskia Uijlenburgh would walk through that same door.

From knowledge of the usages of the time and from the *trouwboek,* or register of applications kept by the commissioners, it is possible to reconstruct the scene.[22] The day was Saturday, August 25, 1590. (Although the entry is preceded by the date of August 30, the latter date does not allow three Sundays for announcing the impending marriage publicly. It is likely that the date was inserted at the wrong point in the page and that the previous date of August 25 applies. Furthermore, Saturday afternoon was the regular time for the commission to meet.)[23] Waiting in the sacristy were two of the marriage commissioners, Dirck Jacobsz. Rosencrans and Cornelis Cornelisz. Heemskerck (a cousin of the father of the jurist Hugo Grotius). There was also the *koster,* or sexton, of the Old Church, who would make the entry in the marriage book. The young couple entered with their witnesses. Arminius was accompanied by a burgomaster, Claes Fransz. Oetgens, and Lijsbet by her father and mother. Arminius is identified in the book as "a minister of God's Word in this city," and Lijsbet is described as "twenty years old, living *opt water in den gulden reael."*

Their promises to each other are affirmed, and they request the "publishing of the banns" for the next three Sundays. Since they are members of the church, the announcements will be in the morning service in the Old Church; otherwise they would have been from the steps of the City Hall on the Dam. They further affirm that they are acting freely, under no coercion, and that they are not related by blood.

[22] *DTB*, no. 405, fol. 162, p. 331.

[23] For a thorough study of marriage laws and statistics in Amsterdam in this period, cf. Leonie van Nierop, "De Bruidegoms van Amsterdam van 1578 tot 1601." The author discusses the meetings of the commissioners on p. 347.

Underneath, at the left, is the signature "Jacobus Arminius." At the right is "Lijsbet Louwerensdoch," which is according to the common practice of spelling phonetically and abbreviating at random. A modern spelling would be "Laurensdochter." The *koster* himself spelled freely and variously. For him, Arminius is "Herminius."

It is worthy of notice that Lijsbet signed her name, and in a clear, even hand. Illiteracy was high in Amsterdam, especially among women. In the preceding entry in the marriage book the bride signed with an X.

The announcement of the impending marriage was made on the next day, Sunday, and on the two following Sundays, by the reader in the morning service in the Old Church. The marriage itself took place on the fourth Sunday, September 16, in the afternoon, after the catechetical instruction and service of baptism. The minister was Johannes Ambrosius, who probably stood in a pulpit slightly elevated above the floor of the choir with the bride and groom standing in front of him facing each other. Family and friends were gathered around, and it may be assumed that there was a large assemblage of the leading citizens of Amsterdam for this marriage of a favorite daughter and the young minister. Of wedding finery there was none, however, for sober Calvinistic custom prevailed. The men were wearing black capes which draped from beneath a ruff to the thigh. They had baggy pants gathered below the knee, and long stockings. They also wore long black hats, the usual custom in church. The women were wearing long dresses with a black mantle hanging from a headband down their backs to the floor. They too wore ruffs.

The minister expounded a grim view of marriage. For the married there are many adversities and crosses because of sin. The purpose of marriage is mutual support in all things pertaining to this life and the next, the begetting of children, and the avoidance of concupiscence. The minister then asked the couple to hold right hands (a contemporary picture shows the man and woman at considerable distance from each other with arms outstretched) .[24] The questions were put to them (the woman "takes him for her lord"—half my readers will regret the passing of that distant age) , and the blessing was given.

Evenhuis reports that such events were so popular that sightseers, who often had had a glass too much, had to be forbidden, by edict of the burgomasters, to climb on the choir screens to watch the ceremony.[25]

The whole proceeding, beginning with the first public announcement, was accompanied by feasting, from the *commissarismaal* on the day of

[24] *ODWA*, II, 69.
[25] *Ibid.*, p. 70.

the first public announcement to the marriage dinner itself on the fourth Sunday. Not uncommonly was there an enormous amount of eating and drinking, with dancing, but it seems highly probable that in the home of the Old Beggar Reael, with the minister as groom, the festivities were subdued. Whatever happened has escaped the notice of the historians. Not even Triglandius manufactures any scandalous episode.

The bride and groom may have lived at first in the Reael home; moving in with parents was common practice in those days. Arminius' bachelor's quarters have not been identified, nor is there any other evidence for the place of residence of the married pair in the first couple of years of marriage. Children soon came, however, and with them a change of residence.

In May, 1593, Arminius and his wife took steps to prepare for the child which Lijsbet was expecting the following month. They left the home of her parents (where it may be assumed that they had been living) to move across town to quarters of their own. The question of the place of their residence has been difficult to solve. I am grateful to Mr. J. G. Kam of Amsterdam for its solution, which required a thorough reading of the financial records of the cloister properties in Amsterdam for the period in question. From these records he has discovered that the couple moved into the St. Ursula cloister in May, 1593, where they remained until they removed to Leiden in 1603.

It had been the practice since the Alteration to house the ministers in old cloister properties (there were some twenty such properties), the income of which now went to the city treasury. Cuchlinus, Hallius, and Ambrosius had lived first in the Franciscan cloister and later in the St. Gertrude cloister. Both these had been destroyed, however, by 1590. The ministers did not pay their own rent; this benefit was provided by the States of Holland. The treasury of Amsterdam billed the States for the rent of their ministers, thereby collecting the income from cloister property occupied by ministers. The first notation of such an obligation for property occupied by Arminius is of a half year's rent of 60 guilders due in November, 1593, for a house in the St. Ursula cloister.[26] From this it is determined that Arminius occupied the house in the previous May. There is another reference in 1594,[27] and again in 1594-95.[28]

The St. Ursula cloister, commonly known as the Eleven Thousand Virgins' cloister after the legendary companions in martyrdom of the

[26] *Thesaurie Ordinaris* 279 (247), *Bagijnen Rapiamus* van 1593, fol. 103 verso.
[27] *Thesaurie Ordinaris* 280 (248), *Bagijnen Rapiamus* van 1595, fol. 105 verso.
[28] *Stadsrekeningen 1594-95*, list no. 61, fol. 32 verso.

saint, had been founded in the early fifteenth century, one of many which sprang up at that time. It was on the north side of the Rusland, a short street connecting the Kloveniersburgwal with the Oudezijds Achterburgwal. The Rusland was at that time the site of the thread and flax market. At its east end was the Raamspoort, an opening in the city wall which led outside to the dye works, noted for their vile odor. North of the St. Ursula cloister was the cloister of the Brothers of St. Paul, whose chapel was in use as the Walloon church. The buildings of the St. Ursula cloister were being taken over for a *spinhuis* or *tuchthuis,* a prison-workhouse for female prostitutes and beggars, a process which may have begun while Arminius still lived there. On ground taken over from the two cloisters was the *dolhuis,* or insane asylum. Street market, dye works, prison, and asylum—a setting somewhat different from the fashionable Warmoesstraat or the bustling commerce "op 't Water," but for all that not too untypical of any part of old Amsterdam. Nor was Arminius without distinguished neighbors. Taffin, the Walloon minister, lived there, as did Ellert de Veer, the pensionary of Amsterdam.[29]

Arminius evidently occupied successively two different houses in the cloister, because there are entries from 1604 to 1614 regarding a house "where Jacobus Herminius [*sic*] had lived," a house whose rent was at the much higher level of 425 to 475 guilders. Mr. Kam has determined that this larger house, made necessary undoubtedly by Arminius' growing family, was that which had been previously occupied by Maarten Block-land, former pensionary and, incidentally, a continuing Roman Catholic who remained in favor with Reformed Amsterdam. He was buried on February 12, 1596, and was honored with an hour-and-a-half peal on the big bell of the Old Church. Arminius moved into the premises on May 1, 1596. The house was located on the corner of the Oudezijds Achterburgwal and the Korte Spinhuissteeg, on the south side of the latter. In 1603 Arminius was paying a rent of 200 guilders a year,[30] and in 1604, after he had moved to Leiden, the house was taken over by the regents of the *spinhuis* for use in the women's prison.[31]

So, from Mr. Kam's researches, we know with reasonable accuracy where Jacobus and Lijsbet lived, raised their children, and made a home to which the young minister could come for domestic solace

[29] For a historical survey of the area, see D'Ailly, pp. 114-17. There are pictures of the *dolhuis* and *spinhuis* in Petrus Schenk (1661-1715), *100 Afbeeldinge der Voornaamste Gebouwen van Amsterdam* (late seventeenth century, recently reproduced by photolithograph). The cloister buildings appear in the pictorial maps of Cornelis Antonijsz. and Pieter Bast's map of 1597, which is contemporary with Arminius.

[30] *Thesaurie Ordinaris* 348 (316), *Bagijnen Rapiamus van* 1603.

[31] *Thesaurie Ordinaris* 349 (317), *Bagijnen Rapiamus van* 1604.

after battling the crosscurrents of civic, ecclesiastical, and theological life. One can look down on the rooftops of the cloister houses in the pictorial maps of Cornelis Anthonijsz. and Pieter Bast and see, in imagination, Lijsbet and her children standing at the door to greet their beloved minister, husband, and father as he makes his way along the Oudezijds Achterburgwal on his way home from the Old Church. But with imagination we shall have to be content, for our only evidence is the rent records. Arminius has written us nothing about his home life in Amsterdam.

The action shifts now, however, from domestic life in the Golden Reael and in the St. Ursula cloister to public life on the Dam, where the burgomasters sat in the tower of the old City Hall, and to the Old Church, where the consistory had its Thursday sessions. Arminius would soon be in the center of attention in both places.

10

THE FIRST ROUND OF STRIFE:
1591-1593

IT IS CLEAR that the theological issues which were to concern Arminius throughout his later ministry were coming to the surface by 1591, and maybe a year or two earlier. Bertius tells a story, which is often repeated, about a complicated train of events whereby Arminius allegedly abandoned an earlier Calvinism and came around to espousing the position of Beza's opponents. No dates are given, but Bertius leaves the impression that this took place around 1591. Caspar Brandt in retelling the same story places its beginning back to 1589. Bertius' story, briefly, is that "certain good brethren who belonged to the Church of Delft" had circulated a pamphlet entitled *An Answer to Some of the Arguments Adduced by Beza and Calvin; from a Treatise concerning Predestination, on the Ninth Chapter of the Epistle to the Romans.* Martinus Lydius, formerly a minister in Amsterdam and since 1583 a professor at the new academy or university at Franeker, in Friesland, sent a copy to Arminius, with a request that Arminius, so recently returned from Geneva, would defend his mentor Beza. This Arminius was pleased to do, says Bertius, and he set himself to a thorough study in preparation for the task. The Delft writers had attempted to defend the doctrine of predestination by modifying Beza's supralapsarianism to a sublapsarian position. Arminius' task, then, was to defend supralapsarianism against sublapsarianism. In the process, according to Bertius, his mind went through two transitions:

But while he was contriving a proper refutation, and had begun accurately to weigh the arguments on both sides, and to compare different passages of scripture together,—while he was thus harassing and fatiguing himself, he was conquered by the force of truth, and, at first, became a convert to the very opinions which he had been requested to combat and refute. But he afterwards disapproved of them, as promulgated by the brethren of Delft, because he did not think the doctrine contained in them to be correct according to the scriptures.[1]

[1] Funeral Oration; *WA*, I, 30.

Bertius goes on to say that the position which Arminius then finally espoused was that of Melanchthon and of the Danish Lutheran theologian Nicholas Hemingius (Hemmingsen), and that "our churches formerly enjoyed the privilege (which is continued to this day in many places) of being always permitted to embrace any one of the several sentiments that have been published on this controversy, which has never yet been decided by the judgment of any ancient Synod or Council." [2] Bertius also mentioned a former Leiden theologian, Johannes Holmannus (Secundus), a disciple of Hemingius, who had taught there from 1582 until his death in 1586.

Underlying this tale of Bertius are some facts. The Delft writers were two ministers, Arent (Arnold) Cornelisz. and Reynier Donteklok. In 1578, in Leiden, they had debated the questions of predestination and of the death sentence for heretics with the humanist critic of Calvinism, Dirck Volckertsz. Coornhert. It was under this pressure that they had felt it necessary to modify Beza's high Calvinism. Their book, *Responsio ad argumenta quaedam Bezae et Calvini ex tractatu de praedestinatione in cap. IX ad Romanos,* had appeared in 1589. It was one of a number of attempts to refute the troublesome (to the Calvinists) Coornhert. Indeed, according to Caspar Brandt, the Consistory of Amsterdam asked Arminius himself to write such a refutation, and Arminius' failure to do so was caused by the intervention of Lydius with his request for a refutation of the Delft ministers.[3] Later writers often carelessly conflate these stories, sometimes to assert that Arminius was trying to refute Coornhert and went over to Coornhert's humanism.

Before attempting to assess the story, other available evidence should be considered. In March, 1591, Arminius wrote a letter to his old friend and teacher at Basel, Grynaeus. "There is a lot of controversy among us about predestination, original sin, and free will," he says. Some refer the decree of predestination to those not yet fallen, indeed, not yet created (supralapsarianism), in either case making some men already liable to damnation. This leads to the question of free will. Does it function in the unregenerate? In conversion is it active or passive? If passive, has it the power to effect conversion; if active, does it precede or follow the divine inworking? But conclusions about free will rest back on views of original sin. Arminius reports that it is being debated whether guilt or depravity comes first. Then a remarkable statement: "Our opponents, who are numerous here, deny it [original sin] altogether." [4]

[2] *Ibid.*
[3] *LA,* p. 61; *KH,* Part 3, p. 103.
[4] The letter is printed in Maronier, pp. 60-61.

His opponents reject original sin, and they are many. Who are they? It is obvious for one thing that he does not refer here to the Calvinists. His opponents are the humanist sympathizers of Coornhert (who had died on October 27, 1590), the so-called "Libertines" who sided with the Calvinists in political opposition to Spain but who opposed them on matters of dogma. They existed among the merchant oligarchy; C. P. Hooft was certainly to be numbered among them. But the precise identity of the reference here is unknown.

What about Arminius himself? If his opponents were the humanists, was he a Calvinist? If a Calvinist, was he a supralapsarian or a sublapsarian? He says to Grynaeus that he has been diligently studying the Scriptures and has come to an affirmation that will not lead him astray nor cause him to mislead others. "I believe that our salvation rests on Christ alone and that we obtain faith for the forgiveness of sins and the renewing of life only through the grace of the Holy Spirit." It is a position that is not Libertine, not supralapsarian, not sublapsarian. The mood of the letter is one of surprise that such subtleties should be raised and that one or another position should be upheld as the one true doctrine. It is from amid the crossfire of these various opinions that he seeks instruction from Grynaeus; indeed, it seems that he seeks support against all the proposed opinions.

There is still further evidence. By 1591 Arminius, in his preaching on Romans, had reached the seventh chapter, and when he came to the fourteenth verse he was faced with one of the questions he had raised with Grynaeus. Verse 14 reads: "We know that the law is spiritual; but I am carnal, sold under sin." The point at issue was the sort of man Paul is describing by such words and by the following passage. It is a man who says, "I do not do what I want, but I do the very thing I hate" (7:15), and, "I delight in the law of God, in my inmost self, but I see in my members another law at war with the law of my mind, making me captive to the law of sin which dwells in my members" (7:22-23). Is such a one regenerate or unregenerate? If he is regenerate, does this not give a low view of the power of God? If he is unregenerate, does this not allow too much good striving in the sinner? The high Calvinists maintained that he was regenerate. Arminius preached otherwise, and the opposition was soon made manifest.

Bertius does not mention this episode. It is Brandt who reports it. Arminius' exposition, he says, "procured him much ill-will, and but little favor with most of his ministerial brethren." [5] He was soon accused from many quarters of Pelagianism and Socinianism and of deviation

[5] *LA*, p. 67.

from the Belgic Confession and the Heidelberg Catechism. The details of his arguments are available to us, and they will be mentioned later. What is important here is that in the course of his preaching in 1591 he had taken a position contrary to the high Calvinists and had drawn their ire.

Finally, there is some negative evidence, or significant arguments from silence, respecting Bertius' story of a theological transition in 1591. First, there is no clear evidence that Arminius had ever accepted Beza's doctrine of predestination and its concomitants. Second, he makes no point of having undergone a theological transition. He constantly portrays himself as teaching an ancient position in the church and one widely held even among the Reformed pastors in the Low Countries. He sees his opponents as innovators, not himself.

All this evidence points to one conclusion: namely, that Arminius was not in agreement with Beza's doctrine of predestination when he undertook his ministry at Amsterdam; indeed, he probably never had agreed with it. The issue had not been raised sharply for him, however, until the events just related here, at which time he took a specific stand against both the high Calvinist positions then proposed—supralapsarianism and sublapsarianism. He suddenly found himself faced with a new set of problems: liberty of conscience, the proper interpretation of the Confession and Catechism, and the authority of the consistory and classis over a minister. What he had learned from his early teachers, what had been widely held in the Dutch churches in the earlier decades, suddenly became controversial, and he was in the middle of the turmoil.

An objection must be met, however. Why was he asked to write refutations of Coornhert and of the Delft ministers? In the case of Lydius, it may have been a lack of information. He could easily have assumed that the recent student of the prestigious Beza was a disciple of the same. The Amsterdam ministers, on the other hand, or especially Plancius, may have been moved by hostility, hoping to put Arminius in a difficult position. They did use precisely this tactic on at least one later occasion. Whatever their motive, the end was attained.

From this same year, 1591, there are two more glimpses into the affairs of Arminius. One shows that he was entrusted with decisive matters in the life of the church. On February 1, 1591, the States of Holland called a conference for drawing up a new church order. Eight politicians and eight churchmen were chosen to serve as a commission. Arminius was one of the eight churchmen, along with Uitenbogaert from The Hague, Arent Cornelisz. from Delft, and five others representing Dordrecht, Leiden, Haarlem, Enkhuizen, and Edam. Arminius was thus

141

the only representative of the Amsterdam church on this important body.[6]

The other event in 1591 was personal and tragic, the beginning of joy and sorrow in his personal life. The first child was born to Lijsbet and Jacobus early in July, a boy whom they named Harmen. The name was selected according to the common custom of naming a first boy after his paternal grandfather. The date of birth was probably July 9 or 10, judging from the fact that the baptism took place on the 11th. Baptisms commonly followed the day of birth and were held in a church. Harmen was baptized in the Old Church, the witness being a "Gyert Jacobs." [7] Witnesses were usually relatives or close friends. There were no Reael relatives by this name, and the most likely conclusion is that this Geertje Jacobsdr. was Arminius' aunt, the sister of the father who was being remembered in the naming of the child.

Infant mortality was high. Perhaps the public baptisms of day-old infants were a contributing factor. The Old Church could be a cold place, even in July. The parents lost their boy at the end of the month, and he was buried in the Old Church on August 1. The entry in the burial book in the customary idiom conveys a vivid pathos: *1 Augusty begraven een kindt onder den arm van Jacobus Arminius ons predicant* —"On August 1 was buried a babe in arms of Jacobus Arminius our minister." [8] Small babies were buried without caskets and were carried to the burial place in the arms of a parent or relative. The burial spot in the church is unknown; it could have been in a Reael family plot or in a plot reserved for ministers and their families. For Lijsbet especially this was the beginning of many personal sorrows, for she was to outlive most of her loved ones.

THE EXACT COURSE of events for the next year is difficult to establish. Sources disagree among themselves and are lacking in precision. The questionable material of Triglandius is repeated uncritically. Caspar Brandt apparently had access to a manuscript of Arminius which is now lost, but he also perpetuates some confusion in Triglandius. Nevertheless, an attempt is made here to trace the course of events in the eventful years of 1592 and 1593.

The dissension over Arminius' sermons on Romans 7, stirred up primarily by Plancius, reached the point that it became a matter of dis-

---

[6] A letter of Arminius to Uitenbogaert of February 10, 1591, concerning this assignment is printed in Rogge, *Brieven van Wtenbogaert*, I, 8-9.
[7] DTB, 2/97.
[8] *Ibid.*, 1042/72.

cussion in the consistory on January 2, 1592.[9] It was decided to try to settle the matter "as much as possible." In a meeting of January 7, of either the classis or the consistory (Triglandius says consistory, but the date is a Tuesday, when the classis would be meeting), it was proposed that the matter be taken up with Arminius. He and Joannes Halsbergius, who had become an Amsterdam minister in 1590 and who appears as an ally of Arminius, refused to discuss it except in the presence of the burgomasters or their deputies, otherwise in the presence of only the ministers, but not with just ministers and elders.[10]

In the meantime, Lydius in Franeker had heard about the troubles and undertook to try to settle the difficulties. He traveled to The Hague to enlist the aid of Arminius' close friend Uitenbogaert, minister at the court of the Stadtholder Maurice, to act as a mediator. Uitenbogaert agreed to make the attempt, and he went to Amsterdam, where he in turn sought aid of Jean Taffin, the minister of the Walloon church.[11]

While this was going on, quite by chance the name of Uitenbogaert was coming up in the meetings of the classis. The church in Amsterdam was in the process of calling an additional minister, Jeremias Bastingius, a moderate Calvinist then in Dordrecht. The burgomasters proposed to the classis that a call be extended also to Uitenbogaert, a move designed to preserve a balance of theological opinions in Amsterdam. The classis considered this proposal on January 14, when Plancius arose to allege that Uitenbogaert held improper views on original sin and other topics. Arminius and some others defended Uitenbogaert and urged acceptance of the burgomasters' recommendation. The classis decided instead to send two elders, Thomas Kronenburg and Jan de Vrye, to inform the burgomasters that they wished to call Bastingius but not Uitenbogaert.[12] Bastingius, by the way, did not accept the call.

Uitenbogaert heard of these proceedings and the accusations of Plancius, and he protested to Plancius about the fallacy of his charges, exacting from Plancius an agreement to rectify the matter before the brethren. This Plancius did on January 23 in a meeting of the classis (or possibly the consistory, it being a Thursday).

The proposed conference between the ministers and Arminius, with neither burgomasters nor elders represented, was held in a meeting of the

---

[9] According to Triglandius, p. 284.

[10] *Ibid.; LA*, p. 68.

[11] Uitenbogaert tells this story in two places: *KH*, Part 3, p. 103, and in the smaller work bound with *KH, Johannis VVtenbogaerts Leven, Kerckelijcke Bedieninghe ende Zedighe Verantwordingh*, p. 6. The latter entry has a marginal note of November, 1590, for the trip of Lydius, but this evidently, from the context of events, should be November, 1591. Uitenbogaert made his trip to Amsterdam in January, 1592.

[12] *LA*, pp. 77-79; Triglandius, p. 284.

classis on perhaps January 7 or 14. It was a solemn occasion, opened with prayer. Plancius then raised his objections. Arminius was teaching Pelagianism, was overly dependent on the early fathers, deviated from the Belgic Confession and Heidelberg Catechism, and held incorrect views on predestination and on the perfection of man in this life. Arminius defended himself on all but the last two charges, denying Pelagianism, defending the authority of the fathers, and denying any departure from the doctrinal formulas. Predestination he refused to discuss on the grounds that there was nothing about it in Romans 7. On the issue of perfection he had already explained himself at such length in his preaching, he said, that nothing more was to be added.[13]

Taffin and Uitenbogaert, meanwhile, made their own attempt to bring about a settlement. They persuaded the concerned parties to come to a conference in Taffin's home, but the conference was unsuccessful. Then they drew up a formula of pacification. It specified that Arminius declare that he was unaware of having taught anything contrary to the Confession and Catechism and agree to stay within the bounds of Scripture as explained in the two formulas. He would agree to submit questions about doctrinal difficulties to his brethren, and, if agreement was not forthcoming, to be silent until the matter could be submitted to a general church council (national synod). The classis, in turn, would agree to keep the peace publicly and privately and to desist from accusations against Arminius.[14]

Taffin and Uitenbogaert appeared at a special meeting of the consistory on January 17 to present this formula. Arminius accepted it, but the majority of the consistory did not.[15]

By this time the burgomasters were doubly alarmed. Their recommendation of a call to Uitenbogaert had been turned down by the ministers, and Uitenbogaert's efforts to gain peace in the church had come to nothing. Accordingly, they summoned Taffin and Uitenbogaert to report to them, and then they decided to call the ministers in as a body for consultation or, better, to summon the ministers to receive advice and instructions from the burgomasters.

The meeting was held on February 11, 1592, at 3:00 P.M., presumably in the tower of the Town Hall. Present were the four incumbent burgomasters—Wilhem Baerdesen, Cornelis Florisz. van Teylingen, Reynier Cant, and Claes Fransz. Oetgens—and the three ex-burgomasters who had stepped down only a week earlier—Pieter Cornelisz. Boom, Cornelis Pietersz. Hooft, and Barthold Cromhout. The ministers were

---

[13] This episode is described in *LA*, pp. 68-70.

[14] *Ibid.*, pp. 73-75, quoting Triglandius, p. 284.

[15] *Prot*, II/73 verso; Triglandius, p. 284.

Cuchlinus, Ambrosius, Hallius, Plancius, Arminius, and Halsbergius. This meeting raised the controversy to the level of an official event, and it may well be called the first Arminian controversy.

It is important to remember who the burgomasters were. Presiding was Cant, who had worked closely with Reael in promoting the hedge preaching of 1566. He had fled Amsterdam the night before Reael in 1567. While he had stoutly resisted the Catholics, he and Reael had also resisted the rioting image-breakers, and he was no friend of rigid Calvinism. He and Reael had sat together at the first table of the first Protestant Communion service in 1566. He had been a member of the first reconstituted city council in 1578, and also an elder of the reconstituted church. Baerdesen had fled in 1567 and had resided with Cant in exile. He was known for his policy of toleration in religion, and at the Alteration he had protected not only Catholics but also Anabaptists, among whom were his own wife and sister. Van Teylingen was also a refugee, the last to be elected to the city council (in 1589). He was married to the sister of another magistrate in the meeting, Barthold Cromhout. Cromhout was the son of the Adriaen Cromhout who had sat at that same first Communion table with Reael and Cant and who had fled in the same leaky boat which perilously conveyed the Reael family to Emden. Oetgens was the paternal uncle of Cromhout's wife. His older brother had died in exile. Boom was the son of one of the leading Reformers of 1566. His brother was married to the widow of Arminius' wife's uncle. Hooft, another exile of 1567, was not a Calvinist in any doctrinal sense but was more of a humanist and "Libertine" in the tradition of Erasmus and Coornhert. In 1597 he was to make a strong plea for religious toleration, and in 1598 a strong attack on the doctrine of predestination advanced by extreme Calvinists.

To put it pointedly, Arminius was surrounded by friends. When the case was taken to the Town Hall, Bre'r Rabbit was in the briar patch.

Cant made the opening statement. As Brandt reports it, from the now-lost manuscript of Arminius, the burgomasters

had perceived with pain from their public ministrations, and that for a considerable time back, as well as from the complaints of several citizens, that they were not at peace among themselves. Dissensions of that kind must be checked in the bud, lest they should issue in results disastrous to the Church, and even to the Republic itself. The honorable senators [burgomasters], therefore, in consideration of the office with which they were intrusted, wished and enjoined that the ministers would diligently apply themselves henceforth to the cultivation of peace and harmony, of which they had hitherto stood forth as an example to other Churches; and avoid giving any one occasion, by their declamatory statements, to suspect that some serious contentions were fostered amongst them. But if they did happen to differ on some points, it was lawful for them to institute amongst themselves private and friendly conferences on such topics; only, they must see to it that these differences do not find their way from the Ecclesiastical Court [consistory] into the pulpit, and thence to the public. Should they fail in this duty, they (the senators) would be obliged to have recourse to other remedies, that no harm might accrue to the Church and the Republic.[16]

The ministers withdrew to consider this statement. When they returned, Ambrosius expressed agreement with the burgomasters' desire for peace. But if any one of the ministers, Ambrosius went on, felt he could be charged with delinquency, it was up to him to clear himself.

Arminius asked permission to speak. He acknowledged that his exposition of Romans 7 differed from some of the Reformed, but he denied that he was outside what was permitted by the Confession and Catechism. He had supposed that he could exercise the liberty enjoyed by all Christian teachers of expounding Scripture according to the dictates of conscience. As for the charge that he was violating the doctrinal standards, he stood ready to discuss this with his colleagues, but only in the presence of the burgomasters themselves, or their deputies, who should act as "righteous arbiters."

Cuchlinus responded at once. He appealed to his thirteen years of service to the church in Amsterdam, and he argued that such a conference should be in the consistory alone. Then the ministers were ordered to retire while the burgomasters deliberated. On their return, Cant spoke for the entire company of burgomasters, reporting

that it was the opinion and decree of the honorable senators, that the Church Court [consistory] should allow this whole matter to rest, and permit whatever discussions had arisen out of it up to this time to be consigned to oblivion. A fresh conference upon it did not appear to them to be suitable, or likely to do good. They (the ministers) must henceforth be on their guard lest any of them should give vent to new doctrines from the pulpit. Should any of them have opinions in which they differed from other divines, and on which they boasted a profounder knowledge, it would be incumbent on them to reserve these to themselves, and to talk them over in a friendly manner with their compeers. Meanwhile, those who think differently, and who cannot be convinced of error, must be calmly forborne with until the points in dispute be decided by the authority of some council.[17]

Cant and Baerdesen then gave the ministers "a very grave and serious admonition" to cultivate fraternal harmony and peace. The ministers expressed their acknowledgments and withdrew.

There are a number of significant points here. Arminius and the

[16] Quoted in *LA*, pp. 81-82.
[17] *Ibid.*, pp. 84-85.

burgomasters stood together in affirming the right and duty of the magistracy to exercise oversight of the internal affairs of the church, at least to preserve its internal peace. The burgomasters accepted the principle of territorialism, at least insofar as they saw unanimity in the church as essential to the welfare of the state, and hence their concern. Plancius was implicitly rebuked, for only he had made "declamatory statements." Arminius was to exercise care in the utterance of "new doctrines," but he was not condemned.

It was affirmed that there might well be doctrinal matters that were not yet settled in the Reformed Church and which should be proper matters for discussion in a council. Thus the oligarchy stood firm (1) in its support of toleration, (2) in its support of its adopted son Arminius, and (3) in support of its own role as the guardian of the peace of the church.

There was apparently relative quiet for the rest of 1592. Arminius continued his pastoral duties. There is only another personal glimpse, the birth of a second son, again named Harmen, on about April 7. He was baptized in the Old Church on April 8, with Lijsbet's mother, Geertje Pietersdr., as witness.[18] Grief once more soon followed joy, for the baby died and was buried in the Old Church on April 19.[19]

Doctrinal controversy revived early in 1593. Arminius was now preaching on Romans 9. A layman, Pieter Dirksen, stayed away from the Lord's Supper because "Arminianism" was preached there (or so Plancius told the story in 1617) .[20] Burgomaster Claes Fransz. Oetgens joined in the complaints, and the matter came up again in the consistory. By now it was apparent that there were two parties in the city. One was a high Calvinist party with Plancius as its theological leader and Oetgens its political leader. The other was gathered around Jan Egbertsz. Bisschop, a prominent Amsterdam merchant, and looked to Arminius for its theological leadership. Jan's brother Rem Bisschop would later be a leading Remonstrant layman, and another brother became the Remonstrant theologian Simon Episcopius.

Finally the matter came formally once again to the consistory. On March 25, 1593, Hallius addressed Arminius sternly, mentioning complaints of the citizens about his sermons on Romans 9, and said that reports were again circulating that the ministers were in disagreement among themselves. Arminius replied that he, too, had heard rumors, but that he had always held himself to teachings consonant with the

[18] DTB, 2/132.
[19] *Ibid.*, 1042/84.
[20] *Prot*, IV/197.

Confession and Catechism. He would prefer to hear his accusers openly, and he felt that the admonition of Hallius was uncalled for. As for disagreements, it was as much the duty of the other ministers to agree with him as for him to agree with them. Other speeches followed, including an intemperate outburst of an elder who accused Arminius of being in conspiracy with some of the city officials to disturb the peace of the church. Arminius responded by calling for names of his accusers and the content of the charges, and by defending the city rulers. He defended his preaching on Romans 9, admitting that he used verse 18 in a manner different from its employment in the margin of the Confession, but in exercising this liberty he did nothing improper and no more than his brethren often did. Cuchlinus spoke, granting the point, but urging "agreement in all those points which constituted the hinge on which the articles of the Confession turned." The talk turned to the duties of elders and matters of ecclesiastical discipline. Arminius and Halsbergius were again accused of holding improper views, and they defended themselves at length. Hallius closed the meeting with a conciliatory statement directed at Arminius, hoping for a happy issue from the whole affair.[21]

Arminius' enemies would not let the matter rest, and a meeting of the consistory was held on April 22 without his knowledge. It was decided that Arminius should be called upon to "declare distinctly and without any circumlocution his opinion on all the articles of faith." [22] Arminius learned of this on May 6, and he decided that he should not reply at once but should petition for a reasonable time for preparation. At the meeting of the consistory on May 20, his enemies brought the matter up, and Arminius came up fighting. He called out in a loud voice, challenging anyone to stand forth and produce anything from any of his sermons which might call for censure. No one accepted the challenge, but one person made the objection "that from the testimony of Martinists [Lutherans], Anabaptists [Mennonites], and even libertines [humanists of the style of Coornhert] themselves, who gloried in his discourses on the ninth chapter of the Romans, it was not unwarrantable to infer that he had taught and maintained something different from that which was taught by his brother ministers and everywhere taught by Reformed divines." Arminius found it strange that no one present could cite an erroneous passage from his sermons. One of the elders replied that Arminius had been on his guard, and that he had used ambiguous expressions. Arminius denied the allegation and de-

---

[21] *Ibid.*, II/106 verso; *LA*, pp. 88-93; Los, p. 65.
[22] *Prot*, II/108; *LA*, p. 93.

manded proof, but no one would attempt to produce any evidence.[23]

Unrest was still apparent a week later, on May 27, and Arminius renewed his challenge. It is evident that Plancius had been the chief instigator of accusations, because when silence prevailed, Cuchlinus asked, "Where is Plancius now? Inasmuch as he had raised doubts about Arminius' preaching, he should now, in the presence of Arminius and of the consistory, speak his mind." Plancius was finally forced to bring his charges. They boiled down to three. First, Arminius, in preaching on Romans 9, had taught that "no one is condemned except on account of sin," which amounted to excluding infants from condemnation. In other words, the doctrine of predestination as Beza taught it was imperiled. Second, Arminius had taught that "too much could not be ascribed to good works, nor could they be sufficiently commended, provided no merit were attributed to them." Third, Arminius had taught that "angels are not immortal."

To the first accusation Arminius replied that Plancius was overlooking original sin. It was an answer well designed to discomfit Plancius, and at the same time it did not require Arminius to deal with the problem of predestination, an action which he still carefully avoided. As for the charge concerning good works, Arminius had nothing to recant; he would stand by the statement. As for angels, Arminius pointed out that he had never mentioned the matter in public but only in private, in Plancius' home in fact, and that his point was that God alone possesses immortality of himself and that the immortality of the angels is not by nature but by sustenance of God. He reiterated his assent to the Confession and Catechism, offering only one scruple—over the interpretation but not the words of the sixteenth article of the Belgic Confession. It is the article on "eternal election," which affirms that God delivers and preserves "all whom he, in his eternal and unchangeable council, of mere goodness hath elected in Jesus Christ our Lord." His scruple was this: Does the "all" refer to believers, or is it an arbitrary decree to *bestow faith?* He accepted the first interpretation and rejected the latter. The terms of the article, however, he accepted.

The consistory found Arminius' statement acceptable and declared the matter closed, urging fraternal fellowship until such a time as a general synod should determine the proper interpretation of the article. And, to a considerable degree, there was peace in the church. Arminius was recurrently the target of accusations, but never again did his preaching become a matter to be discussed in the consistory.[24]

[23] *Prot,* II/110; *LA,* pp. 94-95; Los, p. 52.
[24] These transactions of May 27, 1593, are not in the *Protocollen* of that date but are reported only in the later sources; cf. *LA,* pp. 95-98.

In the months and years to come he carried on his sustained expositions of Scripture, proceeding not only with Romans but also Malachi (which he found good for sixty-nine sermons), Mark, Jonah, Galatians, and Revelation 2 and 3. He finished Romans on September 30, 1601. The only notable incident produced by his sermons arose out of his exposition of the thirteenth chapter, when there were complaints that he granted too much power to the magistrates in matters of religion.[25]

Family affairs again came to the fore in 1593. In the month of May, just when the last round of controversy in the consistory was taking place and when a settlement was finally reached, Arminius and Lijsbet moved to their new quarters in the St. Ursula cloister. Lijsbet was expecting a child again, their third, and this time their joy was unmixed with sorrow. A daughter was born on June 14. At her baptism the next day in the New Church, she was named Engheltien (Engeltje, or Angelica). The witness was Trijn (Katrijn) Cornelisdr.[26] Engeltje (as she is listed in family records) may have been named for Arminius' mother Elborch, with a change to a post-Reformation name of a similar sound, as has been suggested. The usual custom was to name a first son after his paternal grandfather, the second son after his maternal grandfather, the first daughter after her maternal grandmother, the second daughter after her paternal grandmother. A dead parent or close friend could take precedence.[27] In this case, the paternal grandmother was martyred. It will be seen, however, that Jacobus and Lijsbet departed freely from the traditional pattern of naming children.

ARMINIUS' Amsterdam years brought about many more changes in his family. On December 24, 1594, a fourth child was born, a boy, and for the third time they named a son Harmen, after Arminius' father. He was baptized in the Old Church on Christmas Day, with Lijsbet's sister Magteld, wife of Hendrick van Marcken, as witness.[28] A fifth child, Pieter, was born on October 7, 1596, and was baptized in the Old Church on October 10. There were two witnesses, Geertje Jacobsdr., presumably the aunt of Arminius, and another sister of Lijsbet, Dieuwertje, who was married to Andries Prippelnagel. Why the name Pieter? Undoubtedly it came from Lijsbet's side, and her mother's. The name had been used for

[25] *LA*, pp. 99, 124-25.

[26] Dates of birth are from family records kept by Arminius' youngest son, Dr. Daniel Arminius, which were copied by another descendant, Hendrick Sorgh, and reported by van Dam van Hekendorp. Baptisms and burials in Amsterdam are found in DTB. For Engheltien, see DTB, 38/298.

[27] Cf. H. L. Kruimel, "Het Gebruik van Doopnamen in Vroegere Eeuwen."

[28] DTB, 3/45.

at least five generations behind the new baby. Lijsbet's mother's father was Pieter Meeusz. "in den Gouden Reael," and Lijsbet's oldest sibling had been a still-born infant named Pieter. Her next sibling was also named Pieter. There was ample precedent for the name.

Grief once again crowded in on joy, however, for Lijsbet's sister Magteld was buried just fifteen days later in the same church.[29] Two months later, Geertje married the former Amsterdam minister Johannes Cuchlinus in Leiden.

A sixth child did not arrive until August 25, 1598 (should one suspect an intervening miscarriage?). It was a boy. His baptism was delayed until September 1, and the reason becomes apparent from his name and sponsor. He was named Jan, and the witness was Johan (Jan) Uitenbogaert, Arminius' intimate friend from The Hague.[30] Arminius apparently sent for his friend to grace the happy occasion.

Lijsbet's father was evidently prospering and advancing in power and influence during these years. The Reael family had moved to a new location "op 't Water," the present-day Damrak, from number 53 to number 6. The house name moved with them, as was the custom, so that "in den Gouden Reael" was now located only six doors inland from the juncture of the river Amstel with the river IJ (the harbor). This house, three windows wide and five stories high (including the gable), was to be the last of the old buildings on the Damrak to be used as a residence, and the conversion to commercial purposes did not take place until 1936, when the first floor was made into a cafeteria, *De Bock.* Later it became a *brasserie,* or grill, and currently it is the Fiesta Cafe. Behind it is a wooden *pakhuis* or warehouse such as those used by sixteenth-century grain merchants. The house has been much restored but not destroyed; the ancient beams still appear in the ceiling of the cafe. The *pakhuis* is scarcely altered at all. Both the house and the *pakhuis* appear in the 1544 map of Cornelis Antonijsz., and it would appear that these are visible links with the Reael family.[31]

Many more changes were in store the next year, however, with sorrow marring all joy. On May 1, 1600, Reael was appointed a director of the Admiralty of Zeeland, which would mean leaving his beloved Amsterdam again. It would be, indeed, not an exile under duress this time, but an exile of honor and advancement. But a week later his wife, who had borne him thirteen children, was dead. She was buried in the choir of the New Church on May 9, probably in the family

[29] DTB, 1042/180.
[30] *Ibid.,* 38/667.
[31] Cf. D. Kouwenaar, "Het Laatste Heerenhuis op het Damrak Verdwijnt"; I. H. van Eeghen, "De Operatie en de Restauratie van Damrak 6."

plot (it was an expensive burial for the time, costing 8 guilders and 14 stuivers) .[32] This would indicate something of the financial status of the family.

The death of Lijsbet's mother came just as Lijsbet was about to give birth to a seventh child. Laurens (spelled variously Lourens or Louwerens in the church records), named for his bereaved maternal grandfather, was baptized on May 11 in the Old Church. The witness was Pieter Carpentier.[33] Carpentier's wife was from the financially important family of Louis de la Beque, which indicates that Arminius continued to move among the wealthy families of Amsterdam.[34]

Laurens did not live beyond infancy. He was buried in the Old Church on December 27, 1600. When Arminius and Lijsbet buried their first two children, there was no charge for the burial. This time they paid an amount of 1 guilder and 9 stuivers. This could indicate increased financial ability on the part of Arminius.[35]

A few months later death struck again. Laurens Jacobsz. Reael, patriarch of Amsterdam Protestantism and progenitor of one of the two great Reael families of seventeenth-century Holland, died in Middelburg on April 7, 1601. On the following September 20, Lijsbet gave birth to another son, and the name of her father, Laurens, was used again. Laurens was baptized in the New Church on the 23rd, the witness being Willem Bardesius, the son of the recently deceased burgomaster Wilhem Baerdesen.[36] Bardesius, who participated in the revived practice of taking noble titles, was the Lord of Warmenhuizen and Krabbendam and remained a lifelong friend of Arminius. During the illness at the end of his life, Arminius attempted to regain his health by staying for a time at Warmenhuizen, north of Amsterdam.

Jacobus and Lijsbet now had five living children, Engeltje, Harmen, Pieter, Jan, and Laurens. There would be more, but not before they moved to Leiden.

[32] DTB, 1052/161.
[33] Ibid., 3/232.
[34] Carpentier is mentioned in ibid., 409/425, 411/382; cf. van Dillen, *Het Oudste Aandeelhoudersregister van de Kamer Amsterdam der Oost-Indische Compagnie*, pp. 114, 148.
[35] DTB, 1042/260.
[36] Ibid., 38/900.

11

PASTORAL LABORS

AFTER the disputes of the early years of his ministry in Amsterdam, Arminius seems to have settled into the normal but varied routine of pastoral work. He continued in favor with the burgomasters, and he had no more sharp clashes with the clergy. In 1594, when the burgomasters wanted to institute reforms in the Latin schools of the city, Arminius was chosen to draw up a new set of school laws. These were adopted and remained in force well into the seventeenth century; during this entire period they were rehearsed twice yearly by the rectors in a ceremony held in the choir of the New Church. The autograph of the laws was in the possession of the Remonstrant professor Philip van Limborch a century later, but its present existence is unknown.[1]

The name of Arminius appears often in the minutes of the consistory, usually in connection with rather routine matters of church business or pastoral care. With the growth of the city, the pastors found themselves in need of assistants to visit the sick. Thus Arminius reports, on July 13, 1595, that a Frederick Jansz. has been examined to be a *ziekentrooster*, or sick-visitor, by two ministers and two elders, upon which the burgomasters are to be requested to appoint him to the office (and pay his salary).[2]

The bidding of the consistory was usually carried out by a team of one minister and one elder; thus on July 20 Arminius and an elder, Philips Cornelisz., are to warn the marriage commissioners to abide by the regulations, which are being broken daily. There were many regulations surrounding weddings, including laws respecting affinity and consanguinity and the prohibition of ostentatious displays of jewelry and finery, and the consistory was trying to hold the commissioners to stricter enforcement.[3] A week later the consistory decided that a church member named Lieven van Vijnen, who "persisted in a wrong opinion," should

[1] *LA*, pp. 99-100.
[2] *Prot*, II, 175.
[3] *Ibid.*, II, 175 verso.

be warned to change his mind or be excommunicated and dropped from the roll of members. It was evidently a serious affair, for two ministers and two elders were deputed to remonstrate with him. The ministers were Arminius and Plancius. The "wrong opinion" turned out to be his idea that he could get away with sleeping with a woman not his wife, which he tried to defend in the consistory itself on August 24. The consistory was not convinced.[4]

On September 21 Arminius and the elder Walich Sivertsz. were sent to try to reconcile two estranged parishioners—a case which did not yield to quick treatment, for it came up again in October and even in the following April.[5] One of the disputants was the *koster* of the New Church, and his admission to Communion was at stake. Sometimes there were differences between church members and the consistory. On February 29, 1596, Arminius was assigned to deal with such a woman, who wanted from the church a testimonial to be used as a transfer letter. He was to warn and instruct her in the matter. Arminius reported in May that she had left town, and had been reunited with her husband, and again wanted a testimonial. Arminius was instructed to make further investigation before the request was granted.[6] On another occasion Arminius reported that he had had a talk with two Anabaptists, Paulus, a carpenter, and his wife. They persisted in their point of view, he said, and the consistory sent Pieter Dircksz., an elder, and Simon Middelgeest, a sick-visitor, to deal further with them.[7]

Conflict could arise between the clergy themselves and their parishioners. On August 1, 1596, Arminius reported that he himself had been involved in a public fight with a textile worker, Claes Jansz., and the consistory ordered that Claes appear before them personally. This he did on August 15, and it was reported that Claes had been punished for fighting in public (he had probably been drunk), and that he had promised to mend his ways if the consistory would forgive him.[8] The record does not indicate who was the better fighter. It need not be assumed that it was Claes Jansz., for one of the tales circulated about Arminius in the seventeenth century had to do with his courage and physical prowess. He was walking on the dike by the Haarlemerpoort, so the story goes, when shouts of the people made him aware that an escaped prisoner was fleeing near him. Arminius sprang after the man, tackled him, and held him until he could be returned to prison. The story is of uncertain origin. It might be true.

[4] *Ibid.*, II, 176, 178 verso.
[5] *Ibid.*, II, 179 verso, 183, 192.
[6] *Ibid.*, II, 187 verso, 194.
[7] *Ibid.*, II, 194.
[8] *Ibid.*, II, 201, 202.

Whatever differences Arminius and Plancius may have had, they did not necessarily disagree about everything, and they often worked together. On the question of dancing they apparently agreed: they were against it. The courageous Baptista Oyens, who had dared to say that dancing was only a "very small sin," was the object of their joint pastoral care on at least two occasions in 1602. The visits were unsatisfactory, at least to the ministers.[9]

Arminius bore many official responsibilities in the circles of the ministers. He was chosen as *scriba,* or secretary, of the classis as early as April 17, 1589, and he served the classis several times as *quaestor,* or treasurer.[10] He was a delegate of Amsterdam to the Synod of North Holland, first on June 25, 1590, and a number of times thereafter.[11] Mention has been made of his service on the commission to revise the church order of the Dutch Reformed Church in 1591. He was elected secretary of the Synod of North Holland on June 17, 1597, and on June 5, 1600, he served as its president.[12]

In addition to filling these ordinary offices, he was often assigned extraordinary tasks. In 1600 and 1601 he served as representative of both synods, North and South Holland, in some negotiations with the Synod of Gelderland.[13] He was sent by the Synod of North Holland to Hoorn in 1600 to conduct negotiations with Clement Martensz.[14] In 1595 Arminius and an elder, Stoffel Jansz., were assigned tasks related to the call of an additional pastor for Amsterdam. The man desired by the consistory was Jacobus Baselius, then a minister at Bergen-op-Zoom. On September 21 they were deputized to go to Bergen-op-Zoom with "letters of calling." [15] On October 5 they reported that Baselius was willing but that the burgomasters and consistory in Bergen-op-Zoom would not release him. On October 12 the consistory asked Arminius and Stoffel Jansz. to approach the Amsterdam burgomasters to request them to ask the Bergen-op-Zoom authorities to release Baselius.[16] On October 19 they reported that the burgomasters had agreed to write, and on November 16 a letter from Baselius was read, indicating that he had been released. In spite of all this, the call of Baselius was never consummated. In later years he appears as a friend of Arminius; per-

[9] *Ibid.,* III, 82, 83 verso.
[10] Vos, pp. 37, 72.
[11] *APPS,* I, 154.
[12] *Ibid.,* pp. 230, 287.
[13] *Ibid.,* I, 282; IV, 82; I, 289.
[14] *Ibid.,* I, 285.
[15] *Prot,* II, 179 verso.
[16] *Ibid.,* II, 180 verso.

haps it was through these negotiations that their friendship developed.[17] Baselius was a mild Calvinist, although not necessarily in agreement with Arminius at all points. He did not become a Remonstrant. That he did not finally move to Amsterdam does not seem to be tied to doctrinal questions.

On several occasions the advice or help of Arminius was sought by those outside his own locus of responsibility. Utrecht, which had been having internal strife over a variety of issues—doctrine, worship, church order—too complex to relate here, turned to Amsterdam for help. To Amsterdam, yes, but more specifically to Arminius; he was the one they sought as a pastor "on loan," for they believed that he could help them bring some "wandering sheep" back to the fold. The form of the inquiry seemed strange to Amsterdam, however, for it came not from the classis or consistory but was conveyed to Amsterdam in person by some *schepenen*, civil and not religious authorities. Amsterdam wanted to know on what kind of church order such a procedure was based. Utrecht then sent its newly elected elders on the same mission, but now Amsterdam refused to cooperate with Utrecht so long as it had its own church order, which was contrary to that of the other Dutch Reformed churches. Finally, Utrecht sent both its elders and its judges, reporting that peace had been restored in Utrecht but that they needed an outsider, a minister who could come in complete neutrality, to bring the factions in the church together. The request was endorsed by South Holland and by Prince Maurice, and Amsterdam at last consented to lend them a man. But then they sent Ambrosius, not Arminius.[18]

On another occasion it was from within Amsterdam itself that the request came for help from Arminius—from the Walloon congregation not far from Arminius' home. The minutes of the consistory for October 12, 1595, report that Arminius had been asked for advice concerning a member of the Walloon church, of which Taffin was the pastor. Taffin's parishioner had gone over to the English church at Naarden. It was a new kind of problem. Was it a breach of discipline to attend the English church? Was the English church of sound doctrine? It was a contingent of Independents, followers of Robert Browne. Browne and some of his followers had lived in Middelburg in the 1580s, and not long after, they began to appear in Amsterdam. Their rejection of English episcopacy did not lead them to accept the polity of the Reformed churches in Holland. The Reformed never met as an entire congregation; they did not properly observe the Lord's Day; they baptized children of parents

[17] There are references to Baselius in three letters of Arminius to Uitenbogaert in 1599; *Ep. Ecc.*, nos. 48, 49, and 50.
[18] *Prot*, II, 87, 90 verso, 110 verso; reported in *ODWA*, I, 186.

156

not in the visible church; they did not follow the command of Christ in Matthew 18:15-17; they worshiped in the ungodly church buildings of the Antichrist; their ministers were not supported according to I Corinthians 9:14; their consistory was not entirely replaced each year; they performed marriages in the church building; they celebrated Christmas, and Easter, and Ascension. All these criticisms of the church of their hosts, and other criticisms too, the Brownists, as they were known, pushed vigorously. The Dutch did not take it kindly. In the case of the man who had gone over in Naarden, the consistory appointed Arminius, Plancius, and an elder, Arent Boudewijns, to discuss the problem and decide what action to take.[19]

It was not the first time that Arminius had dealt with the Brownists, and this brings up a curious side of his pastoral career. He was often involved with "heretics," sometimes by appointment of ecclesiastical authorities, and often he pushed his assignments with vigor. It was Arminius who had reported in the consistory on July 15, 1593, that an English preacher had preached in the house of one Israel Johnson and would preach there again on the following Sunday. The consistory thought it "an important matter which could not be permitted to continue in silence," and they sent Arminius to speak to Johnson and to report to him that the consistory had ordered that there be no more such meetings.[20] The consistory reported the affair to England, both to the Anglicans and to the Presbyterians, and they sent a deputation to the burgomasters. And when they learned that the Brownists had appeared in Kampen, where they were friendly with the burgomasters, they sent Arminius to warn the consistory there.[21]

There were further difficulties in the Walloon church in 1596. On June 6 Arminius reported to the consistory that Taffin had learned that there would be Brownist preaching in the house of Jean de l'Escluse, a member of the Walloon congregation and a schoolmaster. Arminius and again Boudewijns were sent to tell de L'Escluse that he must not permit the preaching to take place and that the burgomasters would be informed of the matter.[22]

On another occasion Arminius and Taffin met with the Independent leader, Henry Ainsworth, in an attempt to effect an agreement with him. Ainsworth was the young Brownist who had been preaching in the house of Israel Johnson in 1593. A graduate of Cambridge University, he had found it necessary to support himself in Amsterdam by

[19] *Prot*, II, 181.
[20] *Ibid.*, II, 114 verso.
[21] *Ibid.*, II, 119; cf. *ODWA*, II, 224-25.
[22] *Ibid.*, II, 197.

serving as a hired hand in a bookseller's shop. It was discovered that he had great proficiency in Hebrew (the greatest in Europe, claimed his admirers) and ability as a leader. Among his many translations and writings was a metrical version of some of the psalms, which was adopted at once by the Separatists in Leiden, later known as the Pilgrim Fathers. His gifts in Hebrew were not matched by his gifts in poetry; the translation has happily fallen into disuse. When many Separatists in Amsterdam were going over to the Mennonites, or to Baptist views, Ainsworth remained firm in his Reformed beliefs. But he remained firm also in those beliefs, mentioned earlier, which contradicted the polity and practice of the Dutch Reformed churches.

The Brownists were not reticent about pushing their views on the Dutch churches. They had sent a pamphlet containing their views "to all those who profess Sacred Literature in all Christian Universities," a copy of which came to a Leiden theology professor, Franciscus Junius. Junius replied on January 9, 1599, upbraiding them for their attack on "a church which is well furnished with servants of God, whose piety, erudition, and fraternal regard to the members of Christ, are fully known to good men." [23] Two months later, on March 3, Arminius and Taffin, in the name of all the Amsterdam ministers, jumped into the fray on the side of Junius. They directed a letter to him in support of his attack on the Brownists and added some points of their own. At the same time, however, they avoided a total condemnation, and they denied that the Amsterdam clergy had ever denounced the Brownists as schismatics and heretics, as the Brownists had charged.

Of this fact we declare ourselves to be entirely ignorant. We certainly endured, with such a degree of sorrow as was not improper in us, this secession of theirs from our Churches; and we signified the same in their presence, with a fraternal declaration of our sincere regret. But we did not censure their defection with any such ignominious epithets, because we were prohibited solely by our brotherly feeling towards them, and our christian sympathy. Had not these prevented us, more than one occasion would have occurred both of mourning over them, and of making a declaration of a more serious nature against them.[24]

By 1602 it became apparent that no accommodation of the Brownists and the Dutch and Walloon churches could be reached. The Classis of Walcheren had requested information about the matter, and Arminius and Plancius (who also had been active in the affair) gathered their materials together and sent them there.[25]

[23] Quoted in *WA*, I, 151.
[24] Quoted *ibid.*, p. 163; cf. *Ep. Ecc.*, no. 39.
[25] *ODWA*, II, 228.

It is noteworthy that in this controversy with the Brownists, Arminius worked in full sympathy with the moderate Calvinists Taffin and Junius and with the extreme Calvinist Plancius. Indeed, he does not in the decade from 1593 to 1603 seem to be in conflict at all with his colleagues. The Brownist affair was difficult to categorize, however. The Dutch churches were willing to grant that the Brownists were true Reformed Christians, and they did not find fault with Brownist views on the doctrines of salvation. What offended the Dutch was the Brownists' uncompromising and total rejection of the polity and practice of the Dutch churches. Arminius was foremost among the defenders of the Dutch position.

It was not long, however, until the Brownists attacked Arminius and his followers for their alleged defection from true Reformed doctrine respecting salvation. The Pilgrim Fathers who settled in Leiden in 1609 were able to accommodate themselves to the Dutch polity and were known to take Communion in the Dutch church, but on the doctrine of grace they became bitter foes of the Remonstrants. It is supposed by some historians that Brownist antagonism to the soteriology of Arminius stemmed in part from his opposition to them on matters of polity. It is a curious turn of affairs. The Brownists fled England, where they were not tolerated, for Holland, where toleration was extended them. They then attacked their Dutch hosts for having established no true church. When the Dutch Church itself became divided over the question of toleration, the Brownists sided against the Remonstrant supporters of toleration. Arminianism was not tolerated by the Pilgrims who went to Massachusetts for the sake of religious toleration.

During these same years there was another affair in which Arminius played a role in the pursuit of a heretic. The issues were confused, and Arminius was evidently caught between his disagreement with the man in question, on the one hand, and his opposition to persecution, on the other. It became a point of controversy within both the consistory and the city government, and it elicited a speech from the burgomaster Cornelis Pietersz. Hooft which was to lay bare the issues which divided the two emerging factions in Amsterdam.

The center of controversy was Goosen Michielsz. Vogelsangh, a textile worker from Buren. He had gone over to Calvinism at Wesel in the late 1570s and had held to it during a year in Antwerp and a fortnight in Geneva. At Frankfurt, where he had gone next, he married, and this required his joining the Reformed church there. In 1591 he moved back to Wesel for a time, and then to Amsterdam, and then to London, where he brought his church letter to the Walloon congregation. The Walloons required transfer members to make a new confession of faith;

159

Vogelsangh resented this and applied to the Dutch congregation at Austin Friars, where he was received. It was there that he began to express some change in views. The ministers attempted to persuade him to stay with his earlier Reformed orthodoxy, pressing him for an answer. He could not accommodate himself to them, and after nine months he returned to Amsterdam, probably late in 1591.[26]

From a recantation which he made later, in 1598, we know what his new views were. "I maintained," he says in retrospect, "that God is bodily like a man. . . . I held that Adam was God's image because he was a man and that his wife Eve was not made in God's image. . . I asserted that the Son of God is not eternal. . . . I also held that infant baptism is wrong." [27] From the first proposition he had gone on to teach that God consists of body, soul, and spirit and cannot be omnipresent, and from the third he had proceeded to deny the doctrine of the Trinity.

Vogelsangh was not a formally educated man but a maker of velvet, plush, and gold and silver lace. He became so interested in theology, however, that he taught himself Latin, having achieved the sixth class after two years of study in Utrecht. Someone had taught him Greek for four years, and someone else Hebrew for over a half year. He then approached the Bible in the original languages and with a literalist bent, which led him next to find fault with theological doctrines not literally taught in the Scriptures, such as the Trinity, and with the current Dutch translation of the Bible. In Amsterdam he freely advertised his views, causing no small stir in the city. It was when he put his views in writing in a small book, *Het Licht der Waerheid (The Light of Truth)*, that he came to the formal attention of the consistory.

Plancius remonstrated with him to no avail in 1591, and Arminius joined in the attempt to convince Vogelsangh of his errors.[28] Arminius evidently visited him repeatedly. He reported to the consistory that he had warned Vogelsangh not to spread his "detestable errors" lest the church take action against him.[29] Arminius was instructed to see him again, but had to report back that in spite of his "plain texts and good arguments" the man was not to be convinced. Arminius found his words "fulsome and variable," so he asked him to put his ideas on paper. Vogelsangh did so. Arminius found the written sentiments no less acceptable; in fact, they contained such errors, he said, as had never before been seen in Amsterdam. Cuchlinus took his turn, but with no more success than Plancius and Arminius. A couple of years later the

[26] *HRN*, I, 824-25.
[27] *Ibid.*, pp. 834-35.
[28] *Prot*, II, 65; Vos. p. 113.
[29] *Prot*, II, 84 verso; *ODWA*, I, 170, and II, 248-50.

consistory issued a public warning against the views of Vogelsangh, threatening him with excommunication.[30]

Vogelsangh persisted in disseminating his views. On April 13, 1595, Arminius and an elder, Cornelis Jansz. Boecaert, were instructed to warn Vogelsangh personally that excommunication was imminent.[31] The consistory, noting that he did not heed repeated warnings and finding him guilty of "Anthropomorphism, Sabellianism, Arianism, and Samosatenism," finally excommunicated him. This still did not silence him, and the consistory attempted to go even further; they wanted the city government to act. They presented a petition to the burgomasters. There was no response. They prepared a second petition, linking the Vogelsangh case to other problems, and presented it in May, 1597. There were four complaints: Vogelsangh; Lubbert Gerritsz., an Anabaptist who was attracting great crowds to his conventicle; the publication and dissemination in Amsterdam of some attacks on Reformed doctrine; and the practices of conjuring and witchcraft.

The disposition of the latter two complaints is not known. The burgomasters refused to act against Lubbert Gerritsz. The Vogelsangh case remained at the center of attention. The consistory stated its case and then proposed action. "We, therefore, humbly offer it for your consideration whether it would not be advisable that this erring spirit should be cited by your Honors to appear before you in the presence of our representatives or else before our consistory, in the presence of your Honors, and in case he cannot support his gross errors with the Word of God, as we hold that he cannot, he should be hindered from spreading them further according to your Honors' wisdom and discretion." [32]

Vogelsangh was taken into custody. His wife, who was pregnant, was left without means for the care of her five children. The authorities in church and city were divided in their sympathies. There is no direct evidence to show that Arminius approved of this treatment of the man. The indirect evidence of his later statements and of his general sympathies points the other way. What is clear is that one of Arminius' supporters in the government, Burgomaster Hooft, was so enraged by the zeal of the Calvinist clergy against heretics that he made a public statement of protest on October 15, 1597, in the presence of the other burgomasters, who were Wilhem Baerdesen, Cornelis Florisz. van Teylingen, and Pieter Cornelisz. Boom. This statement sheds important light on the developing polarity in Amsterdam, a polarity which pervaded the field in which theological controversies would develop.

[30] *Prot*, II, 127.
[31] *Ibid.*, II, 164 verso.
[32] *HRN*, I, 814-15.

Hooft opened by reminding his hearers that the war against Spain had been fought to gain, in the words of Livy, "a shelter for liberty, but not an unbounded power of invading others." Even Roman Catholics, he went on, had opened the gates to the patriot forces "in a firm persuasion that every man's conscience would be free." Although a government might conceivably have power over a man's conscience, that power should never be exercised in these provinces, which had suffered so much persecution at the hands of the Papists. The land had even then been filled with many different sects, and it would be unreasonable to suppose that in twenty or twenty-five years all these could be persuaded to unite in one church. Therefore, those who repair to the Lord's Supper should not be so strictly examined on so many points, and those who come over to the Reformed Church should not be required to attend the Saturday night confessional sermons before Communion. Some converts, being simple and ignorant, will be confused by the doctrinal intricacies promoted there, and others, more instructed, will be offended by what is taught about predestination and forced either to express dissent, with resultant penalties, or to remain silent, with resultant bad conscience. Furthermore, while in the city government it is wisely ordered that none but natives may hold office, the church has allowed itself to be dominated in the consistory by outsiders who do not understand the nature of Holland, where the virtues of prudence, steadiness, and peace abound more than elsewhere. These imported elders bring with them the quarrels of other places, which is an ungrateful response to the kindness shown them when they came as refugees. And when things do not go well for them, they flee again, or stir up turbulence, as in the time of Leicester. "You are not ignorant, Gentlemen," said Hooft, "that most of the disturbances which have arisen, and do still arise, in any part of the United Netherlands, originate with the admission of foreigners to the government."

The magistrates, he continued, have treated these foreign ministers well. When it comes to poor relief, however, the ministers have made it so that the poor among the ancient burghers get only seasonal relief, while the church poor, consisting mostly of newly arrived Calvinist refugees, are supported the year round, and this with money provided in part by the magistrates. Then the ministers turn around and use the pulpit to level attacks on the *schout*, the burgomasters, the judges, or any of the Thirty-six, not scrupling to indicate which individual is under attack. It would be a shame for Amsterdam to become divided (the possibility was evidently apparent) by the divisive tactics of the foreigners.

It it inconsistent to complain of intolerance under a Popish government and then practice the same intolerance. These foreign ecclesiastics do not understand "the temper of our Hollanders, for we are wont, with the Bereans, to search the Scripture ourselves." A personal note intervenes:

Some, perhaps, will oppose my arguments or reject them altogether because my wife attends the preaching of the Mennonites. But what should one do? At my request she has attended church, but she declares that she is not so well edified there as by the Mennonites. This is a situation I hold in common with many others, men of substance, and it is no occasion for reproach or punishment.

While those of the Reformed faith should indeed be given preference in the city government, it would be dangerous to make this policy unalterable. To do so would be to invite hypocrisy and opportunism, even by unscrupulous Catholics. It was the intention of the Ecclesiastical Ordinances that no Protestant, "in the broadest sense of that term," should be excluded, and it should not be supposed that a single town like Geneva should have a polity which can be adequate or requisite for all other countries.

Again he refers to the struggle for independence. Hollanders, especially those of Amsterdam, should remember that under Spanish oppression all Protestant religious groups suffered exile and persecution equally. It is unbecoming of the ministers and elders, imperfect men like all of us, to set the populace against the magistrates. They should not penetrate too deeply and rashly into the office of civil magistrate, as in the case of witchcraft. Hooft referred to a case where the clergy were ultimately embarrassed by the rashness of their own judgments.[33]

It is a remarkable speech. Hooft sees the original religious purpose of the Alteration to be the establishment of a comprehensive church, broadly Protestant. He resents the influx of refugees, who subvert the church with a coalition of ministers and workers who together dominate the consistory and enforce an intolerant Calvinism on the city. The coalition is strengthened by the ministers' control of poor relief. The result is injustice to old Amsterdam families and the loss of that very toleration for which they had fought. The one doctrinal point that is mentioned is predestination. It is not the only issue, and probably not the central issue, for there are also the questions of clerical domination of the church and religious persecution by civil authority.

For whom was the speech intended? For the burgomasters, to be sure, but among them there would be little disagreement. A wider audience was intended, as is apparent from the fact that Hooft read his speech

---

[33] For the complete text, with slight abridgment, cf. *ibid.*, pp. 817-24.

again on December 20, 1597, to an assembly made up of the judges, burgomaster Boom, and pensionary Ellert de Veer. But who among these would disagree with it? Were there those in the city government who were siding with the "foreign" clergy? The wording of the speech would indicate that there were such persons, that division had crept into the civil government. These divisions will be seen more clearly when attention is given later to the economic developments of the decade. Perhaps they were primarily in the council. Somewhere in the government there had been enough hostility and power to get Vogelsangh taken into custody.

The rest of the Vogelsangh episode is less significant, and nothing of Arminius' role in it is known. On January 7, 1598, Vogelsangh was examined twice by the *schout* and some of the judges (from which testimony is gained the knowledge of his earlier life and thinking). Hooft resisted an attempt to get him sent to The Hague, and on January 26 he made a long speech on the matter to the *schout,* the other burgomasters, the *schepenen,* and the two pensionaries. The church ought to be content, he said, with having excommunicated Vogelsangh. He is now out of her power, and she has nothing more to do with him. He was obviously not a wicked, irreligious man, because someone had called upon his wife and family and found them on their knees at prayer before dinner, sure evidence of the basic piety of the missing husband and father. The clergy are introducing a new intolerance. Vogelsangh's only error is that he is a literalist; but if literalists, on the one hand, and spiritualists, on the other, are to be persecuted, who is to draw the line of that precise center point which alone is to be tolerated? And how can persecution be justified from the New Testament? Furthermore, those who persecute the critics of Calvinistic predestination theory are caught in the contradiction of condemning a man for what he cannot help doing!

Hooft continues. What if Vogelsangh does add insult to injury by propagating his own doctrines? "The same thing is done by all other sects with equal zeal." And if he should be sent off to The Hague, he could not expect neutral justice, for outside Amsterdam, even in Holland, there is no small jealousy of Amsterdam's prosperity. The civil prosecution of heretics leads inexorably to the same kind of persecution so recently practiced by the Papists, for at what point can the process be halted when an alleged heretic persists in his error? The only end is execution. It would be far better to return to the ancient tradition of these provinces, and especially of Amsterdam, and "disturb no man on account of his conscience, but bear with each other's religious mistakes," thereby remaining at peace among ourselves and in unity against our common enemies.[34]

Hooft's second speech convinced many, but it still did not prevent civil action against Vogelsangh. On January 29, 1598, he was banished from the city. Soon he was taken in custody again, this time in Haarlem. The end of the story is anticlimactic: On October 25 and 30 he submitted written recantations to the bailiff, and on November 14 he was permitted to return to Amsterdam. His troubles were at an end. The division in the city which the affair had brought into focus was to continue and increase, however. When Arminius' later statements on toleration and persecution are read, it must be remembered that he had been close to these developments in Amsterdam.

Vogelsangh had found fault with the doctrine of the Trinity, but he was not a Socinian. Two Socinians did appear in Amsterdam—Christophorus Ostorod, a German, and Andreas Voidovius, a Pole. They arrived by sea early in August, 1598, and hired a room at an inn on the river IJ. They had a chest of Socinian books with them. They had been in their room no more than half an hour when the *schout* and his bailiffs appeared, took the books in custody, and announced that the burgomasters would be expecting to see the two men the next day. There they were dispatched, with their books, to The Hague, where the States referred the problem to the Leiden theological faculty. The faculty judged the books to contain Turkish doctrine, and it was ordered that the Socinians leave the country and that their books be burned.[35]

It is noteworthy that not even the "Libertine" burgomaster C. P. Hooft came to the defense of Socinians. Perhaps the possibility of "Turkish doctrine" placed Socinianism beyond the bounds of the tolerable.

It is Triglandius who links Arminius to the affair, specifically to Voidovius. Citing again the unsavory report that Plancius inserted into the minutes of the consistory in 1617, he claims that Arminius had been on familiar terms with Voidovius when the latter had passed through Amsterdam some months earlier while taking some Polish students to study at Leiden. Arminius, reports Triglandius, had said that "the two men, Ostorod and Voidovius, were so outstandingly experienced in the Word of God that he had never seen the like, that they had such forceful arguments for their position that neither Calvin, nor

---

[34] For the complete text, cf. *ibid.*, pp. 825-33.

[35] A comprehensive account of the matter is found in J. C. van Slee, *De Geschiedenis van het Socinianisme in de Nederlanden*, pp. 44-65; cf. C. Sepp, *Het Staatstoezicht op de Godsdienstige Letterkunde in de Noordelijke Nederlanden*, pp. 37-39.

Beza, nor [Peter] Martyr, nor Zanchius, nor Ursinus, nor any of our theologians could refute them, and that they had clearly proved that if the Lord Christ is of one substance with the Father and the Holy Spirit, it must necessarily follow that the Father and the Holy Spirit became man, even as the son of God." [36]

I find no genuine documentation for such a statement, nor is there any hint of such sentiments in all of Arminius' writings. I must concur with the judgment of Evenhuis and van Slee[37] that this report is not to be believed.

Arminius was more often at one with his colleagues in resisting trouble-makers and unorthodox spirits. A case in point is Robbert Robbertsz., who had been born in a Mennonite family in Amersfoort in 1563. In the 1590s he appeared in Amsterdam, where he engaged in a curious mixture of navigational science and theological speculation. At both points he ran afoul of Petrus Plancius. He claimed the gift of prophecy as warrant for some fantastic theories about numerals in the book of Exodus. He developed some strange (and ecumenical) ideas about the church; namely, that all churches were but different doors to the kingdom of God. He had his own children baptized in different churches, including the Roman Catholic. He published an attack on the Mennonites for their banning and shunning, which pleased the Reformed, but then he turned his talents to the Reformed. The Roman Catholic Church, he said, was *het Wees-huys* (the orphanage), the Lutheran Church was *het oude Mannen-huys* (the old men's home), and the Reformed Church was *het Pest-huys* (the plague house). Thereupon he was forced to leave Amsterdam.[38] He had complained earlier that Arminius had said to him that the authorities ought to expel him from the city.[39] When challenged about this, he was unable to prove that Arminius had made the statement.

The allegation was not unreasonable. Arminius was not indifferent to what seemed to him to be error, and he was not averse to exercising discipline in the church and community. In 1593 he had reported to the consistory that he had found a blasphemous book by one Franchoos de Stries, upon which the consistory charged him with responsibility for seeing that all the copies were destroyed.[40] A curious footnote to the affair is that the author was reimbursed for the burned copies.

Arminius did not pursue all so-called heretics, as is seen from his actions respecting the Anabaptists (their modern successors in Holland

---

[36] Triglandius, p. 285.
[37] *ODWA*, II, 250; van Slee, pp. 59-60.
[38] Cf. *ODWA*, II, 238-41.
[39] *Prot*, III, 34 verso.
[40] *Ibid.*, II, 125 verso, cited in *ODWA*, II, 142.

often prefer to be called Mennonites, but I follow the language of
the consistories and synods of the time, which used the term *Wederdoper,*
or Anabaptist). They were having considerable success in drawing off
members of the Reformed churches, and action against them was deemed
necessary. The minutes of the consistory show that Arminius remonstrated with individual Anabaptists in their homes, urging them to return
to the Reformed Church. At the end of the decade, however, a new task
was put to him.

The story begins in the Synod of North Holland, meeting June 21-26,
1599. Arminius was not present because Plancius was the Amsterdam
ministerial deputy that year. It was resolved that arguments against
the Anabaptists should be gathered and published for the instruction
of "the weak." It was further resolved to communicate this plan to the
Synod of South Holland in order that the two synods could collaborate
on the project.[41] In their meeting of August 31 to September 7, 1599, the
South Holland synod concurred, requesting that Arminius be assigned
the task and that his work be overseen by deputies from both synods.[42]
The North Holland synod accepted the suggestion at its next meeting,
June 5-9 1600.[43] Arminius was, incidentally, the presiding officer of that
meeting.

At its meeting of August 15-23, following, the South Holland synod
took note of the fact that Arminius was to write "a short refutation of
all the errors of the Anabaptists" and asked that he share any such
tracts with them.[44] The next year, however, when the northern synod
met in June, no such tract was forthcoming. Arminius did have a progress
report: he had studied all the Anabaptist books he could find and had ab-
stracted the most important doctrinal positions, and he requested the
brethren to share with him any more such books which he might not
have seen.[45] The following August the southern synod took note of the
request.[46]

In the meeting of June 4-12, 1602, of the North Holland synod,
Arminius reported that he had begun the work but had not completed
it, the difficulty being that the Anabaptists had a great many articles
of faith in which many different things were taught (one is reminded of
Luther's answer at Worms). The synod resolved "that he should carry
out the project in the quickest possible manner." [47] In August the South

[41] *APPS,* I, 274.
[42] *Ibid.,* III, 136.
[43] *Ibid.,* I, 280.
[44] *Ibid.,* III, 146.
[45] *Ibid.,* I, 289-90.
[46] *Ibid.,* III, 164.
[47] *Ibid.,* I, 313.

Holland synod requested that he get at least the first part of his writing into print so that their members could know what to expect from the rest.[48]

The synods of 1603 learned that little progress had been made, that in fact Arminius had not done very much at all on the assignment. He promised the North Holland synod that he would get right at it, but he was about to move to Leiden, and he requested that the assignment be carried on by others from Amsterdam. The deputies pressed him to complete the task.[49] In the South Holland synod it was noted that he had promised to pursue the task as soon as he should be settled in his new location.[50]

In 1604 the work was still not done. It was reported to the North Holland synod in June that Arminius had told Werner Helmichius and Adrian Borrius (van der Borren) that the reason he had not finished the assignment was that his time was taken up in preparing for his students the refutation of false papal teaching. The brethren decided, however, that deputies of the synod should speak with him again and call him back to the task which he had begun, in order that this work might be put in print at the first opportunity. And if he should offer the same excuse again, the other professors of theology should be contacted to do the task as something to be expected of men in their office.[51] Later in the same synod there was a report about some new and troublesome Anabaptist books. It was ordered that Arminius be notified and that the books be sent to him.[52] The South Holland synod soon after joined in urging that Arminius complete the refutation of the Anabaptists, "thereby performing a good service greatly desired by the churches of both North and South Holland." [53]

The affair was still dragging on in 1605. In the meeting of the North Holland synod in June it was reported that Arminius wanted to be relieved of the task for two reasons. First, his duties as professor were heavy, and, second, he was now under attack for holding unsound doctrine and he wanted first to clear himself. The brethren rejected both excuses and demanded that he get at the task "with assiduity." [54] The South Holland synod that year heard a report that Arminius had agreed to pursue the task vigorously.[55]

[48] *Ibid.*, III, 188.
[49] *Ibid.*, I, 327.
[50] *Ibid.*, III, 202.
[51] *Ibid.*, I, 346-47.
[52] *Ibid.*, p. 364.
[53] *Ibid.*, III, 214.
[54] *Ibid.*, I, 368.
[55] *Ibid.*, III, 231.

It wasn't until 1606 that the synods began to give in. The North Holland synod noted that Arminius was not going to complete the task, for the reasons he had given a year earlier, and it decided to refer the matter of a refutation of the Anabaptists to the supposedly imminent national synod.[56] In 1607 the matter did not come up, and in 1608 the action of 1606 was confirmed.[57] These actions were noted and confirmed from time to time in the South Holland synod.[58]

It is a curious story of stubborn insistence on the part of the synods and equally stubborn resistance on the part of Arminius. It is correct to conclude that Arminius did not want to write the refutation. But why? Was it because he would not pursue "heretics"? No, for on a number of occasions he had done so. Was it because he had adopted Anabaptist views of the church and sacraments? No, for his theological writings during this period, which are to be examined later, indicate a thoroughly Reformed view of baptism. The reason lies elsewhere.

The controversy with the Anabaptists was now being fought over two issues. One was the old one of the nature of baptism and the church. The other was the questions of grace, predestination, and free will. There are Anabaptist writings from the time on these subjects which show that Arminius would have been reluctant to make a blanket condemnation of all that they were teaching.

Confessions of faith drawn up by Hans de Ries (de Rys, de Rijk) are a case in point and were probably before the eyes of Arminius as he worked on the Anabaptist problem. De Ries (1553-1638) was born in Antwerp. After being under Reformed influence he went over to the Anabaptists, and became a Mennonite minister in Alkmaar, possibly by 1577. He came to be one of the most influential Mennonites of his time. He was a leader of the Mennonite faction known as the Waterlanders (after the region north of Amsterdam, Waterland, in which they first flourished). In 1577 he was one of the five ministers who drew up a comprehensive Mennonite corporate confession of faith, and the next year, when he was in prison in Middelburg, he drew up another confession himself which is similar to that of 1577.[59]

In the confession of 1577 it is stated that "God has known from all eternity all things that happen, have happened, and will happen, both good and bad." "This foreknowledge," it says explicitly, "compels no

---

[56] *Ibid.*, I, 384.

[57] *Ibid.*, p. 429.

[58] *Ibid.*, III, 244, 263.

[59] Cf. W. J. Kühler, *Geschiedenis der Nederlandsche Doopsgezinden in de Zestiende Eeuw*, pp. 353 ff. *et passim*. An English translation of the confession of 1577 is found in Cornelius J. Dyck, "The First Waterlandian Confession of Faith." A translation of de Ries's confession of 1578 is in Dyck, "The Middelburg Confession."

one to sin." Not everything that God foreknows is his will and work, but only that which is good and holy. In Jesus Christ "life and salvation was promised to all men, as many as accepted his word, repented, and believed in him." Those who refuse this salvation do so "of their own guilt and perversity." The confession of 1578 is equally concerned to show that God does not foreordain evil. "Therefore the works of the devil . . . occur without His [God's] ordaining them or willing them."

Both confessions teach that Adam and all his posterity have come under "temporal and eternal death" (1577). There is, however, "a trace of light in fallen man and his descendants" whereby "he is still able to achieve some virtues and avoid some sins, and can, through sensitivity [to this light] and the grace of God, come to a closer walk [with God]." There is, furthermore, a universal gift of Christ to all men which frees the entire human race from the power of original sin, which is death. "We confess man's rehabilitation to equal the fall" (1577). No children are to be damned because of original sin "before the time when man deliberately wills to live by and pursue these inner flaws" (1577). In 1578 de Ries is a bit more careful to ascribe the "trace of light" entirely to grace. "By the grace of God virtue was to remain, all men by grace having sufficient godliness remaining in them that they are without excuse." The responsibility for faith is put upon man: "Man can thereby accept or reject the goodness of God offered through diverse means as the way of life—he can open or close his heart—but not by himself, for of ourselves we can do nothing good without the help of God."

All of this is to say that the Anabaptists rejected the kind of predestination theory that was being promoted by the more rigid Calvinists among the Reformed. Says de Ries in 1578: "It is the good will of God that all men shall be saved; therefore only those shall be damned who despise this grace and lightly turn to sin."

It was over these matters of grace and free will that Arminius had his difficulty. He was sympathetic to the Anabaptist point of view, and Anabaptists were commonly in attendance on his preaching. At the same time, he was trying to avoid direct conflict with his Reformed colleagues by guarding his statements on predestination. It is not that he did not think that the Anabaptists were caught in some errors, but rather that he did not find them to be in error at every point. Furthermore, he suspected that the motives of the synods in requesting his refutation were mixed. He expressed these misgivings in a letter to Uitenbogaert on January 26, 1600:

I have not yet determined any thing respecting the business which has been imposed on me by the Synod. Yet my mind, for certain reasons, is inclined to

170

undertake the task, provided I could ascertain that it has been committed to me with a sincere intent; of which I am compelled to doubt by the perverse and erroneous judgments which some men have formed respecting me. But, whatever intention they may have had, I am of opinion that the labour will be useful to the Church of Christ: Not because these heresies have not been refuted in a learned and solid manner; but because new refutations find new readers. I have not in the course of my previous studies had an opportunity to learn the heresies of the Anabaptists, and their foundations, with so much accuracy as the profitable discussion of this matter requires: This is the only circumstance which slightly interrupts my progress. If any persons feel a persuasion in their minds, that this burden is imposed on me with the sole view of discovering the thoughts of my heart on certain controverted points, they will be frustrated in their wishes. For the necessity of the refutation will not require me to unfold all the views which I hold about Predestination and Free Will, which are, among others, the doctrines concerning which the dispute lies between us and the Anabaptists. But in this affair, I know, you will not fail to lend me your aid, both in furnishing me with books, (if you have any which treat on this subject,) and in giving me the benefit of your advice, as well as correcting my productions.[60]

It is reasonable to conclude that Arminius was no Anabaptist and that he learned none of his theology from them. He was, indeed, opposed to many of their views. He was not unwilling to write against heresy. When he began to write, however, it was not against the Anabaptists but against their Reformed critics. In this affair he was trying to postpone that day.

IN ALL THIS ACCOUNT of the pastoral career of Arminius there is not much about his emotions, his contacts with other human beings, his feeling for his family, his joys, griefs, and fears. The fact is that there is little information about this side of his life. His letters deal almost entirely with matters of theology and church politics. The minutes of the classis, consistory, and provincial synod deal with matters of church discipline. It is known that he officiated at baptisms, marriages, and burials, but little comes through about the human relationships involved. There was grief in his own family, but he has expressed little of this grief in writing. The impression could be that he was humorless and compassionless, a rational theological and ecclesiastical functionary, zealously pursuing the interests of his church and of his own theology. Such an impression would be based on an argument from silence only, and is not sustained by the warm feelings for him expressed by others. Nor is the silence complete; there is at least one point in his Amsterdam years when the warmer side of the man appears.

[60] *Ep. Ecc.*, no. 52; quoted in *WA*, I, 530-31.

171

It was a point at which all Amsterdammers were driven to think of the ultimate meaning of life, a point at which death seemed imminent for all and became real for many. In 1601 the plague struck, as it had done periodically since its first appearance in Europe. It was, in fact, the worst of Amsterdam's plagues, with an estimated 20,000 victims, sometimes as many as 1,000 a day. The burial places in and around the churches proved insufficient, and it was necessary to open three new burial grounds. It was the bubonic plague, and the carrier was the ordinary sewer rat, which thrived in the stagnant waters of Amsterdam's noisome canals.[61]

The plague was the occasion for a great deal of prayer and theological speculation throughout the city. The consistory issued a call for a day when men should call upon the Lord "with fiery prayers." The churches were packed, with hundreds of people standing outside. The *kermis*, or fair, was canceled, and every day was observed with the sobriety for which Sundays alone had been noted. The actions of the clergy were more praiseworthy than their theology. The theology is what would be expected for the times: the plague was a punishment for sin and thus an occasion for repentance, but God spares his own. Arminius attributed it to the miraculous providence of God that the plague had not taken a single one of the "councilmen, judges, treasurers, prefects of orphans, ministers of the Word, elders, deacons, poor-relief superintendents, school rectors, or teachers." [62] The only exception would have been Arminius' friend and neighbor, the Walloon minister Taffin, who died at the time, but presumably not of the plague.

Modern observers, less credulous, have noted that the members of the city government and the officers of the church were from the wealthy sector of the population. They did not live in the water-level cellars of crowded and unsanitary housing where rats often got in the very beds of the people. But if they were fatuous about their own preservation, at least they were grateful.

The actions of the ministers were marked by courage. Arminius praised his colleague Helmichius. "Helmichius does his duty excellently, both in public and in private," he said to Uitenbogaert. There was praise also for Arminius. On one occasion, when he was in a slum district, he heard the sound of crying in a house. He learned that the whole household was afflicted with the plague and tormented with thirst. He gave money to neighbors who were standing by for purchasing water,

[61] H. Brugmans, "De Pest te Amsterdam."
[62] Letter to Uitenbogaert, August 17, 1602; *Ep. Ecc.*, no. 55.

and when none would enter, he took the water in himself "and imparted refreshment, at once for the body and the soul, to every single member of this afflicted family." [63]

Arminius was, if not frightened by the plague, at least made very serious by it. In a letter to Uitenbogaert of October 1, 1602, he says that he is convinced that it is "through your prayers principally and those of our church" that he has remained thus far unaffected by the plague. Furthermore, he is confident that he will be safe from it "through the mercy of God, if he know that my safety will in that case conduce to his glory, to the edification of the church, and to my own salvation as well as that of my family." He was alarmed by the plague, nevertheless.

When this fatal distemper first began . . . my mind was much affected with anxious thoughts about my wife and children, for the small portion of substance which I should be able to leave them was a subject of serious concern. But, by the goodness of God, I overcame that temptation, and I now entertain no doubt that they will be objects of special regard to the Lord God, who is the Father of widows and orphans.

He was also concerned about the disposition of his papers. He had published nothing, but in his study were a great many writings which would be controversial if made public.

While standing on the brink of the grave, I have not been bold enough to order them to be burned, because it is possible that they might be useful to me . . . if I should survive this general calamity. I find much greater difficulty in bringing my mind to the resolution of permitting them to remain as posthumous papers after my decease.

His fear was that they would prove unworthy of inspection, even by such a close friend as Uitenbogaert. But he makes a decision.

But I make this communication to you, and I desire it may stand in the place of my last will, that I wish my papers to fall into the hands of no one, except Jacobus Bruno and yourself, both of whom, I know, will use them with equity and indulgence, and would correct them for the benefit of my heirs, if any part of them, after a slight degree of correction, might see the light. [64]

When Arminius died in 1609, he had made a last will, but its entire contents are unknown, and the disposition of his papers is known only incompletely. Their present existence is also unknown, with a very few exceptions.

[63] *LA*, p. 128.
[64] *Ep. Ecc.*, no. 56; *WA*, I, 174-83.

To get back to Arminius' pastoral role in the plague: in the same letter he tells of two distressing pastoral encounters with dying people. Both were members of the church and, in Arminius' opinion, "true Christians." One was a woman, the other a man, and neither knew the other. "Both of them," reported Arminius, "began to be troubled in their minds because they could not feel in their hearts the assurance of the remission of their sins and the comfortable attestation of the Holy Spirit, especially at that juncture of time when they accounted such perceptions most needful." Both had tried to excite these feelings by recourse to Scripture and prayer, but to no avail. The woman wept; the man "compressed his grief within himself." "I listened to them with a sad heart," said Arminius. He tried to determine the cause of their distress. They gave essentially the same reply, "that they accounted the assurance of the remission of sins, and the testimony of the Holy Spirit, in the hearts of believers, to be that faith by which a man who believes is justified." Since they had no sense of assurance, they feared for their salvation. Arminius questioned each about his fundamental confidence that God had reconciled the world to himself in Christ. Their answer was affirmative. Arminius replied to them, "This is the faith which is imputed for righteousness; but the remission of sins is the fruit of this faith; and a sense of the remission of sins in the heart of a believer necessarily follows it, in the order of nature, at least, if not in that of time." Both then admitted that they had considered the sense of the remission of sins to be faith itself. Arminius held the two to be distinct. "I also explained the causes," he went on, "why this assurance and comfort of the Spirit are not always felt in equal degree." Both were encouraged, he reported, and both were able to commend their souls to God. The man died two days later.

Arminius saw in this a confirmation of an earlier conviction of his, that theological precision is necessary for practical faith, lest confused notions "should produce in the consciences of men uncomfortable uncertainty and perturbation."

A word about Jacobus Bruno (Jacob de Bruyn), who alone with Uitenbogaert was to have the care of Arminius' unpublished papers. He was born about 1572; the place is unknown to me. He was an *alumnus* of Amsterdam, one of the *proponenten* whose theological education was provided at the expense of the city. He studied at the University of Leiden, and in November, 1601, he married Immetje Reael, Lijsbet's next younger sister. At that time he was a minister in Arnhem. The city government of Amsterdam took note of the nuptials by giving Arminius eight *rozenobels* to be conveyed to Bruno as a token of esteem from the burgomasters, this at a cost to the treasury of 74 guilders and 5 stuivers.[65] One may speculate that the *rozenobels* were "golden reals," appropriate gifts for a son-in-law of Laurens Reael. About Bruno little is known. There is no extant correspondence between Arminius and this brother-in-law. The fact that Arminius regarded him as an intimate friend suggests that there is much about the personal life of Arminius which is lost to us.

---

[65] J. C. Breen, "Amsterdams Geschiedenis in 1601"; cf. *De Nederlandsche Leeuw,* XXXIX (1921), 100. Bruno's name does not appear in *BWPGN.*

12

THE EAST INDIAN TRADE

IT WOULD BE a mistake to suppose that these years of pastoral ministry in Amsterdam were tranquil years for Arminius. Much of his work was routine, but the situation in Amsterdam was far from routine. Arminius appears to have been concerned almost exclusively with religious matters. He was not unaffected, however, by the momentous public affairs of the 1590s. The decade was a turning point in Amsterdam's history, and the changes it brought thrust Arminius into an entirely different, and less friendly, political and ecclesiastical setting. It is impossible to understand the nature of his last, beleaguered years without being aware of economic developments in the United Provinces, especially in Amsterdam, and their interactions with political and religious life.

At the beginning of the decade, when Arminius was in the early years of his ministry, Amsterdam was at the end of an era. The radical changes which were imminent may not have been apparent, but the decisive step which was to lead to them had been taken in the Alteration of 1578. The outward form of government did not change then, but the power was in the hands of the merchants, a situation almost unique in all of Europe. The interests of Amsterdam were not seen in terms of hereditary land holdings but rather in the commercial interests of enterprising traders whose economic base was the ships by which they carried on trade with neighboring lands.

The new merchant oligarchy came into power at an unparalleled time in history. When the Hanseatic cities were at their height in the fourteenth and fifteenth centuries, Amsterdam was a minor partner in the Baltic Sea trade. Its fishing economy was to give it the initial leverage which would lead to greater things. The improvement of the process of preserving herring with salt by Willem Beuckelsz. in the early fourteenth century was to make herring a valuable commodity in Europe. It had at least a twofold significance: first, people learned to like salt herring as a food, so that it was in demand in its own right; second, the fact that the fish remained edible for long periods of time made possible longer sea voyages than ever before attempted.

176

The Dutch had acquired strategic fishing rights off the British coasts from Edward I. At first they used salt from peat ash. When the digging of peat in the Low Countries was recognized as destructive of the already scarce land, new sources of salt were needed. Ships were built to haul it from France and Portugal. When the Hanseatic League went into decline, Dutch shippers had the basic equipment to move into a broad range of European trade.[1]

By the second half of the sixteenth century some typical patterns of trade had emerged. The basic pattern was this: Dutch ships carried herring to Baltic ports; there they loaded grain for Spain and Portugal; in Spain and Portugal they loaded salt for Dutch herring packers. Variations on the theme embraced lumber, potash, pitch, and hemp from Norway; flax, cloth, cheese, and hides from Holland; and fruit, cork floats, wine, wool, and iron from the Iberian peninsula. French ports were involved, as has been seen from the Reael ships in Rouen. A newer item of trade was East Indian spices, which had to be purchased from Spanish and Portuguese traders. Bad harvests in southern Europe from 1586 to 1590 gave the Dutch the opportunity to extend their shipping trade into the Mediterranean Sea, where prior to 1585 they had entered only rarely. It was thus far an entirely intra-European commercial system, enterprising but still conservative when compared with what would take place shortly.

A fortuitous combination of factors brought the change, a revolution in trading patterns which was to lead to Holland's Golden Age of the seventeenth century. A simple enumeration of some of the identifiable factors will be useful, quite apart from offering a theory about the rise of capitalism. The war for independence which had begun in 1568 had changed the picture with respect to trade patterns. Trade with the enemy was at once proscribed and tolerated. The argument against it was that it would aid the enemy. On the other hand, it produced needed revenue; furthermore, the merchants argued, if we don't do it, others will. So it was regularized on payment of a license fee, and these fees provided basic capital for the five admiralties of Amsterdam, Rotterdam, Zeeland, the North Quarter, and Friesland. That capital, in turn, helped to finance the war and was to make new trade patterns possible.[2]

Antwerp was declining from its position as a leading port, and this put Amsterdam in a position of leadership. When Parma captured

[1] Very helpful summaries of these developments are found in C. R. Boxer, *The Dutch Seaborne Empire: 1600-1800;* George Masselman, *The Cradle of Colonialism;* and Violet Barbour, *Capitalism in Amsterdam in the 17th Century.*

[2] The great study of the issue of trade with the enemy is J. H. Kernkamp, *De Handel op den Vijand, 1572-1609.*

Antwerp in 1585, he offered its inhabitants a two-year period of grace in which they could choose to leave the city. Many of the Reformed and some of the Roman Catholics took their families and goods and moved north, perhaps as many as 60,000 in number, and Amsterdam was their chief destination. The laborers among them took their manufacturing skills, and the merchants took their capital and their international trade connections. The Reformed took their strict Calvinism.

Some interrelated inventions were significant. The Dutch had departed from traditional ship designs to develop the *Vlie-boot* (English, fly-boat, but named for the channel *Vlie* which led from Amsterdam to the sea), which was improved in 1594 by a shipbuilder in Hoorn, Pieter Jansz. Liorne. The improvement, called the *fluit* (flute), was long, narrow, and shallow, cheap to build, easy to handle, and with a large cargo space. In 1596 the windmill was adapted to the sawing of lumber. The rapid cutting of lumber in standard sizes made possible a massive production of fly-boats and flutes.

At this same time, when trade was producing accumulated capital, there was a shortage of land for investment, and the thrust was toward capital investment in shipping. The capture of Portugal by Spain in 1580, however, had hampered the Dutch shipping trade with Portugal, and this was felt especially in the traffic in spices, the new commodity now in demand. By the early 1590s, then, Amsterdam was exploding with manpower, capital, technology, and capability of trade, but at the same time it was thwarted in the exercise of these potentialities within the existing intra-European trade patterns.

It was Arminus' colleague Petrus Plancius who had the vision and the technical skill to open the way to a new world of trade for Amsterdam merchants. It came about largely by chance. At some point in his career he had learned the art of cartography and had gained scientific knowledge in astronomy and navigation. It has been thought that he had studied under his countryman the Flemish geographer Gerhardus Mercator (1512-1594), although Plancius' biographer Keuning finds this unproved.[3]

Plancius was asked to supply maps for a Bible published in 1590 by the Amsterdam printer Laurens Jacobszoon. The printer included the maps "so that the Christian reader may see the most correct and reliable location of all the countries, cities, and places mentioned in the whole Bible."[4] There were five maps, one of "Paradise, together with the countries, cities, and places mentioned in the book of Creation," another

[3] Keuning, p. 69.

[4] Quoted in *ibid.*, p. 76; a copy of the Bible is in the British Museum, no. 3041. h. 12.

of the Exodus, another of "the Land of Promise as it was in the time of Christ and of the Apostles," another of "all countries, cities, and places mentioned in the Acts of the Apostles and the Revelation of John." A fifth map, the second in order of appearance, was entitled "A description of the whole world, newly improved in many places."

It was this last map which suddenly made Bible scholars out of sea captains. The map itself was based on a late map of Mercator. Its availability and its improvements caused excitement, however, and Plancius was asked by the States General to make a new map of the world, for which they paid him 300 guilders. It was published with a twelve-year copyright in April, 1592, by the Amsterdam printer Claes Claesz. The title promised a lot: "A geographical and hydrographical map of the whole world, wherein all countries, cities, places, and oceans under their respective degrees of longitude and latitude are shown; the capes, promontories, headlands, harbors, shoals, sands, and cliffs the most sharply located and drawn, with the addition of the directions and tendencies of the winds." It created a sensation and was soon reprinted, with an edition appearing in London a year later (only one copy is known to exist now, in Valencia, Spain).[5]

The printer proceeded to publish more of Plancius' maps. At some time between 1592 and 1594—the date is uncertain—Plancius issued a series of detailed maps of parts of the world. In his petition for a copyright the printer stated that Plancius "has obtained a clear description in the Spanish language, showing the secrets of the route to the East and West Indies, Africa, China and similar countries, including the peculiarities of the people, fruits, and other mercantile products."[6] It is not known how Plancius obtained this information, a Portuguese secret hitherto unknown in Holland. Plancius was not unaware of its importance. He prodded three Amsterdam merchants to make the obvious next step, to plan a sea voyage to the source of the spices which they had had to buy from Portugal.

The three merchants and Plancius were neighbors. Jan Jansz. Carel (c. 1545-1616), a dealer in dairy products, had arrived in Amsterdam just after the Alteration and was one of the first elders of the church. He lived just off the south end of the Warmoesstraat on the Dam. Hendrick Hudde, Arentsz. (died 1596) was the son of a wealthy merchant dealing in Baltic grain, Arent Hudde, who had been one of the refugees of 1567. Hendrick carried on the family business at *de drie Coningen* on the Warmoesstraat near the Old Bridge (the present number 56). His name does not appear among the elders or deacons. The third

[5] *Ibid.*, p. 77.
[6] Quoted in Masselman, p. 68.

merchant was a man to watch. He would become one of the most powerful men in Amsterdam, and he would be one of the most bitter enemies of Arminius. At the age of twenty-eight Reynier Pauw (1564-1636) was already a leading merchant in lumber and salt, and he had been made a *schepen* in 1590 and a member of the Thirty-six in 1591. His father, Adriaen Pauw, was from a prominent Gouda family. He was one of the merchant-reformers of 1566 who fled to Emden, and at the Alteration he was the fifth man elected to the council. He lived only until October of that year (1578). Reynier apparently carried on the family business at the original location, *Het Wapen van Lubeck*, near the north end of the Warmoesstraat (the present number 14). Reynier represented the new generation of merchants who no longer knew the temper of the Reformers of 1566, and a new faction in that new generation, ruthless in its drive for power, brilliant in strategy, intolerant in politics and religion. Reynier became a burgomaster in 1605, achieving at one point the unofficial rank of *Magnificat,* or chief among the burgomasters. In 1619 he was appointed by the States General to the Court Extraordinary which sentenced Jan van Oldenbarnevelt to death.

Just when Plancius and Arminius were locked in combat in the consistory, in 1592, Plancius and his three merchant friends were meeting secretly to study and plan for a voyage to the Indies. The Warmoesstraat must have seen some strange goings-on as Plancius, who lived just off the street in the rectory of the Old Church, played his dual role as the public defender of orthodoxy and the private planner of Amsterdam's future mercantile career. Which of his two roles was to be the more important or the more enduring will be a matter of differing opinions. The maps must have been engrossing, for his colleagues later complained that he often entered the pulpit unprepared to preach and talked about sea voyages instead. Maybe that is why there was relatively little friction between Plancius and Arminius in the later 1590s.

One of the plots of the four men was to learn more about Portuguese trade secrets in the East Indies and the Moluccas. A cousin of Reynier Pauw, Cornelis de Houtman, was sent to Lisbon in the guise of a merchant. In the meantime Jan Huighen van Linschoten was serving as a seaman on a Portuguese ship for nine years, and when he returned to Enkhuizen in 1592, Plancius listened with interest to his reports. It was becoming apparent that the Portuguese did not have a firm hold in the East Indies and that Dutch ships could chance a voyage there if they could avoid being intercepted en route. Meanwhile, a refugee from Antwerp, Balthasar de Moucheron, was proposing an expedition by the "Northeast Passage," that is, around Norway and Russia, by which, it was believed, it would be possible to sail south to the Indies.

Plancius supported the plan, at least as a provisional measure. On June 5, 1594, three ships set sail. They failed, of course, but when they returned on September 16, they did not really know how to interpret their experience.

Houtman had returned from Lisbon that same year, and Carel, Hudde, and Pauw, with six other merchants, organized the *Compagnie van Verre,* the Company of Far Lands, to engage in trade with the East by way of rounding the Cape of Good Hope. Plancius, as a minister, did not let his name appear among the investors, but he put 5,400 guilders into the company and seemed to be the deciding voice in many decisions. He also gave courses in navigation for the ship captains, for which he was well paid by the company.

Events moved fast, and for our purposes they must be mentioned only briefly. The company sent out its first fleet, four ships under Cornelis de Houtman and his brother Francis, on April 2, 1595. The ships reached Bantam amidst great difficulties and losses. They returned on August 14, 1597, with only three ships and 89 of the 248 men who started, and with little or no profit. Hopes were high, however, for a successful voyage to follow. On July 2, 1595, a second northern trip was attempted by others who were also tutored by Plancius but backed by Moucheron—Cornelis Nay, Willem Barentsz., Linschoten, Jan Ryp, and Jacob van Heemskerck. They expected to be in China before winter, but they were, of course, forced back by ice and returned in October. The third and last northern venture is the most famous. On May 18, 1596, when the Amsterdam merchants still knew nothing of the fate or fortune of the Houtman expedition around Africa, two ships were sent north under Barentsz. and Heemskerck. Plancius was the chief instigator of this venture. When they reached the west coast of Novaya Zemlya, there was a disagreement between Barentsz. and Ryp. After discovering Spitsbergen (now called Svalbard), they split, Ryp returning home and the others rounding the northern tip of Novaya Zemlya. They were caught in the ice and spent a miserable winter on its east coast, but escaped the next summer in two small boats. Barentsz. died on the return. Heemskerck led them home later in the year.

Was Arminius aware of such happenings? It would be hard for an Amsterdammer to be unaware of them. This trip, especially, caught the imagination of Amsterdam and soon of the whole world, for on the beleaguered expedition was a young man, Gerrit de Veer, who kept a careful journal of all that transpired. His story was published at once and soon translated into several languages. It was a drama of human suffering and courage, on the one hand, and an exciting vista on new possibilities, on the other. Spitsbergen had been discovered; men had penetrated farther north, to 81° latitude, than ever before; and many whales had been sighted. The immediate commercial consequence was the rise of the Dutch whaling industry. Gerrit's father, Ellert de Veer, was a second cousin of the burgomaster Wilhem Baerdesen, and his brother, Dr. Ellert de Veer, town secretary and later pensionary of Amsterdam, was a close neighbor of Arminius at the St. Ursula cloister. When Gerrit's sister, Mientgen (or Mijntje), married Jochim Jansz. Wachter in 1603, Arminius signed their marriage contract as the witness.[7] There is thus every reason to believe that the excitement of the Novaya Zemlya expeditions, and of the other trading ventures, was very well known to Arminius.

The trading excitement was renewed in 1597, with the return of the Houtman expedition from the Indies. The Compagnie van Verre immediately planned a new expedition, but now others were interested. In Amsterdam itself another company, the New Company for Voyages to East India, formed and received from the States General the same privileges as the first. Out of Rotterdam came two companies, and out of Zeeland yet two more. In January, 1598, an attempt was made to coordinate the work of these companies. Zeeland was not cooperative. The Compagnie van Verre and the New Company merged, forming what came to be called the Old Company. It had seventeen directors, headed by Gerrit Bicker, of an old and wealthy family, with Reynier Pauw second in rank. Plancius was heavily involved but did not allow himself to be named a director. Up to this time shipping ventures had been financed by a *rederij*, a short-term joint investment for a limited venture, as small as one voyage of one ship. The Old Company broke with this restricted financing and raised a capital of nearly 800,000 guilders.

On May 1, 1598, it sent out a fleet of eight ships under the capable leadership of Admiral Jacob van Neck, who was from an old Amsterdam merchant family with relationships extending as far as the Coornherts and the Reaels. The fleet split into three sections during the eventful journey. Van Neck returned with four ships in July, 1599, only fourteen and a half months out, and with 600,000 pounds of pepper, 250,000 pounds of cloves, and smaller amounts of nutmeg and mace. The town turned out for a triumphal procession. The crew was led by eight trumpeters to the Dam, where the burgomasters presented van Neck with a gold-plated silver cup and the crew with as much wine as they could drink. The four ships alone had paid for the cost of the entire expedition, with a 100 percent profit besides. Heemskerk returned in May, 1600, and again the church bells rang; and in September, when

[7] *Notariale Archief* 34, fol. 409.

the rest of the fleet returned under Wybrand van Warwyck, the victory was complete. Amsterdam's old trade horizons had been transcended, and the wealth of the East was pouring into her warehouses.

In July, 1598, one of the Rotterdam companies sent out a fleet under Olivier van Noort which rounded South America, entered the Pacific Ocean, and made the first Dutch voyage around the world. The various companies sent out more fleets in 1599 and 1600. Some were successful; some were not. But even success made for confusion, for the competition was driving purchase prices up and selling prices down. In the autumn of 1601 merchants in Amsterdam sought from the States General a monopoly east of the Cape of Good Hope. The States refused, and instead, Oldenbarnevelt called for a consultation of all the companies. This was held in December and January at The Hague, and plans were laid for a united company. Zeeland resisted the longest but finally gave in. The charter of the united company was signed on March 20, 1602. It was called in Dutch *De Vereenighde Nederlantsche Geoctroyeerde Oost-Indische Compagnie,* the United Netherlands Chartered East India Company, and it is often referred to by the initials VOC from which was made a monogram emblem which was stamped on all its property.

The financing of this giant enterprise, which has been called by some historians the first modern joint stock corporation, is a part of our story. The predecessor Amsterdam companies had been the joint enterprise of old Amsterdam merchant families and of newer immigrants from the south. Of the nine merchants who founded the Compagnie van Verre in 1594, six were from old Amsterdam families and three were newcomers. The tenth, silent partner, Petrus Plancius, was from the south as well.[8] When a second Amsterdam company, the so-called New Company of 1597, was organized entirely by Amsterdam stock, it was soon matched, in 1599, by the New Brabant Company, made up of immigrant Brabanders and Flemings led by the vigorous Isaac le Maire. These several companies became the Amsterdam Chamber of the VOC. It was by far the largest of the six chambers, providing over 3.6 million guilders of the total capital of 6.4 million guilders. Zeeland was second with only 1.3 million guilders. Amsterdam was clearly the leader in the new trading era which was opening up, and Amsterdam would reap the greatest benefits. Arminius as a pastor in Amsterdam—indeed, as a favorite preacher of the leading families—was close to the center of the greatest commercial development of the dawning seventeenth century.

More than 1,100 persons invested in the Amsterdam Chamber by the time the books were closed on August 31, 1602. The control of the

---

[8] van Dillen, p. 51.

chamber was shared by old Amsterdam families and newcomers. Of those who invested more than 10,000 guilders, twenty-four South Netherlanders invested 680,000 guilders while twenty-six North Netherlanders invested only 504,000 guilders.[9] Among the "participants," the numerous smaller investors who were not directors, there were 785 northerners and 301 southerners, and the southerners, who comprised 26 percent of the participants, provided nearly 40 percent of the participating capital.[10]

It is instructive to examine the first signatures on the charter of the Amsterdam Chamber. In the first place is Gerrit Bicker from the vast and important Bicker family, brewers, merchants, speculators, and powerful in the city government. In second and third place are Reynier Pauw and Jan Jansz. Carel, plotters with Petrus Plancius before anyone else in Holland even dreamed of the great commercial and colonial empire that was now in the making. Other names were to become the great names of the seventeenth century—Hasselaer, Reynst, ten Grootenhuis, van Baerle, and Bas, to name only a few. Plancius signed the list this time, evidently feeling free at last to identify his financial investments. He was one of the more heavily involved *participanten,* in the amount of 6,000 guilders. Another minister, Arminius' close friend Halsbergius, who in 1599 had been promoted to full minister in Amsterdam, signed for 1,500 guilders. The Reael family invested in the company, although at the outset they do not appear as heavy investors. J. P. Reael, Lijsbet's uncle, invested 6,000 guilders for himself and 900 more for his son-in-law Augustijn Uitenbogaert. Lijsbet's oldest brother, Jacob Laurensz. Reael, invested 3,000 guilders in his own name, 6,450 guilders for his wife's brother (Albert Fransz. Sonck), 1,000 guilders for his mother-in-law, and lesser amounts for other close relatives. These lesser amounts often represented money that was invested by small investors who were not permitted to sign the charter themselves (the number was limited) and who used the offices of friends and relatives to get in on the speculation. It is here that Arminius appears with the modest amount of 600 guilders, which he invested through his brother-in-law Jacob. Investing only 200 guilders was Lijsbet's brother Laurens Laurensz. Reael, who in 1619 would become the third Governor General of the Netherlands Indies.

Missing among the directors and investors of the company were the pioneers of the Reformed Church in Amsterdam, the exiles of 1567. Laurens Jacobsz. Reael, Wilhem Baerdesen, Adriaen Cromhout, Frank de Wael, Cornelis Pietersz. Boom, Adriaen Pauw, Maarten Jansz. Coster,

Reynier van Neck, Egbert Roelofsz., and Reynier Cant were all dead. The leadership had passed on to their sons and to the immigrants from the south. The power of leadership would be tied closely to the new united company. When Wilhem Baerdesen died in 1601, the control of the city council shifted to a triumvirate of the brothers-in-law Barthold Cromhout and Frans Hendricksz. Oetgens and their uncle, Claes Fransz. Oetgens. The latter had become antagonistic to Arminius, and at the political level, at least, the nephews followed their uncle's lead. The emerging leader of the power structure, however, was Reynier Pauw, and when antagonism developed between Oldenbarnevelt and Prince Maurice, he was to side with Maurice's military campaign against Spain against those who favored a truce with Spain.

The stage is set now for the events of the last decade of Arminius' life. In the new Amsterdam of the seventeenth century, propelled to its Golden Age by the impetus of world trade, Arminius could no longer count on the benevolent patronage of the Old Beggars. A new breed was taking over, bold, mad for profits, intolerant in religion, prone toward the Calvinism which had been imported from the south, ready to support Prince Maurice in a holy war against Spain (with attendant profits in view), ready even, in the person of Reynier Pauw, to put the patriot Oldenbarnevelt to death. As professor in Leiden from 1603 to his death in 1609 Arminius often had occasion to express sorrow over the course of affairs in his adoptive city, where attacks on his own integrity could now be made with impunity. Friends he did have there to the end, even in the magistracy, but they themselves were often beset by new forces which they could not control. Arminius' professorial years were to be spent in the tangle of economic, political, and religious strife which the launching of the East Indian trade had ushered in.

13

THEOLOGY IN AMSTERDAM: ROMANS 7

THERE is one more question about Arminius' fifteen years in Amsterdam. What were his theological opinions? From time to time these have come to the surface, but only small glimpses are given us. He was accused of wrong teaching about Romans 7 because he did not follow Calvin and Beza in making it apply to a regenerate man. How did he himself draw different conclusions from the chapter? He was accused of holding wrong views on predestination. What were his views? What did he do in his study? How well developed were his positions and arguments in the years of his pastoral ministry?

Arminius published nothing in his Amsterdam period, and none of his sermons is extant. It is possible by hindsight, however, to know what he was thinking, because the Amsterdam years saw the production of some of his most detailed and closely reasoned writings. Nearly 45 percent of his published theological treatises were written in Amsterdam. These comprise his treatments of Romans 7 and 9, his correspondence with Franciscus Junius, his critique of a book by William Perkins, and two letters to Uitenbogaert which may be regarded as theological treatises. They were all published after his death, and so far as is known with no substantive editing. They deal primarily with the doctrines of sin, grace, predestination, and free will.

At some time during or after his sermons on Romans 7 in Amsterdam, Arminius wrote in Latin a lengthy treatment of the chapter, but in logical rather than homiletical style. It was published in Latin in 1613 under the title *A Dissertation on the True and Genuine Sense of the Seventh Chapter of the Epistle to the Romans* by Godefridus (Godfrey, Govert) Basson. *The Dissertation on Romans 7* was issued with a lengthy dedication signed by "the nine orphan children" of Arminius in which it is stated that Arminius had been revising the manuscript for publication when his final illness overtook him. Included was a large fold-out sheet containing the argument of the book in the form of a Ramist chart. That chart has been dropped from subsequent editions, including the *Opera* and the English translation.

Arminius proposes a five-part treatment. First, he will show that Paul "does not speak about himself, nor about a man living under grace, but that he has transferred to himself the person of a man placed under the law." [1] Second, this position has always had defenders in the church and has never been condemned as heretical. Third, no heresy, including Pelagianism, can be derived from it. Fourth, the position taken by "our modern divines" (Calvin and Beza, for example) was not approved by any of the early fathers or even Augustine. Fifth, the position of Calvin and Beza is "injurious to grace" and "adverse to good morals."

Arminius begins by setting forth firm definitions and proceeds by building clear, logical relationships. In its distinctness and clarity the work is at once reminiscent of Aristotle and adumbrative of Descartes. A man is either regenerate or he isn't. "To be under the law" means not merely to be under its obligations but also to be under its guilt and condemnation. "To be under grace" means to be absolved from guilt and vivified by grace and the Holy Spirit. Arminius appeals to Beza's distinction between "the things which precede regeneration" and "regeneration itself," and to Calvin's concept of "servile fear." [2] He then draws up the resultant definition of a regenerate man, and the definition will determine the exegesis of Romans 7. The regenerate man has "a mind freed from the darkness and vanity of the world, and illuminated with the true and saving knowledge of Christ," affections "that are mortified and delivered from the dominion and slavery of sin," and powers which by the assistance of the Holy Spirit are able "to contend against sin, the world, and Satan." He is able not only to struggle against sin but to obtain the victory over it, so that he "no longer does those things which are pleasing to the flesh and to unlawful desires, but does those which are grateful to God; that is, he actually desists from evil and does good,— not indeed perfectly, but according to the measure of faith and the gift of Christ." [3]

The unregenerate man, on the contrary, is "blind, ignorant of the will of God, knowingly and willingly contaminating himself by sins without any remorse of conscience, affected with no sense of the wrath of God, terrified with no compunctious visits of conscience." But that is not the whole picture of the unregenerate man. He also "knows the will of God but does it not," and he is "acquainted with the ways of righteousness

---

[1] *Writings*, II, 220.

[2] Beza's *Refutation of the Calumnies of Tilman Heshusius*, quoted by Arminius; *Writings*, II, 225. Calvin speaks of servile fear in *Institutes*, 3.2.27 and 3.3.2.

[3] *Writings*, II, 228.

but departs from it." [4] The consciousness of sin, then, is not limited to "regeneration strictly taken" but is included in "things preceding" and "causes" of regeneration. Herein lies a fundamental difference between Arminius and high Calvinism, be it classical or Barthian.

Arminius establishes a connection between Romans 7 and the preceding chapter by means of 6:12-14:

Let not sin therefore reign in your mortal bodies, to make you obey their passions. Do not yield your members to sin as instruments of wickedness, but yield yourselves to God as men who have been brought from death to life, and your members to God as instruments of righteousness. For sin will have no dominion over you, since you are not under law but under grace.

He draws from this an enthymeme:

The antecedent: Sin shall not have dominion over you.
The consequent: Therefore do not yield your members to sin, etc.
Proof of the antecedent: You are under grace; sin will have no dominion over you.
Illustration of the proof from its contrary: For you are not under the law.
Explication and illustration: If indeed you were yet under the law as you formerly were, sin would have the dominion over you as it once had; and, having followed its commands and impulses, you would not be able to do any other than yield your members as instruments of unrighteousness unto sin. But as you are now no longer under the law, but under grace, sin shall not in any wise have the dominion over you, but by the power of grace you shall easily resist sin, and yield your members as instruments of righteousness unto God.[5]

From 6:14 Arminius draws four propositions: (1) Christians are not under the law. (2) Christians are under grace. (3) Sin shall have dominion over those who are under the law. (4) Sin shall not have dominion over those who are under grace.[6] After extended consideration of these propositions he concludes that the reason sin has dominion over those under the law is that "these very men who are under the law are carnal, sold under sin, have no good thing dwelling in their flesh, *but have sin dwelling in them [sed habentes in se peccatum habitans]*." It follows "that they are not themselves the masters of their own acts." It is also an effect of the law, however, to show them their plight, so that "from the showing of the law, having become acquainted with their misery, [they] are compelled to cry out, and to implore the grace of Jesus Christ." [7]

Against the background he has established from Romans 6, Arminius turns to Romans 7:14-25 (he deals also with 7:1-13, but his main concern

[4] *Ibid.*
[5] *Ibid.*, pp. 233-34.
[6] *Ibid.*, p. 234.
[7] *Ibid.*, pp. 244-45.

is with the latter part of the chapter). One of his principal arguments is that the word "carnal" and the phrase "sold under sin" in verse 14 do not apply to a regenerate man. He appeals to Calvin's commentary on the verse in favor of his position, and also to Beza's refutation of Castellio. Calvin had said, "The apostle now begins to bring the law and the nature of man a little more closely into hostile contact with each other," and on verse 15 he had said, "He now descends to the more particular example of a man already regenerate." [8] Beza had said, "St. Paul exclaims that he is not sufficient even to think that which is good; and in another passage, considering himself not within the boundaries of grace, he says, 'But I am carnal, sold under sin.' " [9]

Arminius piles argument on argument, relentlessly. From verse 15, for example, he constructs another syllogism:

He who approves not of that which he does, nor does that which he would, is the slave of another, that is, of sin. . . .
But the man about whom the apostle is treating approves not of that which he does, nor does what he would, but he does that which he hates.
Therefore, the man who is in the place the subject of discussion is the slave of another, that is, of sin; and therefore the same man is unregenerate and not placed under grace.[10]

A further argument is based on the premise that when Paul uses the word ἐνοικοῦσα, "indwelling" (verse 17), he is not speaking of a regenerate man. Arminius distinguishes between two modes of the presence of sin: indwelling (inhabitans) and inbeing (inexistens). Sin as indwelling (inhabitans) is sin as reigning (dominans). Reigning sin is to be distinguished from sin as merely inbeing (inexistens). The man in Romans 7 is marked by peccatum inhabitans which is dominans. Peccatum proptera in regenitis not habitat, quia in illis non dominatur.[11] Arminius does not deny that there is sin in believers, but sin in believers is inexistens. If this distinction were not made, he asks, what would be the difference between the regenerate and the unregenerate? [12]

Arminius draws his most developed argument from verses 22, 23, and 25. I quote them from the King James Version because it preserves a wording which in this case is closer than the Revised Standard Version to the Greek.

---

[8] *The Epistle of Paul the Apostle to the Romans and to the Thessalonians*, pp. 146, 148. The wording I have used is James Nichols' translation of Arminius' indirect quotation of Calvin, but I find no violence done.

[9] Quoted by Arminius, *Writings*, II, 252.

[10] *Ibid.*, p. 253.

[11] *Opera theologica*, p. 695.

[12] Cf. *Writings*, II, 262-66. But the translator has failed to maintain the very distinction for which Arminius contends; hence the necessity of quoting the Latin text.

(22) For I delight in the law of God after the inward man: (23) But I see another law in my members, warring against the law of my mind, and bringing me into captivity to the law of sin which is in my members. (25) I thank God through Jesus Christ our Lord. So then with the mind I myself serve the law of God; but with the flesh the law of sin.

Add to this 8:2:

For the law of the Spirit of life in Christ Jesus hath made me free from the law of sin and death.

The key word in this passage for Arminius is ἀντιστρατευόμενον, "warring against." He sees a battle plan. The warring forces are indicated by the word νόμος, "law." There are generals, and there are armies. When the opposing forces and their chains of command are charted, the result is curiously like an Aristotelian Square of Opposition! [13]

```
The Law of God              directly contrary         The Law of Sin
  (verse 22)                                             (verse 23)
          c             i                      y              c
          o             n                      r              o
          n             d                      a              n
          s             i                      r              s
          e             r                      t              e
          n               e                  n                n
          t               c                  o                t
          a                 t              c                  a
          n                 l                                 n
          e                   y                                e
          o                                                   o
          u                                                   u
          s                                                   s

          &                                                   &

          s                                                   s
          u                   y                                u
          b                   l                                b
          o                 t              c                   o
          r                 c              o                   r
          d               e                  n                 d
          i               r                  t                 i
          n             i                      r               n
          a             d                      a               a
          t             n                      r               t
          e             i                      y               e
The Law of the Mind                          The Law of the Members
  (verse 23)              directly contrary       (verse 23)
```

13 *Ibid.*, 330.

The Law of God and the Law of Sin have the principal dignity. They are the generals. The battleground is the man himself, who finds within two opposing forces or "laws," which are the contending armies, the Law of the Mind and the Law of the Members. The Law of the Mind serves the Law of God; the Law of the Members, the Law of Sin. The military goal of the armies is to bring the man under the control of their respective generals. The man is seen in terms of his will [*voluntatis*]. What, then, is the outcome of the battle?

Man becomes captive to the Law of Sin. Says Arminius:

This is the result of the conflict, the non-performance of good, the non-omission of evil, a token of the impotence of the mind, which commanded good to be done, and forbade the commission of evil . . . and the captivity of man under the law of sin, plainly demonstrating that in this man the party of sin and of the flesh is the more powerful of the two.[14]

The man in Romans 7 cannot be said to be regenerate but rather is dead in sin. This is the actual situation of man apart from Christ, says Arminius. In man as sinner it is the will that is bound by sin. It is inappropriate, then, to contrast Arminius' theology with other Reformed theology in terms of "free will." Arminius agrees that there is no "free will" in the life of sin. This point will receive further development.

Arminius finds Romans to contain something more than the good news of damnation. Man is not left helpless, but if he is to be liberated, the balance of power must shift. A fifth force must intervene, and this he finds in 8:2, the Law of the Spirit of Life. It is the man thus liberated who is regenerate, not the defeated man of Romans 7. The regenerate man has a free will. It is the free will neither of native endowment nor of good residue left over from the fall; rather, it is the gift of grace, the gift of Jesus Christ.

Arminius expresses dismay that his position should be condemned. He lists an impressive roster of supporting witnesses—Irenaeus, Tertullian, Origen, Cyprian, Chrysostom, Basil the Great, Theodoret, Cyril of Alexandria, Macarius, John of Damascus, Theophylact, Ambrose, Jerome, Clement of Alexandria, Vigilius, Procopius of Gaza, Bernard of Clairvaux, Leo the Great, Gregory Nazianzen, and Gregory of Nyssa.[15] Among the contemporary theologians he finds at least partial support in Calvin (*Institutes*, 2.7.9., 2.7.10, 4.20.1, 1.15.3, and his comments on II Corinthians 4:16), Beza, Bucer, Junius, and Piscator.[16] As for Augustine, he finds support in the early writings (*Exposition of Certain Prop-*

[14] *Ibid.*, p. 333.
[15] *Ibid.*, pp. 295-303.
[16] *Ibid.*, pp. 303-5.

ositions from the Epistle to the Romans; To Simplicianus) but less clear support in the *Retractations,* where Augustine permits Romans 7 to apply to regenerate as well as to unregenerate men. Arminius observes, "Wherefore I have St. Augustine in his first opinion fully agreeing with me, and in his latter not differing greatly from me; but those who are opposed to me have St. Augustine contrary and adverse to them in both these his opinions." [17]

In the third section Arminius argues that no heresy is involved with his interpretation; particularly is it free from Pelagianism. Furthermore, there is no Protestant confession which is contrary to it, and he cites those of "the French, the Dutch, the Swiss, the Savoy, the English, the Scotch, the Bohemian, [and] the Lutheran churches." [18]

His final substantive argument is twofold: that the position of his opponents is injurious both to grace and to morality. It gives grace too little power over sin. "Its only effect on the regenerate is to will and not to do." "It is too weak to crucify the old man, to destroy the body of sin, or to conquer the flesh, the world, and Satan." [19] As for morality, "nothing can be imagined more noxious to true morality than to assert that 'it is a property of the regenerate not to do the good which they would, and to do the evil which they would not.' " And then he makes one of his rare shifts from an appeal to logic to an appeal to his own experience:

I truly and sacredly affirm, that this has, in more instances than one, fallen within the range of my experience: that when I have admonished certain persons to exercise a degree of caution over themselves and to guard against the commission of some wickedness which they knew to be prohibited by the law, they have replied, "that it was indeed their will so to refrain, but that they must declare, with the apostle, We are unable to perform the good which we would." [20]

So much for his exposition of Romans 7. His position was to come into favor with later generations of scholars, particularly among the Wesleys and their followers, and in the distinguished volume on Romans in the *International Critical Commentary,* by W. Sanday and A. C. Headlam. The dialectical theology would revert to Calvin and Luther.

[17] *Ibid.,* p. 374.
[18] *Ibid.,* p. 403.
[19] *Ibid.,* p. 420.
[20] *Ibid.,* p. 423.

14

THEOLOGY IN AMSTERDAM:
ROMANS 9;
THE CONFERENCE WITH JUNIUS

THE ISSUE of predestination was just under the surface of Arminius' treatment of Romans 7, but he never let it come to light. It was not until he turned his attention to Romans 9 that he began to express his views in detail and in writing.

There was a long chain of circumstances behind his taking pen in hand. There was in Friesland, probably in Franeker, an ex-priest, Jelle Hotze (which he Latinized to Gellius Snecanus, by which he shall be called here). De Vries calls him "a Zwinglian scholar, highly appreciated in Friesland."[1] Gerard Brandt called him "an elderly, learned and pious church minister."[2] Beza spoke of his impertinence and absurdity.[3]

Snecanus had published a number of books in the 1580s, and in 1590 he issued a book in which he "spoke about predestination according to the sentiments of Melanchthon" and asserted that "the doctrine of conditional predestination is not only conformable to the word of God but cannot be charged with novelty." At the very beginning of the Reformation in Friesland, he said, those who opposed the doctrine were judged to be the innovators. He complained that the harassment he was now suffering smacked of popery and the Inquisition. He was forced to publish secretly. But he boldly addressed his writings to the rulers of Friesland (among whom he was a favorite) —the States, the Stadtholder, and the nobility—and he signed his own name, and this without censure. At the end of his introduction he said, "Let all orthodox professors of theology openly exhort their students not to ascribe to the writings of anyone [and he expressly mentioned Calvin and others] more authority than the rule of faith permits."[4]

[1] *GPCH*, II, 52.
[2] *HRN*, I, 778.
[3] Letter to Uitenbogaert, July 29, 1593, in *GPCH*, II, 52.
[4] Quoted in *HRN*, I, 778-79.

Beza was disturbed by this action of Snecanus, and he wrote to a number of his friends in Holland, including Taffin and Uitenbogaert, complaining about him and urging that he be silenced. Beza seemed to prefer censorship to dialogue, observing that if answers were to be composed to Snecanus, "it would require books big enough to fill a house." [5] Taffin wrote to Beza on December 15, 1593, that an attempt had been made to refute the errors of Snecanus, but in vain, and that it would be useless to try to silence him, for anyone who wanted to publish something would find the means to do it.[6]

In 1596 Snecanus published an *Introduction to the Ninth Chapter of Romans,* and when Arminius saw it he was pleased to find its arguments similar to his own. Accordingly, he wrote a letter to Snecanus, expressing his appreciation for the book and explaining his own views on the chapter. It constitutes Arminius' commentary on Romans 9. The first sixteen pages of the manuscript are housed in the Library of the University of Amsterdam (R. K. T. 62). It was published in 1612 by Godefridus Basson as an appendage to a much larger work, Arminius' examination of a pamphlet by William Perkins, which was written later.

Romans 9 presents problems to a foe of high Calvinist predestination theory. Paul picks up his theme from Malachi—the mystery of Jacob and Esau. "Though they were not yet born and had done nothing either good or bad, in order that God's purpose of election might continue," Rebecca was told, "the elder will serve the younger" (9:11, 12). God "has mercy upon whomever he wills, and he hardens the heart of whomever he wills" (18). "Has the potter no right over the clay, to make out of the same lump one vessel for beauty and another for menial use?" (21). Beza, as has been seen, built on these passages a thoroughgoing supralapsarian, double predestination.

Arminius admits the difficulties. In his opening remarks to Snecanus he says, "I candidly confess that this chapter has always seemed to me to be involved in the greatest obscurity, and its explanation has appeared most difficult." [7] But he had found a clue. He had been preaching it to his congregation, he says, and now the book by Snecanus confirms his position. He is writing to Snecanus "to present my thanks, and to inform you how I have proceeded in explaining this chapter, and what impelled me to take this course." [8] Arminius' *Analysis of Romans 9* is thus a faithful account of the content (it is to be hoped not the *style*) of his preaching from the Amsterdam pulpits. It is tightly reasoned, packed

[5] Letter to Uitenbogaert, July 29, 1593.
[6] *GPCH,* II, 363.
[7] *Writings,* III, 528.
[8] *Ibid.,* p. 527.

again with syllogisms. The syllogisms are primarily hypothetical or disjunctive, often stated in the form of an enthymeme (a syllogism with one of the premises understood but not stated). The adversary is often Beza, and many times he is named. The objective is a theology of grace which does not leave man "a stock or a stone."

It is not feasible here to present all the arguments, but some of them are noteworthy. Arminius begins with a question-and-answer analysis. His opponents, he says, misunderstand the chapter because they look in it for an answer to a question with which it is not dealing. The question they impose on the chapter is this: "Will the word of God fail even if most of the Jews are rejected?" To this question they get the answer: "God indeed, in the word of promise, invited all the Jews and called them to a participation of the covenant, but yet, by His eternal decree and purpose, He determined in fact to make only some of the Jews partakers, passing by the rest and leaving them in their former state." [9] This is the predestinarian theory of Beza. It is, indeed, the answer that the chapter gives to the question. The question, however, is improper; it is not derived from the chapter. The correct question is: "Does not the word of God become of none effect if those of the Jews who seek righteousness not of faith but of the law are rejected by God?" To the question put this way the chapter yields the following answer: "God, in his word and in the declaration of his promise, signified that He considered in the relation of children only those of the Jews who should seek righteousness and salvation by faith, but in the relation of foreigners those who should seek the same by the law." [10] This is the answer Arminius can accept, an answer which he had grounded also in Romans 4:9-10 and Galatians 3–4, "as I presented to my congregation when I treated this subject." [11]

Arminius turns next to Paul's use of types and antitypes. Confusion arises, he says, when Isaac and Ishmael (9:7) and Esau and Jacob (9:9-13) are taken as examples in themselves of God's purpose rather than as types of the children of the flesh and the children of the promise. He admits that his opponents can reply that these individuals themselves belong to the antitypes. If this be so, however, the decree of absolute predestination of individuals as Beza had taught it is upheld. Arminius counters:

It cannot be proved from this passage that they who are types pertain to the antitypes: and if it may, perhaps, be true that Ishmael and Esau belong to the children of the flesh, as thus described, yet that they are such of any divine

[9] *Ibid.*, pp. 529-30.
[10] *Ibid.*, pp. 530-31.
[11] *Ibid.*, p. 532.

purpose is not taught in this place. In this [divine] purpose, as we have explained it, something is determined concerning the children of the flesh and of the promise, but with the explanation which they prefer, something is determined concerning individuals, that these should be the children of the flesh, those of the promise. . . . The question, "Why do some believe and others not? . . . is not here discussed by the apostle, nor has it even the least connection with his design.[12]

This is to say that there is a predestination of *classes* which has priority over (or takes the place of) the predestination of individuals. The classes are marked by a certain kind of quality, that is, those who seek righteousness by works and those who seek it by faith. Ishmael and Esau are types of the class of those who seek righteousness by works; Isaac and Jacob, of those who seek by faith. That they are themselves members of the antitypes is in this context not a part of Paul's argument, according to Arminius.

When God is charged with injustice (which Paul anticipates), it is again important to remember the way in which Paul uses the figures of Ishmael and Esau. "It is true that if the apostle was considering them in themselves and not as types of certain characters . . . there would be an occasion for such an objection." What Paul is saying is this: "God in the word of the covenant and in the purpose which is according to election embraced only those who might be the children of the promise, who should believe in Christ, to the exclusion of the children of the flesh and of those who sought the righteousness of the law." [13] This is grounded in both the "liberty of the divine mercy" and the "illustration of the divine power and glory." Arminius paraphrases 9:15 as follows: "'In the choice and liberty of my will is placed the power of having mercy on whom I will." [14] If there is arbitrariness on the part of God, it is the merciful judgment that salvation shall be by faith, not by works which have been made impotent through sin. Nor must the power of God be limited. "If God can have mercy on whom He will, and harden whom He will, then He is also free to form a purpose according to which He may determine to have mercy on the children of the promise but to harden and punish the children of the flesh." [15] The mercy and power of God are not arbitrary in the sense that a predetermination is made that a particular person shall be a child of the promise or a child of the flesh. That is another question, and a legitimate matter of inquiry. But Paul is not dealing with it in Romans 9.

Arminius goes on. His opponents, "who contend for that absolute

[12] *Ibid.*, p. 540.
[13] *Ibid.*, pp. 541-42.
[14] *Ibid.*, pp. 542-43.
[15] *Ibid.*, p. 546.

decree of God to save certain particular individuals and to damn others," think that they have strong support for their cause in 9:19, "Why does he still find fault? For who can resist his will?" Arminius lays down some fundamental definitions. Sin is the transgression of a law. If the law be unjust, it is not a law. Its transgression would not be a sin. A law is just only if it meets two conditions, "that it be enacted by him who has authority to command, and that it be enacted for him who has the power to obey, not only δύναμει but ἐνέργεια, that is, has ability of such a character as is hindered by no intervening decree." [16] From this it follows "that 'sin is a voluntary transgression of the law,' which the sinner, since he could avoid it (I speak now of the act), commits of his own fault." [17] Arminius presses the point: "An act which is inevitable on account of the determination of any decrees does not deserve the name of sin." It is only those who sin voluntarily and of their own fault who can be held blameworthy.

"For who can resist his will?" The opponents of Arminius had drawn a distinction within the will of God. There are really two wills of God, one secret, the other revealed. As Arminius describes their position (accurately, I might add), "the revealed will has reference to those things which are pleasing or displeasing to God, the secret to those things which he simply and absolutely wills should be done, or not done." Then there arises a dispute, he points out, as to whether the secret will can contradict the revealed will. There are others who say that the divine will is in one respect efficacious, in another respect not. "It is wonderful in what labyrinths they involve themselves, being blinded either by unskillfulness or prejudice, or by both." [18]

Arminius rejects all these proposals as sophistries. The passage at hand does not speak about a hidden will of God. Neither is it unknown who those are whom God wills to harden. "Nothing is more plain in Scripture than that sinners persevering in their sins against the long-suffering of God, who invites them to repentance, are those whom God wills to harden." [19]

Arminius launches his next major attack in connection with the φύραμα, lump, of 9:21: "Has the potter no right over the clay to make out of the same lump one vessel for beauty and another for menial use [dishonor]?" Beza had interpreted the "lump" (massa, in the Vulgate)

---

[16] Ibid., p. 547.

[17] Ibid., p. 548. John Wesley was to adopt this definition of sin when he spoke of "sin properly so called (that is, a voluntary transgression of a known law)" in his Thoughts on Christian Perfection (1766); quoted John Wesley, ed. A. C. Outler, p. 287.

[18] Writings, III, 548-49.

[19] Ibid., p. 550.

to mean "mankind not yet made, much less corrupted" (supralapsarianism). Arminius prefers to follow Augustine, interpreting it as a *massa perditionis,* the aggregate of fallen men.[20] The objects of God's mercy and judgment are men as sinners. What is God's part in making a man a vessel for dishonor? Arminius discusses the question at length and then summarizes: "God makes man a vessel; man makes himself an evil vessel, or a sinner; God determines to make man, according to conditions satisfactory to himself a vessel of wrath or of mercy, and this he in fact does, when the condition is either fulfilled or perseveringly neglected." [21]

What, then, is the message of Romans 9? It is the message of justification by faith. It is the message of the freedom of God's mercy, whereby he alone determines who shall be saved, namely, the believer. This is an affirmation of predestination: God has predestined to salvation all who believe in Christ. Arminius stands firmly in the tradition of Reformed theology in insisting that salvation is by grace alone and that human ability or merit must be excluded as a cause of salvation. It is faith in Christ alone that places a sinner in the company of the elect.

Arminius closed his letter to Snecanus with a poem, which William Nichols, admitting that his version is "neither sublime nor pathetic," renders thus:

> If any man will show to me
> That I with Paul do not agree,
> With readiness I will abstain
> From my own sense, and *his* retain:
> But if, still further, one will show
> That I've dealt faith a deadly blow,
> With deepest grief my fault I'll own,
> And try my error to atone.[22]

WHAT WAS HAPPENING in the 1590s is that the Calvinists, seeking to impose their theology on the Dutch churches, ran into constant resistance from the older Reformers and their sympathizers. Snecanus and Arminius were not alone in their refusal to capitulate to the pressures of Beza and his disciples in Holland. The controversy which was beginning to flare in many quarters now caused some consternation among the more "orthodox" Calvinists themselves, who found their colleagues taking positions which seemed to them to be too extreme to be defended.

[20] Augustine, *Against Two Letters of the Pelagians,* Book 2, chap. 13 [vii].
[21] *Writings,* III, 558.
[22] *WA,* III, 519.

One who had misgivings about the extremism of Beza's disciples was a professor of theology at Leiden, Franciscus Junius.

Junius (François du Jon) was born at Bourges on May 1, 1545, one of nine children of a local nobleman. He studied at Bourges, Lyons, and Geneva, where he matriculated on March 17, 1562 (while Calvin was yet living). In 1565 he accepted a call to be the pastor of the secret Reformed church in Antwerp. He was associated with Marnix and Gillies le Clercq in a committee for spreading political and religious literature—for which the authorities put a price of 300 guilders on his head. He fled to Breda only a half hour before his house was raided, and he was one of the first Reformed ministers there. He was forced by circumstances to be much on the move for the next few years, during which time he produced numerous writings. In 1584 he became a professor and doctor of theology at Heidelberg. In 1592 he returned to the Low Countries to be a professor of theology at Leiden. His was an irenic voice amid the more strident controversialists, as evidenced in his *La Paisible Chrestien, ou de la paix de l'Eglise Catholique. Comment il faut garder sainctement la paix, la nourrir, et entretenir, mesmes en la diversité et difference d'opinions* (Leiden, 1593). He finished out his career at Leiden in spite of invitations to be a minister at La Rochelle, a professor at Geneva, and a professor at the new university of Franeker.[23]

It was through a matter of family circumstance that Arminius first met Junius. Arminius' erstwhile colleague in Amsterdam, Johannes Cuchlinus, had gone to Leiden in 1592 to be regent of the *Statencollege* of the university. In 1596, on December 10, he was married in Leiden for the fifth (and last) time. His bride, the widow of Govert Dircksz. Steencop, was Geertje Jacobsdr., the sister of Arminius' father Harmen Jacobsz. Cuchlinus now was to become Arminius' uncle by marriage! Arminius went to the wedding, and there he struck up a friendship with Junius. He learned that Junius was proposing some revisions of Beza's predestination theory, and this pleased Arminius. They agreed to carry on the discussion by letter and to keep the correspondence confidential lest it cause trouble in the church.[24]

Arminius began the correspondence with a statement of his views about the position taken by Junius (the English translation runs about

---

[23] On Junius see *BWPGN*, IV, 604-16, and *GPCH*, I, 73 *et passim*.

[24] The family circumstance is worthy of note. The registry of the marriage indicates only the bride's name, her birthplace of Oudewater, her late husband's name, and her previous residence in Dordrecht and Rotterdam (*Huwelijksaantekeningen*, December 10, 1596 [C. 173]). That she was Arminius' paternal aunt is known from a letter he wrote to Uitenbogaert on February 7, 1597, telling of the matter with Junius. He speaks of *meae amitae* (*Ep. Ecc.*, no. 19).

twelve pages). Junius divided Arminius' missive into twenty-eight parts, an introduction and twenty-seven propositions. To each of these he wrote a reply, considerably longer than the propositions themselves. Junius, as was the custom with Leiden professors then and now, had students living in his home. With one of them he shared this correspondence, and the student took advantage of the situation to copy it out and show it to his fellow students. News of this reached Arminius, who felt that the agreement of confidence had been violated. He accordingly took the twenty-eight replies of Junius and wrote to each of them an even longer reply. Junius never answered, the reason unknown. Partisans of Arminius liked to say that he didn't because he couldn't. It is just as well; the correspondence as it stands now runs some 250 pages.

The material was edited after Arminius' death and published in the separate sections, each beginning with a proposition by Arminius, followed by the reply of Junius, and that followed by the comments of Arminius.[25] The introductory epistle signed by "the nine orphan children" of Arminius (but probably not written by any of them), addressed to the rulers of the Province of Utrecht, complains about Junius' failure to answer Arminius' comments. It states also that Arminius "increased and amplified" the material after the death of Junius. This probably refers to Arminius' addition of twenty theses on predestination which Junius had published in 1593. On each of these Arminius makes short comments. In the preface of the Dutch editor (identity unknown) Junius comes in for some rather bitter criticism—"how curiously he examines all things, how speciously he distinguishes, how shrewdly he shuns some points, how dexterously he dissimulates." [26] From this one might suppose that there was considerable bitterness between Arminius and Junius, but this does not seem to be the case. Arminius praises Junius highly in a letter to Uitenbogaert,[27] and there is evidence to suggest, in spite of allegations to the contrary, that Junius in his last days was not averse to seeing Arminius appointed to a professorship at Leiden.[28]

Junius draws back from a full supralapsarianism, which in the hands of Beza had really meant that predestination precedes not only the

[25] It was published in Leiden in Latin in 1613 by Godefridus Basson under the title of *Friendly Conference of James Arminius with Francis Junius about Predestination carried on by means of Letters.* It is included in the *Opera.*

[26] *WA*, III, 11. The dedication and preface, which are both in the *Opera,* are missing from the American translation by Bagnall. Bagnall's translation will be followed here for the main text, however, because of its more general accessibility.

[27] *Ep. Ecc.,* no. 19.

[28] *BWPGN,* IV, 612-13.

lapsus but also the *creatio*. It is the latter point that Junius avoids. He is willing to see the object of predestination to be man as created. As for the fall, he wishes to avoid a direct answer by saying that man is considered *in puris naturalibus*, "neutral-natured." [29] His position approaches that of Arminius in that it does not predetermine a man yet uncreated to a certain eternal destiny. It falls short of Arminius' position in that it does not refer predestination to man as a sinner. Arminius pointed out on the one hand that Junius' position was not that of Calvin and on the other that it still ran the difficulty of making God the author of sin. In the ninth proposition Arminius says:

I do not present as a matter of doubt the fact that God has elected some to salvation, and not elected or passed by [*praeterierit*] others, for I think that this is certain from the plain words of Scripture; but I place the emphasis on the subject of election and non-election;—Did God, in electing and not electing, have reference to men considered in their natural condition [*in puris naturalibus*]. I have not been able hitherto to receive this as truth.[30]

Junius replied that those who follow his position "have only desired that the contemplation of supervenient sin should not affect the case of election and reprobation, according to the declaration of the apostle, 'neither having done any good or evil' (Rom. 9:11), and according to those words *in puris naturalibus,* mean only the exclusion of any reference to supervenient sin from the case of election." [31]

Arminius affirms in turn what has been seen already in his *Analysis of Romans 9;* namely, that the object of predestination is man as sinner and that grace is an act or affection of God toward sinful man and no other. Arminius' eleventh proposition sums up his position:

Election is said to have been made in Christ, who was ordained as mediator for sinners, and was called Jesus because he should save not certain individuals considered merely *in pura natura* but "his people from their sins." He is said to have been foreordained, and we in him, and he, in the order of nature and causes, before us. He was ordained as Savior, we, as those to be saved. . . .
Election is said to have been made of grace, which is distinguished from nature in a two-fold manner, both as the latter is pure and considered abstractly, and as it is guilty and corrupt. In the former sense it signifies the progress of goodness towards supernatural good, to be imparted to a creature naturally capable of it. In the latter sense it signifies the ulterior progress towards supernatural good to be communicated to man as corrupt and guilty, which is also in the Scripture called mercy. In my judgment the term grace is used in the latter sense in the writings of the apostles, especially when the

[29] The term is found in Thomas Aquinas, who used it to indicate a state where grace and all supernatural gifts are absent.
[30] *Writings,* III, 94.
[31] *Ibid.,* pp. 94-95.

subject of discussion is election, justification, sanctification, etc. If this is true, then election of grace was made of men considered not in a merely natural state but in sin.[32]

Junius objects to this argument, denying that Christ is mediator only for sinners. Christ is the head of all creation, including nonsinful angels, for example, and he is the mediator of all creation. He is head by reason of our relation to him, and he is mediator by reason of our relation through him to the Father. The two facts are really one fact: to be head is to be mediator. Christ is both, and to all creation. Therefore, the grace of God in Christ is given to all in neutral nature, not to sinners only.

Arminius replies that nonsinners stand in no need of a reconciler and redeemer, that Christ was not considered by God as a mediator of redemption except as he was appointed such for those who sinned, and that the election of men by God is not made except in a mediator. His chief complaint about Junius' position is that it, no less than Calvin's or Beza's, introduces the necessity of sinning in order that the decree of election may be executed. This, in effect, makes God the author of sin. If man considered *in puris naturalibus* is elected and reprobated— that is, predestined to be redeemed from sin and predestined to be punished for sin—sin must necessarily intervene between the decree and its execution. Sin cannot be committed except by one who is both subject to the law and able to perform it. "But it could not be committed, of necessity and with certainty, by a free and contingent cause (which could commit sin or refrain from it), if it was not circumscribed and determined by a more powerful agent surely and with certainty moving or impelling the cause, in its own nature free and contingent, to the act of sin, or else withholding or withdrawing that which was necessary to the avoidance of sin."[33] Thus God, by leaving the creature in his own nature (in which sin necessarily follows), determines that the creature must sin. Therefore, God is the author of sin.

Junius concludes his answer to Arminius with an appeal in the irenic spirit for which he was noted:

I have thus, my brother, in this subject, used the diligence and promptitude which was possible in view of the duties which have not rarely interrupted me. Receive my effort with kindness, if it may not answer your expectation. May the God of truth and peace seal on your mind that saving peace more and more and graciously guide both of us and all his servants in the way of truth to his own glory and to the edification of his church in Christ Jesus our Savior. Amen.[34]

[32] *Ibid.*, pp. 133-34.
[33] *Ibid.*, p. 220.
[34] *Ibid.*, pp. 260-61.

Arminius concludes his "reply to the reply" in a similar spirit but with obviously more relish for prolonging the debate:

I have thus presented my objections to your answers to my propositions not so much with the thought of refuting them as with a desire to elicit from you more extended answers and explanations by which I might perhaps be satisfied and my mind freed from its difficulties on this subject. I, therefore, beseech God that if I have written anything contrary to the truth, he may pardon me concerning it and may reveal the truth unto me; if I have advanced anything agreeable to the truth, that he will confirm me in it, and that he will grant to me yourself, assenting to my views and aiding me, that, by means of you, the truth may daily gain greater authority.[35]

Quite apart from the content of the arguments in the correspondence, one gets the impression of Arminius as a dogged controversialist. Junius, in this case the gentler spirit, never quite answers Arminius' questions.

THE CORRESPONDENCE with Junius probably took place in 1597. The next year Arminius wrote a letter to Uitenbogaert which should be numbered with his theological works, although it has appeared in print only in the *Praestantium ac eruditorum virorum epistolae ecclesiasticae et theologicae*.[36] There are about fifty extant letters of Arminius to Uitenbogaert, and most of them deal with theological matters. This one, coming in the aftermath of the correspondence with Junius, takes on special interest, for it shows Arminius to be aggressively pursuing the matter of predestination.

Except for brief personal words at the beginning and end, it is a series of Ramist charts probing the logical possibilities regarding predestination. Such charts had begun to appear in the early 1590s. Johannes Piscator may have been the first to make use of such a visual aid, and they were used also by the Cambridge theologian William Perkins.[37] Arminius first puts forth all the possible combinations of "possible, not possible, certain, not certain" with "to be saved, not to be saved, to be damned, not to be damned." He then works out a table of agreements, showing how they agree or differ with each other with respect to the reprobate and the elect. This takes up some seven charts. Then he makes some comments, and a few of the comments will serve to illustrate his logic at work:

Nothing pertains at the same time to both the elect and the reprobate as such, for in this they are distinguished from each other. But although it is not con-

---

[35] *Ibid.*, pp. 261-62.
[36] *Ep. Ecc.*, no. 26. The manuscript is in the Remonstrant collection housed in the University of Amsterdam, R. K., III E, 1 7.
[37] Breward, p. 71.

tradictory to hold together "possible to be saved," "to be saved," and "certain to be saved," it is not proper to describe the elect as "possible to be saved," for not enough is thus said when they are actually "certain to be saved."

Then more charts. He is concerned to distinguish between what can be said about the elect and the reprobate *qua* man from what can be said about them *qua* elect, etc. It is, in fact, a pastoral necessity.

From this it is clear enough how circumspectly one must speak before the common people about this matter, for they do not know how to distinguish between these aspects. . . . Thus there can only be an upsetting of the mind tending toward desperation if what is said about the reprobate *qua* reprobate be understood as said about man *qua* man. Or it can tend toward a dangerous complacency if what is affirmed about the elect *qua* elect is affirmed about man *qua* man.

At the end he raises some leading questions, such as "whether providence acts in all this equally toward men, generally and individually, at least so that all and each are able or could be able to be saved and not damned," and "if the decree of providence denies some men sufficient and necessary means for salvation, how can these men be justly damned?" And he makes a significant remark in passing. "For it is our presupposition that no one is saved except through an act of predestination." Arminius is never caught in the denial of the presupposition, but he doggedly seeks to understand what it means.

On March 3, 1599, Arminius wrote another letter to Uitenbogaert which was in fact a theological treatise, and this one was included in the *Opera,* where it is entitled *A Letter on the Sin against the Holy Ghost.*[38] Uitenbogaert had been planning to preach on this subject to his congregation in The Hague, and he had written to Arminius asking for help. Arminius' reply is noteworthy partly for his own reticence and hesitation. "I know that my contemplations on this question are such as cannot satisfy you, since, in fact, they are not much approved by myself." [39] His analysis of the problem and of the possible answers is, as usual, lengthy and complex. He does arrive at a succinct answer. In isolation from the arguments it is lacking in full meaning, but it is offered here as an example of Arminius' work when he is not caught up in controversy with predestinarian opponents.

The sin against the Holy Ghost is the rejection and refusing of Jesus Christ through determined malice and hatred against Christ, who, through the testifying of the Holy Spirit, has been assuredly acknowledged for the Son of God (or, which is the same thing, the rejection and refusing of the acknowledged

[38] *Ep. Ecc.,* no. 45.
[39] *Writings,* II, 511.

universal truth of the gospel), against conscience and committed for this purpose: that the sinner may fulfill and gratify his desire of the apparent good which is by no means necessary, and may reject Christ.[40]

It is a clear piece of writing throughout, but important now primarily as a period piece, as when he deals with Uitenbogaert's question: "Have Cain, Saul, Judas, Julian, Francis Spira, etc., perpetrated this crime?" Arminius answers no for Cain, no for Saul, yes for Judas, yes for Julian, and no for Francis Spira.[41]

[40] *Ibid.*, pp. 528-29.
[41] *Ibid.*, pp. 533-36.

15

THEOLOGY IN AMSTERDAM: THE *EXAMINATION* OF *PERKINS' PAMPHLET*

ARMINIUS produced one more major writing during his Amsterdam ministry; in fact, it is in many respects his most important single composition. The story behind it crosses over to England and opens up the whole question of the relationship of English Arminianism to Dutch Arminianism. That question itself lies beyond the scope of this book, but the circumstances behind Arminius' *Examination of Perkins' Pamphlet on the Order and Mode of Predestination* will bear upon it.

England was not unacquainted with the controversy over predestination. In 1555, some four years before the birth of Arminius, there had developed a polarity among the Marian exiles in Frankfurt—Puritans all, indeed, but with tendencies which would diverge and grow farther apart. The leaders were John Knox and William Whittington, on one side, and Richard Cox and John Jewel, on the other. A. G. Dickens calls them "Genevan Puritans" and "Prayer Book Puritans" respectively, and he sees them not yet participating in but foreshadowing the dichotomy within the Church of England between Erastian prelatists and Calvinists which would be so divisive by the end of the sixteenth century and on into the seventeenth.[1] Between the foreshadowing and the fulfillment there would be a crystallizing of positions on both sides, the "Coxians" drawing nearer to the defense of the Prayer Book and the "Knoxians" drawing nearer to Presbyterianism and Calvinism. The issue of predestination would become entwined in matters of politics, and the Prayer Book party would support the prerogatives of the supreme magistrate, the Crown, in the government of the church.

The issue of predestination itself had arisen in England also at an early date. Among the prisoners in England during the Marian persecution were some men who came to be called "Free-Willers"—John Trewe,

---

[1] A. G. Dickens, *The English Reformation*, p. 292.

Henry Hart, John Kemp, M. Gybson, Chamberlain, and Abingdon. John Strype reports that "they were men of strict and holy lives, but very hot in their opinions and disputations and unquiet." [2] Another prisoner, John Bradford, took the predestinarian side. He appealed for support to Archbishop Cranmer, Bishop Ridley, and Bishop Latimer, who were also in prison. He did not hear from Cranmer and Latimer, and Ridley gave him a discouraging reply. The turbulence of the times prevented sustained debate, and the tracts of Trewe and Bradford were not published until 1819. Trewe's objections to Calvinist teaching on predestination are markedly similar to those raised much later by Arminius.[3] While it may be true, as O. T. Hargrave maintains, that no direct connection can be established between the Free-Willers and later English Arminianism, the significance of the existence of this early dissent from Calvinism cannot be denied. Hargrave is correct in asserting that they anticipated the Arminianism of a half-century later.[4]

The controversy was to break out with clarity in Cambridge in the 1590s. Cambridge had become a stronghold of Calvinist, Puritan sentiment, especially in the person of William Perkins. Perkins (1558-1602) was perhaps the first important English theologian since the Reformation. He was a moderate Puritan, a moral theologian of considerable importance, an Erastian in polity, and a predestinarian in soteriology. His teaching on predestination did not go unchallenged, however, for another professor took sharp exception to Perkins. Peter Baro (1534-1599), a native of France and a licentiate in the University of Bourges, had fled to England and in about 1574 had been elected to Peterhouse and appointed Lady Margaret Professor of Divinity. In that capacity he had resisted the Calvinism of William Whitaker, Richard Vaughan, and Perkins. So bitter did the controversy become that a student of Baro's, William Barrett, was denied the B.D. degree in 1595 because he would not accept Perkins' views on predestination. That was the year that the Lambeth Articles were drawn up in an attempt to commit the Church of England to strict Calvinism. Baro criticized the articles, and in 1596 he was forced to resign and move to London.

At the time of this trouble, which from his point of view could be viewed only as persecution, he wrote a letter to a friend and ally, Nicholas Hemingius, professor of theology at Copenhagen. Hemingius, who was highly esteemed by Arminius, had been a student of Melanchthon and has been accused by his Danish Lutheran colleagues of being a crypto-Calvinist in his views of the Lord's Supper. He had,

[2] Strype, *Memorials of Thomas Cranmer*, I, 502.
[3] Cf. *WA*, I, 648-55.
[4] "The Freewillers in the English Reformation."

however, opposed Calvinistic predestination theories. "Do the elect believe, or are the believers elect?" he had asked.[5]

Baro enclosed with his letter to Hemingius (of April 1, 1596) an analysis of "three opinions concerning predestination" which set forth arguments and conclusions almost precisely the same as Arminius would advance in his *Declaration of Sentiments* in 1608. When Baro died in London three years later, there was a magnificent funeral procession attended by all the London clergy. Why this honor to a discredited ex-professor from Cambridge? In 1599 the ailing Archbishop Whitgift, who had supported the Calvinist cause, turned over his administrative duties to the Bishop of London, Richard Bancroft, a nonpredestinarian, conservative, Prayer Book churchman. Thus the power was shifting back to the non-Puritan, non-Calvinist element prefigured by Cranmer, Hooker, and even Cox. Bancroft, at the Hampton Court Conference of 1604, was able to resist the efforts to append the Calvinist Lambeth Articles to the Thirty-nine Articles. Dickens observes that this and other events at the time marked "the undermining of the Anglo-Puritan dominance and the recovery of a medial tradition, which eschewed the rigours of orthodox Calvinism, deprecated bibliolatry, stressed the role of reason in interpreting the Christian Faith, and resisted the demands for changes in liturgy, church-government and the Articles." [6] This tradition in England would later be called "Arminianism."

In the meantime Perkins, a prolific writer, was writing a book on predestination. It was an attack on an earlier book critical of predestination. The earlier book and who wrote it are unknown, but it is probable that Baro was the author. The book in question may even have been Baro's letter to Hemingius. Perkins' book was published first in 1598 in Cambridge under the title *De praedestinationis mode et ordine,* and it was published again in 1599 in Basel as *De praedestinationis mode et ordine: et de amplitudine gratiae divinae.* While Perkins wanted to make the doctrine of predestination more "reasonable" than it is in Calvin, his logical rigor drove him to a supralapsarian point of view in which the creation and fall become means for carrying out the prior decree of election or damnation. He went so far as to say that "no good thing can be done unless God doth absolutely will and work it" and "no evil can be avoided unless God do hinder it." The will of God is known, he said, "not only by the written word, or by revelation, but by the event. For that which cometh to pass doth therefore come to pass because God hath willed that it come to pass." [7]

---

[5] Quoted in James Nichols, *Calvinism and Arminianism Compared in their Principles and Tendency,* p. i.

[6] Dickens, p. 314.

[7] Perkins, *Works,* II, 605.

Arminius bought the book eagerly, for he was an admirer of Perkins, but he read it with dismay. He took pen in hand to write to Perkins: "I thought I perceived some passages of yours which deserved examination by the rule of truth. Wherefore I deemed that it would not be amiss if I should institute a calm conference with you respecting that little book of yours." [8] He then proceeded to volunteer his comments on the pamphlet—over two hundred pages in the English translations. Before he could finish them and send them to Perkins for a reply, Perkins died, in 1602. The manuscript lay dormant until after Arminius' death. It was published in 1612 in Leiden by Godefridus Basson. Both it and the complete text of Perkins' pamphlet were issued in Dutch translation in Gouda in 1617 (just before the Synod of Dort), and it was included in the Latin *Opera*.

The *Examination of Perkins' Pamphlet* is perhaps the most difficult of Arminius' writings. It follows the course of Perkins' theses, which in turn had been an attack on the earlier work (of Baro?). (It is significant that the position which Perkins attacks is always defended by Arminius. There is no evidence that Baro, if he were the author, knew the work of Arminius.) Arminius goes to it with a barrage of analyses and arguments about sentences, phrases, words, and even grammatical constructions. He plays the new game of logic to the full. No stone is left unturned to show where Perkins is, in Arminius' opinion, unbiblical, inconsistent, ambiguous, deceived, or otherwise in error. In the midst of the complexity and disorder of this incoherent document, however, are the most complete ingredients of Arminius' doctrines of grace. The arguments are worked out in greater detail here than in his later academic disputations in Leiden. It is the basic document of Arminianism.

To follow the course of the contents of the *Examination* would duplicate the stylistic difficulties of the original. It will be sufficient to present some of the principal theological positions it contains. The translation by William Nichols will be followed.

Grace applies to man as sinner. Arminius reiterates and emphasizes what he had affirmed in his earlier writings, that evangelical grace has to do with man as sinner. Perkins had begun his pamphlet with this definition of predestination: "Predestination is the counsel of God touching the last end or estate of man out of this temporal or natural life." [9] Arminius objects to this for a number of reasons, foremost of which is the point in question. He counters by pointing out that "the predestination of which the Scriptures treat is of men as they are sinners." [10]

[8] *WA*, III, 266.
[9] *Works*, II, 606.
[10] *WA*, III, 274-75.

It includes the means by which those who are predestined will be "certainly and infallibly" saved, "but those means are the remission of sins and the renewing of the Holy Ghost and his perpetual assistance even to the end, which means are necessary and communicable to none but sinners." [11] Predestination must then refer to sinners, and it has its ground only in Christ. "Since God can love to salvation [*ad salutem amate possit*] no one who is a sinner unless he be reconciled to himself in Christ, it follows that predestination cannot have place except in Christ." But Christ was given for sinners, so that "it is certain that predestination and its opposite, reprobation, could not have had place before the sin of man,—I mean, foreseen by God,—and before the appointment of Christ as Mediator, and moreover before his discharging, in the foreknowledge of God, the office of Mediator, which appertains to reconciliation." [12]

Does Perkins make God the author of sin? If grace is not thus restricted, God is in effect the author of sin, says Arminius. The point is raised in connection with the question of the divine permission. Unless the fall is a free act, not predetermined by the predestinating will of God, the divine permission is nothing but the divine will, which means that God wills sin. Perkins had said that the fall is "permitted" by God but that it "comes to pass only by God willing it." [13] Arminius asks in reply "how God can at once *will* the fall to happen, and *permit* the same; how God makes use of his volition about the fall both mediately and immediately; mediately by willing the permission, immediately by willing the fall itself." In other words, Arminius wants to kmow "how the fall can happen by God willing it, and the will of God not be the cause of the fall." [14]

Perkins had made certain distinctions: that God wills the fall not as it is sin but as it is a means of illustrating his glory; that he wills it not by his revealed will, but by the will of his good pleasure—his hidden will. Arminius rejects these distinctions as useless subtleties, for he sees in them no escape from the fact that whatever God wills he effects, and if he wills sin, no matter under what species, he effects sin.

Arminius felt that one major point of confusion in Perkins was his doctrine of "permission." Arminius dealt with the question at great length in a section which William Nichols in his translation has subtitled "Arminius's Treatise on Permission." It offers a definition of permission in general: "An act of the will by which the permitting party

[11] *Ibid.*, p. 278.
[12] *Ibid.*, pp. 278-79.
[13] Quoted *ibid.*, p. 287.
[14] *Ibid.*, p. 288.

suspends any efficiency within his power, by the exercise of which any act of his to whom permission is granted would be circumscribed or actually stopped, to perform which act the latter has inclination and strength sufficient." God's permission, then, "is an act of the divine will whereby God suspends any efficiency possible to him, whether by right or by ability or in both ways, which efficiency, if it were made use of by God, would either circumscribe or actually prevent a certain act of the rational creature for the performance of which act the same creature has inclination and strength sufficient." [15] The permission of God, however, is threefold: "one by which God makes any act a matter of choice for the rational creature, not binding it by law; a second, by which he permits an act to the ability of the creature; a third, by which he permits an act to the affection and will of the creature." [16]

God's permission of sin is not according to the first mode, for sin is forbidden by the law. The divine permission of sin must be in a mode which is a suspension of impediments which prohibit sin. Those impediments are the revelation of the divine will and the persuasion to obey that will. The divine permission of sin is the suspension of either or both. But God does not thereby will sin. One must not say that God performs "no act sufficient for the hindrance of sin, when sin is actually not prevented." Nor should one say that God unwillingly permits sin, when God produces acts sufficient for preventing sin which occurs. Arminius concludes: "For the sole consideration of efficacious prevention, by the suspension of which permission is properly and adequately defined, causes us to perceive that God neither wills sins, on account of some impediments being employed which are not efficacious, nor yet unwillingly permits sin, because, besides those sufficient hindrances, he possesses efficacious ones also in the storehouse of his wisdom and power, by bringing which forth sin might be surely and infallibly prevented." [17]

There are two general reasons for God permitting anything, including sin. One is "the liberty of the will [*libertas voluntatia*], of which God made the rational creature a partaker." The other is "the display of the divine perfection." At this point Arminius picks up a classical theme about God's overruling of evil. The divine perfection is such "that it cannot only effect and hinder anything for his own glory, but also so reduce to order the acts of rational creatures which are permitted, and which often go much beyond the bounds of the order prescribed and laid down for them, that wisdom, justice, and power may shine out

[15] *Ibid.*, p. 390.
[16] *Ibid.*, p. 397.
[17] *Ibid.*, p. 399.

far more brightly." In support of this Arminius quotes Augustine's dictum that "God judged that it was the province of his most omnipotent goodness rather to produce good from evils than not to allow evils to be." [18]

The extent of election. Another way to come at these problems is to ask about the extent of God's election. Has God elected everyone, or has God elected only some? Arminius tries to steer between Pelagianism and necessitarianism. He denies what many of his critics and some of his friends have alleged that he held—that there is a universal election to salvation. Perkins had alleged that to say, "God wills all men to be saved if they believe, and to be condemned if they do not believe," involves both a universal election and a universal reprobation.[19] Arminius replies that, on the contrary, it involves the particular election of believers and the particular reprobation of unbelievers.

This is to say that saving grace is not universal. Saving grace is given only to those who are saved, and only those who believe are saved. Arminius shows here how close to Calvin he is: men are not saved because they will to be saved; they are saved because they are those whom God has predestined to save—that is, believers. But Calvin did not make the last point clear. Arminius says:

In Rom. 9:6, where it is said, "Not of him that willeth nor of him that runneth, but of God that showeth mercy,"—"righteousness" is understood. For it is there argued concerning those to whom righteousness is properly imputed, not working, but believing: that is, it is not he that wills, or he that runs, who obtains righteousness, but he to whom God has determined to show mercy, that is, the believer. The passage, Mt. 13:11, proves that the same grace is not given to all.[20]

Common grace and peculiar grace. Who then can be saved? Is this not simply predestinarian high Calvinism? If saving grace is given only to a few, what has happened to universal salvation? Arminius speaks to these issues when he criticizes the distinction between "common grace" and "peculiar grace" (or "special grace") and when he makes a distinction between salvation as sufficient and salvation as applied.

Perkins had distinguished between common grace and peculiar grace. Common grace is that which is common to believers and others who repudiate the same grace; that is, it is the grace which is shared by the elect and the nonelect. Peculiar grace, by contrast, is that operative, ef-

[18] *Ibid.*, p. 408.
[19] Quoted *ibid.*, p. 441.
[20] *Ibid.*, pp. 449-50.

fectual grace which is given only to those who had been predestined to receive it. Perkins had said that "God will not have to be praised if men should embrace the blessing even by the help of common grace," [21] meaning that man, by embracing salvation without the aid of peculiar grace, would have contributed something of merit to his salvation.

In his logical rigor Perkins is both faithful to Calvin and unfaithful. Calvin had spoken of two kinds of calling, universal and special:

There is the general call, by which God invites all equally to himself through the outward preaching of the word—even those to whom he holds it out as a savor of death [cf. II Cor. 2:16], and as the occasion for severer condemnation. The other kind of call is special, which he deigns for the most part to give to the believers alone, while by the inward illumination of his Spirit he causes the preached Word to dwell in their hearts.[22]

It is that phrase "for the most part" [*ut plurimum*] which marks off Calvin from his more rigorous disciples. Calvin, in fact, goes on to say of the special call that "sometimes he also causes those whom he illumines only for a time to partake of it; then he justly forsakes them on account of their ungratefulness and strikes them with even greater blindness." [23] Arminius would agree thoroughly.

Perkins, then, like Plancius, like Franciscus Gomarus at Leiden, retained a position more logical, more rigorous, than Calvin's. If the believer embraces salvation by means of a kind of grace which is not always effective, he is meriting salvation. Arminius asks:

Who has merited that the blessing should be offered to himself? Who has merited that any grace whatsoever should be conferred on himself? . . . Do not all these things proceed from the gratuitous divine favor? . . How does it affect this matter to any great extent whether a man has embraced the offered blessing by the aid of common grace or by the aid of peculiar, if both the one and the other have gained by his free assent [*adsensum liberum*] and were foreknown by God as certainly about to gain it? . . . Peculiar grace ought so to be explained as that it may be consistent with free will [*libero arbitrio*], and that common grace is so to be explained that men may by its repudiation be held worthy of condemnation and God be shown to be averse from injustice.[24]

If these qualifications are maintained, Arminius is saying, the distinction between common and peculiar grace breaks down. What is needed is a different distinction, between salvation as sufficient and salvation as applied. Perkins had said that Christ had not died for every

[21] Quoted *ibid.*, p. 445.
[22] *Institutes*, 3.24.8.
[23] *Ibid.*
[24] *WA*, III, 445.

man, but only for the elect, and he supported his position with this syllogism:

The expiatory victim sanctifies those for whom it is a victim; for the victim
  and the sanctification appertain to the same persons:
But Christ sanctifies only the elect and believers:
Therefore Christ is the victim for the elect and believers only.[25]

Arminius replies that a distinction must be made between the offering of the victim (referring to Hebrews 9:13-14) and the application of the benefits, or between salvation provided and salvation applied. He says:

Between the oblation . . . and the application or sanctification, it is necessary for faith to intervene. Wherefore the offering up of the victim was made not for believers, but for men as sinners; yet with this condition, that it does not sanctify any but those who believe in Christ.[26]

Here, then, is a universal salvation and a particular salvation. The offering up of Christ is salvation provided, sufficient, or, as Arminius puts it, "recovered" [recuperatio]. When faith intervenes, the blood of the victim is sprinkled (to use the language of Hebrews); or, as Arminius puts it, salvation is efficacious and applied. The first is the oblation; the second, the sanctification. The first is universal; the second, restricted. But in it all there is one kind of grace, not two.

What about "faith intervening"? What is the "cause" of the faith? Are all men able to believe? Is the ability to believe a native ability, an inherent goodness, an act of a will which is free to do the good, a good work, an act of merit?

Perkins had taken the position that the "promise of the Messiah" or the offer of salvation made by God and the "commandment to believe" are to be distinguished, and that the command is more general than the promise. To this Arminius takes sharp exception:

In this . . . assertion you are, in my opinion, mistaken. For the promise, as made, and the command to believe, extend equally widely. For if the promise is not made to all to whom the command is given to believe, then the command is unjust, vain, and useless. Unjust, for it requires from that that he have faith in the promise,—not general faith [fidem generalem], that it belongs to others, but special faith [fidem specialem], that the promise was made even to himself. This command is vain, for it is concerning nothing, for it commands to believe but presents no object of faith. Whence the command itself is also useless, for in no way can it be performed by him to whom the promise as made does not belong.[27]

[25] Quoted ibid., p. 335.
[26] Ibid., p. 336.
[27] Ibid., p. 307.

Thus there is given a universal command to which obedience is possible. But the possibility is a possibility of grace, not of works, and the obedience is faith, not earning.

Arminius urges the same point in another way: that God wills nothing contrary to his command. The command to believe cannot be reconciled with the divine predestination of someone who cannot believe. The reprobation, on the contrary, is the consequence of the nonobedience to the command, to a real command.[28]

Does Arminius make man the author of salvation? Back to the earlier question: If all men are able to believe, and if their election or reprobation turns on their decision (a word Arminius does not use) to believe or not to believe, does not then man elect himself, and is this not Pelagianism? The objection can be put another way: If Perkins, speaking for supralapsarianism, is guilty of making God the author of sin (as Arminius alleges), is not Arminius guilty of making man the author of salvation?

Perkins had argued that if there is only one kind of grace, and if this grace can be accepted or rejected by the same man, "sin, Satan, the world, death, and hell are more mighty than Christ the Redeemer." [29] Arminius counters by pointing out that "in the first place, they could not prevent Christ from offering himself to the Father as a sacrifice, from obeying the Father, and undergoing death," thereby obtaining reconciliation and redemption. It is indeed true that sin and Satan hinder many from believing in Christ, "yet God is not 'overcome' thereby." Why? Because it is God's free decision not to bring men to faith by an irresistible act.[30] But does not man still *elect* himself? What, precisely, is it that man *does* to be one of the elect? Does he make an act of free will?

The place of free will. Arminius moves here with an obliqueness which indicates his unwillingness to go too far toward either the denial of free will or a Pelagian affirmation of it. Perkins had accused the author who is under attack of teaching that the will is capable of contrary choice. "This doctrine," he said, "attributes to every man a free will, flexible to either side by grace [*liberum arbitrium flexibile in utramque partem*]." [31] Arminius asks in reply whether free will is not flexible to either side even without grace, for it is the very meaning of free will to be flexible. But, he adds, free will in man as sinner is "addicted to evil," and "it will not be bent to good except by grace." Grace is as a

[28] Cf. *ibid.*, pp. 318 ff.
[29] Quoted *ibid.*, p. 447.
[30] *Ibid.*, pp. 447-48.
[31] Quoted *ibid.*, p. 470.

form which brings into actuality the potentiality of the free will to goodness. In a sinful man the free will is sufficient for only evil choices. Thus Arminius says that "grace is present with all men, by which their free will may be actually bent to good; but that there is in all men such a will as is flexible to either side upon accession of grace." [32]

In sinful man free will is addicted to evil, but upon the accession of the grace of God that appears to all men it becomes flexible to either side. Grace rescues free will, but not without the choice of the will thus rescued. It is free will that is saved, and the saved free will concurs in its salvation. If it did not, it could not be said to be saved. "It is unavoidable that the free will should concur in preserving the grace bestowed, assisted, however, by subsequent grace, and it always remains within the power of the free will to reject the grace bestowed and to refuse subsequent grace, because grace is not an omnipotent action of God which cannot be resisted by man's free will." Perkins had charged this position with being Pelagianism. Arminius replies: "The Pelagians attributed the faculty of well-doing to nature wholly, or only in part to grace; but this doctrine attributes it entirely to grace." [33]

Perkins had also objected that to make one kind of grace universal is Pelagianism. Arminius replies by distinguishing between "the ability to believe" and "believing." "The ability to believe belongs to nature; believing, to grace." Thus it is incorrect to allege of this position, as Perkins had done, "that nature and grace are of equally wide extent." And to deny that man can resist grace is to go against Scripture. "Is man, then, a log which by mere and pure natural necessity assents to grace?" If not, then why the scriptural threats and promises? Arminius bursts out into an expression of weary but intense feeling: "I wish that those who now-a-day treat of the dogma of predestination would prove that their doctrine does not infer 'fatal necessity.' " [34]

The part man plays in salvation is believing. Evangelical belief is the free choice to receive offered grace, which offered grace makes the free choice possible. In all of this man does nothing apart from grace: he earns nothing; he contributes nothing; but he chooses freely, and it is a choice which he can refuse to make, for grace is not an irresistible force.

Falling from grace. Perkins raises a matter with which Arminius had not previously dealt. He charged his opposition with the necessity of saying that saving faith may be lost, or that a believer may fall from grace. In more recent language, Perkins upheld the doctrine of eternal security.

[32] *Ibid.*, pp. 470-71.
[33] *Ibid.*, p. 470.
[34] *Ibid.*, p. 482.

It was evidently a new issue with Arminius, and he approaches it cautiously. He says that it is an open question, and that Perkins has not settled it. "I should not readily dare to say that true and saving faith may finally and totally fall away, although several of the Fathers often seem to affirm that." [35] What he does not "readily dare to say" he is quite willing to probe, however, and at considerable length (seventeen pages in the English text) he gives detailed consideration to Perkins' arguments for eternal security, or the "perseverance of the saints." The discussion is very much a battle of proof texts, but students of this controversy in the intervening centuries will find the discussion illuminating, with some surprising turns in Arminius' arguments.

Perkins had proposed seven arguments for the doctrine of the perseverance of the saints. The first was based on Peter's confession and Christ's response to it, particularly the words, "On this rock I will build my church, and the powers of death shall not prevail against it" (Matthew 16:18). Taking the words quite literally, Perkins derived from them three proofs: (1) that if faith is a rock, it remains firm; (2) that the gates of hell will not prevail against it; and (3) that the promise of the passage is made to all who are built on the rock. Arminius responds in kind and charges that Perkins has used the word "faith" equivocally. Faith, says Arminius, means either Peter's confession about Christ or trust placed in that confession. In the former sense, faith is the rock which remains unshaken. In the latter sense, faith is inspired in believers by the Spirit and the word. And while believers are built on the rock, and the gates of hell shall not prevail against it, "it is one thing for the gates of hell not to prevail against the rock; quite another for those who are built upon the rock not to fall away from the rock." [36] Furthermore, says Arminius, falling away "does not take place on account of the power of hell, but by the will itself of the person who falls away." [37]

Perkins' second argument was based on Matthew 6:13 ("And lead us not into temptation, but deliver us from evil"); 10:32 ("So every one who acknowledges me before men, I also will acknowledge before my Father who is in heaven"); and 24:24 ("For false Christs and false prophets will arise and show great signs and wonders, so as to lead astray, if possible, even the elect"). To the argument that Christ provides deliverance from temptation to all who ask for it, Arminius replies that not all believers necessarily ask for it. To the argument that Christ acknowledges the elect, Arminius replies that "the elect" and "believers" are not convertible terms unless perseverance be added to faith. To

[35] *Ibid.*, p. 454.
[36] *Ibid.*
[37] *Ibid.*, p. 455.

the argument that believers cannot fall because the elect cannot be deceived, Arminius answers that being deceived is not the same as departing from Christ.[38]

In his third argument Perkins had held that entire defection from true faith would require a second ingrafting if the one thus defected should be saved. Arminius cites Romans 11:23, "God has the power to graft them in again." He also denies that rebaptism is necessary, "because baptism once conferred on anyone is a perpetual promise to him of grace and salvation, as often as he returns to Christ." [39]

Arminius finds Perkins' fourth argument the most convincing. It is based on I John 3:9, "No one born of God commits sin; for God's nature abides in him, and he cannot sin because he is born of God." Arminius appeals to Augustine, who referred the verse to those who are called according to the divine purpose and regenerated by the decree of divine predestination. Says Arminius: "If you affirm that it is here said respecting all who are born of God, that they sin not, and that the seed of God remains in them, I shall take the word 'remains' as signifying indwelling, but not the continuation of indwelling." As long as the seed remains in him, he does not sin unto death, but by degrees the seed may be taken out of his heart. "But this argument, I allow, is the strongest of all which can be adduced to this purpose." [40]

The rest of the arguments are similar in content and method. When Perkins appeals to the parable of the sower to prove that believers cannot fall from faith inasmuch as the seed sown in their hearts is immortal, Arminius says that the seed indeed may be immortal, but it can be removed, &c. Much the same sort of things goes on about the figure of the vine and the branches in John 15:2.

After presenting his arguments, Perkins had asked, "What is the cause why faith does not perish?" His answer: "That it is not from the nature of faith, but from the gift of confirming grace, which has been promised to believers." [41] Arminius again points out that the covenant of God (Jer. 23:4) "does not contain in itself an impossibility of defection from God, but a promise of the gift of fear, whereby they shall be hindered from going away from God so long as that shall flourish in their hearts." [42] Similar arguments are set forth around John 10:28, "No one shall snatch them out of my hand." The sheep can defect, says Arminius, and then they are seized by Satan.

[38] *Ibid.,* p. 456.
[39] *Ibid.*
[40] *Ibid.,* p. 457.
[41] Quoted *ibid.,* p. 458.
[42] *Ibid.*

218

Arminius had said earlier in his *Examination of Perkins' Pamphlet* that he "should not readily dare to say that true and saving faith may finally and totally fall away." At the end of the discussion, however, he takes a stand:

In the beginning of faith in Christ and conversion to God the believer becomes a living member of Christ; and, if persevering in the faith of Christ, and keeping a conscience void of offence, remains a living member. But if it happens that this member grows slothful, is not careful over itself, gives place to sin, by little and little it becomes half-dead; and so at length, proceeding still further, dies altogether, and ceases to be a member.[43]

Arminius continued to skirt this issue throughout his career. He dealt with it again during his Leiden years, and then he took a slightly different approach to the problem.

Divine foreknowledge of future faith. Arminius raises also the question of the divine foreknowledge of future faith or unbelief. In his later writings he deals with the question at great length, but even here his general position is evident. Both Perkins and Arminius, along with the overwhelming majority of theologians up to their time, assume such a foreknowledge. The issue between them turns on the relation of foreknowledge to predestination. Perkins had held that "election is not according to the foresight [*praescientia*] of faith, since the cause why God foresees faith in one man, and not in another, is the mere will of God, willing to bestow faith on the one, and not on the other." [44] In this Perkins was following Calvin when he said that God "foresees future events only by reason of the fact that he decreed that they take place." [45] Arminius answers that it is necessary to make a twofold distinction with respect to predestination itself. The predestination which is absolute and without respect to foreknowledge is this: that "believers shall be saved, unbelievers shall be damned." But when predestination is made to refer to individual men, one must "premise the foreknowledge of faith and of unbelief, not as a law and rule, but as properly precedent." [46] In other words, predestination of classes is absolute or without qualification; predestination of individuals is with respect to foreseen faith. It was at this point that Arminius' colleague in Leiden, Gomarus, would raise serious questions. The present-day theologian will raise still more.

---

[43] *Ibid.,* p. 470.
[44] Quoted *ibid.,* p. 453.
[45] *Institutes,* 3.23.6.
[46] *WA,* III, 451.

ARMINIUS the Amsterdam pastor was, in the quiet of his study, a thoroughgoing theologian, deeply enmeshed, on paper at least, in the battles which raged among the epigones of Calvin in the dawning new age of reason. His paperwork was not disconnected from his preaching. In many cases it was an elaboration of it. In other cases it was the probing of ideas which would provide the basis for preaching. It was the raising to self-consciousness of the dogmatics implicit in the early Dutch reformers such as Veluanus, Gerard Blokhoven, Coolhaes, Hermannus Herberts, Cornelis Wiggerts, Snecanus, and many of the merchant-reformers of Amsterdam. He had been able to develop his arguments in relative privacy. His exposition of Romans 7, an extension of his preaching to be sure, was not published. His exposition of Romans 9 was written to a sympathizer. His conference with Junius was relatively confidential. His letters to Uitenbogaert were to a bosom friend. Perkins died before Arminius could send the *Examination*.

In 1602, however, the days of privacy and confidentiality were coming to an end. Arminius would soon be thrust into the constantly public life of a professor. His theology would move from the study to the lecture hall and to the arena of national and international debate. His writings would become more precise, more systematic, often more guarded. Before turning to that new and final stage in his career, however, it will be useful to enumerate some of the fundamental ingredients of his thinking in 1602, as found in the *Examination of Perkins' Pamphlet*.

1. Evangelical grace is God's affection to man as sinner.

2. Predestination is subordinate to the appointing of Christ as mediator; believers are predestined *in Christ*.

3. To fail to restrict evangelical grace to sinful man is to make God the author of sin.

4. Sin is permitted by God in that he suspends the impediments which prohibit sin, but not in that he provides nothing sufficient for the hindrance of sin.

5. Saving grace is not universal; it is given only to those who believe.

6. The distinction between common grace and peculiar (special, efficient) grace is denied.

7. The necessity of a distinction between salvation as sufficient and salvation as applied is affirmed.

8. That which intervenes between sufficient salvation and applied salvation is faith.

9. The promise of salvation and the command to believe are of equal extent.

10. The act of believing is a choice of the free will which has been brought from its addiction to evil to a point of flexibility by grace.

11. The salvation of the free will by grace involves the choice of the free will, or else the free will could not be said to be saved.

12. This doctrine is not Pelagianism, for it attributes every good thing to grace and nothing to man apart from grace.

13. That believers may fall from true faith is a possibility that Perkins had not disproved.

14. By an absolute predestination God wills to save those who believe and to damn those who persevere in disobedience; by a conditional predestination God wills to save those individuals whom he foresees as believing and persevering and to damn those whom he foresees as not believing.

16

QUESTIONS OF CHURCH AND STATE

THE THEOLOGICAL ISSUES with which Arminius dealt in his Amsterdam writings were abstruse enough in his own time and may seem well-nigh beyond recovery for the modern reader. The final verification of theories about predestination must certainly lie in eternity. Arminius saw that there were practical, pastoral consequences of these theories, to be sure, but one may still ask what larger significance they had in the realm of time and history. The first decade of the seventeenth century was to see predestination theory merge with matters of grave practical concern in both church and state, and the decade after Arminius' death in 1609 was to see the whole nation embroiled in a bitter internal hostility over the complex of theological-political questions. The discussion would continue after 1619 and spill over into British theology and politics as well.[1] When Arminius disputed about the exegesis of Romans 7 and 9 and about the predestination of classes and individuals, the other issues were just under the surface. Before we move on to the events of his Leiden professorship, it will be helpful to show how this was so.

The ecclesiastical and political dimensions of Arminius' thinking about grace, sin, and predestination in his Amsterdam years may be indicated by a series of questions, each one leading to the next.

1. Did Arminius' views conform to the teachings of the Belgic Confession and the Heidelberg Catechism?

2. What authority did these two confessions have in the Dutch Church? What is the relation of confessional authority to scriptural authority?

3. By what synodical structure could authority be given to these formulas?

4. Had there been, in fact, a national synod with authority to adopt the confessions?

5. Could and should a new national synod be called?

6. For what purpose should it be called—to enforce conformity to

---

[1] That larger and later story is told well in Douglas Nobbs, *Theocracy and Toleration, a Study of the Disputes in Dutch Calvinism from 1600 to 1650.*

the confessions? To interpret the confessions? To revise the confessions?

7. By what authority can a national synod be called? By the church alone? By the ruler? By the States General?

8. What is the relation of church to state? Of church to ruler? What is the function of the ruler in the government of the church?

9. What is the doctrine of the church which functions in such decisions?

10. What shall be said about the ecclesiastical, political, and even spiritual status of dissenters from the official or dominant religion?

These are formal questions; materially, they were embedded in the actualities of changing structures of power, the rise of the East Indian trade, the war with Spain, divergent goals and ambitions of the military leader Prince Maurice and the civil leader Oldenbarnevelt, and leading personalities among clergy and laity in the church.

Arminius avoided a direct attack on the doctrinal formulas. They dated back to a time when the issues with which he was dealing had not been made fully explicit. Although he seems to show less attachment to the Confession and Catechism than do his opponents, he is unwilling to grant the weight of their (undetermined) authority to the supralapsarians. In later years he spoke to the issue directly. In Amsterdam he did not, and the task at hand is to see what the formulas said at the crucial, mooted points.

The Belgic Confession, Article 14, states that man "has willfully submitted himself to sin and thereby to death and the curse." [2] Arminius could appeal to this in support of his contention that sin is not necessitated by a divine decree, and he did so in 1608.[3] The same article speaks of false teaching about free will, "seeing that man is nothing but a slave of sin and has no receptivity or ability unless it is given him from heaven." Arminius could agree.

Article 16 deals with election.

We believe that whereas the whole posterity of Adam is fallen into ruin and damnation through the guilt of the first man, God showed himself to be such as he is, namely, merciful and just. Merciful, in that he delivers and saves out of this ruination those whom he in his eternal and unchangeable council, through his pure goodness, has foreseen [wtuersien] and chosen in Jesus Christ our Lord, without any consideration of their good works; and in that he leaves the others in their fall and ruin wherein they themselves have cast themselves.[4]

[2] My translation of the Dutch text of 1562 in Bakhuizen van den Brink, *Nederlandsche Belijdenisgeschriften*, p. 83. In order to avoid both anachronism and distortion of the issue I do not use here the text of the Synod of Dort (published in Latin in 1620, in Dutch in 1621) or other texts from after the period in question.
[3] *Writings*, I, 219.
[4] Bakhuizen van den Brink, *Nederlandsche Belijdenisgeschriften*, p. 89.

223

Arminius has not contradicted this article, but his writings do raise a question of interpretation. What is the referent of "those whom he . . . has . . . chosen"? The answer Arminius has given is that they are believers. If that interpretation be granted, he has no quarrel with the Confession.

The Heidelberg Catechism has even less about predestination, but Questions 20 and 54 are to the point:

20. Q. Will all men then be saved through Christ as they were lost through Adam?
   A. No, only all those who by an upright faith are incorporated into him and accept all his benefits.
54. Q. What do we believe about the universal Christian Church?
   A. That the Son of God has gathered, protected, and preserved for himself from the beginning of the world to the end, out of the whole human family, through his Spirit and Word, a community chosen to eternal life, in unity of the true faith, and that therefore I am and shall eternally remain a living member thereof.[5]

Question 20 seems to be well accommodated to Arminius' thesis that salvation is willed for the class of believers. Question 54 permits the interpretation and makes no specification of the mode of election. The question about Arminius' theology and the two formulas may well take another turn: not, Could the statements be stretched to accommodate Arminius' views? but, Could they be stretched to accommodate his opponents' views? It was, indeed, this second question which disturbed the upholders of the older and milder Dutch theology. Should not the confessions be revised to remove the ambiguities under which the supralapsarians took cover? In defense of this position it can be said again that the formulas were written before the issue of supralapsarianism had been raised, just as Calvin himself gives no clear answer as to whether he is supra- or sublapsarian. I conclude that Arminius felt himself to be in essential disagreement with the Confession and Catechism, that he made no attack on them, but that he was nevertheless not entirely pleased with them because of their ambiguity.

There was the related matter of the authority of the formulas. Were they binding on the Dutch churches? Here there was even greater ambiguity. Had there been a national synod with authority to make them binding? The synods at Wesel (1568) and Emden (1571) were indeed important, but at several points they failed to be "national synods." They were held outside the country. They had not been called by the States General. They had not been accorded universal recognition. Several provinces were unrepresented at the Synod of Dordrecht of

⁵ Ibid., pp. 157, 173.

1574. The Synod of Middelburg in 1581 lacked the backing of the States General. The Synod of The Hague in 1586 was dominated by Leicester and the strict Calvinist clergy, and with the fall of Leicester it was in discredit. Among all parties it was agreed that a genuine national synod must be held at the behest of the States General, and such a synod there had never been.[6] Until such a synod should occur, it was possible to refer all questions about the authority and interpretation of the Confession and Catechism "to the forthcoming national synod."

At that point the agreement ended. Those who were lukewarm to the Confession and Catechism (and Arminius must be included) could point out that they were not Dutch documents but imports from foreign churches. They were not considered statements of the consensus of the Dutch Church but were put into use hurriedly in a time of stress. The Belgic Confession had been written in 1559 by Guido de Brès (1523-1567), assisted by Adrian Saravia, H. Modetus, and Godfrey van Wingen, as a defense of the "churches under the cross" in the southern Low Countries. Saravia had taken a copy to Geneva for approval, which was not given. Only after Article 36 on the civil magistracy was altered by Franciscus Junius to Geneva's liking was it approved there. It was adopted at Wesel, Emden, and Dordrecht (1574), but with the un-certainties just enumerated. The Heidelberg Catechism had even less claim on the Dutch churches, written as it was in the Palatinate. The supporters of supralapsarianism wanted the formulas endorsed by a national synod; the opponents wanted them "revised in the light of the word of God."

In 1597 the Synods of North and South Holland petitioned the States General for a national synod. The States refused. From their point of view the earlier synods had too often moved in the wrong direction by putting undue limits on the role of the magistrate in the calling of pastors and in other functions of oversight in the church. More to their liking was Oldenbarnevelt's church order of 1591. Arminius had served on the commission which drew it up. It was based on a compromise between the demands of the church and the demands of the state. The calling of pastors, elders, and deacons was in the hands of a commission of four secular deputies and four church deputies. The secular deputies were responsible to the city government. The church deputies were chosen with the approval of the city government. Meetings of the consistory, classis, and provincial synod were permitted as long as nothing but church business was transacted. Nothing was said about a national synod. There was no stipulation that ministers must subscribe to the

6 Cf. G. J. Hoenderdaal, "De Kerkordelijke Kant van de Dordtse Synode."

Confession and Catechism, only that they declare that they would preach Bible doctrine as it is summarized in the Catechism. The power of censure rested finally with the provincial synod, but it could be enlarged with as many deputies as the States should wish, and the majority ruled.[7]

The States General feared that a national synod would give occasion for the Calvinists to introduce a Genevan polity whereby the church ruled itself entirely while still calling on the state to protect and maintain it. This could in turn introduce a reign of religious intolerance which would divide the nation.[8] The Holland ministers then turned to the States of Holland, asking permission to have a national synod. It was their purpose (at least of the majority) to use such a gathering to gain official approval of the Confession and Catechism in order that they might exercise discipline against ministers in Haarlem and elsewhere who were allegedly "dissenting" from the formulas.

The move backfired. The States of Holland granted the permission, with a proviso: that in the national synod the Dutch confession should be revised in the fear of God, and that it should be considered how best to establish, maintain, and increase peace and unity in the Dutch Reformed churches, and at the same time to do away with the difficulties which had arisen.[9] Although the Holland ministers were willing to go ahead on this basis, there was immediate protest from other provinces, especially Utrecht, who reminded Holland that it had only one vote in the States General.

The question was now out in the open, however. Should a national synod meet to enforce the Confession and Catechism or to revise them? All the other questions were tied up in this. What was the original "charter" of the Dutch churches? Were they committed to Calvinism? If so, what kind? Could there be dissent within the church? How much? Could there be dissent outside the church? And what was the ultimate standard of faith, the confessions or the Bible?

By 1600 the questions were manifest in actions in Haarlem, where the rigorists were pursuing their less "orthodox" brethren. They raised the suggestion "whether it would not be advisable that the ministers of the churches should annually renew their subscription of the Confession and Catechism, seeing individuals might be found who, though they had subscribed on being installed into office, nevertheless, at a subsequent period, gave manifest evidence of having changed their mind." [10]

---

[7] Fruin, *Tien Jaren uit den Tachtigjaren Oorlog, 1588-1589*, p. 170.
[8] *APPS*, I, 249; III, 70; cf. *HRN*, I, 808-9.
[9] *HRN*, I, 809.
[10] *LA*, p. 122.

Arminius was indignant, and he expressed himself heatedly to Uiten-bogaert: "I wonder at the improvident minds of these men who do not perceive that by this method they not only call in question the fidelity of all ministers as persons that must be compelled to constancy in the Faith by annually subscribing their names and likewise sow the seeds of daily dissension." And what if there should be a man who as time goes on has doubts about some article? Must he be forced to extricate himself before time for subscribing again? He might need more time. And isn't this an inquiry into crimes not yet committed? "But do not such actions as these seem like the foundation of a new Spanish Inquisition, or one of the Council of Trent?" He says that his protest does not arise because he would refuse to subscribe but because of the nature of the proposal itself. Then his indignant sarcasm comes to the surface:

It seems to me that many persons are so afraid of appearing not sufficiently anxious concerning ecclesiastical matters that they meditate whole nights and days whether they likewise cannot propose something for discussion in different synods. Such men ought to be reminded of the apostolic admonition: Give attendance to reading, to exhortation, to doctrine.[11]

IT IS TIME now to leave Amsterdam. What has happened to the lad from Oudewater whose personal tragedies combined to throw him into the company of theologians, churchmen, rulers, merchants, and parishioners? In 1603, when his Amsterdam tenure was interrupted, he was some forty-four years old, a vigorous pastor, active in the councils of the church, busy in matters of pastoral care and discipline; studious, producing lengthy, dogged, relentless probings of theological matters; a skillful logician; the emerging leader of a newly articulate theological school built on the old foundations of Dutch Protestantism, linked with the new age of logic and reason; valiant for truth but not afraid of tolerance, and at the same time Erastian and aristocratic. He was also a family man, whose wife, daughter, and four sons were his responsibility and his comfort. And by this time he may also have contracted the disease which would take his life, for it is not long until we hear of his "colds," which were probably the first stages of tuberculosis.

---

[11] *Ep. Ecc.*, no. 53; quoted *WA*, I, 135-36.

PART III
PROFESSOR

17

THE CALL TO LEIDEN

It was the frightening plague of 1601-2 that brought a momentous change in the life of Arminius. Although most of the clergy in Amsterdam had been spared, in Leiden the plague was less discriminating. On August 28, 1602, it took the life of the elder Lucas Trelcatius (born 1542), a professor of theology at Leiden since 1587 and pastor of the Walloon church there. Friends of Arminius began at once to seek his appointment to the vacant post. Hugo Grotius, then a nineteen-year-old law student under J. Scaliger at Leiden, wrote to Uitenbogaert, then serving as chaplain to Maurice's forces in the field in Brabant, urging him to persuade Arminius to accept the professorship if offered. He was seconded by the elder Antonius Thysius, a professor of theology from Harderwijk, who called Arminius "a light of the Netherlands and born to the school."[1]

Uitenbogaert wrote to Arminius about the matter in September, and Arminius replied on October 1. This is the letter in which he tells about the plague in Amsterdam. The latter part deals with the Leiden proposal. He frankly considers Uitenbogaert's suggestion that he, Arminius, is a fit man for the post.

I will not begin to say that you are greatly in error, lest I appear in your eyes desirous of producing petty excuses if I labor to evade that function; yet those which I do make shall be real excuses. I yield at once to your supposition that I shall not be totally unfit for promoting theological studies, if I be diligent and studious and devote my entire powers to this matter.[2]

He has a number of objections. One is the close mutuality which exists between himself and the church in Amsterdam. "You know likewise the amazing difference between the intense affection which sheep evince towards their shepherd who is always with them and that temporary affection which even the most virtuous of students manifest towards a man who is their instructor only for a few years." There is also the

[1] *KH*, Part III, p. 102.
[2] *Ep. Ecc.*, no. 56; quoted *WA*, I, 180.

"personal sanctification" which cannot but come to a man who sincerely carries out the holy offices of the pastoral ministry. Already in Amsterdam he has been hindered in exercises contributing to private holiness by the investigation of difficult theological topics. "What will become of me," he asks, "when I shall have dedicated myself to that employment which prefers far larger demands for the contemplation and discussion of difficult topics?"

Again, he enjoys a happy relationship with the magistrates in Amsterdam. Under them he can "with the greatest ease and without any stain of conscience or molestation give complete satisfaction." "I am resolved," he goes on, "always to preserve an upright and unbiased spirit, and not to force my conscience for the sake of any man living." But in Amsterdam there is seldom a necessity to displease the magistrates for the sake of conscience. In Leiden it could be different.

Very important to him is his family. It is not a matter of scraping together immense riches; that, he says his friend will know, he has never done. In Amsterdam he gets a good salary, and he is sure that the city would increase it whenever necessary. And there is no need (granted there is little opportunity) to develop an estate for his children to inherit, for he is sure that the church in Amsterdam will make necessary provision for them in the event of his death.

Finally, there is a contractual problem. He is committed to the service of Amsterdam for life. Whether the university should approach the burgomasters or the consistory, it will be reminded of the prior claim of Amsterdam on his services.

Arminius makes a counter proposal: that Thysius himself be appointed. Thysius, who had been in France, had recently accepted a professorship in the new academy at Harderwijk; Arminius had suggested back in 1600 that he be appointed to Leiden.[3] He closes the letter with personal greetings. God, he says, "with his own right hand has hitherto powerfully preserved me and my family in the midst of the excessive carnage and masses of dead bodies."

There were others who proposed Lucas Trelcatius the younger to succeed his father. Junius wrote to Uitenbogaert warning against the son. His reason is not known. It may have been that he thought the thirty-two-year-old son too young, or he may have questioned his competence (with reason). Perhaps he, too, wanted Arminius to have the post, but that cannot be proved. Young Trelcatius was appointed in 1603 to continue his father's lectures as *professor extraordinarius* (he became *professor ordinarius* in 1606 and died the next year).

[3] *Ep. Ecc.*, no. 53.

On October 23, 1602, Junius himself died of the plague. Gomarus ministered to him in his final illness and delivered the funeral oration. He let it be known that he did not want Arminius appointed, and he gave it out that this was the dying sentiment of Junius as well. Gomarus' biographer, J. P. van Itterzon, argues that there was nothing personal in Gomarus' opposition to Arminius, that it was entirely a matter of guarding against heresy and preserving peace in the faculty.[4] Arminius, so Gomarus maintained, would bring dissension. The argument is specious. There was now peace and unity in the theological faculty; Gomarus was the only remaining *ordinarius*. That Arminius was a heretic was a moot point. That difference of opinion would be Arminius' fault and not Gomarus' was gratuitous. That Gomarus would oppose Arminius is understandable. Even that his motives were a concern for the peace of the church and the purity of her doctrine may be granted. That he had a correct assessment of the nature of either the peace or the purity remains the question.

On October 29, 1602, Arminius wrote to Uitenbogaert in dismay about the death of Junius. The university and church were already sorely wounded by the death of Trelcatius, he said, and a still graver injury is the loss of the most excellent and learned Junius. Where can they turn for help? Not France, because it is in such dire straits that it can't handle its own problems. In Germany it is not much better. Pezelius in Bremen is too old. Grynaeus is already over sixty. Paraeus in Heidelberg is bound to the Palatinate. The only remaining option there is Piscator, at Herborn. He says nothing in this letter about himself as a prospect for the job.[5]

At about this very time, however, others were mentioning him. Uitenbogaert had returned from the battlefield to The Hague, and there was a dinner at the house of one of the *raadsheren* (judges of the High Court), Nicolas Cromhout. There were two other judges, François Francken of Gouda and Rombouts Hoogerbeets of Leiden, and an Arnhem burgomaster de Voocht and a Leiden curator, Cornelis van de Nieuwstadt (Neostadius). These assembled members of the government spoke favorably to Uitenbogaert about Arminius. A few days later Nieuwstadt told Uitenbogaert that he had received a letter from Nicolaas van Zeyst, the Leiden pensionary, reporting that the university students were unanimous in support of Arminius.

If support was building up for Arminius, so was opposition. Gomarus spearheaded the opposition, and he was joined by Cuchlinus, the regent of the *Statencollege* or Theological College of the university and

[4] *Franciscus Gomarus*, p. 82 *et passim*.
[5] *Ep. Ecc.*, no. 57.

Arminius' uncle by marriage. In the background was Plancius. Active locally was a Leiden minister, Festus Hommius. The subregent of the Theological College, the younger Petrus Bertius (who was married to a daughter of Cuchlinus by an earlier wife), favored Arminius.

The curators met on November 9, 1602, in the town hall of Leiden to discuss the matter. The board included, in addition to Nieuwstadt, the university's first curator, Jan van der Does (commonly known by his latinized name Janus Dousa), Lord of Noordwijk and Kattendijk, and Joannes Grotius (de Groot), the father of Hugo Grotius. The rector, Paulus Merula, appeared and requested permission for Gomarus to speak in the interests of his faculty. It was granted.

Gomarus first presented a copy of his recent funeral oration on Junius. He alleged that Junius had not favored Arminius for an appointment. Arminius was bad enough in Amsterdam; in Leiden he would spread his infection throughout all the churches. Even if he promised amendment, he was not to be trusted. Were there no men who could maintain peace? He recounted the possibilities: Amandus Polanus in Basel, David Paraeus and Bartholomaeus Keckerman in Heidelberg, Johannes Piscator in Herborn (a more likely prospect, he said), Henry Rowlands and William Perkins in England. Within the country there were Arent Cornelisz., minister in Delft; Werner Helmichius, Arminius' colleague in Amsterdam; the young Trelcatius; and Guilhelmus Coddaeus, a Hebrew scholar in Leiden. Arminius was not on the list.[6]

The curators were pleased neither by the content nor by the vehemence of the address. They questioned Gomarus. Had he known Arminius personally? He had greeted him only once, at a distance. Had he read the correspondence with Junius? (Gomarus was related by marriage to Junius, his second wife being a sister of Junius' third wife; hence some expectation of familiarity.) He had only scanned it, but he had heard a bad report of it. Who had put him up to making these charges? Plancius.

The curators then sought the advice of Oldenbarnevelt and Uitenbogaert, and the latter made before them an impassioned plea for Arminius' appointment. On November 11 they decided to move ahead with the call. There was too much support in high places for their decision to be blocked. Uitenbogaert, the court chaplain, was an intimate friend of Arminius. The High Court judge Nicolas Cromhout was a friend from Geneva days and a brother of the Amsterdam burgomaster Barthold Cromhout (although it must be said that in later years he was

---

[6] van Itterzon, pp. 82-83; *WA*, I ,185-86; *LA*, pp. 136-39; Uitenbogaert, *Kerckelijcke Bedieninghe*, p. 18.

a foe of the Remonstrants at the Synod of Dort and one of the judges who condemned Oldenbarnevelt). Also in the government at The Hague was Adrian Junius, who had traveled with Arminius to Italy. In Leiden he had the support of the prestigious Dousa, and of the elder Grotius and of van Zeyst in the city government. The consummation of the appointment would require much negotiation, but the die was cast.

There were conferences with Arminius, apprising him of these events. On November 19 two deputies of the curators, Nieuwstadt and van Zeyst, approached the burgomasters of Amsterdam (C. van Teylingen, P. C. Boom, Claes Fransz. Oetgens, and C. P. Hooft), who were not cooperative and refused to let the deputies approach the consistory. Three of the burgomasters, at least, were friendly to Arminius, and it may be assumed that they simply did not want to lose a friend and valuable minister.

The deputies of the synods, a continuing body with ill-defined powers of oversight in the church between synodical meetings, who had previously used Gomarus as their agent of hostility to Arminius, now tried to enlist Uitenbogaert. At an extraordinary session their chairman, Arent Cornelisz., brought his complaints. Arminius was too young, was inexperienced, was prone to quarrels. Uitenbogaert was incensed. "Too young!" he exclaimed. "And his hair already turning grey; too inexperienced! and fifteen years he has stood at the head of the Amsterdam congregation." The exchanges which followed were long and bitter, and Uitenbogaert excused himself from the meeting. The others proceeded to communicate their hostility to Arminius to Oldenbarnevelt.[7]

The curators, meanwhile, persisted in their plans. When Arminius was in Leiden on business of the Amsterdam classis on January 21, 1603, they asked him if he would accept the professorship. He repeated the answer he had given earlier, that he could answer such a question only when he should be released from his obligations in Amsterdam.

Cornelisz. was in Amsterdam on January 27. Arminius complained about the procedures against him in the meeting of the deputies, suggesting that "that method of acting did not appear to be sufficiently Christian, and that another ought to be adopted, of a more positive sort, and more in accordance with Christian candor."[8] The deputies kept up their attack, however, and toward the end of February renewed their complaints to Oldenbarnevelt.

In the meantime Gomarus was complaining of his heavy duties as sole *professor ordinarius* in theology. In an unpublished letter of Feb-

[7] *LA*, pp. 145-49; Rogge, *Wtenbogaert*, I, 213-14.
[8] Letter to Uitenbogaert, January 28, 1603, *Ep. Ecc.*, 3rd ed. Supplement, no. 1; *LA*, pp. 150-51.

ruary 19, 1603, he recounts his duties: every fourteen days public disputations, private disputations two times a week, and practice sermons to hear three nights a week, and all that without any help.[9] The negotiations dragged on. More charges against Arminius. Now he was not sufficiently anti-Roman—so alleged Arminius' Amsterdam colleague Helmichius. This gratuitous accusation was resented in Amsterdam, where it was remembered that Arminius had recommended Helmichius for a place in the ministry.

In early March, Arminius himself was incapacitated by a severe cold (was it tuberculosis?).[10] Progress was made on March 13, however, when Oldenbarnevelt provided Uitenbogaert with credentials to represent him in approaching Amsterdam for the release of Arminius. On April 5 Uitenbogaert and Nicolas Cromhout appeared before the Amsterdam burgomasters, who were still reluctant to lose their favorite minister. Amsterdam was full of dignitaries in the cause of Arminius; Dousa, van Zeyst, and Nieuwstadt were there, too. On April 8 they appeared before the consistory, which was reluctant to see their least favorite minister promoted to a professorship. The deputies made a proposal: if Arminius were released, they would try to get Baselius in Bergen-op-Zoom released to go to Amsterdam (Amsterdam had tried once before to get this preacher who was noted for his eloquence). On April 11 the consistory refused. Now Arminius' back was up. The next day Hallius reported to the consistory that Arminius had declared that even if the dismissal were refused, under the circumstances he could no longer serve the church in Amsterdam.[11] Arminius offered to repay the city the money that had been applied years earlier for his theological education. It was a momentous step for Arminius, for he was casting away one security with no assurance yet of another.

The burgomasters themselves now became alarmed, fearful "lest Arminius should suffer in his health from taking the refusal of his dismission too deeply to heart." The burgomasters approached the consistory, urging reconsideration, and the consistory now showed itself to be internally divided over the matter, some defending Arminius. On April 13, at the close of the evening service, the Leiden deputies approached the consistory again, this time with a harder line. Uitenbogaert was the spokesman. It was evident, he said, that the consistory was holding back because Arminius was thought to hold bad doctrine. The deputies would abandon the call at once if the consistory would

[9] Manuscript in the Bibliotheca Thysiana, Leiden, reported in Bakhuizen van den Brink, "Arminius te Leiden."

[10] Letter to Uitenbogaert, March 3, 1603; *Ep. Ecc.*, no. 58.

[11] Triglandius, p. 286.

make a specific accusation. The consistory now backed down, and the next day they gave their consent with three provisos: (1) that Arminius should not leave Amsterdam until another minister had been obtained, preferably Baselius; (2) that Arminius should have a meeting with Gomarus and "wipe away all suspicion of heterodoxy by a candid explanation of his own opinion"; and (3) that if he should ever leave Leiden, "or should necessity urgently demand his services for the church in Amsterdam," he should be free to resume his ministry.[12]

In all of this there were numerous consultations back and forth between the deputies, the consistory, the burgomasters, the former burgomasters (the new burgomasters in 1603 were Barthold Cromhout and Gerrit Bicker, and Barthold's brother Nicolas was one of the deputies), and the *Vroedschap*, or Council of Thirty-six. The deputies were concerned about the conference with Gomarus. Where and under what conditions should it be held? The consistory specified that it should be in the presence of synodical deputies. The university regarded this as an encroachment on its autonomy. The burgomasters pointed out that it was a necessary concession for gaining the release of Arminius.

On April 15 the burgomasters approved the release with the concurrence and seal of the Thirty-six. The university deputies expressed their pleasure and thanks, and they departed. The burgomasters absolved Arminius of any obligation to repay the money granted years earlier for his theological education. Both the council and the burgomasters entered statements of appreciation in their minutes, and he was given a gift of 25 guilders on his departure. Furthermore, the burgomasters passed a resolution granting his widow, should he die, the same pension at the cost of the city as other widows of ministers there, namely, 200 guilders a year.[13]

There has been considerable discussion about Arminius' role in all these proceedings. Did he actively seek the new position? The question itself is ambiguous. Surely in the first instance he was not seeking a professorial appointment. There is no indication that he expected to do anything other than to fill out his days in the ministry in Amsterdam. The deaths of the elder Trecatius and Junius did not change the situa-

[12] *LA*, pp. 167-68.

[13] The resolutions are quoted in Rogge, *Wtenbogaert*, I, 223, n. 1. The primary sources for our knowledge of these complex negotiations are, among others, the minutes of the Amsterdam consistory, the acts of the burgomasters and council, records of the university, contemporary letters, and the later accounts of Uitenbogaert and Triglandius. Triglandius, as usual, draws on the highly biased material inserted in the minutes of the consistory in 1617. Thorough collations and evaluations of the evidence are found in Rogge, *Wtenbogaert*, I, 194-226, and Maronier, pp. 128-78. For an account less sympathetic to Arminius, cf. van Itterzon, pp. 78-96.

tion. It was the vigorous efforts of others which put his name in the hopper. Then, when the opposition to his appointment took the turn of casting aspersions on his integrity and orthodoxy, he was concerned to be vindicated. It is nothing amiss in his character that he came to the point where the appointment was something to be desired. If one is to believe Triglandius, he connived and maneuvered to get it, putting pressure on powerful people in Amsterdam to secure his release. The evidence for this is not forthcoming. On the contrary, in a letter to Uitenbogaert, Arminius reflects on the whole situation with quite a different spirit. He was disturbed to be the center of a *cause célèbre*, to have put so many highly placed people to so much trouble. On April 26, 1603, he wrote to Uitenbogaert:

My beloved friend, there is one thing which vehemently distresses me. How shall I be able to satisfy such a great expectation? How shall I be able to prove myself to be in some measure worthy of having so mighty a movement set agoing on my account? But I console myself with this consideration alone, that I have not courted the professorship, and that the curators were warned of those things which have happened before they had determined any thing on the subject of my call.[14]

Upon the return of the deputies to The Hague they, together with Oldenbarnevelt, set the conference with Gomarus for May 6 at the home of Dousa in The Hague, with Arminius to be accompanied by Uitenbogaert and Hoogerbeets. The North and South synods were represented by Helmichius and Cornelisz. respectively. The Consistory of Amsterdam was invited to send deputies but did not do so. The curators were there, and two Leiden burgomasters. Oldenbarnevelt himself attended.

The conference lasted two days. Discussion centered on Arminius' exposition of Romans 7 and on his correspondence with Junius. Gomarus objected that no one was present from Amsterdam, although the curators had sent them an invitation. His discomfort was due to the fact that Plancius had put him up to the whole affair, and now he alone had to carry the battle, not being even yet thoroughly informed about Arminius' writings. Arminius defended his exposition of Romans 7. At one point he drew from his pocket his manuscript on the chapter for anyone to inspect. No one accepted the challenge. The Church of Rome was discussed, and the correspondence with Junius. Gomarus admitted that Arminius' views on Romans 7 were admissible if not preferable. The meetings finally ended with the concurrence of all in Arminius' appointment, and the curators treated the company to a dinner at the

[14] *Ep. ecc.*, no. 62; quoted *LA*, p. 172.

castle of the court (the Binnenhof), where the conclusion of the matter was celebrated "with all modesty and merriment."

On May 8, the curators and Leiden burgomasters, who always at that time acted in concert regarding the university, officially appointed Arminius to be professor of theology. Three days later they named the younger Lucas Trelcatius to be *professor extraordinarius*. Thus they continued their policy of maintaining balance in the faculty between the two theological tendencies in the Dutch churches.

18

LIFE IN LEIDEN

ARMINIUS was faced now with the difficult process of breaking ties with family and friends in Amsterdam. The distance to Leiden was not great, perhaps around twenty-five or thirty miles by road, but it would suffice to separate the family from their familiar environment for all but occasional visits. The move itself must have been difficult. The five children were all under ten years of age, the youngest under two, and Lijsbet was in the ninth month of another pregnancy. The move may be dated at about early June of 1603.

Leiden was a beautiful city, although for the seventeenth-century dweller the charm of antiquity would not have the same appeal as it does today. It was not only a university town but a burgeoning center of the textile industry, attracting workers from the southern provinces both by its political liberty and by its opportunities for employment. The population had grown rapidly since the time of the siege. A census of 1622 reported nearly 45,000 inhabitants, and it would reach at least 70,000 later in the century. When England took the lead in textiles, Leiden declined and did not regain its former size until after World War I.

It was a tightly defined town with little suburban sprawl. Growth was planned and systematic, section by section. The most recent growth when Arminius returned there was northward, across the Old Rhine. Here the Flemish textile workers streamed in, living in mean laborers' houses, too many of which are extant. The town was now bounded by walls, with fortifications and windmills on them, and the walls were surrounded by a circuit of *singels,* canals which served at once for drainage, transportation, and defense. Outside the *singels* were fields used as *blekerijen,* "bleacheries," where there were rows of racks for drying and bleaching textiles. Beyond them was the flat, rich farmland of the Rijnland polder.

As in Amsterdam there were two great churches. The grandest and oldest was the Pieterskerk (St. Peter's Church), midway between town hall and university in the oldest part of Leiden. Parts of it date from the fourteenth century, and it was completed in the early sixteenth. In the next oldest part of town stood the Hooglandsekerk (originally St. Pancras, called the "highland church" for a slight rise of ground on which it stood). It lacked a nave. There was a third church, smaller and newer, the St. Mary's Church, more to the north.

Near the Hooglandsekerk was Den Burcht, a medieval circular castle from the twelfth century on an earthwork mound of possibly ancient origin. In the oldest part of town was the Breestraat, still Leiden's main street, and where it was intersected by the Pieterskerk Korsteeg (choir alley) the town had been traditionally divided in four quarters. Embedded in the spot was the *blauwesteen,* the blue stone, a customary fixture for a place of judgment and execution. Falsifying a measure could cost a merchant his hand, in medieval times.

In 1581, just as Arminius was ending his student days in Leiden, the university had taken over the cloister of the Dominican (White) nuns, whose buildings dated from 1516. The cloister church was on the west side of the canal called the Rapenburg at the Nonnenbrug (nun's bridge), where the Kloksteeg (bell alley) issued from the churchyard of the Pieterskerk. Chief functions of the university took place there or in the nearby Pieterskerk. It was also the location of lectures in theology. The university already spilled over into other buildings. Across the canal was the Falijde Begijnhof Church, which housed not only the library but also the anatomical theater of Dr. Pieter Pauw, with its cadavers and skeletons, both human and animal. The Theological College, where Arminius' hostile uncle Cuchlinus and his school friend Bertius held forth, was south of the Rapenburg in the former church of the Cellebroeders' cloister.

Arminius' duties in Leiden would be fairly well circumscribed by these buildings, but he had friends in the city government, too. The burgomasters, four of them, sat in the newly enlarged town hall on the Breestraat. It had been remodeled and richly decorated in the new Golden Age style by Lieven de Key and Luder van Bentheim. Then there were the shops, the markets, the textile workshops, and the houses many of them but hovels, which would fill out such a town at that time. Throughout the town were Leiden's most unusual institution, the many former convents now converted to almshouses, or *hofjes,* for widows and other indigents. They were quadrangular affairs with gatehouse and chapel, and Leiden had some three dozen of them.

The decline of Leiden after the seventeenth century had the happy side effect of preserving the old city quite intact. There is much there today that Arminius would have known. The modern visitor could use Orlers' map of 1614 to find his way today. The two great churches are there, and the university building, the Latin school, Den Burcht, and some thirty almshouses (some rebuilt, but usually along the old lines). A medieval castle adjacent to the Pieterskerk, the Gravensteen, is now the university law school. The Begijnhof Church is still a part of the university library, and the oldest books are there. Even the Cellebroeders' church was there until 1969, although for the past century and a half it had been used as a riding academy.

A lovely town, we say now with romantic hindsight. In Arminius' time, however, the air of romance was subdued by the stench of the canals, and the graceful beauty of canals lined by linden trees was not sufficient to cover over the ugly reality of death by plague and tuberculosis. Arminius would have seen the beginning of the building of magnificent facades along the Rapenburg, but he apparently had little time or sensitivity for the beauties of nature, antiquity, or architecture. At least he has left us no literary clue.[1]

Where did Arminius live? Such a mundane detail does not appear in his correspondence, but the more prosaic town government has kept records which help us. From the chimney tax records of 1606 we know one place of residence, presumably his first, and from other records we know where he lived from about 1607 until his death. At first he was a tenant in a house owned by Jan van der Does (Dousa), the aged curator, on *de oulde oisterling plaets,* a market street named for the *easterling* (Baltic) merchants who had done business there. Later it was called the *Garenmarkt,* the Thread Market, its present name. The house was a sizable one for the time and place, about 45-foot frontage and running deep into the block. It was on the west side of the street, four doors south from the canal known as the Steenschuur, a continuation of the Rapenburg. The Oosterlingplaats or Garenmarkt is in an enlargement of the city made from 1389 to 1396. Dousa died in October, 1604, and the house was sold to Pieter van der Velde. In 1606 Arminius paid a chimney tax of 7 guilders and 5 stuivers, for five fireplaces (his rival Gomarus had eleven chimneys).[2]

The house may have lasted until 1807, but in that year everything in

---

[1] A description of Leiden in 1613, remarkable for its detail and its accuracy, is provided by J. J. Orlers, *Beschrijvinge der Stad Leyden.* Orlers, who was the nephew of Jan van Hout, secretary of Leiden during the siege, included two maps and pictures of the major buildings. See also P. J. Blok, *Geschiedenis eener Hollandsche Stad,* III, 1-33 *et passim.*

[2] *Bonboek,* fol. 448 verso. The premises are shown in detail in the magnificent handdrawn, water-color maps of streets and canals made by S. D. van Dulmanhorst and Simon Fransz. van Merwen in 1578, preserved in the Leiden archives. These were reproduced in color by photolithograph by W. Pleyte (Leiden, 1874).

the area was demolished when a bargeload of dynamite exploded (with tragic loss of life). On its location today the visitor will find the Geological Museum, adjacent to the Van der Werff Park.

It is possible to reconstruct the typical daily routine of Arminius. He tells of reading until 9:30 in the morning (it may be assumed that he was an early riser) and of meeting a class from 10:00 to 1:30. Home again (and if it is safe to read back from the life of a modern Leiden professor, a light lunch with a glass of wine, and perhaps a nap), and then he is back at his lecturing (he speaks of expounding Matthew in this case) from 4:00 to 7:30. Home again, a meal, and letters to write.[3] The walk from his home to the university would take from five to ten minutes. Sometimes there would be a university event at the Pieterskerk, and Sundays there would be public worship. If he ever went shopping with his wife, he has not admitted such a mundane detail in writing. Probably he did not. As a professor he lived in a very special and often segregated society. If he had any contacts with others than members of the university and the government, we do not know it.

It was a rising industrial city, Leiden, but ever dominated by the presence of its university. If there was town-gown strife, it did not divide the *curatoren en burgemeesteren* who so often acted in concert. What kind of university was it now, and what role did it play in Dutch national life?

It was two-sided, at one and the same time. It was the stronghold of the Latin tradition of Renaissance humanism, and it was the seedbed of Dutch culture and language. On the surface, the Latinity was dominant. Almost all academic discourse was in Latin, and this made it possible for the university to draw to its faculty and student roster leading scholars from all over Europe. That in itself would have left it merely an enclave in a foreign terrain had not the wealth of scholarship burst the bounds of Latin and spilled over in Dutch. When Prince Maurice established a school for engineers at the university in 1600, it was stipulated that instruction would be in Dutch. Dutch was also the language of the *Statencollege,* and the time came when the great Latin scholars deigned to write poetry in Dutch. This paralleled what was growing out of the Chamber of Rhetoric in Amsterdam, where Laurens Jacobsz. Reael and other Old Beggars had already broken ground for a true Dutch literature. There is a direct cultural line from Reael and C. P. Hooft to their sons Laurens Laurensz. Reael and Pieter Cornelisz. Hooft, who with Roemer Visscher, Caspar van Baerle, Gerard Vossius, Constantijn Huygens, Joost Vondel, Jacob Cats, Samuel Coster, and Jan Sweelinck gathered at the castle at Muiden for the promotion of

[3] Letter to Uitenbogaert, February 3, 1607; *Ep. Ecc.,* no. 98.

Dutch letters. The influence of Leiden merged in with the *Muiderkring*, bringing to it the full strength of its classical learning.[4]

The university was defined in terms of its distinguished faculty. The guiding hand in its development was the curator Dousa, himself an eminent humanist. Other curators have been mentioned. Among the burgomasters (who functioned as *ex officio* curators) who rotated in and out of the four posts in the decade were Laurens Adriaansz. van Swaansdijk, Foy van Broekhoeven, Jan IJsbrandtsz. van der Nesse, Isaak Nicolai, Arnold Duyk de Jode, Frans Duyk de Jode, and Frank van Thoornvliet. The famous burgomaster of the siege of 1574, Pieter Adriaansz. van der Werf, had died five years earlier, but his son Adriaan Pietersz., was rising in the ranks of town leadership. Both Nicolaas van Zeyst and Rombouts Hoogerbeets served the city in the capacity of pensionary.

It was Dousa's great pride that he had brought to the university the renowned historian Justus Lipsius. In 1592, however, pride turned to embarrassment when Lipsius, after having become embroiled in a bitter controversy with Coornhert, left the country and sent word back that he was returning to the Roman Catholic Church. Now who would shine where this bright star had gone out? This time Leiden sought the man who had the reputation of being the greatest scholar in Europe, the French classicist Joseph Justus Scaliger, then, at age fifty-two, entering the prime of his career. The curators were successful, and with great pomp, accompanied by noblemen, Scaliger took up residence in Leiden in 1593. He was more than a professor; he was a distinguished scholar-in-residence. No teaching was required or expected of him. It was enough that he should live in Leiden, pursue his studies, and be available for counsel to the faculty. He is said to have memorized the whole of Homer in twenty-one days, the rest of the Greek poets in three months, and the entire body of Greek literature in two years. He was skilled in thirteen languages, including Hebrew, Chaldee, Arabic, Syriac, Persian, Russian, Greek, and Latin. His was the Olympian voice over and above all the lesser gods of the professorial pantheon.

It is interesting at least, if not assuredly significant, to see what he thought of the professors of theology. Junius he held in contempt. After Scaliger died, it was found that he had written in the margins of his copies of Junius' books remarks such as "ass," "dumbhead." [5] And as for Junius' relative Gomarus, Scaliger said, "He thinks he is the most learned theologian of all. He understands chronology [Scaliger's specialty] like I understand counterfeiting," and, "This great Doctor Go-

[4] Cf. P. J. Blok, *Geschiedenis van het Nederlandsche Volk,* IV, 381; Geyl, pp. 283-88.
[5] Sepp, *Godgeleerd Onderwijs,* I, 90.

marus, who talks about everything that he doesn't understand." What of Arminius? *"Arminius est vir maximus."* [6] It was high praise from a man who praised almost no one. But Scaliger never became a principal in the theological debates. He stood aloof over all that.

It should not be supposed that it was a one-man faculty. There was a host of luminaries in the Leiden heavens when Arminius taught there. Cornelis Grotius, professor of law, brother of Joannes Grotius and uncle of Hugo Grotius, was the *Rector Magnificus* in 1603. Gomarus and Trelcatius taught theology, with Cuchlinus and Bertius in the Theological College. There were Gerardus Bontius in anatomy, botany, astronomy, and mathematics (a universal man!); Petrus Pauw in medicine (he had grown up next door to Lijsbet "op 't Water" in Amsterdam); Carolus Clusius in medicine (an herb garden is named for him); Rudolphus Snellius in mathematics (Arminius' former teacher), and his even more distinguished son, Willibrord Snellius, still a lecturer. In history was Paulus Merula, with Bonaventura Vulcanius in Greek (he was secretary of the Academic Senate), and Guilhelmus Coddaeus in Hebrew. The librarians, later professors, were Daniel Heinsius and Johannes Meursius. Heinsius wrote verse in both Latin and Dutch, and Meursius preserved archival remains of inestimable value for our knowledge of the early years of the university. The secretary of the *Vierschaar,* a body consisting of the *Rector Magnificus,* the burgomasters, two *schepenen,* and four professors, was Jan van Houten. There were others.

Gomarus (François Gomaer) was to dominate Arminius' Leiden years. He was born in Brugge on January 30, 1563, and was thus three or four years younger than Arminius. He had two younger brothers and possibly a younger sister. He learned Greek and Latin at an early age in Brugge, but the school is unknown. Brugge had known Protestant preaching since 1521. Pieter Gabriel, who later was in Amsterdam, was preaching there at mid-century. By the 1570s, at the latest, Gomarus' parents had embraced the Reformed religion, and under Spanish pressure had to flee the city for the Palatinate in 1577 or 1578. Gomarus, however, went to Strassburg, where at age fourteen he began three years of studies with the renowned German humanist Johannes Sturm. From there he went to Neustadt, where the Calvinist professors of Heidelberg had been forced to go when the Elector Ludwig would tolerate no one but Lutherans. Here he studied Hebrew under Junius, Greek under Simon Stenius, Latin under Lambertus Pithopoeus, philosophy under Fortunatus Crellius and Johannes Jugnitius, and theology under Hieronymus Zanchius (an Italian), Daniel Tossanus, and Zacharias Ursinus, the

---

[6] Quoted by van Itterzon, p. 148, who adds that he cannot understand why Scaliger didn't like Gomarus.

Franciscus Gomarus. Engraving from life.
By permission of the Iconographisch Bureau, The Hague

author of the Heidelberg Catechism. There is some question as to the extent of the influence of these men on Gomarus, for he was a much more extreme Calvinist than they. Gomarus was in Neustadt from 1580 to 1582.

In the autumn of 1582 he went to Oxford in order to study under John Rainolds. It is possible that he did not become a member of the university, for his name does not appear on the matriculation register. It was a time of low interest in theology at Oxford, and in 1583 he left for Cambridge. There he bypassed the two-year requirement for taking the baccalaureate examination and received the degree at once. He immediately petitioned to go on to a master's degree, and he was promoted to that on June 20, 1584. In Cambridge he studied under the supralapsarian William Whitaker. It is not certain that he knew William Perkins. It is possible that he studied Ramist logic under William Temple. Whether he did or not, Gomarus did become a dedicated Ramist. Scaliger later commented on the large number of Ramist books in Gomarus' library, which to Scaliger was no asset. Gomarus was unhappy at Cambridge and had unkind words for it in later life. The English he learned there he later used to preach to the English congregation in Leiden.

When the Elector Casimir replaced his brother Ludwig in 1583, the Calvinist professors were restored at Heidelberg. Grynaeus, under whom Arminius had studied at Basel, came from that city. Georgius Sohnius came from Marburg, and Junius came from Neustadt. Gomarus enrolled in 1585. One of his fellow students was Antonius Thysius. Gomarus was now surrounded by countrymen and at least some kindred spirits theologically.

In 1587 Gomarus was called to the refugee Walloon church in Frankfurt, which had been established in 1555 by Marten Micron and Johannes à Lasco. There he was married for the first time, to an Antwerp girl, Emerentia, daughter of Gilles and sister of Abraham Muysenhol. She died after the birth of a son in 1591. In the summer of 1593 he remarried, to Maria, a daughter of local nobility. This led to dissension in the community (Gomarus was no stranger to dissension before Arminius went to Leiden) due to the fact that Gomarus was not a citizen and hence was ineligible to marry Maria. There were many troubles in Frankfurt, including the dispersal of his congregation under persecution by the Lutherans, and he left in early January of 1594. Before the month was out, he had been called to Leiden to be professor there. In April he was officially received by the curators at a feast marked by an abundance of Rhine wine, and in June he gave his inaugural oration on the covenant of God.

In his theology he was at one with Beza and Plancius, a supralapsari an. In his temperament he was, by almost all accounts, fractious in the extreme. Junius himself, later related to Gomarus by marriage, delivered this judgment: "That man pleases himself most wonderfully by his own remarks. He derives all his stock of knowledge from others; he brings forward nothing of his own: or, if at any time he varies from his usual practice, he is exceedingly infelicitous in those occasional changes." [7] Perhaps nothing brought him into so much personal discredit as his violent attacks on the character of Arminius after the latter's death.[8]

Professors were in a class by themselves at the university, but they were not the only persons of influence. There were the beadles, two of them, an unique office combining functions of official messengers with those of notaries and deans. During Arminius' tenure as professor the office was held by father and son, Louis (Ludovicus) and Matthijs Elzevier, the famous printers. When Matthijs was chosen beadle in 1607, it was a victory over a rival printer, Thomas Basson.

The printers were always seeking close association with the university in order to have access to the publishing of disputations and other university projects. There was a third printer in Leiden, Jan Jacobsz. Paedts, who often had the custom of the university. Paedts was the first to publish any writings of Arminius, beginning with his first public oration in Leiden, a set of theses on the nature of God delivered on July 7, 1603. Still another printer received some of the printing orders of the university. Thomas Basson, an Englishman who supported the Arminian cause, began printing disputations of Arminius in 1609, before Arminius' death. When he died around 1613, his son Godefridus carried on the business.[9] The printers had taken over the premises of an earlier university printer, Christoph Plantin, and occupied a number of buildings along the Kloksteeg, from the Rapenburg to the Templum Salomonis (site of a medieval library foundation and a bookstore to the present day).

With apologies to all students who read this, I observe that to canvass the 800 students is a task beyond the reach of this study. Certain names will appear in special circumstances.[10]

Then there were the ministers of the Reformed churches in Leiden. Festus Hommius opposed Arminius vigorously. Adrian Borrius was a

---

[7] Quoted in *WA*, I, 171.

[8] The important modern study of Gomarus is by van Itterzon, from which this biographical material is derived.

[9] Cf. J. A. van Dorsten, *Thomas Basson*.

[10] For a complete listing of the students in all faculties, cf. *Album Stud. Acad. Lugd. Bat* (The Hague, 1875).

friend and later the first signatory to the Remonstrance of 1610, still later a Remonstrant exile. Johannes Arnoldus Corvinus (Raven) came in 1606, also a supporter of Arminius and later a signatory to the Remonstrance who suffered deposition and exile in 1619. Corvinus was instrumental in getting the works of Hugo Grotius published. Adolphus Sprankhuysen was also a minister. Egbertus Aemilius came in 1604, and Daniel Colonius in 1605 to the Walloon church. An English church was not formed until 1609.[11]

Leiden was proud of its university, but at the same time the university was a world apart from Leiden. There were two points of contact, however. Not only did the *curatoren en burgemeesteren* work closely together, but the townspeople took the students into their homes for room and board, a tradition which is only now diminishing significantly. But to be a member of the university marked a person apart. John Robinson, pastor of the Scrooby Separatists, achieved this status in the following decade. The professors apparently had little contact with the common life of the town. It is doubtful that Arminius could have been aware of a child born in 1606 to a miller, Harmen van Rijn, and his wife Neeltgen, a short distance north of the university, a son whom they named Rembrandt. More to his interest would have been some one hundred English Separatists and their pastor, John Robinson, who moved to Leiden from Amsterdam in the spring of 1609; but Arminius was then in his final illness and could not take the measure of these Calvinists, some of whom would become America's Pilgrim Fathers. He lived in a very special world where professors dealt with books and ideas, students and colleagues. But it was not a peaceful world at the center of the nation's intellectual life. The crosscurrents of ideas produce storms no less severe than those which buffeted the merchant ships making their way into the port of Amsterdam. Bustling Amsterdam would have offered Arminius more tranquillity than he would know in Leiden.

Not all the battles of life in Leiden would be lofty, however. There is an old apocryphal tale about Arminius (I do not vouch for its truth) which tells of an encounter with his colleague Professor Dominicus Baudius. Baudius was fond of drink, and on this occasion he was lying drunk in a Leiden gutter. Arminius came upon him, and in distaste exclaimed, "O pestis Academiae!" The drunken Baudius, ever in com-

---

[11] On the officials of the university and town, cf. Soermans, *Academisch Register . . . Leiden.* On the university itself, in addition to works mentioned earlier in this chapter, cf. P. C. Molhuysen, *Bronnen tot de Geschiedenis der Leidsche Universiteit;* Sepp, *Godgeleerd Onderwijs;* and A. Eekhof, *De Theologische Faculteit te Leiden in de 17de Eeuw* (Utrecht, 1921).

mand of his wit and his Latin, replied, "O pestis Ecclesiae!" This story was supposed to show that Baudius had bested Arminius. If so, it was a Pyrrhic victory, for Baudius died some time later of delirium tremens.[12]

A few more developments in the family life of Arminius can be related here before the theological matters are faced again. More children came to the couple during the Leiden years. After moving to Leiden in early June, 1503, Arminius took his doctoral examination on the 19th. On June 20 little Jacob was born. Baptismal records from these years are not extant, and knowledge of names and dates comes from family records.[13]

Jacob was followed by Willem on May 2, 1605, at 4:30 A.M. On that day Arminius wrote a letter to Uitenbogaert telling of the birth. *"Uxor mea hodie mane ante semiquintam filium mihi peperit nonum, & septimum continuata serie."* James Nichols has misunderstood this to mean a ninth child and seventh son. Willem was the ninth son and the seventh living child (but not in a continuous series). Arminius goes on to quote an Antonius Asaldus, who had said that a masculine seventh child will have the power to cure "wens and scrophulous affections," a power shared with the kings of France. If any credence can be given to this, Arminius said whimsically, Willem will be a doctor.[14]

Ansaldus missed it, for Willem never became a doctor. But Daniel did. Daniel was born on November 28, 1606. Arminius mentions the event in a letter to Joannes Narsius on December 27, a tenth son *"ex ordine sine interruptione octavi."* He does not mention his name.[15]

At some time between the chimney tax of 1606 and the end of his life, Arminius moved his family to a new house, one much more convenient to his work. It was the rectory (*paterhuis*) of the old Begijnhof Church which had been taken over by the university. It faced the churchyard at the west end of the Pieterskerk, precisely opposite the west door. The house has long since disappeared, and the spot is occupied now by a nondescript school building.

It was probably there that Geertruyd was born, their twelfth child and second daughter, on September 12, 1608. There would be no more children; their family was now complete. Engeltje, the oldest, was fifteen years old. After her came seven sons, Harmen, Pieter, Jan, Laurens, Jacob, Willem, and Daniel. Daniel and Geertruyd would not remember their father.

[12] "Oude Professoren Anecdoten," *Leids Jaarboekje,* 1917, p. 51.

[13] These are recorded in the articles by D. W. van Dam van Hekendorp and W. M. C. Regt.

[14] *Ep. Ecc.,* no. 76; *WA,* I, 309.

[15] *Ep. Ecc.,* no. 87.

The Leiden years were marred by illness. Earlier writers have been prone to see Arminius' bouts with sickness as the result of tension and overwork, but the simple fact is that he had tuberculosis. This judgment is made on the basis of interpreting the descriptions of his disabilities in the context of the prevalence of the disease. When Gomarus delivered a speech on predestination, attacking Arminius in process, on October 31, 1604, Arminius was sick.[16] In March, 1606, the family went to Amsterdam for a week, visiting the family of Lijsbet's uncle J. P. Reael.[17] It was a relief from the pressures of Leiden, but later in the year he had a spell of sickness lasting five weeks.[18] In May, 1607, when his close friend the Amsterdam minister Halsbergius died, he wrote to his friend burgomaster Dr. Sebastian Egbertsz.:

But justly do you remark that he has gone before: we shall every one of us follow, each in his own order,—the thought of which is constantly impressed upon my mind by a catarrh which now assails me at no rare intervals, affecting sometimes the chest [*in trachaeam*], sometimes the bowels [*in praecordia*], sometimes the stomach [*in ventriculum*]. He who is ready to administer final judgment on all mortals has sent this as a warning; and thereby he orders me to moderate the grief I feel for the decease of my friend, whom, perhaps, after not many years I shall follow.[19]

A sharp attack on February 7, 1609, showed that the disease was far advanced, giving the physicians cause for alarm and hindering Arminius in his work. The end came later that year.

From time to time Arminius sought relief outside Leiden. In addition to visiting in Amsterdam, he went to Utrecht for some rest. In a letter written from there to Borrius he reported that he had no catarrh, felt no lassitude, and was enjoying the pleasant air. He had found it necessary to travel by water and not by land, however, because he could not endure the jolting of the carriage.[20] At other times he rested at the country place of his good friend Willem Bardesius.

All of this is to say that in Leiden, Arminius was blessed with family and friends but cursed with illness and conflict. We turn now to his professional life and writings, the locus of the conflict.

---

[16] *LA*, p. 201.
[17] *Ep. Ecc.*, no. 84.
[18] *Ibid.*, no. 86.
[19] *Ibid.*, no. 101.
[20] June 23, 1608; *ibid.*, no. 116.

19

THE FIRST YEARS OF TEACHING: 1603-1604

DOGMATIC theology and the politics of church and state are intertwined in the six years of Arminius' life as a professor at Leiden. To tell everything that happened would be tedious, but to treat the theology out of the context of the events of those years would be inadequate. The plan adopted is to give first, at least in outline, the course of events which constitutes the matrix for the theological writings, indicating in each case something of the theological positions taken. After that, a more systematic account of the dogmatics of Arminius will be in order.

IT WAS DECIDED that Arminius should present himself for a doctoral examination before undertaking his duties. It was held on June 19. In a letter never published and now lost (since the nineteenth century), Arminius tells of the event.

I was examined on Tuesday by Gomarus, in the presence of the illustrious [Joannes] Grotius and [Paulus] Merula. He performed his part actively and honorably. I answered his questions as well as I could at the time. He, and the other two who were present, expressed themselves satisfied. The examination turned on questions relating to the substance of theology; and he conducted himself quite as he ought, and in the manner I could have wished.[1]

After Arminius' death, Gomarus said that he regretted the approval that he had given, alleging that if he had known of Arminius' *Examination of Perkins' Pamphlet* he would not have granted it. Later writers have followed Gomarus in accusing Arminius of dissembling before the examiners. Triglandius leads the pack, and he is followed by many Dutch Reformed writers, including G. J. Vos, F. J. Los, and, unfortunately, R. B. Evenhuis (the only major flaw in his fascinating and helpful history of the Reformed Church in Amsterdam, *Ook Dat Was*

---

[1] Quoted in *LA*, pp. 180-81.

252

Amsterdam). Gomarus was speaking with hindsight; he wished afterward that he could have foreseen the full meaning and power of Arminius' positions. Arminius, on his side, was careful, trying to avoid offense without compromising his position. I find no reason to disagree with the judgment of H. C. Rogge when he says, "Arminius was cautious, sometimes almost too diffident, but he never spoke other than what he thought." [2] As for Gomarus' withholding approval in 1603, it is doubtful that he could have done this unchallenged in the presence of the two witnesses, Grotius and Merula.

The next step toward the doctorate was a public disputation on the morning and afternoon of July 10. The topic was the nature of God. The opponents were Petrus Bertius and three ministers, Festus Hommius of Leiden, Jacobus Crusius (de la Croix) of the Walloon church in Delft, and Nicolas Grevinchovius of Rotterdam, who was later a Remonstrant. The performance, in which Arminius had to respond extemporaneously with syllogisms to objections made by his critics, was acclaimed by all present. The disputation is lengthy; perhaps Gomarus, granted that he was present, did not notice what was being said. One of the principal arguments was that the foreknowledge of God does not predetermine what is known. God foreknows some things as necessary, others as contingent. The point will need further discussion when the broad structure of Arminius' thought is studied. What is important here is that at this public occasion Arminius took a position which was contrary to the Bezan theory of predestination. "Though the understanding of God be certain and infallible, it does not impose any necessity in things, nay, rather it establishes in them a contingency." [3]

On that day a diploma or bull conferring the title of Doctor of Theology was signed by Bonaventura Vulcanius, secretary of the Academic Senate, to be presented the following day at an academic convocation. Notice was taken of Arminius' performance in private examination and public disputation, and he was given "authority to interpret publicly and privately the Sacred Scriptures, to teach the mysteries of religion, and to dispute, write, and preside at discussions on points of the Christian faith, as well as to solve theological questions; also to perform all public and formal acts pertaining to the true office of a Doctor in theology; in fine, to enjoy all the privileges and immunities as well as prerogatives which, whether by right or by custom, are due to this order and dignity." [4]

At the convocation the next day, July 11, Arminius delivered an

[2] *Wtenbogaert*, I, 255, n. 1.
[3] *Writings*, I, 447.
[4] Quoted in *LA*, pp. 183-84.

oration, "The Priesthood of Christ." It draws heavily on the imagery of sacrifice and priesthood, especially as these are developed in Hebrews, and points to the final consummation in which Christ's expiatory sacrifice passes over into his offering to God of all the church of the faithful. It was not controversial. At the close, Arminius offered a prayer and expressed his gratitude to his promoter Gomarus and the others present, including the students.

Bertius in his funeral oration says that Arminius was "the first person that had been publicly presented" with the title of doctor at Leiden. There had been one earlier doctorate conferred, however, on the elder Lucas Trelcatius. Unless Trelcatius had not received his title "publicly," Bertius was in error at this point.[5]

After the convocation there was a great feast, at which Arminius was, according to tradition, the host. All professors had the right to be guests at such a dinner, which made it a costly affair. The curators evidently saw Arminius' financial plight, for they made him a grant of 200 guilders to offset the costs of his doctoral promotion and dinner.

The favor of the curators was shown in other ways. His beginning annual salary was 800 guilders, some 200 to 400 guilders more than some other professors, and it was gradually raised to 1,200 guilders. He was also given a rent allowance of 150 guilders which was raised in stages as his family grew to 300 guilders. It was also a time of inflation, and these increases may not have meant much gain in purchasing power. The figures for Gomarus' financial benefits during this period are missing, so it cannot be determined how Arminius' income compared with that of his rival colleague. It can be assumed that Gomarus did well, for in his earlier years in Leiden he lived adjacent to the university itself, where he owned the premises just west of the university building. At the time of the chimney tax of 1606, he lived in a house of eleven chimneys on the west side of the Rapenburg, three doors south of the Groenhasengracht. A revealing insight into the financial and administrative policies of the curators is given in 1609, when Arminius and Gomarus were at the height of their controversy. In order that each might have the resources to present his case fully to the university, the curators granted each an honorarium of 250 guilders for the preparation and presentation of a public disputation; as Bakhuizen van den Brink observes, "so even-handed was the distributive justice of the curators." [6]

Other honors and tokens of esteem were given. The curators expressed

---

[5] *WA*, I, 33; Bakhuizen van den Brink, p. 4, citing Molhuysen.

[6] Bakhuizen van den Brink, p. 4, where all these financial arrangements are recounted.

their appreciation to Uitenbogaert for his efforts in behalf of the call of Arminius by presenting him a silver bowl with the arms of the university on it (at a cost of 100 guilders). A solemn presentation was made by Nieuwstadt and van Zeyst. Dousa celebrated the appointment by honoring Nicolas Cromhout with a poem in Latin for his part in bringing Arminius to Leiden. Dousa, as A. W. Harrison aptly puts it, "even achieved the impossible by getting the name of Wtenbogaert into another poem on the same subject." [7]

After the promotion Arminius had to return to Amsterdam to wind up affairs there. Baselius had not been obtained for a replacement, and Arminius was obliged to await his successor, Jacobus Rolandus. The assumption that he had moved his family to Leiden in early June is based on the fact that the birth of his son Jacob is not recorded in the baptismal records in Amsterdam, but Arminius himself was not free to remain permanently in Leiden until September.

In Amsterdam hostilities were abating, and instead there was a mellowing time of mutual farewells and expressions of esteem. On September 1, 1603, the Classis of Amsterdam wrote a brief but thoroughly cordial letter of commendation. It speaks of the fifteen years during which "he has taught sound doctrine" and of his faithful and effective work in all the functions of the ministry. "To this day" he has "adorned his holy calling by the probity and the honorable and virtuous tenor of his life." He is commended for "the transcendent and luminous endowments of his genius, and the rare and singular gifts which he possesses." It was signed by two Amsterdam ministers, Halsbergius, the president of the classis, and Hallius, the secretary. [8]

A week later the consistory wrote a longer letter in the same vein. Arminius had requested a testimonial letter, it says, and this ought not be refused. "We desire to testify to all and every one," it goes on, "that the high integrity of the above-named most accomplished . . . , the soundness of his doctrine, and the propriety of his manners, has by means of an uninterrupted acquaintance and constant intercourse been . . . fully known, tried, and confirmed by us." It speaks of his counsel, aid, conversation, intimacy, cheerful labors in all aspects of the ministry, piety, consummate probity, and rare erudition. It is flowery, to be sure, but that was the style of the times. It concludes: "We commend to all men of piety, honor, and learning, this most respectable gentleman and most venerable brother in Christ, and it is not possible for us to frame any recommendation with greater affection and favor." It was

---

[7] Harrison, *Beginnings of Arminianism*, p. 55.

[8] The entire text is included in Bertius' funeral oration, *WA*, I, 36.

signed by Johannes Ursinus, the president of the consistory, and by Hallius and Halsbergius.[9]

These testimonials have caused great concern among the enemies of Arminius, and numerous attempts have been made to explain them away. Ursinus and Hallius themselves began the process when they attested to the rewritten history in the minutes of the consistory in 1617. There it was asserted that the testimonials were given only because Arminius had solemnly pledged to teach nothing new at Leiden and to submit his views to a national synod. This line is taken up by Triglandius, and later by Vos. Vos discounts the letter from the classis on the ground that the classis was not directly involved in the controversy. As for the consistory, the letter meant merely that Arminius had given no offense in recent years.[10] Evenhuis is more moderate. He does not object to the testimonials themselves but only to their form—overstated and flowery. Such letters were customary, he says, and were not intended to be taken in all respects literally.[11] In that he may be right, but a strong protest must be made against the Calvinist rewriters of history in 1617. H. C. Rogge has shown that the testimonial from the consistory had been in the acts of the consistory in 1603 and had been *removed* in 1617.[12]

The later efforts to discount the testimonials have clouded the picture. To mention them is necessary but anachronistic. What is important for the narrative is that Arminius did receive the testimonials, and amid those expressions of esteem, fond farewells were made as he undertook his work in Leiden in September.

Late September of 1603 is the probable time for Arminius' assumption of duties in Leiden. He began his teaching with three orations on theology: *The Object of Theology, The Author and End of Theology,* and *The Certainty of Sacred Theology.* In the first he makes reference to the process of his call, his own inability to judge its propriety, but his confidence that it had been "divinely instituted and brought to perfection." [13]

He seeks the prayers of his friends that he may discharge his obligations well, and he thinks it wise to begin with some discourses on the subject of his professorship. He respects the work of his colleagues in other fields and knows that they will understand that he means no disrespect to their disciplines. "For to every kind of study in the most noble theater

[9] Quoted *ibid.,* pp. 34-35.
[10] Vos, p. 51.
[11] *ODWA,* I, 199-200.
[12] *Wtenbogaert,* I, 226. Cf. his earlier findings in *Algemeene Kunst- en Letterbode,* 1859.
[13] *Writings,* I, 53.

of the sciences I assign, as it becomes me, its due place, and that an honorable one; and each being content with its subordinate station, all of them with the greatest willingness concede the president's throne to that science of which I am now treating." [14] The theological faculty at Leiden still marches at the head of academic processions, but it is undoubtedly more a matter of tradition than of concession to the Queen of Sciences. But Arminius could make his claim without hindrance. Gomarus, at least, would not complain.

The discipline of theology is defined in the Ramist tradition. Since God, the object of theology, cannot be received in his infinity, the discipline must be accommodated to our finite capacity. Theology is in the realm of grace, not of glory. Theoretical theology is for the world of glory; in this world theology is practical and through faith, not sight. "For this reason we must clothe the object of our theology in such a manner as may enable it to incline us to worship God and fully to persuade and win us over to that practice." [15]

In the first instance, then, God is the object of theology, and in man's primeval state this was simply so. The theology of primeval man was "legal theology," but when man had broken the law, legal theology no longer sufficed. Another revelation was required, entailing a new creation, a new providence, a work of redemption, and the restoration of the Spirit of grace, and this was provided through the Mediator. In Christian theology, then, there are two objects of theology, God and Christ. How are they related? "Indeed, these two objects are not of such a nature as that the one may be separated from the other, or that the one may be collaterally joined to the other; but the latter of them is, in a proper and suitable manner, subordinate to the former." [16] This is to say that God, who with the demise of legal theology is no longer accessible to us, has unfolded all his goodness in Christ, so that in Christ we see the mystery of God. Christ is the middleman in communicating God's benevolence, his gracious decree, and his saving efficacy. Faith in Christ is thus necessary for obtaining salvation from God and for qualifying men to receive this salvation.

This raises the question of the salvation of those who have not heard of Christ, a question which had been largely ignored by the first Protestants but which now, with the rise of exploration and trade, could not be suppressed. Arminius does not bow to the argument that the requirement of faith in Christ violates the justice of God, but his own answer is oblique: "The necessity of faith in the cross does not arise

[14] *Ibid.*, pp. 54-55.
[15] *Ibid.*, p. 60.
[16] *Ibid.*, pp. 68-69.

from the circumstance of the doctrine of the cross being preached and propounded to men; but, since faith in Christ is necessary according to the decree of God, the doctrine of the cross is preached that those who believe in it may be saved." [17] This would seemingly lead to a theology of missions, but Arminius did not move on to make such an application explicit. Oddly, it was Plancius, the predestinarian Calvinist in Amsterdam, who proposed Christian missions as one of the purposes of the East Indian trade. The reasons for this curious reversal lie beyond available evidence, and speculation as to motives, be they religious or financial, is useless.

Arminius is content with admonishing his hearers (and the hall of the university was crowded), especially the students, to strive to become eligible for the worthy occupation of "teaching, instructing, and edifying the Church of the saints," spending "whole days and nights in acquiring a knowledge of God and of his Christ," remembering that they are forming an entrance into the communion of the angels themselves, the heavenly messengers. To this end they may well take the apostle Paul for their example.[18]

The language is scriptural throughout. There is almost nothing of technical theological language. Indeed, as Maronier points out, Arminius does not use Trinitarian language. He confines himself to Scripture in speaking of the relation of Christ to God. Neither is there any Calvinist language; predestination is mentioned only once and in a general way. His raw material is Scripture itself, with the form of oratory and argument defined in classical terms (references are made to Euripides and Isocrates).

In the second oration Arminius makes the author of theology to be the same as its object. God is the author of legal theology; God and Christ are the authors of evangelical or Christian theology. The Holy Spirit is also the author of theology, but only in the role of the Spirit of Christ the Mediator. "The revelation of evangelical theology is attributed to Christ in regard to his mediatorship, and to the Holy Ghost in regard to his being appointed substitute and advocate of Christ the Mediator." [19]

The end or purpose of legal theology in its strictest sense is the union of God with man, "to the salvation of the one and the glory of the other." [20] The end of evangelical theology, on the other hand, is "God and Christ, the union of man with both of them, and the sight and

[17] *Ibid.*, p. 77.
[18] *Ibid.*, p. 81.
[19] *Ibid.*, p. 94.
[20] *Ibid.*, p. 101.

fruition of both, to the glory of both Christ and God." [21] This is to say that the union of Christ and his church, begun here on earth, will never cease but will at length be consummated and perfected.

The oration ends with a solemn charge to the students:

God has destined you to become "workers together with him" in the manifestation of the gospel and instruments to administer to the salvation of others. Let the majesty of the Holy Author of your studies and the necessity of the end be always placed before your eyes. . . . You cannot prophesy unless you be instructed by the Spirit of Prophecy. In our days he addresses no one in that manner [referring to Amos 3:8] except in the Scriptures.

No one can be directed to the end of theology, union with God, except by the way of truth, a truth which is taught by theology alone. Let the Scriptures then be your example: "Read them in the night time, in the day time read them [*Nocturna versate manu, versate diurna*]." [22]

The third oration, *The Certainty of Sacred Theology*, is the most time-bound of the three. It deals with the "evidences of Christianity" which were to be put forth so often in the Age of Reason. Everything turns on revelation, but how may we know that there has been a revelation? The necessity of it may be inferred from the nature and condition of man in terms of man's capabilities and needs, or from Christ in terms of his goodness and power. But how does one move from necessity to certainty? How may we be assured of the divinity of the word of revelation? Arminius has nine answers or supports.

First, Scripture attests to its own divinity. It deals with a divine object, God, and it attests to the person of Christ "in such a manner that the human mind, on beholding the description, ought to acknowledge that 'such a person could not have been invented or devised by any created intellect.' " [23]

Second, all the parts of sacred doctrine agree among themselves, as in the congruence of all the predictions concerning Christ. Commands, interdicts, enactments, prohibitions, rewards, and punishments all fit together in a superhuman congruity, while poetry such as Psalm 104 far outshines the best that the Greeks and the Romans could produce.

Third, prophecies are fulfilled with utmost precision, just as Moses proved when he cited the promise made to Abraham that the deliverance from Egypt would take place at the end of 430 years, "on that very day" (Exodus 12:41).

Fourth, the divinity of biblical revelation is seen in the miracles;

[21] *Ibid.*, p. 102.
[22] *Ibid.*, p. 111.
[23] *Ibid.*, p. 124.

to deny miracles which have the testimony of both Jews and Gentiles who were the enemies of true doctrine "is an evident token of manifest impudence and execrable stupidity." [24]

Fifth, Christian truth is verified by its antiquity. Arminius cites Tertullian's doctrine that the oldest is the truest. Christian truth is not only the oldest, but it has survived innumerable perils along the way.

Sixth, the word of revelation has been administered by men of sanctity; that is, those whose personal desires were set aside in order to witness to a truth which was indeed often to their own discredit—Moses, Paul, David, Samuel, for example.

Seventh, the confessors of the word have been constant in persecution and have often sealed their testimony with their lives. They have been caught up in the duel between God and Satan, the result of which is that "the divinity of God's word has been raised as a superstructure out of the infamy and ruin of Satan." [25]

Eighth, the church witnesses to the divinity of the word, although it does not *bestow* such divinity. "Authority is derived from an author: but the church is not the author; she is only the nurseling of this word, being posterior to it in cause, origin, and time." [26]

Ninth and finally, there is the internal witness of the Holy Spirit. Here Arminius speaks with fervor:

We declare, therefore, and we continue to repeat the declaration till the gates of hell re-echo the sound, that the Holy Spirit, by whose inspiration holy men of God have spoken this word, and by whose guidance they have as his amanuenses consigned it to writing—that this Holy Spirit is the author of that light by the aid of which we obtain a perception and an understanding of the divine meanings of the word and is the effector of that certainty by which we believe those meanings to be truly divine, and that he is the necessary Author, the all-sufficient Effector.[27]

The argument remains ever circular. Scripture itself says that the Holy Spirit is the author. When the Jews make the same claim for the Talmud or the Cabala, and when the Turks do so for the Koran, it is a matter of their opinion, for it is only the Holy Spirit which gives knowledge.

Circular it is, and prescientific. "It is necessary that the sun be borne along from the east to the west by the diurnal motion of the heavens," Arminius says, adding that it was, however, "more necessary that Hezekiah receive by a sure sign a confirmation of the prolongation

[24] *Ibid.*, pp. 130-31.
[25] *Ibid.*, p. 137.
[26] *Ibid.*, p. 138.
[27] *Ibid.*, p. 140.

of his life. So the sun turns back ten degrees, thus Isaiah 38:8." [28] Arminius was quite unaware of the new astronomy about to come in, quite unaware that his countryman in Middelburg, Lippershey, was about to invent the telescope. The oration is truly a period piece, but a good one. There is no eccentricity, no carelessness, no pious slogans. And its purpose is not merely to prove something about Scripture. We can give no greater praise to Scripture, Arminius says, than "the application of our minds to an assiduous contemplation and a devout meditation on the knowledge of such a noble object." Theology issues in practice.

So Arminius finished his three orations. They were polished productions, noncontroversial, and widely applauded. He was launched on his teaching career, and the storm clouds were for the moment not visible.

His FIRST regular lectures were prelections (a reading of the text with comments) on Jonah, adapted from his earlier sermons in Dutch on Jonah and delivered now in Latin. The text is lost. It was actually during the course of these lectures, according to Caspar Brandt, that the curators offered their thanks to Nicolas Cromhout and Uitenbogaert, with the gifts and poems mentioned earlier. On October 28, 1603, he began another of his tasks when he presided at theses offered publicly by two students. One student, Corranus, spoke on justification; the other, Gilbert Jacchaeus, on original sin. The students did well and elicited little intervention from Arminius, according to Brandt. On the heels of this, however, and possibly as a result of seeing the students' overweening attempts to solve theological intricacies, Arminius consulted with his colleagues, urging the abandonment of "the cumbrous mass of scholastic assertions" and the return to "the earlier and more masculine method of study" which appealed directly to Scripture.[29]

His counsel, Brandt reports, was not taken kindly by those who still suspected him of heresy. Gomarus continued to watch for an occasion for taking offense, and he imagined that he had found it early in 1604. Arminius, in expounding Jonah, made reference to the New Testament. Gomarus, who shortly before Arminius' appointment to Leiden had been made *professor primarius*, claimed that Arminius was infringing on his sole right to expound the New Testament. "You have invaded my professorship," he said. Arminius denied the charge and defended his right, by authority of the curators themselves, to give prelections on

[28] *Ibid.*, p.116.
[29] *LA*, pp. 191-92.

the New as well as the Old Testament, provided he did not encroach on
Gomarus' particular topic at the time. In this he was sustained, but it
was evident that he would not have peace with Gomarus.

The professors now worked out mutually a schedule of public disputations. On February 7, 1604, it was Arminius' turn, and his subject
was predestination. Now for the first time in the university he would
speak directly on the topic which had become the focal point of the
disputes between the theologians. How would he handle it?

In a word, positively. There is no attack on the doctrine. There are
the affirmations which he feels he can and must make on the basis of
Scripture. He speaks only of the predestination of the elect, acknowl-
edging a predestination to damnation (double predestination), but preferring to call the latter reprobation. On the basis of Ephesians 1 and
Romans 9 he sets forth a definition: "Predestination . . . is the decree of
the good pleasure of God in Christ by which he resolved within himself
from all eternity to justify, adopt, and endow with eternal life, to the
praise of his own glorious grace, believers on whom he had decreed to
bestow faith." [30] It is not legal but evangelical. God alone is the cause,
not man. The foundation is Jesus Christ the Mediator. It is an eternal
decree "because God does nothing in time which he has not decreed to
do from all eternity." [31] The object is twofold: spiritual blessings and
believers. Here Arminius insists on what he had said in Amsterdam
about believers. "The word 'believers' . . . presupposes sin: for no one
believes on Christ except a sinner, and the man who acknowledges himself to be that sinner." Believers, furthermore, are not "those who would
be such by their own merits or strength, but . . . those who by the gratuitous and peculiar kindness of God would believe in Christ." [32] This
is to say that faith is not a work.

The corresponding "double" decree is reprobation, which is "a decree
of the wrath, or of the severe will, of God by which he resolved from
all eternity to condemn to eternal death unbelievers who, by their own
fault and the just judgment of God, would not believe, for the declaration of his wrath and power." [33] This doctrine is practical, for it establishes the glory of the grace of God, consoles afflicted consciences, and
terrifies the wicked, driving away their security.

Thus Arminius rounds out his statement. No one is attacked. No opposing positions are defined and rejected. No mention is made of Calvin
or Beza or Confession or Catechism. The appeal is entirely to Scripture.

[30] *Writings*, I, 565.
[31] *Ibid.*, p. 566.
[32] *Ibid.*, p. 567.
[33] *Ibid.*, p. 568.

The doctrine, he says, ought to resound in private walls and schools and also in the public worship of the church. But he does offer a warning: "One caution ought to be strictly observed, that nothing be taught concerning it [predestination] beyond what the Scriptures say, that it be propounded in the manner which the Scriptures have adopted, and that it be referred to the same end as that which the Scriptures propose when they deliver it." This Arminius believes he has done.[34]

It is a masterpiece of brevity, clarity, and restraint, and at the same time positive and uncompromising. It distills the massive work of his *Analysis of Romans 9* and his *Examination of Perkins' Pamphlet*. All the syllogisms are gone; what remains is affirmation.

On May 29 he spoke again, delivering theses on the church, and in July he offered theses "On the Sin of Our First Parents." The first may be what is known as Public Disputation 18 in the *Opera*, although the title is different from that reported by Brandt, and the second seems to differ from Public Disputation 7, judging from reports on it in Brandt. It was at the second disputation, in July, Gomarus and Trelcatius being present, that he pressed hard the point that the first sin was contingent and not necessary. Opposition to him began to be manifest, and some present objected to his saying "that there is no absolute necessity in things, besides God; yea, that not even fire burns necessarily, but that every necessity which exists in things or events is nothing else than the relation of cause to effect." [35] Helmichius was in Leiden not long after, and he too pressed the point with Arminius, but after a long discussion they parted on good terms. For that matter, Arminius' colleagues had as yet made no trouble for him. Gomarus was lecturing on Romans 9 and had pledged publicly that he would present all positions before arguing for his own. Arminius responded by offering to recant his own position should Gomarus' arguments appear to him the stronger. Arminius was aware of opposition, however, and he mentioned it in letters to Uitenbogaert. He reacted also to the new imputation theory of Johannes Piscator, finding it full of confusion.

It was not until October 31, 1604, that the theological battle in Leiden began in earnest. Gomarus touched it off by holding a public disputation on predestination, out of turn and not a part of the established schedule. He began with an "acrimonious preface," according to Brandt, excusing his speaking out of turn on the grounds that error was abroad—no direct mention of Arminius, but the message was plain. He then proposed his theses, which covered essentially the same position taken by

[34] *Ibid.*, p. 569.
[35] *LA*, pp. 195-97; *Ep. Ecc.*, nos. 69 and 70.

Beza. The object of predestination is man as "salvable, damnable, creable, liable to fall, restorable," so that the decree of creation and all that follows is for the purpose of carrying out the prior decree of predestination or reprobation.[36] That means that in God there is "definite prescience," with the emphasis on the *definite*. "For God's prescience is as it were a book on which God's will for predestinating has inscribed the things predestinated (Rom. 17:8; Jude 4). For God foreknows definitely future things because he has foreordained them by decree." [37]

Arminius took it hard. He was in physical pain at the time, but the mental anguish caused by this public and, he felt, unwarranted attack caused him to take pen in hand the next day and pour out his feelings to Uitenbogaert. He has done nothing to give offense to Gomarus, he says, and he would like to return to his favor, and to that of Plancius too, for it is not right for him to hate anyone. "Be this my brazen wall— a conscience void of offence." But the disciple is not above his master, and he will gladly suffer and die for the truth. "No new thing is this, for the truth to be rejected even by those whom such conduct least beseems and who least of all wish to incur such a charge." [38]

Arminius did not waste time in self-pity; he set forth an answer to the theses of Gomarus, the last of his long, closely reasoned analyses of the writings of an opponent. Nothing was published at the time, however. The two disputations, Arminius' and Gomarus', were published together in 1609, probably before Arminius' death, and again in 1610. His *Examination of Gomarus' Theses on Predestination* was published in 1613 and 1645 but was not included in the *Opera* of 1629, 1631, or 1635. The English translation by William Nichols is in the third volume of the London *Works* (1875).

---

[36] Thesis 13, quoted by Arminius in his *Examination of Gomarus' Theses on Predestination; WA,* III, 564.

[37] Thesis 16; *ibid.,* p. 572.

[38] Letter to Uitenbogaert, November 1, 1604, *Ep. Ecc.,* no. 74; quoted *LA,* pp. 201-2. Brandt takes the "brazen wall" phrase and makes the passage to be Arminius' motto.

20

CONFLICT CONTINUED:
1605-1606

IN 1605 the battle became intense. In early February Arminius was chosen *Rector Magnificus*, chief officer of the university, elected annually. The election reflected the esteem of a majority of his colleagues, but the attacks on him continued. Caspar Brandt reports that all his words and deeds were subjected to minute scrutiny by his enemies, who were searching for a basis for accusations. If he so much as duplicated an argument used by a Catholic, Lutheran, or any other outside the Reformed churches, it was said that he had gone over to the enemy. When he followed the practice of the late Franciscus Junius and handed to his students written theses for their examination, it was charged against him as a crime. Although his public statements were frank enough, his opponents took to alleging that he taught privately things other than he spoke publicly. Reports spread throughout the country that new doctrines were being taught at Leiden. The Leiden pastor Hommius led the pack, and finally Arminius challenged him. In the presence of Uitenbogaert and Hommius' colleague Borrius, Arminius answered Hommius' charges. Hommius was silenced for the moment and agreed "to institute an inquiry after truth." He told his friends later, however, that upon returning home, he had prayed to God for light and it had been revealed to him to continue in his opinions. Arminius wrote to Uitenbogaert: "Well done, worthy investigator of the truth! As if God, forsooth, grants his Holy Spirit at one prayer in such large bestowals as to impart the ability to judge, in matters so great, without any liability of error!" [1]

Early in the year there were several occasions on which the controversy broke out in public. The first of these involved a student from Dordrecht, Joannes Narsius, who was studying theology at Leiden as a protégé of Amsterdam, as Arminius had been years before. He had been examined by the brethren in Amsterdam in 1604, to their satisfaction,

---

[1] Letter to Uitenbogaert, May 20, 1605, *Ep. Ecc.*, no. 77; *LA*, pp. 211-12.

but the enemies of Arminius, presumably Plancius and his friends, supposing that his studies under Arminius at Leiden would corrupt his beliefs, submitted questions in writing to Narsius, requiring replies. This plan was drawn up in the consistory on January 13, 1605. The questions were obviously designed to elicit either an affirmation or denial of Arminius' positions. Narsius was astute in his answers. He could affirm original sin and deny free will; Arminius had done the same. At other points, such as, Is the power to believe given to all who hear the gospel announced? he could reply that he could find no explicit answer in the Confession or Catechism. The design of the questions and the strategy and astuteness of his answers is illustrated in the third question: "Whether whatsoever things come to pass contingently in respect of men . . . also come to pass thus contingently in respect of providence and of the divine decree." The trap was this: if man believes contingently, then God's decree is contingent on man's choice and is not absolute. Narsius answered:

I have to request, brethren, that, seeing the word *contingently* is not to be found in the Sacred Volume, nor in the Belgic Confession, nor yet in the Palatine Catechism, and is moreover used in a variety of senses by scholastic writers, you will submit to rest satisfied with this my confession: "Nothing comes to pass by chance; but whatsoever things come to pass, whether of great account or small, whether good or bad, are subjected to the government and direction of Divine Providence; in such a manner, indeed, that those things which seem to us to be uncertain, and to happen by chance, nevertheless, in respect of the most wise and omnipotent providence of God, and of his eternal decree, happen certainly and immutably; although, of the evil itself which is committed, he is in no respect the author." [2]

It was a cautious answer, discomfiting in its reminder that the Confession and Catechism were silent on the mooted point, both conciliatory and firm in its denial of chance and its reminder of the danger of making God the author of sin. The answer did not satisfy the Amsterdam investigators. The affair served to bring Arminius under further suspicion. Narsius never was accepted at Amsterdam and later sided with the Remonstrants, but he did not become a minister.[3]

Another incident involved a student from Voorburg, Abraham Vlietius. On April 30, 1605, he presented theses on divine providence, with Gomarus presiding. He offered arguments against the position of Gomarus, and Gomarus reacted bitterly, intimating that Arminius had set him up with his arguments. Gomarus' allies joined in the attack, main-

---

[2] *LA*, p. 215.

[3] On Narsius' later career, cf. Joannes Tideman, *De Remonstrantsche Broederschap,* pp. 336-38.

taining that the student had done something improper by differing from the presiding professor. Arminius, fearing that harm would come to Vlietius, supplied him with a letter of testimonial:

> That Abraham Vlietius, in a disputation concerning Divine Providence held on the 30th April, 1605, was bound, from the office he then undertook in the college of disputants, to offer objections; and that, in objecting, he kept himself within the bounds of modesty and advanced nothing unworthy either of himself or his auditory, and consequently gave no just occasion of complaint, I hereby testify as requested.
>
> Jacobus Arminius
> Rector of the University for the time being, and myself an eye and ear-witness[4]

The turbulence was coming from all sides. Now Cuchlinus entered the fray. He changed the schedule of his prelections to coincide with those of Arminius, and he required the students who were dependent on him for their scholarships to attend his classes. Arminius had to appeal to the burgomasters to get this petty hindrance set aside.[5] And just at this time, on May 2, Willem was born.

Two days later Arminius made a counterattack by offering for his public disputation some theses "On the Righteousness and Efficacy of the Providence of God Concerning Evil" (Public Disputation 9 in the *Opera*). It is a long disputation defending the providence of God vis-à-vis the existence of sin. It deals with the nature of creatureliness and sin, the action of God regarding sin in hindering and permitting, and the punishment and pardon of sin. God permits sin, but God overcomes sin. "God permitted Judah to know Tamar his daughter-in-law both as it was an act and as it was a sin: because it was the will of God to have his own Son as a direct descendant from Judah and at the same time to declare that nothing is so polluted as to be incapable of being sanctified in Christ Jesus." [6] It is not a controversial piece respecting Gomarus, for it attacks those who deny the justice of God who allows evil to exist. The only offense Gomarus might take was that Arminius offered his defense tacitly as an alternative to the kind of defense a supralapsarian could offer. And what could a supralapsarian say? It was a shrewd maneuver.

THE NEXT ROUND in the conflict was instigated by the deputies of the synods of North and South Holland. Five of them, all ministers, called

---

[4] *LA*, p. 220.

[5] *Ibid.*, pp. 220-21; letter to Uitenbogaert, May 2, 1605, *Ep. Ecc.*, no. 76.

[6] *Writings*, I, 502.

on Arminius on June 30, 1605—from North Holland, Jacobus Rolandus of Amsterdam and Joannes Bogardus of Haarlem; from South Holland, Franciscus Lansbergius of Rotterdam, Libertus Fraxinus of The Hague, and Daniel Dolegius of Delft. They apparently were acting on their own, for no mandate for their visit is indicated in the minutes of the preceding sessions of the synods. They explained their errand to Arminius by reporting that rumors were circulating throughout the churches about his unsound doctrine and that young men examined before their classes were giving novel answers and claiming Arminius as their authority. They feared that the integrity of the Reformed theology was being undermined. They wished, accordingly, to enter into a friendly conference with Arminius.

Arminius objected. Should he submit, he said, there would be no end to such annoyances. If in the future the brethren should hear from a candidate an answer which violated the Confession or Catechism, they should arrange for a meeting of the classis, the student, and himself, for the sake of which he would go at his own expense to the meeting at any place proposed.

Lansbergius, speaking for the group, did not accept Arminius' answer, upon which Arminius defended his refusal at length. The deputies, he pointed out, represented the synods and would report to them. He, on the other hand, was subject not to the synods but to the curators, and he could not submit to synodical authority without their permission. Furthermore, he was not conscious of teaching anything contrary to the Scriptures, the Confession, or the Catechism. It was the deputies' obligation either to prove otherwise or to apologize. If they wished to lay aside their official role and speak with him as pastors only, he would be glad to enter into conference, provided both he and they should enjoy the same liberty in expounding their own opinions. If agreement were not thereby reached, no report would be made to the provincial synods, but the whole matter would be referred to a national synod.

The deputies did not accept his second counterproposal, and as they were leaving, their objective unfulfilled, Arminius made still a third proposal: that they visit Gomarus and Trelcatius with the same proposition which had been made to him. He insisted that he had given no more occasion for such annoyance than had his colleagues. The deputies consented and later reported that they had so done. If so, it would have been the the mere shadow play that Arminius expected it to be, for it was probably Gomarus who, with Plancius' support, had put them up to the whole scheme in the first place.[7]

---

[7] This is how Arminius recounted the episode in 1608 in his *Declaration of Sentiments; Writings*, I, 196-97.

On July 23, 1605, Arminius held another public disputation with theses "On the Free Will of Man and Its Powers" (no. 11 in the *Opera*). He spares nothing in describing the loss of free will in the state of sin. "In this state the free will of man towards the true good is not only wounded, maimed, infirm, bent, and weakened, but it is also imprisoned, destroyed, and lost." Its powers are not only weakened, but "it has no powers whatever except such as are excited by divine grace." The mind is dark, the affections are perverse, and there is no power to do good or refrain from doing evil. But when man is in a state of renewed righteousness, he loves what is good and begins to perform it in deed, yet all of this is begotten within him by the Holy Spirit.[8]

The theses went as far as Arminius could go toward conciliating his enemies. They leave no room at all for an initiation of repentance and faith by free will. Few of those who called themselves Arminians in later centuries could have accepted a position so strongly Calvinistic. And yet these theses did not deal with certain topics. There is nothing there about the universal call of the gospel and its effect on the bound will. Such a universal and effective call is not denied; it is simply not discussed. Had Arminius abandoned his earlier position? Was he dissembling his views? Why the one-sidedness of the disputation?

Two days later, in a letter to Adrian Borrius, he reveals his thinking on these questions.

I transmit you my theses on free will, which I have composed in this [guarded] manner, because I thought that they would thus conduce to peace. I have advanced nothing which I consider at all allied to a falsity. But I have been silent upon some truths which I might have published, for I know that it is one thing to be silent respecting a truth and another to utter a falsehood, the latter of which it is never lawful to do, while the former is occasionally, nay very often, expedient.[9]

Those hostile and those sympathetic to Arminius have divided on the ethical question. On the one hand, he was holding back some of his views; on the other, he was seeking peace in the university and church under the most difficult provocations from his enemies.

On July 28 Arminius was visited again, this time by two deputies from the Consistory of Leiden. They were elders, Burgomaster Foy van Broekhoven and Professor Paulus Merula, and they urged him "with gentle terms" (according to Brandt) to confer with his professorial colleagues, in the presence of the consistory, about their doctrinal differences. If he would consent, the elders would approach the other pro-

[8] *Writings*, I, 526-29.
[9] *Ep. Ecc.*, no. 78.

fessors; if not, nothing more would be done. It was a quite different approach from that of the synodical deputies a month earlier.

Arminius did not comply, however, for again he pleaded the necessity of seeking the permission of the curators (of which Broekhoven was one) and the uselessness of such a conference for the church. According to Brandt, the elders were convinced and the matter was dropped.[10]

The Synod of South Holland was about to meet, and among the *gravamina,* or messages, to be addressed to it was one from the Classis of Dordrecht. It was a complaint about controversies within the university and church at Leiden, asking the synod to take steps to bring the troubles to an end at once in order to do away with schism and scandal. The curators were alarmed at this prospect of synodical interference in the internal affairs of the university and also fearful of an attack on Arminius, and they called the three theology professors together. Had they observed any such controversies? The professors considered the matter and came up with a unanimous answer to the effect "that they could have wished that the Classis of Dordrecht had acted in this matter in a better and more orderly way." They admitted that there was more disputation among the students than they liked, but among themselves, they said, there was no disagreement on the essentials of doctrine. They signed a document to this effect on August 10, obtaining the concurring signature of Cuchlinus in the Theological College.

It was a remarkable turn of affairs, especially in view of the public attacks on Arminius by Gomarus, sometimes from the pulpit. Had Gomarus had a change of heart? Or Arminius?

The fact is that there was in mid-1605 some degree of peace between the two men. On June 7 Arminius had written of it to Uitenbogaert:

Between Gomarus and me there is peace enough, unless he lend an ear to him who seems to act only for this, that he may not be found to have been a false prophet. On the other hand, I will do my best to make my moderation and equanimity manifest to all, that I may have the superiority at once in the goodness of my cause and in my mode of action.[11]

Who was the agitator who, Arminius feared, would keep Gomarus stirred up in order to cover his own prophecies? Plancius, undoubtedly. It was reported that Gomarus himself recognized this, remarking to his friends "that he could easily have been induced to cultivate peace with Arminius, but for the importunity of the churches and their deputies." [12]

When the Synod of South Holland met in Rotterdam at the end of

[10] *LA,* pp. 230-31.
[11] *Ep. Ecc.,* no. 77.
[12] *LA,* p. 235.

August, it struggled with the matter, trying to find some way to exercise control until there should be a national synod. It was decided to request the curators to require the professors to declare their views on controversial topics.[13] The task was committed to the synodical deputies, Lansbergius and Hommius, who on November 9 presented the curators with nine questions and a petition that the curators would require answers to these questions from the theological professors. The curators refused. If anyone had complaints, they said, they should submit them to a national synod. The deputies then asked for permission to submit the questions directly to the professors, but this too was refused. Arminius reported afterward that the whole matter was done with such secrecy that he had known nothing of it until the deputies had departed.[14]

It was a strange controversy, difficult to judge from a modern perspective. For good or for ill, the deputies represented the official channels of church government. They were pursuing a matter both theological and ecclesiastical, doctrine and ministerial education. The curators were guarding the integrity of the university against outside interference and against the imposition of dogma. Had the deputies prevailed, Arminius might have been deposed and the university would certainly have been compromised. The curators prevailed, and the deputies were frustrated in getting at the problem which concerned them. On both sides, however, the desire for a national synod was rising.

A copy of the nine questions came into Arminius' possession, possibly through one of the curators, and he proceeded to write a reply, matching each question with a counter question and adding short comments. Then on January 31, 1606, he wrote a letter to Uitenbogaert commenting further on his earlier comments.[15] The whole body of material—questions, counter questions, and comments—was included in the *Opera*. James Nichols added the epistolary comments in the *Works*. One new point is raised: Can believers perfectly obey the law of God in this life? Arminius' answer will be considered later.

In the same letter of January 31 Arminius also spelled out some views on faith which were consonant with his views, indeed, necessary implicates of them. He draws on the distinction, made by earlier Reformers, between historical faith and saving faith. Corresponding to it is the distinction between Christ as Savior and actual salvation. The foundation of faith is in the union of our duty (to believe) and the divine reward (life eternal). "If therefore I believe, as I am bound to do,

[13] *APPS*, III, 326-37.
[14] *Declaration of Sentiments; Writings*, I, 198-99.
[15] *Ep. Ecc.*, no. 81.

that Christ is constituted a Savior, that is, possesses the power, ability, and will to save, and if I thus through faith deliver myself up to him, I shall in this case actually obtain salvation from him, that is, remission of sins, the Spirit of grace, and life eternal." The point is that historical faith passes over into saving faith *when exercised.* No one need be left with a mere historical faith.

At about this time he presented more theses publicly in a disputation "On the Comparison of the Law and the Gospel" (no. 13 in the *Opera*). It was a discussion of the old and new covenants and should have elicited no controversy, but someone gratuitously interposed the objection "that man could not but transgress the law, seeing that the decree of God, which determined that he should transgress, could not be resisted." [16] It was a harassment, and Arminius took steps to avoid its repetition.

Harassments came from other quarters constantly, not least from the Amsterdam pulpits where Plancius held forth. Plancius kept up a running attack on Arminius and his friends, calling them Coornhertians, Neo-Pelagians, and the like. The controversy spilled over into the streets, which dismayed the scholars, for now the intricacies of theology done in Latin were in danger, so it was felt, of becoming crudities in Dutch. The fact is that the issues were distorted in the process, with examples in later years of party labels suffering at times a complete reversal in the minds of some people.

As 1605 drew to a close, Arminius completed his prelections on Jonah. The text is not extant. One wonders what could detain him so long in that book.

IN EARLY 1606 Arminius began prelections on Malachi. Here again he was going over territory he had covered in Dutch from the pulpits of Amsterdam. Jacob and Esau appear in the second verse, so the problem of predestination was present. The problem of predestination was present throughout the Dutch churches, clearly out in the open by now. It has been shown that this was not so up until this time. Why, then, should it occupy the center of the stage now? Why should the controversy rage not only in lecture hall and pulpit but also in the streets, with passions inflamed, houses divided, indeed, the nation about to be divided?

Two easy answers must be rejected for their oversimplicity. It was not a matter of mere disagreement in the realm of ideas. Disputes about ideas can scarcely be sustained without something more empirical to

[16] *LA,* pp. 241-42.

carry them along. Neither was it a "historical accident," just one of those things which arise from time to time to occupy men's minds and exercise their competitive tendencies.

A deeper answer will consider, among other things, the personalities involved. The Amsterdam minister Plancius and the Leiden theologians Arminius and Gomarus were strong personalities. Plancius was many-sided, energetic, jealous. Arminius was logical and tenacious. Gomarus was brilliant and choleric. The trio occupied chief places in Dutch public life, and each had powerful supporters and disciples. But they were, after all, theologians, not statesmen or even merchants (although Plancius had his oar deep into the financial waters). There have been many theologians whose disputes and quarrels have not been projected into the national life. And out of all the theological matters about which disputes could arise, and indeed did arise in early seventeenth-century Holland, why should predestination be at the center?

Insofar as an adequate answer can be comprehended and delineated, it will be rooted in the polarity in Dutch religious and national life which goes back to the refugee flights of the latter part of the sixteenth century. This polarity has been seen in connection with Arminius' relationship to Amsterdam. Now, in the seventeenth century, the polarity was taking new forms and intensities. Robert Cardinal Bellarmine may well have touched it off when he attacked the Reformed doctrine of predestination. Here he found the soft underbelly of the Protestant enemy, and his jabs hit home. It was partly to offset these Jesuit attacks that the Theological College had been established at Leiden. Then, when someone else, especially a Reformed professor of theology, took his own jabs at the underbelly, it was regarded as a defection to the archenemy of the true faith, a sell-out to the papal Antichrist. This very charge would soon be made about Arminius. It was in this context that tales about his having kissed the Pope's toe in Rome were circulated. All of this served to make predestination a touchy issue, for it seemed to strike at the very foundation of both the Reformed religion and the national struggle for independence. How could the church tolerate someone who joined Bellarmine in rejecting Beza's supralapsarianism? It mattered not that basic disagreements with Bellarmine might remain; it was enough that aid and comfort had been given to the enemy.

This is still in the realm of ideas, however, and one need not be a Marxist to look for a socio-economic matrix in which the ideas stood for political realities. The country was a loose confederation of provinces which sent delegations to the States General, each delegation possessing one vote. The province of Holland bore the brunt of the financial burden of government and of its major preoccupation, the war with

Spain, and Holland usually dominated affairs of state. These affairs were of two kinds: civil and military. Oldenbarnevelt, as grand pensionary of Holland, personified and exercised the civil power. Prince Maurice, as the military commander, represented the military. There was no clear understanding of the mutual relationships between them, but they had usually worked together out of common goals and necessities.

After 1600, however, this informal but effective duality began to show signs of strain. Maurice had for ten years distinguished himself with military victories to the point that the Dutch campaign was moving from the defensive to the offensive. Spain was beginning to weary of this long war so far from home, and in June, 1602, she had made a small overture for a truce. The conditions were not realistic enough to be taken seriously by the Dutch, although they too were becoming weary of the inconclusive war.

Maurice's military offensive continued, with the costly battle of Nieuwpoort and the Siege of Ostend in 1602, and offensive raids toward the south and the capture of Sluis in 1604. The goal, of course, was still to unite all the provinces, north and south, in an independent nation. Realists, however, sensed that the prospects were not bright, that Spanish power in the south was too strong, and patriotic, Reformed resistance too weak there, for the uniting of the country to occur within the lifetime of anyone then living. Dutch patriotic historians and Protestant historians in general tended for years to regard this as the consequence of the moral vigor of Protestants in the sober north and of the moral and religious flabbiness of the fun-loving south. The modern observer will be more impressed by Pieter Geyl's thesis that the great rivers which came out at Rotterdam played a crucial military role.[17]

Maurice and Oldenbarnevelt, each in his way, were realists. Maurice never abandoned his goal of military conquest, but he quietly consolidated his political power with the goal of establishing himself as a royal sovereign in the north. Oldenbarnevelt, suspecting that the south could never be captured, was willing to entertain the idea of a truce with Spain. The new commercial interests in the seaport towns, anxious to get on with world trade, watched the issue from a financial perspective: which course would be good for business? The clergy asked many questions, each to his own preference. What would be good for the nation? What would do the greatest harm to the Spanish agents of the papal Antichrist? While Maurice and Oldenbarnevelt quietly moved under the surface to undercut each other, all these issues began to

[17] Geyl, *The Revolt of the Netherlands.*

coalesce. There would be a war party, militaristic, staunchly Calvinistic and anti-Catholic, predestinarian, centralist, politically even royalist, and ecclesiastically presbyterian. There would be a peace party, trade-minded, theologically tolerant, republican, and Erastian. The first would support the war and fight Arminianism; the second would support a truce and fight Calvinism. These pure types are a bit overdrawn; there were many who had crossed affinities, but there were many more who fit perfectly in one type or the other.

If these party lines were not openly apparent at the beginning of 1606, the realities behind them were developed enough to make predestination a fighting issue. By 1608, at the latest, it became the linguistic convention by which many people talked about the whole complex problem of the future of their national, economic, social, and religious life.

ARMINIUS' TERM as *Rector Magnificus* ended on February 8, 1606, and according to the custom he gave the rectoral oration. He chose the topic "On Reconciling Religious Dissensions Among Christians." It analyzed the causes of dissension and the cures proposed, and it culminated in a call for a national synod and some specifications for such a gathering. It was one final national plea for a degree of tolerance and inclusiveness in the church which would not be known in the lifetime of anyone present. A survey of this most significant statement of Arminius' views on religious conflict will be in order.

Since sin entered the world there have always been both blessings and evils in human history. The present blessing is the fact that now the knowledge of Christianity shines everywhere (was Arminius thinking of Europe alone or also of the new lands where traders went?—he does not say). The evil is that the very people who are called the sons of peace are divided into factions. According to the proverb "Where a man hurts, there he puts his hand," it is appropriate to devote this rectoral oration to the hurt of the hour, religious dissension.

Religious dissension is the worst kind of dissension, for it strikes at the very altar itself. It engulfs everyone; each must take sides or else make a third party out of himself. It prolongs itself and is almost beyond solution. People think that their very salvation is jeopardized if they make the smallest concession, and each party supposes that the other party denies it the right to eternal salvation. Cynical rulers have known this and have often deliberately stimulated religious dissension while they centralized power in themselves.

Dissension damages both the minds and hearts of men. It creates doubts about religion, leading to despair, and despair leads to atheism, and atheism to Epicureanism. At the affective level it creates estrangements, schisms, factionalism, persecution, slanders, and ultimately war. Then everyone regards his dissenting brother as the most hateful, dangerous person in the whole world. Leaders then set themselves up to claim blind obedience from the masses. "Thus not without reason one is led to exclaim, 'Oh, how much evil is caused by religion!'"

The causes of religious dissension are threefold: accidental, productive, and perpetuating and preventing. Christian faith itself is an accidental cause because its foundation is the word of the cross of Christ, which is a stumbling block and folly. In a stricter sense, however, dissension is produced by Satan, who disseminates falsehood, and by man, who becomes the instrument of Satan by giving way to sinful affections, including pride, anger, inordinate curiosity, avarice, lust, love of glory and riches and pleasure, and hatred of peace. Dissension is perpetuated when we suppose our enemies to be malicious rather than merely in error, stubbornly defend what we have said once we have said it, curse and reproach our adversary, or exaggerate and distort his opinions.

False remedies are too often proposed, such as the sufficiency of implicit faith, whereby the Roman Church commands belief without knowledge, or the conceit that all religions are of equal worth, or the prohibition of controversy, or the failure to interpret Scripture, being content with the mere reading of it. Rome asks us to accept the authority of the Catholic Church, but it channels this authority into substitutes—the Pope, cardinals, and bishops. Some persons appeal to the consensus of the fathers, but such consensus does not exist. Others want the truth confirmed by a miracle, or they abjure the devil, which is a mark of an ultimate desperation.

There are true remedies—prayers to God, amendment of life, giving place to humility, contentment, benevolence, patience, and a proper kind of search for knowledge. "Let sobriety in acquiring wisdom restrain the desire for knowledge; and let study take the place of learned ignorance." In accomplishing this, one must keep four things in mind: first, it is very difficult to discover truth and avoid error; second, people who err are more likely to be ignorant than malicious; third, those who err may be among the elect; and fourth, it is possible that we ourselves are in error. It will help, furthermore, to consider all the points on which agreement is possible; this will put the smaller number of disagreements in a more proper perspective.

The ultimate remedy is a council, "an orderly and free convention of the parties that differ from each other, where, after the different opinions have been compared and the reasons weighed in the fear of the Lord, let the members deliberate, consult, and determine what the word of God declares concerning the matters in controversy, and afterwards let them by common consent communicate the result to the churches." [18] This is Arminius' appeal for a national synod, but he has more than a general appeal; he has also some specifications for the raising and ordering of such a synod. His Erastianism is given full expression:

The chief magistrates who profess the Christian religion will summon and convene such a synod by virtue of the official authority which they possess by divine mandate and according to ancient Jewish practice, which was afterwards taken over by the Christian church and was continued nearly to the ninth century, until the Roman Pontiff began, through tyranny, to arrogate this authority to himself. Such a procedure is required by the public good, which is never committed with greater safety to the custody of any one than to his whose own interests are not involved. [19]

The statement embraces the various components of Arminius' Erastianism. First, magistrates possess a divine mandate. Second, this is according to Old Testament practice. Third, the early church followed this practice until perverted by the Pope. Fourth, it is implied, as Coornhert had suggested, that to deny the magistrate this role in favor of consistorialism or presbyterianism is to develop a papacy of the presbytery. Fifth, the magistrate, being a layman, is a disinterested observer of the conflicts among ministers and theologians. Sixth, religious peace and tolerance are requisites of public order.

Arminius moves on with some more proposals. Only men of wisdom and holiness, zealous for God and for the salvation of man, lovers of truth and peace, discerners of truth and falsehood, and obedient to Scripture, will be admitted to the synod. The synod will include both clergy and laymen. If the first requirement about wisdom and holiness seems to beg the question, Arminius clears himself by advocating the admission of representatives of all parties. Would he include Lutherans? Anabaptists? Catholics? He does not say. Rhetoric takes over now: the hall is to have over its porch in gold letters the Platonic motto: "Let no one who is not eager for truth and peace enter." Then God is to place his angel with the flaming two-edged sword "at the entrance of this paradise," and the president of the synod will be Christ through his Holy Spirit, who has promised to be where two or three are gathered in his name. In the chief chair, to symbolize this spiritual reality and remind the delegates of the ultimate authority in the synod, there is to be placed a Bible.

[18] *Writings*, I, 183. Nichols' translation is modernized throughout this section.
[19] *Ibid.*

Then Arminius comes down to earth. For the sake of order there will have to be subsidiary presidents, preferably the magistrates or someone appointed by them, otherwise someone elected by the whole synod. These chairmen would convene the assembly, propose the agenda, call for opinions, collect votes (using tellers), and ensure accurate debate and the equal privilege of the floor to each delegate. Debate will be according to the rules of logic, not of rhetoric, concise and not impetuous. Every speech is to be read from a manuscript. The agenda must not digress from religion to consider political matters such as a war against the Turks, but must deal with matters of faith, morals, and church order. Dogmas must be assessed in terms of their truth and the degree of necessity that exists for believing them. Since church order is a matter of positive law, not divine law, it can be handled quickly through mutual accommodation.

Now for the crucial issue: the Confession and Catechism. Nothing is more obstructive to the investigation of truth than prior commitments to partial truths. Let all the delegates, then, "be absolved from all other oaths directly or indirectly contrary to this [supreme allegiance to the divine word] by which they have been bound either to churches and their confessions [Belgic Confession and Heidelberg Catechism?], schools and their masters [Geneva, Calvin and Beza?], or even to princes themselves (except in matters of their proper jurisdiction) [Prince Maurice?]." [20]

Arminius believes that such a synod will produce a consensus on at least the greater part of dogmas, "especially those supported by clear testimonies from the Scriptures." But what of the others? Two courses of action remain: either it is granted that brotherly love may exist where there is difference of opinion, or it is agreed that party zeal will not pass over into bitterness and derision. If anyone violates this, let the vengeance of God be called down, "but the snyod will not assume to itself the authority of forcing upon others the resolutions it has passed unanimously," for it may even at such a point be yet in error. This will do more to win dissidents than will the use of force. Lactantius is quoted: "Faith should be by persuasion and not by compulsion," [21] and Tertullian: "Nothing is less religious than to force religion." [22] Arminius closes with an appeal to his hearers to face the issue: the choice is theirs; will they have dissension or peace?

How should such a proposal for a synod be assessed? Was Arminius too confident about the power of reason and persuasion, too oblivious

[20] *Ibid.,* p. 187.
[21] *The Epitome of the Divine Institutes,* chap. 54.
[22] *To Scapula,* chap. 2.

to the depth of sin in man? Was he, on the other hand, cynically trying to set up a magisterially controlled assembly where his own views would prevail? Or was he on a dead-center realism, offering a program which could take place and succeed?

Maybe there was a little of all three, or some mixtures thereof. Certainly, if he took his proposals with utmost seriousness, he was too sanguine about the realities. As for the magistrates, it was his conviction that they did indeed have the divine right and obligation to summon a synod and preside over it. In his mind's eye he would have seen Oldenbarnevelt in this role. The question of the religious sympathies of the grand pensionary has been often mooted. He did not involve himself directly in the theological disputes, but from the circumstances up to 1606, and certainly from the later course of his life, including the final tragedy of his death, there can be little question that he sided with Arminius and later the Remonstrants, at least politically. So Arminius was indeed safe in proposing such a magisterially controlled synod. It is not necessary to term this cynicism, although it certainly had a large ingredient of naïveté in it—if he meant it in all seriousness. That seriousness needs to be considered, however.

What was Arminius' *serious* intent in making this proposal? At one level he did seriously want such a synod as he had described to take place. At another level, however, he must have known that his opponents would resist it. What he accomplished was to set forth, in the most public forum possible, a vision of dedication to scriptural truth in an open assembly which would stand in judgment upon any reality which came short of that vision. In that he was entirely successful. There was a national synod, nine years after his death, the Synod of Dort of 1618-19, and so far was it from the vision of Arminius that the Arminians themselves were never even seated as delegates, but were only summoned as culprits to appear before it for condemnation. Arminius may have been, in 1606, the complete realist, knowing that at every point he was describing the kind of organization, procedure, and agenda which in its universality, disinterestedness, and loyalty to Scripture alone would not be acceptable to the supralapsarians. In 1606, nevertheless, he was still hopeful. On February 12 he wrote to his friend and student Narsius:

According to the custom . . . I resigned my office of Rector on the eighth instant. My successor is Pavius [Pieter Pauw, the professor of medicine]. The oration which I pronounced was on Religious Dissension, and I explained its nature and effects, its causes and remedies, with that freedom which the subject itself and the state of the church require. Many people highly approve of what was said, while it is a copious source of blame and grief to others. I hope to be able to afford you a sight of this oration the next time you come to Leiden, when you will confess that it is not the production of a timid orator. For I perceive that the suspicions and calumnies of these men have the effect of imparting fresh courage to me, which is much strengthened by the synod that is soon to be convened.[23]

Arminius was confident that the synod would convene soon, and there was good reason for the hope. Both parties were agitating for it. Earlier in the winter, on November 30, 1605, the deputies of the two synods had requested the States General to call a national synod, and now Arminius, in the capacity of *Rector Magnificus,* had made a public plea for the same. The next month, on March 15, 1606, the States General granted their approval. Far from bringing the two parties together, however, it drove them even farther apart, for the supralapsarians were dismayed by the wording of the sanction. The States General had authorized the calling of a synod on the same terms as those laid down by the States of Holland in 1597; namely, that in the national synod the Confession and Catechism should be revised.

The synodical deputies were furious. "By that single clause," they complained, "the entire doctrine comprehended in these summaries was called in question." This would give an opening to those who wanted to change the doctrine of the Reformed churches, they feared. On April 19 they addressed a letter to the churches of all the provinces telling how hard they had worked to get the clause for revision removed.[24] When the Synod of South Holland convened on August 8, the deputies reported the action of the States General. The synod urged the deputies to see that the church was treated justly in the matter. A new tactic was urged: even if the synod were to have the mandate to revise the Confession and Catechism, the formula specifying such a revision should be removed from the sanction and replaced by milder words which would give less offense to the church.[25] The synod also ordered that all ministers examine the Confession and Catechisms closely and report any difficulties in it to the next meeting of the classis. This action was fought by Uitenbogaert, delegate from The Hague, but it was defended by the president, Johannes Becius from Dordrecht. Other churches and synods in the United Provinces were to be alerted. Most pointedly, the professors of theology and the heads of the theological colleges (in addition to the *Statencollege,* or Dutch Theological College, there was also at Leiden now a French Theological College) were to examine closely, with their students, the Confession and Catechism for the purpose of promoting peace and unity in the church. It was hoped

---

[23] *Ep. Ecc.,* no. 82.
[24] *LA,* pp. 250-54.
[25] *APPS,* III, 243.

by this means to isolate the critics of the creeds and achieve a consensus of support that would render useless the sanction for revision. A committee for approaching the professors was appointed—Uitenbogaert, G. Coddaeus, N. Marlandus, and E. Aemilius. Uitenbogaert was safely surrounded by opponents of Arminius.[26]

The committee visited Leiden in December and called on Gomarus first, asking him to submit his judgment on the Catechism and Creed. He was cordial enough, but he hesitated, holding that it would be more proper for the entire theological faculty to be convened by their dean, who at the time was Arminius. Trelcatius gave the same answer. The committee protested these evasions, and then asked Arminius for his opinions on the creeds. He commended the synod and its representatives for its action, reported that he was busily engaged in examining the Creed and Catechism and that when and if he had any criticisms, he would submit them at the proper time and place. As for convening the faculty, there was no point in it, since what the committee was requesting was the individual opinions of the professors. The most the committee could get was individual promises to study the creeds. Bertius, since the death of Cuchlinus the previous June the head of the Dutch College, also agreed to study the matter. Colonius, at the Walloon College, would promise nothing until he had conferred with the Walloon Synod.[27] Thus the matter bogged down in delays and evasions at the end of 1606.

For Arminius this new development meant that he had to fight now on two fronts: the doctrine of predestination and its implicates, and the politics and procedures of the proposed synod. To make matters worse, a third front opened up also in 1606. Arminius had held a public disputation "On the Divinity of the Son," and in the debate which followed a student had proposed that the Son is αὐτόθεος [autotheos]; that is, that he has his divine essence from himself and not from the father. Arminius was in an awkward position, for Trelcatius had taken that position in his recently published Common-places,[28] and Arminius had no high opinion of the book of his younger colleague. The student's objection had to be answered, however; so Arminius pointed out that αὐτόθεος is not a scriptural term, but since it has been used by Epiphanius and others, it was not entirely useless if rightly understood. If it were taken to mean "truly God," it was acceptable; if "God of himself" (the closer etymological sense), it was contrary to Scripture

[26] Ibid., pp. 254-55.
[27] LA, pp. 265-68.
[28] Trelcatius, Scholastica, et methodica, locorum communium S. Theologiae institutio (1610).

and to the early fathers. The student was implying that Arminius was unorthodox in his Trinitarian theology. Arminius was maintaining that while the Son is true God, there is in Scripture and the patristic writers a certain subordinationism. The term αὐτόθεος itself stems back to Origen's *Commentary on St. John,* where he had applied Philo's distinction between the sole αὐτόθεος and the lesser or derivative θέοι to the distinction between the Father and the Son in the Godhead.[29] The student cited Trelcatius for his authority. Arminius replied that to say that the Son is αὐτόθεος is a novelty in the church, that the early church had held that the Son possesses his divinity by eternal generation from the Father. Trelcatius' position would lead either to tritheism or Sabellianism. Hence the necessity for a certain subordinationism.[30] Arminius was in a strong position, too, for although he had to disagree with his colleague Trelcatius he could point out that both Beza and Gomarus had concurred in his position.

This did not hinder the enemies of Arminius from accusing him of Socinianism. Some time earlier, when this charge was in the air, Arminius had caustically observed that he would be better able to answer it if he had ever seen anything written by the Socinii. Narsius reported later, however, that at about this time Arminius did read the Socinian literature and presented to his students persuasive arguments against it.[31] But the third front had opened up. Arminius had to defend himself on predestination, on the issue of a national synod, and on the doctrine of the Trinity. As the controversy passed beyond the bounds of academic halls to pulpits and streets, it made no difference what defense he made. It was enough to conclude that "where there is smoke, there is fire." [32]

On this note the year came to a close. In late March, Arminius had spent a week with Johan Pietersz. Reael in Amsterdam. Later in the year he had had a five-week siege of illness. A curious sidelight in the year is a letter written to Narsius in which he discusses Nebuchadnezzar. The story is not to be taken literally, he says. Nebuchadnezzar was mentally ill. Such a rationalizing exegesis would scarcely have been tolerated at that early date, and Arminius did not publish it.[33]

---

[29] Cf. Philo, *De somniis,* I.3.30, and Jean Daniélou, *Origen,* pp. 252 ff.

[30] For corroboration of Arminius' judgment concerning the fact of subordinationism in the patristic writers, cf. R. L. Ottley, *The Doctrine of the Incarnation,* p. 286, and L. Hodgson, *The Doctrine of the Trinity,* p. 88. Both these writers decry, however, what Arminius tolerates.

[31] Narsius to F. Sandius, September 10, 1612; *Ep. Ecc.,* no. 198.

[32] On this episode, cf. *LA,* pp. 257-65; also Arminius' letter to Uitenbogaert of September 1, 1606, *Ep. Ecc.,* no. 88.

[33] July 20, 1606; *Ep. Ecc.,* no. 86.

IN THE WORLD of trade, the first ships of the VOC to return from the Indies arrived in Amsterdam in July, 1606, with some full cargoes but also, and more important, reports of new trade areas opened up. As to the war, there were contrary pressures. The "Lords Seventeen" (directors of the VOC) put pressure on the States General to launch a raid on the Spanish fleet. Others wanted to negotiate a truce with Spain. The motives were largely the same in each case: to get on with the East Indian trade.

21

THE TRUCE AND
THE NATIONAL SYNOD: 1607

THE NEXT YEAR was eventful in every way. The Spanish archdukes Albert and Isabella had authorized secret but now serious moves toward a truce. On the night of February 6, 1607, there was a stealthy visit to the house of the secretary of the States General, Cornelis Aerssens, by a Brussels relative of his, the merchant Werner Cruwel. Cruwel bore a message from a Franciscan, Jan Neyen, who was the son of an old retainer of William of Orange and hence well known in the north. Neyen's letter indicated that the archdukes would consider a truce of ten or twelve years with the United Provinces, "in the capacity of, and as taking them for, free lands, provinces, and towns, against which they claim nothing," provided the Dutch refrain from their East Indian trade. It was only a truce that was offered, not peace, and the demand was well-nigh intolerable, but it was nevertheless impressive that mighty Spain was willing to treat with the tiny rebel provinces at the far north end of its vast empire as an independent entity.

Aerssens knew that this was a big matter, and he hurriedly made it known to Oldenbarnevelt. The latter agreed to meet with Cruwel, but he wanted a witness. He chose none other than Maurice himself. The meeting took place on February 8. It was intended that everything be secret for the time being, the proceedings being known in the south only to the archdukes, Spinola, Neyen, and Cruwel, and in the north only to Aerssens, Oldenbarnevelt, and Maurice. Maurice opposed a truce, for it would reduce his base of political power as a military commander. He resented Oldenbarnevelt, who through the States General had thwarted him in his designs to become the sovereign of the United Provinces. Oldenbarnevelt, on the other hand, had the care of raising money for the war. The bulk of it had to be provided by his own province, Holland, whose debt had risen to some 26 million guilders, and he estimated that the annual shortage was running some 1.1 million guilders.[1] The war was forty years old, with no end in sight.

Maurice did agree to meet Neyen. The story of Neyen's arrival is known in detail from his own diaries and letters. Neyen, a skilled and probably unscrupulous negotiator, arrived late in February in Rijswijk disguised as a burgher. A carriage took him by night to Aerssens' house. There he found Maurice and Oldenbarnevelt, and the negotiations began. The secrecy soon broke down. Who let the news out is unknown, but possibly both Maurice and Oldenbarnevelt were guilty, each seeking support for his position. It was inflammatory news, coming as a rumor, involving a Jesuit priest, jeopardizing the East Indian trade, and yet holding out the prospects of peace and independence.

In Amsterdam there was dismay. This apparent threat to the burgeoning VOC was not received kindly. The Amsterdam Chamber of the VOC controlled eight of the seventeen votes of the Lords Seventeen. Reynier Pauw was the powerful leader of the eight and hence on the way to becoming one of the most powerful men in a nation increasingly dominated by its merchants. He was an ardent Calvinist, an opponent of Arminius, and a friend of Maurice. His Calvinism gained him the support of the new working class, which resented the ingrown merchant oligarchy which ruled in Amsterdam, and there was soon a clear alliance between Calvinism and the war interests of Maurice. The war discomfited the oligarchy, advanced Maurice's power over that of Oldenbarnevelt, and damaged the hated Spaniards, all at once. Maurice, who was no theologian, to say the least, now became a Calvinist.

On March 22 the burgomasters of Amsterdam drew up a resolution condemning the proposed truce, arguing that it would eventually destroy the country. They could point to the damage done to England's East Indian trade by her truce with Spain. Furthermore, there was a strong contingent in Amsterdam, led by Pauw, which wanted to get from the States General a charter for a West India Company. The trade pattern they envisaged for it was opportunistic to the utmost. They planned to capture a portion of the sparsely inhabited Brazilian coast, build plantations there, and man them with slaves from West Africa. This would bring wealth to Holland and frustrate the aims of Spain and Portugal (the latter now being annexed to Spain). Religiously, it would plant the Reformed faith rather than Catholicism in the New World. And there would be a side benefit—the capture of Spanish silver galleons. This was, in fact, the chief motivation of many of the agitators for a West Indian Company. The truce would preclude this direct af-

[1] Frits Snapper, *Oorlogsinvloeden op de Overzeese Handel van Holland 1557-1719*, p. 63.

front to Catholic Spain and this direct approach to Spanish gold. The States General refused a charter to the proposed company, and there was increased hostility toward Oldenbarnevelt in high Amsterdam circles.[2]

This is not to say that all the merchants opposed the truce. Oldenbarnevelt himself, after all, had played the major role in the formation of the VOC. He, and some Amsterdam merchants who sympathized with him, believed that the truce offered a basic gain, independence, which in the long run would serve trade better than the continuation of the war. The differences which developed among politicians and merchants were partly over strategy, partly over the power struggle between Maurice and Oldenbarnevelt, and partly over the religious issue of a holy war against the Catholics.

During these months of February and March, Arminius was probably scarcely aware of these affairs of state and had no inkling that he would soon be caught up in the middle of them. His letters continue to deal with matters of biblical exegesis, and he mentions his illness.[3]

In spite of the intervention of the Amsterdam authorities, the affair must have been still quite a secret in early April, for Admiral Jacob van Heemskerck set forth with a Dutch fleet in pursuit of the Spanish fleet. On April 11, 1607, a preliminary armistice was drawn up, but Heemskerck could not know it. In ignorance he attacked the Spanish fleet off Gibraltar on April 25. Although Heemskerck was killed in the battle, the Spanish fleet was defeated, which suddenly put Holland in a new position of strength. On May 4 the States General signed a provisional eight-months' armistice, and in June the VOC expedition under van Warwyck returned with a moderate amount of cargo but with still more contacts made for trade in the East. The VOC was not going to be frustrated by the truce, and they made plans in the autumn to send out a large expedition under Pieter Verhoef. The Lords Seventeen gave him two sets of instruction, one for public consumption, the other for action. The first called for routine trading; the second was kept sealed until Spain was safely behind. Crews were mustered, at very low pay, from the least prosperous segments of the Dutch population. Military men as well as sailors were employed. The fleet did not get away until December 22. When finally the secret orders were opened, it was discovered that the company was calling for aggressive action against the Portuguese in the East. By now, of course, the eight-months' truce would have expired.

[2] Cf. David Hannay, *The Great Chartered Companies*, p. 88; Masselman, pp. 180 ff.
[3] To Uitenbogaert, February 1, 1607, *Ep. Ecc.*, no. 99; to Narsius, March 29, 1607, *Ep. Ecc.*, no. 100.

ARMINIUS' TIME was taken up more and more with the matter of a national synod. Before a consideration of that problem, there is a personal circumstance worth noting. On May 1, 1607, he wrote to the town of Oudewater informing the town fathers that the widow of the elder Petrus Bertius, Jacomyne Bertius, was planning to reside there. Arminius speaks of the many years he has known her, and he commends her to the town as a worthy and honorable lady.[4] This opens up the possibility that Arminius continued his relationship with Oudewater during his adult life. It is known that his aunt, now the widow of Cuchlinus, spent her last years in Oudewater, where she was listed in the annual register of the survivors of the massacre of 1575. Perhaps Arminius himself had arranged for the widow of Bertius to move to Oudewater. Also in 1607 the authorities in Oudewater sought the advice of Arminius on another matter, the calling of a minister. Johannes Lydius, a son of Martinus Lydius, had been called in 1602. In 1607 Levinas de Raadt was added. This irritated an Oudewater *schepen*, van Galen, who wanted his son, just promoted at Leiden, called. Arminius advised against calling the younger van Galen, and the call was not given.[5] Van Galen, by the way, later supported the Remonstrants. These two glimpses suggest that Arminius was not out of touch with his native city.

All this was peripheral to the religious controversies which were raging. Now, when the populace was aroused over Oldenbarnevelt's dealing with a priestly agent of Spain, Arminius was accused of advising his students to read the works of the Jesuits and of Coornhert. The two rumors should have canceled each other out, so far apart were the parties named, but logic does not prevail when passions are high. Arminius wrote to his friend Burgomaster Sebastian Egbertsz. in Amsterdam that the rumors were nothing but lies.

So far from this, after the reading of Scripture, which I strenuously inculcate, and more than any other (as the whole university, indeed, the conscience of my colleagues will testify) I recommend that the *Commentaries* of Calvin be read, whom I extol in higher terms than Helmichius himself, as he owned to me, ever did. For I affirm that in the interpretation of the Scriptures Calvin is incomparable, and that his *Commentaries* are more to be valued than anything that is handed down to us in the writings of the Fathers—so much so that I concede to him a certain spirit of prophecy in which he stands distinguished above others, above most, indeed, above all.

[4] The letter is in the Gemeente Archief, Oudewater, and was brought to light and published by R. C. H. Römer in *Nieuw Archief voor Kerkelijke Geschiedenis*, I, 174-76.

[5] den Boer and Schouten, p. 82.

Johan Uitenbogaert. Etching by Rembrandt.
By permission of the Rijksprentenkabinet, Rijksmuseum, Amsterdam

Arminius esteemed Calvin's *Commentaries.* What about Calvin's other writings?

His *Institutes,* so far as respects Commonplaces [*loci communes*], I give out to be read after the Catechism as a more extended explanation. But here I add —*with discrimination,* as the writings of all men ought to be read.[6]

It was also in May, 1607, that the curators and burgomasters increased his rental allowance to 300 guilders a year, and this may mark the point at which he moved into his new quarters on the Pieterskerkhof, the former *pastorie* of the Falijde Begijnhof Church.

In the midst of all this, the matter of the national synod was being pushed. Late in February, 1607, the synodical deputies requested permission of the State General for a Preparatory Convention to lay plans for the national synod. Permission was granted, and the States General notified the States of the provinces to send ministers to a meeting at The Hague on May 22. The session of the Preparatory Convention actually began on May 26. Holland was represented by Gomarus, Arminius, Becius, Uitenbogaert, Helmichius, and Hermanus Gerardi (Gerhardsz., a minister in Enkhuizen). There were delegates also from Zeeland, Utrecht, Overijssel, Groningen, Amelandt, and Friesland— seventeen in all. Friesland sent two extreme Calvinists, Professor Lubbertus and Johannes Bogerman, minister at Leeuwarden. The latter was in the next decade the president of the Synod of Dort.

The States put eight questions to the conference—about the manner of submitting *gravamina;* when they should be submitted; how many delegates there should be and how they would be qualified; whether ministers who were not delegates could appear before the synod; whether the Walloon churches should be represented; whether the delegates should be free to express themselves as bound to nothing but the word of God; whether delegates could withdraw when things occur about which they have scruples; and how the synod may contribute to the well-being of the church.[7]

Agreement was quickly reached on a number of points. The synod should convene in early summer of 1608 in Utrecht. *Gravamina* should be sent by the provincial synods. Each particular synod would send four ministers and two elders, although men not elders could be substituted for elders if they were otherwise qualified and professed the Reformed religion. The Walloon churches in the United Provinces were to be invited, and also the refugee Dutch churches in Germany and

---

[6] Letter to Egbertsz., May 3, 1607; *Ep. Ecc.,* no. 101.
[7] Uitenbogaert describes these proceedings at considerable length in *KH,* Part III, pp. 124-26.

France. The States General were requested to send delegates of their own. Professors were to be included, and ministers who were not delegates could appear before the synod.

The delegates divided on question six: Should the delegates be bound only by the word of God? Thirteen delegates wanted to bind the delegates to the Confession and Catechism as well as to Scripture. Four delegates submitted a minority report with a simple *yes* to the question. They were Arminius, Uitenbogaert, and two Utrecht ministers, Everhardus Bootius and Henricus Ioannis. This was the crux of the matter: whether Scripture should be the supreme authority in terms of which Confession and Catechism could be revised, or whether the Confession and Catechism should be determined *a priori* to be so conformable to Scripture that not even Scripture could judge them. Arminius and his friends were outvoted. The majority argued that the Catechism was of Palatine origin and that the Dutch Church had no authority to change it. The minority argued that the foreign origin of the Catechism was reason enough for the Dutch to revise it. And they could point to other lands where confessions were revised, including France and England.

Professor Hoenderdaal points out that the deeper issue behind all this was the doctrine of the church.

Arminius and Uitenbogaert wanted a church that would be free from what was already a too-confining confessional authority. They wanted to recognize a plurality of confessions. In this they were not un-Calvinistic, for Calvin himself was willing to recognize more confessions, including the Augsburg.[8]

On the eighth question there was also serious divergence, with the lines drawn as earlier. The purpose of the synod, the way it could serve the welfare of the church, according to the minority, was to revise the Confession and Catechism. The majority agreed that this was a possible function of the synod, should the synod itself so decide, but that the specification of this purpose should be removed from the call issued by the States General. The purpose of the synod, they said, should be "the confirmation, the unified acceptance, and the propagation of pure doctrine for the maintenance of good order and peace in the churches, together with the furthering of piety among the residents of the country."[9]

Arminius and his friends at last agreed to the omission of the controversial clause about revision provided the omission should not be taken to preclude the revision itself at the time of the synod.[10]

[8] Hoenderdaal, pp. 351-52.
[9] *KH*, Part III, pp. 124-26.
[10] *LA*, p. 281.

It was a defeat for Arminius and Uitenbogaert, and soon they were to learn that the majority would press for far more restrictive measures than those they had proposed in the Preparatory Convention. The next year Arminius wrote in alarm to his friend Burgomaster Egbertsz. that his opponents were pressing to restrict the synod to the "orthodox" party only, who would rise up against all who wanted to change the Confession and Catechism. Rather than being a peaceful synod it would be controlled by the self-appointed accusers of heretics who would suppress and ban anyone they deemed persuaded by "unorthodoxy." [11]

This meant the collapse of hope for Arminius, the rejection by the church of his rectoral oration "On Reconciling Religious Dissension Among Christians." Arminius did not live to see his fears completely realized, but when the synod was finally called, in 1618, they were justified beyond measure.

It was an unhappy year for Arminius. He was under attack from all directions. In a letter to Egbertsz. he reported, "There is nothing, according to their own confession, which certain zealots leave unattempted here and elsewhere, both at home and abroad, in Germany and France, that they may move an insignificant creature like me from my chair and put me to silence." Amsterdam, he said, was the chief source of the trouble, where they say things publicly (he was referring to Plancius and Helmichius) which no one in Leiden, where he taught daily, would dare whisper.[12]

Another source of trouble was Lubbertus at the University of Franeker in Friesland. He wrote a letter on July 1, 1607, complaining about Arminius to the successor of John Knox in Scotland, Andrew Melville of St. Andrews. Melville, however, was in the Tower of London, and the letter did not reach him, being received by the Earl of Salisbury instead. He decided that it was an affair of church, not of state, so he gave it to the Archbishop of Canterbury. The Archbishop gave it to the Dutch ambassador, who passed it on to Oldenbarnevelt. Oldenbarnevelt gave it to Uitenbogaert, who showed it to Arminius. Arminius and Uitenbogaert were disturbed and hurt, and they wrote a lengthy reply to Lubbertus on April 12, 1608, pointing out that he had distorted and suppressed facts; that he had, in fact, as many errors as sentences; and that he had omitted the fact that Arminius and Uitenbogaert had finally consented to the omission of the phrase about the revision of the Confession and Catechism from the synodical call of the States General.[13]

[11] December 14, 1608; *Ep. Ecc.*, no. 124.

[12] May 3, 1607; *Ep. Ecc.*, no. 101.

[13] Both letters are in *Ep. Ecc.*: Lubbertus' is no. 104; the reply of Arminius and Uitenbogaert, no. 105.

Lubbertus was chagrined, to say the least, to be caught in this circuitous manner.

Complaints about Arminius and Uitenbogaert were also circulated among the French Reformed churches, and young men were warned against studying theology at Leiden. On November 9, 1607, Uitenbogaert wrote a defense of Arminius and himself to the minister at Charenton, Pierre du Moulin. It was a lengthy letter, in French, patiently answering the charges (made, so it was learned, by Lubbertus and Trelcatius) and pleading for understanding and unity.[14]

There were other attacks and counterattacks. Arminius attempted to gain the understanding of a younger Reformed theologian, Conrad Vorstius, professor at the new Reformed "Illustrious School" at Steinfurt. He wrote him a lengthy letter on August 25, 1607, explaining his views on the controverted topics, including necessity and contingency, and the term αὐτόθεος.[15] Vorstius must have listened carefully, for he became a sympathizer of Arminius and was, in fact, his successor at Leiden.

There is a curious quirk of history in another letter written to Vorstius, on September 21, by Henricus Rosaeus, minister at The Hague, expressing his fear that the church will be torn apart by dissension unless greater liberty of thought is tolerated.[16] The curiosity, if it can be called such, is that a few years later Rosaeus became a firm Contra-Remonstrant and led a schism from the church in The Hague *because* toleration was practiced there.

When the Synod of North Holland met in June, 1607, evil reports about Arminius and Uitenbogaert abounded. One of the actions of the synod was to order that all ministers should expound the Catechism every Sunday afternoon, and, more pointedly, show greater zeal in refuting the "Anabaptist tramps" (*Wederdoopscher looperen*).[17] It was was a non-too-subtle reminder that Arminius had never written his refutation of the Anabaptists.

On the heels of that synod, which became a disseminator of evil rumors about the two men, Arminius and Uitenbogaert felt it necessary to send a letter to each of the classes of North Holland defending the minority report of the Preparatory Convention. The same intolerant spirit was shown in the Synod of South Holland in August, where one delegate held that the government could not be truly Christian until it had driven all sectarians out of the country. By implication Arminius and Uitenbogaert were now sectarians. Matters were not helped when

[14] *Ep. Ecc.*, no. 108; cf. Harrison, pp. 90-95.
[15] *Ep. Ecc.*, no. 105. There is a fine treatment of Vorstius in Harrison, pp. 165-89.
[16] *Ep. Ecc.*, no. 106.
[17] *APPS*, I, 418-19.

Uitenbogaert refused to report on the Preparatory Convention on the grounds that he had participated not as a deputy of the synod but of the States. It was a bitter session throughout. Again Arminius and Uitenbogaert felt it necessary to defend themselves, and they wrote a defense of the minority report to Oldenbarnevelt. The majority, through seven of them who met in Amsterdam in October, countered with a defense of the majority report. Both reports were received by the States General on December 5.

The same Synod of South Holland created more confusion when it petitioned the States of Holland for permission to have a *provincial* synod made up of delegates from North and South Holland. It was felt by many that this was an attempt to preempt the national synod. The States denied the request on September 14.

There were many other maneuverings and outbreaks of conflict in 1607, but only one more needs to be mentioned. The ministers of Gouda, finding the Heidelberg Catechism not entirely suited for the instruction of the young, because of both its complexity and its ambiguity, drew up a simpler and less technical catechism, published it in 1607, and proposed it for use in the elementary schools. It was entitled *A Short Instruction for Children in the Christian Religion.* The authors, a father-and-son team in the ministry, Hermannus Herberts and his son Theodorus, had consulted Arminius about the project. It was simple in its language, confined almost entirely to words of Scripture, and Arminius had expressed his approval. He had not, however, had a hand in its writing. Caspar Brandt expresses surprise that this should have created a public uproar,[18] but it could hardly do otherwise, just when the whole nation was exercised over the question of the revision of the Heidelberg Catechism. The little book was widely attacked by the opponents of Arminius and Uitenbogaert; and one of them, Reynier Donteklok, who in 1589 with Arent Cornelisz. had tried to solve the predestination problem with a sub- instead of supralapsarianism, now the rector of the Latin school in Brielle, published an attack on the Gouda Catechism, as it came to be called. In his *Examination of the Gouda Catechism* (1608), he charged it with being so loose doctrinally that it was "a shoe that fits all feet." He accused Arminius of having helped draw it up.[19] The whole incident served only to add more fuel to the fire of controversy.

---

[18] *LA,* p. 296.
[19] *BWPGN,* II, 542-43.

22

POLARIZATION IN
CHURCH AND STATE: 1608

THE TRUCE negotiations begun in 1606 had continued throughout 1607, resulting in an eight-months' truce entirely to the advantage of the United Provinces. In 1608 the negotiations took a new turn. Hitherto they had been carried out ostensibly by South Netherlanders led by the Brabander priest Neyen. Now the Spanish overlords themselves would appear, and publicly, in The Hague.

The envoys of the enemy arrived at Rotterdam on February 1, 1608, and proceeded to Delft and The Hague in a great procession. Ambrosio Spinola, the Spanish military commander in the south, was there, and Don Juan de Mançiçidor. The South Netherlander Jean Richardot was in the group, and the earlier negotiators Neyen and Verreyken, who were now in the background. The credentials of the chief negotiators were impressive at the diplomatic level, but at the popular level there was something even more impressive: a retinue of 166 brilliantly attired noblemen, numbers of servants, and all their baggage. The Dutch did their part, too. Prince Maurice led a procession out from The Hague to meet the visitors. He was accompanied by his cousin William Louis and his brother Frederick Henry, and they were surrounded by numbers of famous military commanders and members of the government. The road from Delft to The Hague was lined with throngs of Dutch people who had come to enjoy the drama of the encounter of the most notable military commanders of the age. The two processions met at the Hoornbrug near Delft, and Maurice escorted the guests to their quarters in The Hague.[1]

The gaudy parade inflamed the Dutch populace. They were the sons of the iconoclastic rioters of 1566, refugees from Spanish tyranny in the south, relatives of soldiers in the army, and sober Calvinists, and this display of "popery" was too much for them. The combination of secrecy and ostentation fed the fires of anti-Catholicism, and before long the

[1] Blok, *Geschiedenis van het Nederlandsche Volk*, III, 518-19.

Calvinist preachers were thundering sermons against Spain, the Pope, the Catholic religion and its theology, the Jesuits, and the truce. There was a mass of critical pamphlets, many of them reminders of the atrocities committed by the Spaniards in previous years. Caught in this barrage of invective was, of course, Oldenbarnevelt, and with him his friends.

At a more substantive level, the truce was opposed on the issue of the East Indian trade. That was the stickler. The Lords Seventeen of the VOC issued a remonstrance defending the necessity of the trade, and Willem Usselincx, who was promoting the idea of West Indian trade, did the same, pointing to the advantages of war. At the popular level, then, and in financial circles, the truce was the volatile topic of the day. The country was becoming sharply divided into two factions, a war party and a peace party.

Against this background of national agitation Arminius had continually to ward off attacks from his enemies. A rumor was circulated that the Pope had written to him and to Uitenbogaert, offering them a large bribe if they would return to Rome. Such a rumor traveled far on the wave of hysteria set off by the truce negotiations. It was also rumored that Arminius recommended to his students the writings of the Jesuit Suarez.

These things had been going on since 1607, but early in 1608 there was the beginning of more. Lubbertus had been at it again, this time spreading his evil reports about Arminius by a letter to David Paraeus in Heidelberg. The Palatine ambassador to The Hague, Hippolytus à Collibus, decided to look into the matter, so he invited Arminius to visit him at The Hague. Arminius explained his views in answer to the charges of Lubbertus, and the ambassador was so pleased with them that he asked for a written draft. This Arminius provided in a letter of April 5, 1608.[2] It was published in 1613 and included in the *Opera*. It deals with five topics—the divinity of the Son of God (the αὐτόθεος problem), the providence of God (the problem of the necessity of sin), predestination, grace and free will, and justification (the problem of imputation). It constitutes a brief account of the views of Arminius in early 1608 on the topics which were in question.

In his introductory greetings he defends his orthodoxy at two levels. "I confidently declare that I have never taught anything, either in the church or in the university, which contravenes the sacred writings that ought to be with us the sole rule of thinking and of speaking, or which is opposed to the Dutch Confession of Faith, or to the Heidelberg Catechism, that are our stricter formularies of consent."[3] The perora-

---

[2] *Ep. Ecc.*, no. 114.
[3] *Writings*, II, 460-61.

tion is a passionate appeal for understanding and justice. "This one favor I wish I could obtain from my brethren . . . that they would at least believe me to have some feelings of conscience toward God." His only ambition, he goes on, is "to inquire with all earnestness in the Holy Scriptures for divine truth . . . for the purpose of my winning some souls for Christ, that I might be a sweet savor to him and may obtain a good name in the church of the saints," this in spite of the fact that at the moment he is a reproach to his brethren and "made as the filth of the world and the offscouring of all things." He longs to participate in a Christian conference, where he will manifest "moderation of mind and love for truth and peace." Otherwise, he would prefer that his brethren prefer charges against him before a proper authority, so that the dissension might be terminated. He would consider "any assembly whatsoever," of all the ministers in the United Provinces, or of delegates, or of Holland and West Friesland alone, "provided the whole affair be transacted under the cognizance of our lawful magistrates." "I am weary of being daily aspersed with the filthy scum of fresh calumnies." Unlike the heretics, he says, who shun such a confrontation, he is eager for it.[4]

It was a pattern with Arminius that after a crisis he would write a letter about the whole matter to a close friend. The day after this passionate outpouring to the Palatine ambassador, Arminius again wrote such a letter, this time to Johannes Drusius, professor at Franeker and opponent of Lubbertus. He commends the professor for his serious studies and especially for two qualities he possesses:

You have two qualities, above all others, which I cannot but extol: the first is that you openly declare that you are still in doubt and suspend your judgment, where, after the arguments have been produced, you are afraid of giving full assent; the second is that you do not refuse at this period of life to change your opinions. . . . I love these two properties in you so much the more because they approach the more nearly to my own intentions. . . . Neither am I ashamed to have occasionally forsaken some sentiments which had been instilled by my own masters, since it appears to me that I can prove by the most forcible arguments that such a change has been made for the better.[5]

The last sentence, by the way, is the sole occurrence known to me of any report by Arminius that he had once adhered to views he now rejected. He does not specify who the teachers were, or which sentiments.

In the same month, April, Arminius and Uitenbogaert sought relief from the constant attacks of their enemies by petitioning the States of Holland to use their influence with the States General to get the national synod convoked. They defended the minority report which had

---

[4] *Ibid.*, pp. 475-78.
[5] *Ep. Ecc.*, no. 115; cf. *WA*, I, 168.

brought so much trouble on them, professed their allegiance to Scripture, and denied any intention of bringing about "a new state of things." They promised that they would adhere to the Reformed church and religion "till their last breath." [6]

When Arminius saw that no action was being taken, he drew up a petition in his own name requesting a legal inquiry into his situation. For all the trouble he was in, no one had filed any charges, no tribunal had accepted any responsibility, and he was without the means of facing his accusers and defending himself. This time the States of Holland and West Friesland acted. They set a meeting for May 30, 1608, at which Arminius and Gomarus were to appear, along with the other four delegates from Holland to the Preparatory Convention, and all this in the presence of the High Court. The court was to determine whether the differences between the two principals could not be settled by friendly dialogue and report their findings to the States.

The synodical deputies, as might be expected, objected, and on May 14 they proposed that there be called instead a provincial synod of both North and South Holland. On the same day Bertius wrote a letter to the chief judge of the court, Rombouts Hoogerbeets, commending the court for agreeing to the hearing. He reported that the theological students in the university who went on record as favoring Arminius' views were subject to harassment and suspicion, with no small hint that their careers would be blocked in the synods. It is a pressing matter: there are several young men even now ready for entering the ministry. Unless the controversy is settled, there will be nothing but trouble and no hope of public peace. And since he is so closely involved in the troubles as regent of the Theological College, he would appreciate permission to sit in the back benches at the hearing as a spectator, not out of curiosity but out of a desire to discharge his duties properly. Would Hoogerbeets please use his influence with Oldenbarnevelt to that end? [7] Hoogerbeets' response to the request is not known.

The meeting was held on schedule, with Arminius and Gomarus present, and the four deputies—Becius, Helmichius, Uitenbogaert, and Gerardi. The members of the court in addition to Hoogerbeets were Francken, Johan van Santen, Simon van Veen, and Rochus van den Honert. Gomarus now broached his objections. It was a civil court before which he appeared, and it did not have jurisdiction over matters spiritual. The court replied that no decision was being made in religious matters, but only an inquiry into the seriousness of the breach between the two principals. Gomarus then found it unjust that he should appear

[6] *LA,* pp. 308-9.
[7] The letter is quoted verbatim from the autograph in *LA,* pp. 311-15.

in the role of a prosecutor of Arminius, for they had lived in peace together in Leiden and he was ignorant of what his colleague had written or spoken in public. Since Arminius had mentioned some scruples, he should present them himself. Arminius expressed his astonishment that after all the trouble that had been caused him, charges against him were still not forthcoming. Gomarus then tried to make a charge, quoting a statement of Arminius that "in the justification of man before God, the righteousness of Christ is not imputed for righteousness, but faith itself [is imputed, etc.]." Arminius did not abjure the quotation, but he offered a positive statement to be placed in the record: "I profess that I hold as true, pious, and sacred, that doctrine of justification before God effected through faith to faith, or of the imputation of faith for righteousness, which is contained in the Harmony of the Confessions by all the Churches." [8]

It was a strong and shrewd statement, for it put his opponent in the position of setting the Dutch Church over against the other Reformed churches. But that was not all. Arminius offered to put his views on justification in writing and submit them for investigation by the churches. He promised that if it should be shown that his opinion was wrong, he would either desist from holding it or resign his office. Gomarus conceded nothing. Arminius then quoted the answers to Questions 60 and 61 of the Heidelberg Catechism as his own sentiments on justification. Gomarus still quibbled, and the court was put out with him, since they perceived that for Arminius no less than Gomarus it was not human works but the grace of God that effects justification. The court then enjoined Gomarus to put his position on disputed points in writing; then let Arminius do the same, and let each write his comments and criticism of the statement of the other. The meeting was adjourned, and the court reported to the States that the differences between the principals were not fundamental but had to do with subtleties that might better be omitted or at least tolerated.

The States, upon receiving this report, summoned the two men. Oldenbarnevelt, their grand pensionary, made a speech which in retrospect looks fatuous, to the effect that the States were pleased to learn that no fundamental differences existed between the two theologians and that now they were enjoined to live in peace and teach nothing contrary to Scripture or the Confession and Catechism. Gomarus was not content

---

[8] *LA*, p. 319. He was referring to Salnar's *Harmonia confessionum fidei orthodoxarum et reformatorum ecclesiarum,* a compilation of extracts from the principal Reformed confessions designed to be a Reformed counterpart to the Lutherans' Formula of Concord (1577). Commissioned by the churches of Zurich and Geneva to unite the Reformed churches in a common front against Roman Catholics and Lutherans, it includes, nevertheless, excerpts from the Augsburg, Saxon, and Würtemburg Confessions.

with that and made an inflammatory statement. He would not want to stand before God his judge with the theological opinions of Arminius, and unless they were suppressed, there would be civil strife "province against province, church against church, city against city, citizen against citizen." Arminius again protested both his orthodoxy and his good faith in maintaining the peace of the church.[9]

It was not a happy meeting. A layman present is reported to have remarked that he would rather appear before God the judge with the theology of Arminius than with the love shown by Gomarus. Uitenbogaert was depressed and remarked to Hugo Grotius that he saw nothing but trouble ahead for Arminius, the same kind of trouble that befell Castellio in Geneva, who finally had to earn his living by sawing wood.[10]

There was very little happiness for Arminius in those days. His enemies—for the term "opponents" is now not strong enough—had created an atmosphere of hysteria in which he was to be blamed for everything that went wrong. It was as if he were the scapegoat on which all the sins and troubles of church and state were to be laid, so that if only he could be driven out, there would be no more problems.

Some of the hysteria had sinister effects; sometimes there were petty annoyances; often it created the extra burden of hard work for Arminius as he had to take pen in hand and patiently answer charges leveled at him.

An example of the first was a student riot in December, 1607. A law student, Assuerus Hornhovius, had just passed his promotion examination on a morning when in some kind of disturbance, probably a drinking celebration, he was shot and killed by a soldier of the watch. This touched off a round of student riots that lasted throughout the winter. The enemies of Arminius were able somehow to pin the blame on him, and placards to that effect were posted on the walls of the town and on the doors of the university. The students were incited even to try to break down the door of his house at night. Hommius exulted in this turn of affairs. "His influence is beginning to wane," he observed. Maronier, who relates these events, comments aptly, "His enemies had thus reached their goal." [11]

Less important but annoying nonetheless was a rumor about ghosts in his house. Arminius and his wife had gone to Amsterdam for "several months," so the story went, leaving the children home with the maid.

[9] *LA*, pp. 316-25; Rogge, *Wtenbogaert*, I, 359-63.
[10] Rogge, *Wtenbogaert*, I, 365, citing a letter of Uitenbogaert to a certain N. R.
[11] Maronier, pp. 289-90.

(The exaggeration of "several months," which is chronologically impossible from what is known of Arminius' activities, casts doubt at once on the story, not to mention other doubts that will arise in the mind of the modern reader.) One day they heard a frightful noise in the professor's study. Engeltje and the maid, fearing that a thief had broken in, "climbed up" to look in the study (to look over the door? to get up to the attic study?), but what they saw was a fearsome ghost in human form. They called the neighbors and threw a key out the window so that the neighbors could come in to help, but no one found anything. This story was told by none other than the Leiden minister Hommius in a letter to Lubbertus at Franeker. Lubbertus must know of this event, says Hommius, because when a heretic has dealings with an evil spirit it is a sure sign that heresy exists! [12]

A more substantive harassment occurred in 1608 when someone circulated thirty-one theological propositions, a sequence of twenty and a sequence of eleven, and attributed them partly to Arminius, partly to Borrius, and partly to both. The purpose was to attribute heresy to the alleged writers. This sort of thing was not new, for five of these articles, and then seventeen more, had circulated two years earlier, and Arminius had seen them. Some persons ("men of wisdom and authority," according to Caspar Brandt) showed Arminius a copy of the thirty-one articles, and he felt it necessary to draw up an extended answer to this device, making comments on each of the articles. His friends persuaded him not to release the reply at the time, however, lest his thorough answers serve only to drive his enemies to still more extreme tactics. His answer was not published until the appearance of the *Opera* in 1629. It may have been circulated in manuscript during Arminius' lifetime, however. James Nichols suggests that this may have occurred in early 1609.[13]

It was the second of the only three apologetic pieces Arminius issued during these troubles, the first being his shorter ("mercifully short," as Harrison puts it) letter to Hippolytus à Collibus, the third being his *Declaration of Sentiments*. It deserves some scrutiny.

In the introduction he tells something of the history of the articles without naming anyone as the presumed author. There are grounds for suspecting Lubbertus, for they are similar to the charges he had made in his letter to Paraeus in Heidelberg. Arminius had long been silent, he says, but lest his silence be interpreted as a confession of guilt, he must now reply. "Whatever I know to be true, I will confess and defend. On whatever subjects I feel hesitation, I will not conceal

[12] October 10, 1608, quoted in Maronier, p. 290.
[13] *WA*, I, 669.

my ignorance. Whatever my mind dictates to be false, I will deny and refute." [14]

The body of his answer is lengthy and intricate; some of its content will be mentioned later. It is not as dispassionate as some of his earlier writings, however, for he bursts out indignantly against the tactics of his enemies. Of the twenty-fourth article, which he found particularly ambiguous and confusing, he said, "I do not know what I can most admire in this article—the unskillfulness, the malice, or the supine negligence of those who have been its fabricators!" [15] At another point he complains that what he regarded as a private consultation with a minister was immediately publicized by that minister. In the conclusion he offers again to confer with anyone who is not satisfied with his answers. He deals also with those who reproach him for hesitancy at some points. Hesitancy was not the style of his enemies, and they blamed him when he did not have ready and fixed answers to all questions. Arminius replies:

The most learned man, and he who is most conversant with the Scriptures, is ignorant of many things and is always but a scholar in the school of Christ and of the Scriptures. . . . It is better for him to speak somewhat doubtfully than dogmatically about those things of which he has no certain knowledge, and to intimate that he himself requires daily progress and seeks for instruction. . . . Not everything which becomes a subject of controversy . . . is of equal importance. Some things are of such a nature as to render it unlawful for any man to feel a doubt concerning them. . . . But there are other things which are not of the same dignity. [16]

Helmichius died in Amsterdam on August 29, 1608. He had been no friend of Arminius, although he had felt the grief and pathos of the division in the church. In his last illness his friends heard him cry out on numerous occasions, "Oh Uitenbogaert, Uitenbogaert!" They asked him, "Dominee Helmichius, why do you cry so much for Uitenbogaert? Arminius is always at the bottom of the trouble." He replied, "What is Arminius to me? But Johannes, Johannes Uitenbogaert, whom I have loved as a mother loves her child that she carries under her heart, oh Uitenbogaert, who causes such grief to the church!" [17]

Further trouble arose out of Alkmaar. It had three ministers—the relatively uneducated Pieter Cornelisz., a former basketmaker; Cornelis van Hille, from the Dutch refugee congregation at Norwich, England; and a newcomer (in 1597), Adolphus Venator (Adolf de Jager).

[14] *Writings,* I, 277.
[15] *Ibid.,* p. 355.
[16] *Ibid.,* p. 377.
[17] J. Hania, *Wernerus Helmichius,* pp. 84-85.

Venator brought new life to the church with his oratorical and clear preaching, not to mention his scholarship (van Hille reported that Venator carried an unpointed Hebrew Bible with him on pastoral calls). Rivalry developed between van Hille and Venator, stimulated partly by theological differences but even more by their wives. Venator had taught that it is not enough to belong to a church where the pure word is preached and the sacraments properly administered, but each person must examine himself to see if there be in him faith, hope, and love, of which the last is the greatest. He tried to get permission for the banned former minister, Cornelis Wiggerts, to preach. Then he took in students and taught them the classics and even had them act Terence's comedy *Andria*. When his colleagues objected, he reminded them that Plancius also engaged in an outside trade, mapmaking. Venator was temporarily suspended.

All that was in the early 1600s, but in 1608 the trouble flared up again. The Classis of Alkmaar demanded that all its ministers sign the following statement: "We the undersigned declare that the doctrine contained in this [Heidelberg] catechism, which is accepted unanimously by the Reformed church, as well as the Thirty-seven Articles [of the Belgic Confession], agrees entirely with the word of God and accordingly with the doctrine of salvation." Venator was ill, but four other ministers, supporters of Arminius, refused to sign. They appealed to the States of Holland, who ordered them reinstated. The classis refused on the grounds that it was an ecclesiastical matter, and referred it to the Synod of North Holland meeting at Hoorn on October 28, where the actions of the classis were upheld. During the synod the ministers had a dinner at the home of Arminius' friend Willem Bardesius. During the dinner Plancius, expressing the hysteria of the day, remarked that the Catholics were as dangerous enemies as Jews and Turks (two other prejudices of the times). Venator objected, defending the Christian character of Rome. He was in real trouble now, and at the next meeting of the classis the declaration concerning the Catechism and Confession was put to him. He refused to sign and was suspended from the ministry. The town council reinstated him. Many of the tensions in the Dutch Church were now played out in open conflict in Alkmaar—the authority of magistrates versus ministers, attitudes toward Rome, the nature of Confession and Catechism. Unfortunately, the issues got confused with some woman trouble. It was a *cause célèbre* throughout the country, and served to put more pressure on Arminius, who deplored the pledge demanded by the classis of the ministers.[18]

[18] On the Alkmaar affair, cf. *KH*, Part III, pp. 186-90; Rogge, *Wtenbogaert*. I, 318-32.

The Catholic issue was played to the hilt by Arminius' enemies. Under the pressure of rumors that he was sympathetic to Rome, Arminius wrote almost vehemently against Rome. In a public disputation on "The Case of All the Protestant or Reformed Churches with Respect to Their Alleged Secession" (Public Disputation 22), given on August 1, 1607, he had defended the legitimacy of the Reformed churches vis-à-vis Rome. It was typically thorough, leaving no loopholes, but it did not satisfy his enemies, for at one point he had said, "We conclude, therefore, that neither with respect to faith and worship nor with respect to charity have the Reformed churches made a secession from that of Rome, so far as the Romish church retains anything which is Christ's; but they rejoice and glory in that separation so far as she is averse from Christ." [19] It was more than the anti-Catholic hysteria of the day could bear to concede that in some respects the Roman Church might have retained something of Christ. In the frantic days of 1608 Arminius was accused again and again of favoring Rome, of being an agent of the Jesuits; and by one person he was blamed for causing in the country a spirit of weakness which enabled the Spanish troops to capture several towns from the United Provinces. Arminius could find no effective avenue of protest. To a friend he wrote that should Prince Maurice be assassinated (he was remembering the assassination of William of Orange) tomorrow, he was sure that he would be blamed for that!

He did make another attempt to clear himself. Shortly after the hearing before the High Court on May 30, 1608, he held a public disputation "On the Roman Pontiff, and the Principal Titles which are Attributed to Him" (Public Disputation 21). It did not matter that scarcely a year earlier he had scourged the Roman Church generally and the Pope in particular in a disputation "On Idolatry" (Public Disputation 23). Now he would try once again to convince his enemies that he was no friend of the Pope. He began by denying the Pope such titles as spouse, head, and foundation of the church, the vicar of God and Christ, and the prince of pastors and bishops. He concurred entirely, he said, with those who disparage the Pope with titles such as "the adulterer and pimp of the church, the false prophet, the destroyer and subverter of the church, the enemy of God and the Anti-Christ, the wicked and perverse servant, who neither discharges the duties of a bishop nor is worthy to bear the name." [20] He actually defends at length each title specifically. Has he, then, abandoned or suppressed the slight qualification which had enraged his enemies earlier? No, for in a

[19] *Writings*, I, 631. This disputation was later published in Dutch translation as *Een cort, ende bundich Tractaetgen* . . . (The Hague, 1609).

[20] *Writings*, I, 609.

concluding remark he says, "It is a part of religious wisdom to separate the Court of Rome from the church [of Rome] in which the pontiff sits." [21] That is to say, it is possible that in spite of the sins of the Pope, there are possibly Roman Catholics who are Christians; or to put it less individualistically, that the Church of Rome is in some sense a true church. In another place he used the language of Deuteronomy 24:1, 3, "bill of divorcement," and said that he was not sure that God had granted the Church of Rome, in spite of her sins, a bill of divorcement.

The disputation did not accomplish its purpose but only fed fuel to the fires of hate. Arminius was attacked from the pulpits of Amsterdam, where he was accused of teaching that the Pope is a member of the body of Christ. He wrote a protest to his friend Burgomaster Sebastian Egbertsz.; it is significant for its firmness, both against the Pope and against the bigoted anti-Catholics. And he draws on some Dutch history in his remarks:

I openly profess that I do not hold the Roman Pontiff to be a member of Christ's body, but to be an enemy, a traitor, sacrilegious, a blasphemer, a tyrant, and most violent usurper of a most unjust domination over the church; as the man of sin, as the son of perdition, as that most notorious outlaw, etc. I understand, however, by the Pope one who exercises the Pontificate in the usual manner. But if some Adrian of Utrecht, supposing him to be elevated without dishonorable artifices to the Pontifical chair, were actively to set about the reformation of the church, making a commencement with himself the Pope, and with the Pontificate, and with the Court at Rome, and assuming nothing more than the name and authority of Bishop—though holding the pre-eminence over all other bishops by virtue of ancient statutes of the church—him I should not dare to call by the above appellations.[22]

He went on to say that he did not expect the papacy to reform itself. He was taking a position of principle, however, which would be centuries in making itself acceptable in Reformed circles—which indeed has been seldom acknowledged in Protestant circles until the advent of Pope John XXIII. Few people could hear him in 1608, although the memory of Adrian should have helped.

THE NEW TRUCE negotiations in the Trèves Chamber of the Binnenhof in The Hague were proceeding throughout 1608, and the events there constantly roused the two factions in Holland to new levels of anxiety and anger. There were small irritations. The Spanish envoys continued

[21] *Ibid.*, p. 619.
[22] September 14, 1609; *Ep. Ecc.*, no. 118.

to use the seal of the seventeen United Provinces. Different languages were used—the enemy used French, the States used Dutch. It took some time to agree on a uniform system with dual transcription of the proceedings. Many smaller matters, nevertheless, could be settled—boundaries, reparations, and the like. But on two major points the differences remained vast and bitter—the East Indian trade and religion. A great deal was said about the first issue; the other loomed large but did not dominate the discussions. The religious issue boiled down to the question of the toleration of Catholics in the north, for their numbers were diminishing due to conversions to the Reformed religion and to social and governmental sanctions against the Roman religion. Catholicism appeared headed to a minority position numerically, if not extinction, and the Spanish envoys wanted to ensure the legal toleration of remaining Catholics.

On the trade issue it was decided to send Neyen to Spain to try to persuade the "peace party" there to gain concessions for the north. The temporary armistice was extended, to the disgust of Maurice and William Louis. The negotiations dragged out through the summer, while the envoys awaited the return of Neyen. Others used the time industriously if not helpfully by turning out a flood of inflammatory pamphlets against the truce. There were fictional "conferences between the Pope and the King of Spain," an alleged "letter from a baker to the Pope," and all manner of devices for exciting the populace against the truce.[23] Furthermore, there were facts for the public to ponder, for the proceedings of the negotiations were published daily. Finally, on August 22, the French diplomat Pierre Jeannin brought a message from the Spanish government: an offer of perpetual recognition of independence for the United Provinces with two provisos—trade with the Indies should cease, and Catholic worship should be permitted without hindrance. It was a blow to the hopes for peace and further excited the war party. Then, when military actions were resumed on the border, the north suffered some serious losses, including the death of young Count Adolf of Nassau. The whole business might have come to a standstill had not a most peculiar circumstance arisen.

In an apartment in The Hague where the Spanish envoys had recently been living there was discovered in a drawer of letter of instructions which had been left behind. The discovery might possibly convince the north of the good faith of the archdukes—unless it was a ruse. That was the question, and everyone had his opinion. Never had the country

[23] Many of these are extant and may be seen in the Royal Library in The Hague; cf. W. P. C. Knuttel, *Catalogus van de Pamfletten-verzameling Berustende in de Koninklijke Bibliotheek,* I, 271 ff.

been more aroused by a public issue. The missive, in fact, had probably been contrived by Richardot.

This was in September. The whole country was in a state of agitation, not least the churches. Arminius could find no peace for mind or body. At times he was so sick that he could not stand the jostling of a carriage. Accusations flew all around, but he could find nothing to pin down, no responsible body to hear him. Finally, just when the truce negotiations were at their most inflammatory stage, he had his opportunity.

23

THE *DECLARATION OF SENTIMENTS*

THE AFFAIR really began with the conference of Arminius and Gomarus before the High Court on May 30, 1608, when at the conclusion of that meeting the court had ordered the two men to submit their opinions in writing. Arminius later asked the States of Holland that he be permitted to submit his opinions to them not only in writing but in person. At the meeting of the Synod of South Holland in Dordrecht on October 14-18, 1608, it was decided that all ministers would have to submit their opinions on the Confession and Catechism to their local classis within thirty days. This was in effect an inquisition, and it was contrary to orders of the States of Holland.[1] The States moved quickly now, and on October 20, in a letter signed by their secretary, A. Duyck, they invited Arminius to appear before them on Thursday, October 30.[2]

Arminius had just ten days to prepare his statement. He read his *Declaration of Sentiments* before the full assembly of the States of Holland and West Friesland at the appointed time in the Binnenhof in The Hague. He spoke in Dutch from a manuscript which is extant.[3] It was published the year after Arminius' death by Thomas Basson.[4] A translation into Latin, not by Arminius, was included in the *Opera*. With the *Answers to Nine Questions* it was the first of Arminius' writings to appear in English, translated by Tobias Conyers, who in his preface begs Oliver Cromwell to have a more favorable view of Arminians.[5] James Nichols' translation of 1825 is from the Latin text of the *Opera*. The Dutch text was reissued a second time, 350 years after the first printing, with introduction and notes by Professor G. J. Hoenderdaal.[6]

The *Declaration* represents the mature views of Arminius. He spoke

---

[1] *APPS*, III, 280-81.

[2] *KH*, Part III, p. 181.

[3] Collection of the Remonstrant-Reformed Church, Rotterdam, 2201, no. 29, in the City Library, Rotterdam.

[4] *Verclaringhe Iacobi Arminii* . . . (Leiden, 1610).

[5] *The Just Man's Defence* . . . (London, 1657).

[6] *Verklaring van Jacobus Arminius* (Lochem, 1960).

firmly and openly, attacking what he found in the church that he felt was wrong, and offering a clear exposition of hiw own views at those points which were controverted. The diffidence is gone; he knows that the time to speak has come. Arminius had made a shrewd move in asking for a public hearing before the States, and the States were no less shrewd in granting it. The eyes of Holland were turned to the event, for here was the symbol, at least, of the divisions which were tearing the country apart. While Arminius patiently explained his views on God and man, grace and free will, the divinity of the Son of God, and evangelical perfection, his listeners were hearing it with ears attuned to the issues of war and peace, Spain, the papacy, the fruits and risks of privateering, the East Indian trade, the West Indian trade, the stealthy negotiators nearby, the growing rivalry between Oldenbarnevelt and Maurice, and the truce.

The *Declaration* begins with remarks about the occasion of Arminius' appearing before the States and proceeds to a detailed account of the controversy over doctrine and the proposed national synod, beginning with the visit of the synodical deputies to him on June 30, 1605. He recounts the persistent efforts of the synods to summon him to account for his views and of his equally persistent refusal to yield to their demands. When the Preparatory Convention made the same attempts, he still refused, he says, because (1) he was under the jurisdiction of the curators, not the synods, and (2) there would be a lack of equity because he would be outnumbered, they would be "armed with public authority," and the deputies were not free to make their own judgments in the case but were bound to the opinions of their superiors. He proceeds to tell of the rumors that have been spread about him. Then he turns to the doctrinal matters themselves.

First, he deals with predestination. Under eight headings he describes the supralapsarian position—accurately, it must be added. For purposes of analysis he reduces it to four heads which, because his own position will be presented under four heads, should be indicated here:

1. God has decreed to save and damn certain particular persons.

2. In order to carry out that decree, God determined to create Adam and all mankind in him in a state of original righteousness, "besides which he also ordained them to commit sin" and thus be deprived of original righteousness.

3. God decrees not only the salvation of the elect but the means to it so that they can do no other than to believe, persevere in faith, and be saved.

4. God decrees to deny these means to the reprobate.[7]

[7] *Writings*, I, 216.

Arminius now comes out fighting. No longer is he content to say merely that many views should be tolerated in the church; he finds this position intolerable, and he says why. Twenty reasons, in fact, are offered. Logic and history come into play. This doctrine is not the foundation of Christianity, for it "is not the decree of God by which Christ is appointed by God to be the Savior, the Head, and the Foundation of those who will be the heirs of salvation." The logic works like this: The certainty of salvation depends on this decree (stated as a syllogism) :

They who believe shall be saved;

I believe;

Therefore, I shall be saved.

But this doctrine of predestination contains neither the first nor the second member of the syllogism.[8]

Then the history. The doctrine described "was never admitted, decreed, or approved in any council, either general or particular, for the first six hundred years after Christ." [9] He does a comprehensive survey: Nicaea, Constantinople I, Ephesus, Chalcedon, Constantinople II, Constantinople III, and the local councils of Jerusalem, Orange, and Mela. Furthermore, none of the orthodox theologians of the first six hundred years taught or approved this doctrine. He mentions Augustine, Prosper of Aquitaine, Hilary, Fulgentius, and Orosius. It does not agree with Salnar's *Harmony of the Reformed Confessions* published at Geneva, nor does any single confession in the *Harmony* teach precisely this doctrine. It is not mentioned at all in the confessions of Bohemia, Würtemburg, and England, nor in the First Helvetic Confession and the Confessio Tetrapolitana. The confessions of Basel and Saxony mention it only briefly, in three words. The Augsburg Confession speaks of it in such a manner that the Genevan editors find it necessary to make a warning annotation. The Second Helvetic Confession has to be stretched to accommodate this doctrine, and yet it is approved in Geneva itself.

But history gets us to the here and now, and that raises the issue of the Belgic Confession and the Heidelberg Catechism. Arminius quotes Article 14 of the Confession, that man "wilfully subjected himself to sin . . . giving heed to the words of the devil." "From this sentence," Arminius says, "I conclude that man did not sin on account of any necessity through a preceding decree of predestination." [10] Likewise with Article 16. As for the Catechism, Question 20 is noteworthy: "Will all men, then, be saved through Christ as they became lost through

[8] *Ibid.*, pp. 216-17.
[9] *Ibid.*, p. 218.
[10] *Ibid.*, p. 220.

Adam? No. Only those who, by true faith, are incorporated into him and accept all his benefits." Arminius makes the observation now familiar from his earlier writings: "From this sentence I infer that God has not absolutely predestinated any men to salvation; but that he has in his decree considered them as believers." [11] Similar treatment is given Question 54.

There are other reasons for rejecting this doctrine of predestination. It is contrary to the nature of God, particularly his wisdom, justice, and goodness. It is contrary to the nature of man, who has been created in the image of God with freedom and an aptitude for eternal life. It is opposed to the act of creation, which is a communication of good. It is inconsistent with the nature of sin as the disobedience which is the meritorious cause of damnation. It makes sin a means by which God executes the decree of damnation.

Arminius is not through yet. This doctrine of predestination is contrary to the nature of grace, to the glory of God, to Jesus Christ our Savior, and to the salvation of men. On the last point, it

prevents . . . saving and godly sorrow for sins, . . . it removes all pious solicitude about being converted, . . . it restrains . . . all zeal and studious regard for good works, . . . it extinguishes the zeal for prayer, . . . it takes away all that most salutary fear and trembling with which we are commanded to work out our own salvation, . . . [and] it produces within men a despair both of performing that which their duty requires and of obtaining that towards which their desires are directed.[12]

There is still more. The doctrine is in open hostility to the ministry of the gospel, it subverts the foundation of religion generally and of the Christian religion particularly, and it has been rejected by the greater part of Christians both historically and in the present. "However highly Luther and Melanchthon might at the very commencement of the Reformation have approved of this doctrine, they afterwards deserted it." He cites the letter of Melanchthon to Caspar Peucer:

Laelius writes to me and says that the controversy respecting the Stoical fate is agitated with such uncommon fervor at Geneva that one individual is cast into prison because he happened to disagree with Zeno. O unhappy times, when the doctrine of salvation is thus obscured by certain strange disputes! [13]

[11] *Ibid.*, p. 221.
[12] *Ibid.*, pp. 230-31.
[13] Quoted *ibid.*, p. 239. Not all Lutherans, of course, attacked Calvin's predestination theory; the early Luther himself had held to an absolute double predestination in his controversy with Erasmus. Reinhold Seeberg and others have pointed out, however, that even here Luther's purpose was different from Calvin's. Seeberg says, "Luther used predestination chiefly as an argument against the Pelagian doctrine of

Arminius cites especially the Danish Lutheran theologian Nicholas Hemingius.[14] He makes the point also that the "Papists, Anabaptists, and Lutherans" all use this doctrine to bring discredit on the Reformed churches. Finally, it has been mixed up in every one of the difficulties and controversies which has plagued "these our [Reformed] churches" since the Reformation.

To illustrate this point, he refers to four controversies—the affairs of Coolhaes at Leiden, of Hermannus Herberts at Gouda, of Cornelis Wiggerts at Hoorn, and of Tako Sybrants at Medemblik. "This consideration," he says, "was not among the last of those motives which induced me to give my most diligent attention to this head of doctrine and endeavor to prevent our churches from suffering any detriment from it, because, from it, the Papists have derived much of their increase." [15]

The last point is a reminder that he, no less than his enemies, is unwilling to see the Catholics gain ground in the country. But who is "aiding and abetting the enemy"? Not he, but his opponents.

The mention of Coolhaes, Herberts, Wiggerts, and Sybrants is the second time they have been named in the *Declaration*. Earlier, when he was recounting the efforts made to get him to "confess" his views before the synodical authorities, he had reminded the deputies of the jurisdictional disputes between consistory and magistrates in these four cases. The double mention of their names shows that Arminius saw in them kindred spirits.

The case of Coolhaes has been described in connection with Arminius' days as a university student at Leiden. Hermannus Herberts (1540-1607) had incurred the hostility of the extreme Calvinists as far back as 1582, when he had been accused of favoring the Anabaptists. In 1586, at the national synod at The Hague, he was accused of holding improper opinions on Christian perfection and on predestination, and a controversy ensued for some seven years. Attempts were made to

---

sin; Calvin, against the Pelagian doctrine of grace" (*Text-book of the History of Doctrines*, II, 407 n.). Melanchthon was more prone to attack predestination in its Calvinistic form. On the nature of Luther's assent to Melanchthon's so-called synergism, cf. Clyde L. Manschreck, *Melanchthon, the Quiet Reformer*, pp. 293-302. Arminius was probably thinking here also of the Lutheran theologian Tilman Heshusius (he mentions him elsewhere) who attacked the Calvinist doctrine in 1560, and of Johann Marbach, who did the same a year later. For recent treatments of Luther's views on predestination, free will, and cooperation, cf. Gustaf Wingren, *Luther on Vocation*, pp. 123-43, and Gordon Rupp, *The Righteousness of God*, pp. 274-85.

[14] A pupil of Melanchthon, Hemingius (1513-1600) dissociated himself from Calvin's predestination theory in his *Tractatus*, with the result that he became a favorite of the Arminian party in the Low Countries.

[15] *Writings*, I, 240-41.

excommunicate him, but as pastor at Gouda, since 1582, he was protected by the magistrates and freely taught moderate views of predestination.[16]

Cornelis Wiggerts (died 1624) had been charged with improper opinions on original sin, the perseverance of the saints, predestination, free will, and related points, and he was suspended by the Synod of North Holland in 1587. A drawn-out controversy ensued, during which Wiggerts preached regularly in a private house. He was excommunicated in August, 1598, but his private meetings continued for many years.[17]

Tako Sybrants (died 1615) had been a minister in Utrecht from 1582 to 1586 and thereafter at Medemblik. He had been accused of heterodoxy on much the same grounds as the others. The affair came to a head in 1598-99, and Sybrants was finally left unmolested.[18]

These were all instances of the retention in the Dutch Church of an older, indigenous theology which came under fire when the largely refugee Calvinists gained control of the church. Even in 1608, however, their control was by no means absolute, and Arminius was now thrust into the position of leader and spokesman for the older theology, playing out the role of these earlier men on a national scale and with greater theological skill.

Arminius turns next to two other forms of the doctrine of his opponents, but in briefer fashion (mercifully). One is a modified supralapsarianism, and the other is a sub- or infralapsarianism. The second position does not predetermine anyone to damnation but simply leaves the nonelect in their helplessness. The third position is that which Arminius faced early in his Amsterdam career when the two Delft ministers, Arent Cornelisz. and Reynier Donteklok, had modified their supralapsarianism under the pressure of controversy with Coornhert. Arminius makes short criticisms of these positions at the points where they differ from the first one.

He is now ready to make a positive affirmation of his own doctrine of predestination. It is surprisingly brief. In short, God has decreed to appoint his Son as the Savior, to receive into favor those sinners who repent and believe in Christ, and to administer the means that are sufficient and efficacious for such faith; he then decrees the salvation and damnation of particular persons on the basis of the divine foreknowledge of the belief and perseverance, or lack thereof, of the individuals.[19] Arminius defends this way of putting it with twenty short

---

[16] Cf. Rogge, *Coolhaes*, II, 152 ff.
[17] *APPS*, I, *passim;* Rogge, *Coolhaes*, II, 198-219; *HRN*, I, 793-95.
[18] *APPS*, I, *passim;* Rogge, *Coolhaes*, II, 183-91; *HRN*, I, 795-96.
[19] *Writings*, I, 247-48.

arguments which correspond to his twenty criticisms of the doctrine first described. His position corresponds to the sum and content of the gospel, clearly contained in the Scriptures, never contradicted by the early church, and in agreement with Salnar's *Harmony*. "It agrees most excellently with the Dutch Confession and Catechism," [20] and it is in accordance with the nature of God, of man, of creation, of eternal life and death, of sin, and of grace. It contributes to the glory of God, the honor of Jesus Christ, the salvation of men, and the preaching of the gospel. It is the foundation of the Christian religion, and it "has always been approved by the great majority of professing Christians." [21]

Arminius then turns briefly to four related doctrines. He defines the providence of God with relation to God's will and God's permission: "God both wills and performs good acts," but "he only freely permits those which are evil." [22] Man in sin is unable to exercise his will to do any good at all except he be regenerated and continually aided by grace. The grace of God is a gratuitous affection, infusion of the gifts of the Spirit, and perpetual assistance which is "the commencement, the continuance, and the consummation of all good," but it is not an "irresistible force." [23] On the perseverance of the saints, he is cautious: "I never taught that a true believer can either totally or finally fall away from the faith and perish, yet I will not conceal that there are passages of Scripture which seem to me to wear this aspect." [24] On the assurance of salvation, "it is possible for him who believes in Jesus Christ to be certain and persuaded, and, if his heart condemn him not, he is now in reality assured that he is a son of God and stands in the grace of Jesus Christ," this by the inward testimony of the Holy Spirit, the fruits of faith, and the "testimony of God's spirit witnessing together with his own conscience." [25]

On a fifth related doctrine he speaks at greater length: Is there a perfection of believers in this life? After analyzing Augustine's position, he gives a qualified answer: Yes, but "in no other way than by the grace of Christ." [26] His full teaching on this point will require reference to other writings and will be presented later.

Arminius feels it necessary to deal with the question of the divinity of the Son of God. At considerable length he defends his refusal to

[20] *Ibid.*, p. 248.
[21] *Ibid.*, p. 250.
[22] *Ibid.*, p. 251.
[23] *Ibid.*, p. 253.
[24] *Ibid.*, p. 254.
[25] *Ibid.*, p. 255.
[26] *Ibid.*, p. 256.

ascribe the term αὐτόθεος to Christ. This section is taken over from his *Apology Against Thirty-one Articles.*

He also defends his criticisms of Piscator's theory of the imputation of Christ's righteousness. He objects to the formula, finds it unscriptural, and prefers to affirm simply: "To a man who believes, faith is imputed for righteousness through grace." He will be willing, he says, to subscribe to what Calvin has said on this in the third book of his *Institutes.*[27] That point, too, will need further treatment.

Arminius turns now from the content of doctrine to the matter of the revision of the Confession and Catechism. He defends the clause of the States General specifying that a national synod shall have the task of revising the formularies. It gives honor to the word of God, which is supreme over all. Since the Confession and Catechism are human pamphlets, they are liable to error. A national synod has the task of determining whether all things in the church be in a proper condition, and this should not exclude the church's doctrine. An examination of the creeds, whether it results in their confirmation or in their revision, will leave them in a stronger position, with greater value for the church, when it is perceived that they conform to the word of God. The Augsburg Confession has been revised, and the Swiss and French churches have "enriched their confessions with one entirely new article" only "two or three years past." [28] The Belgic Confession itself had been revised.[29]

He recounts the arguments against his position: that the church's theology will be called in question, which is neither necessary nor proper because (1) it has already been approved by many learned men, (2) it has been sealed with the blood of many thousand martyrs, and (3) revision will bring confusion within the church and ridicule upon it.

Arminius replies. There is nothing wrong in "calling in question" that which is not "unquestionable." It is possible for learned men and even martyrs to err. As for the martyrs, they died for "the fundamental articles of the Christian religion" which have gained the unanimous consent of those of the Reformed religion, not for subjects of controversy among the various parties within the church. He gets specific. One of his critics had said that the critic's own (Calvinistic) interpretation of Romans 7, which could be found in the marginal notes to the Belgic Confession, was thereby that which "the martyrs had with their own

[27] *Ibid.,* p. 264.

[28] The Synod of Gap in 1603 has inserted an article in the Gallican Confession of 1559 declaring the Pope to be the Antichrist. This had been removed in 1607, however, by the Synod of La Rochelle.

[29] Franciscus Junius had abridged Article 16, and numerous other changes had been made in various editions.

blood sealed." Arminius denies this. If you go through the entire French *History of the Martyrs*, he says, you will not find a single instance of a person being examined on Romans 7.[30]

It may be asked what changes Arminius really wanted to make in the Confession and Catechism. He addresses himself to this question, particularly with respect to the Confession, which is unique to the Netherlands, unlike the Catechism, which comes from Heidelberg. Someone had objected that if a national synod could revise the Confession every time it met, the church would have nothing firm on which to depend. Arminius answers that the church always has the Scriptures, on which every doctrinal question must finally be resolved. As for the Confession, it has some things that "are certain and do not admit of doubt." Others are the cause of continual dissension. The second category should be reconciled with the first. Then "let it be attempted to make the confession contain as few articles as possible." Remove the "explanations, proofs, digressions, redundancies, amplifications, and explanations." Retain only "those truths which are necessary to salvation." The consequence of such brevity will be fewer errors.[31]

The revision of the Catechism will be necessary only if it is elevated to the status of an authority equal to the Confession. Otherwise it can remain as it is, but with liberty of explanation.

There is a curious duality in all of this. On the one hand, Arminius claims that his views are consonant with the Confession and Catechism. On the other hand, he wants them revised, reduced to the "essentials," so that there is no longer any basis in them for the views of his opponents (for this surely must have been his intention). He denies that the creeds teach what his opponents teach, but he wants to remove the ambiguities under which they take cover. Would he have permitted them, had the decision been his to make, to continue to preach supralapsarianism? Probably so, but only as an individual interpretation, not as the doctrine of the whole church and something necessary to salvation. In his peroration he says again that two questions must be raised: Is a doctrine true, and is it necessary to salvation? He promises to abide by these two questions, with the Scriptures as the norm. If his own doctrine should prove true and necessary (as he supposed), would he enforce it on his brethren? He says no, "unless I have plainly proved it from the word of God and have with equal clearness established its truth and the necessity unto salvation that every Christian should

[30] His reference was to Jean Crespin, *Le Livre des Martyrs depuis Jean Husz jusqu'en 1554.*
[31] *Writings*, I, 272.

entertain the same belief." [32] He is sure that if his brethren will adopt the same point of view, there will be no more controversy.

Thus far it could appear that he was both naïve and arrogant—naïve in expecting that his position would surely win in any fair-minded assembly, arrogant in expecting that his "true and necessary" doctrines should be made to replace the views of his opponents. In the midst of his own self-assurance of the equity of his cause, however, he expresses humility and deference. "I am not of the congregation of those who wish to have dominion over the faith of another man, but am only a minister to believers, with the design of promoting in them an increase of knowledge, truth, piety, peace, and joy in Jesus Christ our Lord." And if a proper synod should decide against him, no schism would be formed on his account. "In patience will I possess my soul [Luke 21:19], and though in that case I shall resign my office, yet I will continue to live for the benefit of our common Christianity as long as it may please God to lengthen out my days and prolong my existence."

Once again Arminius offered, under certain conditions, to resign his office. He was committed now to the struggle, exposed at the head of the battle line. And there is a pathos in his reference to the length of his days. He must have sensed from the progress of his illness that he did not have many left—less than a year, as it turned out.

He closed the *Declaration* with a line in Latin: *Sat ecclesiae, sat patria datum.* "Enough given to church and country." [33]

---

[32] *Ibid.*, p. 274.
[33] *Ibid.*, p. 275.

24

THE LAST YEAR: 1609

A NEW NAME appears in the story at about this time. On the day before
Arminius gave his address to the States of Holland, he wrote a letter
to Rem Bisschop, a merchant in Amsterdam. Bisschop (c. 1571-1625)
was an Amsterdam merchant who had long been disaffected with clergy
such as Plancius and had been a friend of Arminius. He was from a noteworthy family. His parents, Egbert Remmensz. Bisschop and Geertruyd
Jansdr. van Lingen, were among the early Reformed laymen in
Amsterdam. His brother Jan was a merchant. A younger brother Simon
(1583-1644) had shown signs of unusual intelligence, and a way was
sought for him to enter the Latin school in Amsterdam. His father,
a *snijder,* or carver, did not have the means, but his oldest brother,
Rem, already a successful merchant, and a former burgomaster, Cornelis
Benningh, provided the money. At the urging of the ministers Cuchlinus
and Arminius, and against the initial opposition of his parents, Simon
was sent to the University of Leiden as an *alumnus* of Amsterdam,
as Arminius had been before. He studied there the prescribed six years,
from 1600 to 1606, concluding his work with a thesis written for Snellius
on the question, "Is the study of philosophy necessary for the theological
candidate?" After 1606 he remained at Leiden to study theology under
Arminius and Gomarus. The city fathers of Gouda who had supported
Herberts desired the young man for their minister, and clearance was
received from Amsterdam. It was in the Synod of South Holland, however, that the move was blocked. From this circumstance alone it is
evident that Simon had become a disciple of Arminius. As a scholar
he had, according to the custom of the times, latinized his name. He
is known to history as Simon Episcopius, upon whom the theological
mantle of Arminius fell, the first Remonstrant professor of theology.[1]

Arminius wrote numerous letters to Rem Bisschop in the closing
months of his life, letters evidently unknown to Philip van Limborch
when he edited the *Epistolae Ecclesiasticae* in 1704, for none has been

[1] There is a very useful study of Episcopius in English: Frederick Calder, *Memoirs
of Simon Episcopius.*

published (one is cited in Caspar Brandt's *Life of Arminius*) .[2] Later events show that both Rem Bisschop and Simon Episcopius were among the firmest supporters of Arminius.

In the days after Arminius' *Declaration* events moved fast. The peace negotiations with Spain were now focusing down on a truce of twelve years. Maurice and Oldenbarnevelt were further estranged and yet continued to work together while they maneuvered against each other.

The States of Holland, meanwhile, had to deal with the defiance of the Synod of South Holland in its October meeting. On November 23, 1608, the States issued a countermand: any ministers who had objections to the Confession and Catechism were to address them to the States, not to a classis or local synod, and the States would forward them to a national synod, or at least to a provincial synod, one of which they hoped would be called soon. Now there was a direct conflict between the church and the state. The conflict served to delay the time when a national synod could be held. It went quite beyond the question of predestination to the doctrine of the church itself; indeed, the theory of the state, of the United Netherlands, was at stake.

Professor Hoenderdaal makes an important point when he reminds us that the Remonstrance of 1610, signed by the supporters of Arminius the year after his death, was not an act of insurgency by those who were against the church. It was an act of ministers of the church, addressed to the States of Holland, in response to the action of the States on November 23, 1608. And while the doctrinal portion of the Remonstrance, the famous "five points," dealt with matters of God, man, and salvation, the underlying issue was the politico-ecclesiastical issue, the question of a free church subject only to Scripture, its integrity as such to be preserved by the Christian magistrate. That issue was made plain in 1610 by a small book by Uitenbogaert, *Tractaet van 't Ampt ende Authoriteyt eener hoogher christlicker Overheyt in Kerkelike saecken,* in which he made explicit the latent political and ecclesiological implications in what may now be called the "Arminian" position. His book has been aptly termed "the sixth point of the Remonstrance." [3]

Professor Hoenderdaal grants, properly, that this position on church and state is not defensible in a modern perspective. Arminius and Uitenbogaert thought in terms of an older "Christian society," where the magistrates were thought to function as believers in their office as

[2] There are nine of these letters dated from May 8, 1608, to August 26, 1609. The manuscripts are in the collection of the Remonstrant Church, Amsterdam, R. K., L. 3. c.-i., k., l., housed in the Library of the University of Amsterdam.

[3] Cf. G. J. Hoenderdaal, "De Kerkordelijke Kant van de Dordtse Synode," pp. 353-55; Rogge, *Wtenbogaert,* II, 26 ff.; and Nobbs, whose entire book is devoted to this issue.

well as in their private persons. Neither side in the controversy anticipated what was just around the corner, the modern secular state. The issue in 1608 was still put in terms of the church and the magistrates rather than the church and the state. And when the enemies of Arminius gained control in the next decade, it was with full reliance upon the magistrates to enforce their position.

Gomarus now petitioned the States of Holland for permission to appear before them. It was granted, and he gave his speech on December 12, 1608. It was an attack on Arminius throughout. Arminius had departed into the errors of the Pelagians and Jesuits on grace and free will, on justification and sanctification, and on the law of God. He accuses Arminius of teaching that faith comes not from grace but from man's natural ability, that we are justified not by imputed righteousness of Christ but by our act of faith as a work of our own righteousness, and that believers can perfectly fulfill the law of God. One detects in each case the subtle distortion of oversimplification. I am reminded of a question often asked by my early teacher, Dr. H. Orton Wiley, "Why is faith faith for a Calvinist and works for an Arminian?"

Gomarus continues. Arminius was in error on predestination, on the doctrine of foreseen faith (Gomarus doesn't deny the foreknowledge, but he places the ground of foreknowledge in God's election), on original sin, on the possibility of a believer falling from grace, the authority of Scripture, the Trinity, the providence of God, the Incarnation, the satisfaction of Christ, regeneration, the church, and good works. Then comes the clincher: Arminius does not teach all these heresies openly in the university; some of them he teaches only privately to his students in his house! He explains away the scriptures that are contrary to his views. Those to which the Jesuits appeal, he supports. He sows doubt about the falsity of heresy and about the truth of orthodoxy. He puts truth and error side by side on the scales, as if one could merely choose which he preferred. "From this it is evident," says Gomarus, "that my colleague covers up his views in order to make them acceptable to whatever hearers are present."

Arminius is also inconstant, Gomarus goes on. He says one thing and then another about the Jesuits and about the Pope. And he is wrong in going past the synodical authority to appeal directly to the magistracy. He has even argued that a heathen magistrate could preside over a Christian synod. Arminius has borrowed his doctrine of predestination from the Ubiquitists (a derogatory term applied by the Reformed to the Lutherans), whose doctrines had never been found in the church or university. And so it went. The States should take care lest they be misled as was Constantine, by a court preacher, at the Council of

Nicaea. That was a low blow—or a telling blow, depending one one's sympathies—designed to estrange the States from Uitenbogaert and, in passing, reinforce suspicion about Arminius' doctrine of the Trinity.[4]

By all accounts the States were offended by Gomarus' speech. He was acrimonious and too passionate in his attack; Arminius had been soft-spoken. Arminius had impressed them with his piety, and they could not believe him to be the two-faced person Gomarus pictured him to be. Arminian historians interpret this as a vindication of Arminius. Calvinist historians, including van Itterzon, attribute it to the gullibility of the States. In either case, Arminius had won his way with the States, which was little surprise, for he was supporting the prerogatives of the magistrates in the oversight of the church. If a modern "objective judgment" is possible on the relative merits of the two presentations, it would have to say at least that Arminius was the more able strategist. Without claiming objectivity, and following Gomarus' advice not to put truth and error on the scales as if either may be chosen, I make bold to say that Arminius' *Declaration,* while not without flaws, manifests a candor, a clarity, and a charity which are missing in Gomarus.

While Gomarus was blasting Arminius from The Hague, constant attacks were made back in Amsterdam. On December 10, 1608, Arminius wrote of them to Burgomaster Egbertsz. His wife's brother Jacob Laurensz. had written him, he says, that an elder in the church was circulating seven articles in his name, articles designed to mark him as unorthodox. But who is the elder? No one will come out and say, because they do not want to goad the elder into more vicious actions.[5] So it is Arminius who must exercise patience. "But beware," he warns his friend, "lest by your connivance and indulgence these stings increase so fast as to cause you afterwards to utter vain lamentations about the punctures which they make and the pain they excite. . . . I therefore now desire you to give this intimation in my name to your colleagues." He is not addressing the college of burgomasters directly and formally, he says, but only informally through his friend, so that there may be "as little noise and exertion as possible." "Yet if you think otherwise, I will write to the bench of the magistrates." [6]

Four days later Arminius wrote to Egbertsz. again. He put his finger

[4] This summary of Gomarus' *Vertoog [Remonstrance]* is derived for the most part from van Itterzon, pp. 131-34; cf. *KH,* Part III, pp. 184-85; Triglandius, p. 420; *HRN,* II, 87; Rogge, *Wtenbogaert,* I, 368-70. Gomarus' *Vertoog* was published in his *VVaerschouwinghe,* and it was this which prompted the friends of Arminius to publish the *Declaration of Sentiments* the following year.

[5] I have been unable to determine which elder was in question. Of the twelve in office at that time, none appears among the known opponents of Arminius.

[6] *Ep. Ecc.,* no. 123.

on another aspect of the problem. Gomarus and his friends are trying to pack the church assemblies with opponents of Arminius and Uitenbogaert and treat Arminius and his friends as if they are not the church. That is, they are trying, with no justification at all, to set Arminius over against the church. It was a prophetic insight, for that is exactly what the Contra-Remonstrants were able to do a decade later.[7]

At the turn of the year the truce negotiations were making better progress. At the end of November, Oldenbarnevelt had gained the support of most of the cities, with Amsterdam and Delft holding out. By the end of December, Amsterdam and Delft came across. Maurice finally conceded and persuaded Zeeland to do likewise. Negotiations were resumed in February, 1609, in Antwerp this time, with the representatives of the States General arriving from Bergen-op-Zoom on March 25. On April 9 the Twelve Years' Truce was signed. The terms were generally favorable to the north. Its independence was recognized, at least provisionally, and the clause about the East Indian trade was vague enough to satisfy Spanish pride and Dutch ambition at one stroke. Catholic worship was to be tolerated in the north. But with the cessation of hostilities, there was relief from military expenditures of every kind, such as the increase of troops, protection of navigation, and the building of new forts. Many of the merchants were now won over to the plan, but there remained a bitterness between Maurice and Oldenbarnevelt which would poison the life of the country for years to come, affecting matters of religion no less than matters of state. While Oldenbarnevelt came under the suspicion of treason, the friends of Arminius would be charged with heresy, and the two charges would intermingle.[8]

On February 7, 1609, Arminius had a sharp attack of illness, and it alarmed his doctors. He was attended by Pieter Pauw (Pavius), the boyhood neighbor of Lijsbet in Amsterdam and builder of the anatomical theater in the Falijde Begijnhof Church. Other doctors attended Arminius as well—Reynier Bontius, son of a professor of medicine who himself later became a professor of physics and of medicine; Henry Saelius, whom I cannot identify; and, in Amsterdam, his friend the burgomaster, Dr. Sebastian Egbertsz. For a time he was almost completely incapacitated.

It was just at this time that he was caught up in the pamphlet war

---

[7] Cf. his letter to Dr. Sebastian Egbertsz. December 14, 1608; *Ep. Ecc.*, no. 124.

[8] For the text of the truce terms, cf. (among others) van Meteren's Book 30 of his *Historie van de Oorlogen en Geschiedenissen der Nederlanden*, X, 101-13. The effect of the truce is discussed in Blok, *Geschiedenis van het Nederlandsche Volk*, III, 529 ff. An important modern study of the question of Oldenbarnevelt's alleged treason is H. Gerlach, *Het Proces tegen Oldenbarnevelt en de "Maximen in den Staet."*

that had been raging. The curators and burgomasters decided, in view of the wild and inaccurate rumors that were circulating, that theses of Arminius and Gomarus on predestination which they had given in 1604 should be published. On February 8 each man was granted 250 guilders for the task. The theses were translated from Latin into Dutch and published by the university printer, Jan Paedts, in one binding. Thus the governors of the university maintained their impartiality, and at the same time every reader could know what the two men had taught.

On Sunday, March 15, Arminius wrote to Uitenbogaert the last such letter known to us. He reports that he is feeling better, although he still has bowel trouble, fever, and loss of appetite. He hopes to be able to go out soon. He has continued his studies, although he regrets the time that has been lost. If only his sickness of soul could be healed, he would not complain over the other losses. He laments his duties only partly fulfilled. It is not a cheerful letter. Lijsbet, with nine children and a sick husband to tend, was entering deep waters. He tells of his writing and his teaching, however, with some notes of hope. Then there is a greeting: "Farewell, and be strong, for God is with you." The letter must have been written early in the morning, as was his custom, for he adds a postscript: "After breakfast I shall try to go out to the church to give thanks to God for the grace I have until now enjoyed." [9] It would be an exertion to go to the church—and the church was no more than a hundred yards distant. That indicates something of his physical condition.

Two weeks later he wrote to Conrad Vorstius. He discusses the accusations against his theology that are made in every quarter, the need for revising the Confession, his approval of the Gouda Catechism. He is not yet completely over his severe illness. He can't understand how people invent rumors about his alleged pro-Roman sentiments. There are other such matters. "We live in the church with the same right as anyone else," he protests, "and no one is to lord it over the belief of another, for our only Master is Christ." [10]

The Dutch printing of the theses on predestination by Arminius and Gomarus sold out quickly but only gave rise to further pamphleteering. Coolhaes, now seventy-five years old, appeared in print once more, urging peace in the church. No one paid attention. The enemies of Arminius now took the initiative, led by Donteklok, who in turn was answered by Corvinus. Corvinus did not sign his pamphlet, and it was taken for Uitenbogaert's. Donteklok replied to it. Arminius' supporters responded by publishing more of Arminius' public disputations in

[9] *Ep. Ecc.*, no. 125.
[10] March 30, 1609; *Ep. Ecc.*, no. 126.

Dutch translation, including his theses of 1605 and 1607 "On the Righteousness and Efficacy of the Providence of God Concerning Evil." Another was "On the Free Will of Man and its Powers," bound with Bertius' disputation "On the Heresy of Pelagius and Coelestius." To offset the rumors that he was secretly a Papist, they published his theses of February 22, 1606, "On Indulgences and Purgatory." Also on the Roman question, his theses of August 1, 1607, on the denial that the Reformed churches had seceded from Rome. At least one more work was published in 1609—whether before his death I cannot ascertain— a collection of twenty-four disputations. These were published again in 1610 with the addition of one more, "On Repentance." Hence the "Twenty-five Public Disputations" found in the various editions of the *Opera* and *Works*.

The publication of the twenty-four disputations must have been after July 25, for on that date Arminius made a public appearance, delivering one of the sets of theses included therein, "On the Vocation of Men to Salvation." It was his last public service to the university.

It is largely a restatement of points he had made earlier. Vocation is God's gracious act in Christ whereby he calls "sinful men who are liable to condemnation." The instrumental cause is the word of God, either by the ordinary method of human preaching and writing or by the extraordinary circumstance of the word "immediately proposed by God inwardly to the mind and the will." The man who is the subject of vocation is "unworthy to be called, and unfit [*inepti*] to answer the call." It is only by the estimation of God that such a one may be accounted worthy and rendered fit. The form of vocation is in the administration of the word and of the Holy Spirit, and God has instituted it according to both his justice and his mercy in Christ. Here Arminius proposes a doctrine of "unequal grace." In implied response to his enemies who had accused him of teaching that God's grace is given equally to all, Arminius turns the tables on them by denying the same. God reserves for himself, says Arminius, the "full and free power ... of bestowing unequal grace on those who are equals, and equal grace on those who are unequal, nay, of employing greater grace on those who are more wicked." Here Arminius (or his editors) cites Romans 9:24-26; 10:17-21; 11:25, 29-33; Ezekiel 3:6; Matthew 11:21, 23. In another passage on "unequal grace" he quotes Romans 5:20: "Where sin increased, grace abounded all the more."

The *terminus a quo* of vocation is man not merely in his natural or "animal" condition [*status vitae animalis*] but in his state of sin, guilt, and condemnation. The *terminus ad quem* is a state of grace in the present life and, afterward, a state of glory. The proximate end is that they who have been called may believe; the remote end is the salvation of the elect. Here he makes a point which would lead to a curious debate after his lecture. "The answer by which obedience is yielded to this call is the condition which, through the appointment of God, is also requisite and necessary for obtaining the end." [11] There are two requisites for eternal life, vocation and the answer to vocation.

Vocation is partly external, partly internal. External vocation is by the ministry of men; internal vocation is the inward illumination of the Holy Spirit. Those who are called and answer to the call constitute the church; but just as vocation is both external and internal, so the church is both visible (confession with the lips) and invisible (belief with the heart—Romans 10:10). But the external word must not be regarded as merely preparatory, as the spiritualists say. It is truly vocation, just as is the inward word.[12]

What happened at the conclusion of his reading of the theses is known from a letter written by Adrian Borrius, who was present, to Simon Episcopius, who had just the month before gone to Franeker to study Hebrew under Drusius. The session had started at 9 A.M. After some two hours of desultory discussion between Arminius and two appointed opponents, another party spoke up. He gave his name as Adrianus Smetius (Smith), and it was rumored that he was a priest, possibly a Jesuit. After an opening analysis of the debate, Smetius came to the heart of the matter. If there is sufficient grace given to every man, what distinguishes the man who answers the divine call from one who does not? If it is something of grace, then the man who *does not* answer *cannot* answer. If it is something on the part of man, then man determines his own salvation. This challenge aroused Arminius to the vivacity of former days, and he engaged in a rather long exchange with his challenger. Man determines himself, said Arminius, but not without grace, for free will is in concurrence with grace. One does not act without the other. The exchanges continued, using an analogy introduced by Smetius from the medicine of the day. If one man moves six degrees more than another man, does he not add something to what the other does? Arminius answered that more grace is bestowed on him who acts the more, not preveniently but in accompaniment to it. Smetius responded that the man who acts the more (referring to the human response to the divine call) has something of which he may boast. Arminius countered by pointing out that faith by its nature excludes boasting. As the exchange ended, "the Jesuit muttered between his teeth, 'This is a very trite reply.'"

[11] *Writings,* I, 573.
[12] For the entire disputation, cf. *ibid.,* pp. 570-74.

The Jesuit was not the only one muttering, however, for Gomarus throughout the episode made visible signs of his displeasure with Arminius' answers, sometimes gesturing, sometimes writing notations, sometimes whispering to a professor of medicine, Everard Vorstius, sometimes muttering suppressed exclamations. Afterward, outside the hall, he exclaimed, "The reins have been given up to the Papists in fine style today!" He had sharp words for Arminius, who offered to discuss the matter publicly and added, "I am fully persuaded that the doctrine of irresistible grace is repugnant to the sacred Scriptures, to all the Fathers, and to our own confession and catechism." [13]

Borrius also reported some alarming news about Arminius. After the disputation he went to Oudewater to get some rest and try to regain his health. That evening he had a "most serious paroxism" and relapsed into even worse health. "I am much afraid that this most excellent light will be taken away from us before the time. . . . Let us importunately apply to [God] in ardent prayer, and add fasting to our supplications, that God may at least not so speedily deprive us of his presence."

Episcopius immediately wrote a long letter to his dying teacher and friend. He is profuse in his professions of esteem and affection, regrets that Arminius' illness is not only worse but is aggravated by the attacks of his enemies. He tells of his own experiences in Franeker during the past month and a half. It is a fascinating tale. The whole town was awaiting his arrival, his renown as a student having gone before. Although Arminius had advised him not to get involved in public disputations on predestination, he had found it impossible not to yield to the entreaties of the students, and he had tackled the great Professor Sibrandus Lubbertus. Lubbertus had later said that "Arminius himself could not more accurately, or more forcibly, have presented his arguments and proofs than he had done." Lubbertus, he reported, was, unlike Gomarus, both cordial and straightforward. But he was not so sharp in controversy. He "stood before an opponent with a species of stupid simplicity which exposed him to every dart that was aimed at him." [14]

Arminius came close to ending his days in the town where they had begun, but he recovered sufficiently to return to Leiden. This visit to Oudewater confirms the impression that he maintained contacts there, possibly with the town fathers, judging from the earlier correspondence, and certainly with his aunt Geertje Cuchlinus and the widow Jacomyne Bertius.

[13] Adrian Borrius to Simon Episcopius, July 30, 1609; *Ep. Ecc.*, no. 130, quoted in part in *WA*, I, 301-2; II, 230-31; and in *LA*, pp. 351-52.

[14] C. August 1, 1609; *Ep. Ecc.*, no. 131; cf. Calder, pp. 55-60.

His days were to be short but not uneventful, and the events were the new developments of the weary dissension. The synodical deputies had written to Arminius on February 18, 1609, reminding him that he had not sent in his criticisms of the Confession and Catechism. He replied early in April that although he had promised to do so in writing, the States had intervened by ordering them sent to the States, sealed. The States, however, now trying to avoid a national or provincial synod, tried to bring about a settlement or accommodation between the two Leiden professors by summoning them for a "friendly conference" for an exchange of views. Each might select four ministers to stand beside him for counsel.

The meeting began on Thursday, August 13, in The Hague, at 7 A.M. Arminius had with him Uitenbogaert, Borrius (from Leiden), Grevinchovius (Rotterdam), and Venator, who had been in the eye of the storm in Alkmaar. Gomarus was accompanied by Hommius (Leiden), Acronius (Schiedam), Rolandus (Amsterdam), and Bogardus, from the same stormy town of Alkmaar. Some incumbent and former burgomasters of Amsterdam were also present—Jacob Boelensz., C. P. Hooft (who had pleaded for toleration in 1597), Barthold Cromhout, Dr. Egbertsz., and Gerrit Jacobsz. Witsen—as well as Arminius' former Amsterdam neighbor, the pensionary Ellert de Veer. This may be taken as a direct response to his appeal to Egbertsz. for support from the magistrates there. Significantly, two incumbent burgomasters hostile to Arminius were not there—Claes Fransz. Oetgens and Reynier Pauw.[15] When the meeting began, with Arminius and Gomarus at opposite ends of a long table, their advisers at the sides, Arminius was in the company of powerful friends of long standing, both among the States and especially among the Amsterdam burgomasters, sons of the Old Beggars of 1566.

Oldenbarnevelt made an opening statement. The sole purpose of the conference, he said, was to determine the doctrinal differences between Arminius and Gomarus so that these could be the better referred to a synod. Gomarus spoke next. There was not so much difference between him and Arminius as there was between Arminius and the doctrine of the church. Arminius replied by repeating that he had held himself within the Confession and Catechism. Uitenbogaert thought it necessary to remark that he and the three other advisers of Arminius had come not as partisans but as brethren, to see whether the affair could be handled in a friendly fashion. But Gomarus and his team had already planned their attack, and they launched it. Bogardus made the first

[15] The attendance of these burgomasters is known from Arminius' unpublished letter to Rem Bisschop, August 26, 1609, Manuscript R. K., L. 3. e, Library of the University of Amsterdam; cited in *LA*, p. 363.

sortie: this conference must not in any way curtail the freedom of the church to exercise its own judgment in the matter. Then Gomarus and his friends protested the presence of Venator, who had been deposed by the Synod of North Holland for his failure to submit to the synod his opinions on the Confession and Catechism. Oldenbarnevelt, speaking for the States, intervened. The synodical action had been in conflict with the authority and express command of the States, who had ordered such opinions sent to them; the deposition of Venator was invalid and hence irrelevant in this conference. This brought the conference squarely around to the conflict between the synods and the magistrates. Thus it went until 11 A.M., when the meeting was adjourned until the next day.

The issue of the revision of the Belgic Confession with its implications for the problem of synod and magistrate was finally set aside in the second session, when Arminius agreed to move on to the theological issues. Gomarus wanted justification to be discussed first, and he wanted all these proceedings put in writing, to be judged later by the national synod. The States agreed partially, specifying that the proceedings themselves should be conducted *viva voce,* with the advisers submitting their written reports of the same to the States, who would deliver them to a provincial or national synod.

All the old arguments were rehearsed—on justification, predestination, irresistible grace, free will, and final perseverance—and nothing new turned up. The sessions recessed for the weekend, resuming on Tuesday the 18th. Arminius took sick and had to go home. The States, seeing that no continuation would be possible, cut short the conference on August 21, ordering each of the principals to submit to them in writing his own opinion, the arguments for it, and the refutation of the contrary opinion within fourteen days. Then the States called before them in a separate meeting the eight advisers, asking for their opinions about the importance of the controversy and the means for correcting it. Gomarus' advisers found it very important and saw no remedy short of a provincial or national synod. Arminius' advisers found the dispute over justification of no real importance at all, and they thought that Arminius' views on predestination were the closest to Scripture and the most practical for pastoral consolation and instruction. "In favor of Arminius was the entire tenor of the gospel; while the opinion of Gomarus transcended the gospel."

Uitenbogaert then spoke, and he wasn't brief. He dealt with Venator, the revision of the Confession, the cases of Wiggerts and Herberts, and earlier precedents going back to Anastasius Veluanus. After a lengthy

327

recital of the problems of the present moment, he called for a remedy. There is a *medecijnmeester,* the doctor, and there is the medicine. God is the doctor. But he administers medicine through officials. Those officials are the Lords States, who have the responsibility and authority not only to cleanse the temples of images but to install ministers, to call church meetings, to exercise church discipline, and to make church laws. There must be an end to the collaterality of church and magistrate, which now divides the country. It was an unbounded Erastianism he proclaimed, far beyond anything Arminius had said. Some propose the medicine of a national synod, he went on. Let it be, but be sure that Satan does not preside over it (a phrase borrowed from Beza). The synod should have the following goals: a friendly and brotherly conference over the present differences, to find out why "Popery" is increasing among us (each side blamed the other for that alleged growth), and to reestablish church discipline under the authority of the high magistrates.[16]

Gomarus turned in his written work on time; Arminius never finished his. He was confined to his sickbed in what was to be his final illness. On September 12 he wrote to the States, the last of his letters known to us. He explained the severity of his illness, which was the reason for his failure to send in his document. A considerable part of it was finished, but he had had to break it off. If he should recover, he would finish it. If not, he was making arrangements that they should have the unfinished document in its incomplete condition. He was confident, however, that what he had taught was the truth. Far from having any doubts about it, he believed it to be in thorough agreement with Scripture. "By God's grace I have persisted in it, and I am ready to appear with this conviction before the judgment seat of Jesus Christ the Son of God and Judge of the living and the dead." The final line: "Out of my sickbed in Leiden, this 12th of September." [17]

Episcopius heard in Franeker about the deteriorating condition of Arminius, and he hurried back to Leiden to be with him. He spent many hours by the bedside, but at the end of September, being told that Arminius might linger a long time yet, he returned to Franeker. The symptoms were sinister: fever, cough, swelling of the abdomen, difficult breathing, indigestion, insomnia, and gout or arthritis. There were intestinal pains in the ilium and the colon and impaired vision of the left eye. This quasi-medical description is from the funeral oration of

[16] This account is collated from two reports of the speech, the first part from *KH,* Part III, pp. 191-94, the latter from *HRN,* II, 98-104; cf. *LA,* pp. 357-66.
[17] *KH,* Part III, p. 196.

Petrus Bertius, but the doctors themselves of that day wouldn't be much more precise.[18]

Bertius tells some miserable stories about the behavior of Arminius' enemies during the final illness. His affliction was seen by some as an apt fulfillment of Zechariah 11:17 and 14:12. The first passage reads:

> Woe to my worthless shepherd,
>   who deserts the flock!
> May the sword smite his arm
>   and his right eye!
> Let his arm be wholly withered,
>   his right eye utterly blinded!

Never mind the left eye. And they played equally miserable games of anagrams, both sides, scrambling the letters of a name to determine the man's character. James Nichols suggests that this bad habit was left over from the earlier Reformation game of scrambling the Pope's names or titles to get the beastly number 666. IACOBUS ARMINIUS became VANI ORBIS AMICUS, a friend of this vain world. Supporters, adding an H for Harmensz., made HABUI CURAM SIONIS, I have had a care for Sion.[19]

Arminius maintained his dignity. He was clear in his mind, cheerful in his temper. He was in pain, but he was concerned for the needs of his family, preparing Lijsbet as best he could for his departure by trusting "in the God of the widow." He testified to his friends of his hope in Christ. He often prayed aloud. Bertius reports some of the repeated forms:

O thou great Shepherd, who by the blood of the everlasting covenant has been brought again from the dead, Jesus, my Lord and Savior, be present with me, a sheep of thine that is weak and afflicted!

O Lord Jesus, thou faithful and merciful High Priest, who wast pleased in all things to be tempted as we are, yet without sin, being taught by such experience how hard and painful a thing it is to obey God in sufferings, that thou mightest be touched with the feeling of our infirmities,—have mercy upon me, succor me thy servant, who am now laid on a bed of sickness and oppressed with these numerous maladies. O thou God of my salvation, render my soul fit for thy heavenly kingdom and prepare my body for the resurrection! [20]

He kept a clear mind to the end, and he tended to his affairs as best he could. We know little of the details of these arrangements, but it is likely that he arranged for his friends to see about a pension for his widow and children, and he may have arranged for the sale of his

---

[18] *WA*, I, 42.
[19] *LA*, pp. 369-70.
[20] *WA*, I, 44-45.

books. He called in a notary to make his will. Bertius quotes only the pious commendation of his soul to God, and in the notarial remains in the archives in Leiden there is no trace of the document. But even the piety is of interest, for Arminius remained the firm proponent of his views to the end:

> Above all, I commend my soul, on its departure out of the body, into the hands of God, who is its Creator and faithful Savior; before whom also I testify that I have walked with simplicity and sincerity and in all good conscience in my office and vocation; that I have guarded with the greatest solicitude and care against advancing or teaching anything which, after a diligent search into the Scriptures, I had not found exactly to agree with those sacred records; and that all the doctrines advanced by me have been such as might conduce to the propagation and increase of the truth of the Christian religion, of the true worship of God, of general piety, and of a holy conversation among men,—such as might contribute, according to the word of God, to a state of tranquillity and peace well befitting the Christian name; and that from these benefits I have excluded the Papacy, with which no unity of faith, no bond of piety or of Christian peace can be preserved.[21]

One last protest against those who accused him of crypto-Catholicism!

In his very last days he was surrounded by family and friends— Uitenbogaert and Borrius especially, and also Bartholomeus Praevostius, who became a Remonstrant minister. Praevostius lived until 1669 and often spoke of the vivid impression the deathbed scene left upon him.[22]

Another visitor was a professor from Bremen, Matthias Martinus. He described his visit:

> I spoke with him particularly about the articles which, I had heard, had been lodged with the States and which were unjustly ascribed to him to the damage of his name. He was then already sick, but out of bed, so that I had to spare him and not tire him. He appeared to me to be a truly God-fearing man, learned, very experienced in theological controversies, skilled in the Holy Scriptures, shrinking from expressing theological matters in philosophical terms. What his errors concern, which, how many, and on what grounds they are, I cannot judge. God knows about that.[23]

In his home on the Pieterskerkhof at about noon, Monday, October 19, surrounded by his family and by friends, Jacobus Arminius of Oudewater peacefully died. He was about fifty years of age at his death. Lijsbet, his widow, was just forty years old. Their oldest child, Engeltje, was sixteen. Then came her seven brothers and little Geertruyd, only thirteen months old.

[21] *Ibid.*, pp. 46-47.
[22] *LA*, p. 372.
[23] Letter to Conrad Vorstius, n. d.; *Ep. Ecc.*, no. 133.

In the midst of their sorrow, their family and friends rallied to help with the burial arrangements. Lijsbet's brother Laurens, now a judge and council member in Amsterdam, took charge and wrote to Uitenbogaert in The Hague to ask which friends from there should be invited to the burial; he assumed Hoogerbeets and Adrian Junius, but who else? They were also unsure which Amsterdam burgomasters to invite, he said. He would leave that, too, to the judgment of Uitenbogaert.[24]

The burial took place on Thursday, October 22, across the way from Arminius' home, in the Pieterskerk, where his body was laid to rest by weeping friends and wife and children beneath the paving slabs of the church floor. There was evidently no marker, and the exact location is not known. The entry in the town burial book reads only "Armijnius opt Kerkhoff" (referring to his address).[25] On the same day, at the request of friends and of the Academic Senate of the university, Petrus Bertius delivered a funeral oration in the Great Auditorium of the university. The professors were there, including Gomarus. Arminius' old friend Rudolphus Snellius was probably there, and the curators, the burgomasters, friends from The Hague, and friends and relatives from Amsterdam—and friends and relatives from Oudewater, where this story began.

Toward the close of his eulogy, Bertius uttered these oft-quoted words: "'There lived in Holland a man whom they who did not know could not sufficiently esteem, whom they who did not esteem had never sufficiently known.' And he closed his address with words from John: "Beloved, let us love one another."

[24] October 20, 1609; in Rogge, *Brieven van Wtenbogaert*, I, 94.
[25] *Register van der Overlijden Personen binnen der Stad Leiden*, III 1609-1617),
7, Gemeente Archief, Leiden.

25

ARMINIUS' THEOLOGY REVIEWED

AT THE RISK of some repetition, but for the purpose of establishing first some historical background, a closer look at Arminius' theology has been held off until this point. Now a comprehensive survey can be made, drawing upon any or all of Arminius' writings, but especially on his Leiden works.

Not all his writings have been mentioned. Appended to the first printing of his letter to Hippolytus à Collibus was a collection of theological propositions, something over two hundred, under twenty-nine doctrinal headings. They clearly arise out of the controversies of the time. Some are in the form of affirmative theses; others, in the form of leading questions. They are included in the *Opera* as "Certain Articles to be Diligently Examined and Weighed." A subtitle adds: "because some controversy has arisen concerning them among even those who profess the Reformed religion." A further note explains that "these articles are partly either denied or affirmed in a decisive manner, and partly either denied or affirmed in a doubting manner, each of which methods is signified by certain indicative signs which are added to the different articles." [1] These signals are missing in the *Opera* of 1631 (the edition available to me) and in the English translations, making these articles difficult to interpret. The propositions on predestination were taken over bodily into the *Declaration of Sentiments*. The "Certain Articles" must be used with caution in establishing Arminius' position.

A more important item in the *Opera* is the section of Private Disputations. They were first published in 1610 with the Twenty-Five Public Disputations. They are shorter and more numerous—seventy-nine in all. They are thought to be an outline or syllabus for the private lectures which Arminius gave in his home (a usual custom for professors at that time); hence it is noteworthy that they contain no "secret teachings," as Arminius' enemies alleged. The series is incomplete, ending with the Sixth Commandment in an exposition of the Decalogue,

[1] *Writings,* II, 479.

evidently broken off by the death of the author. The editor of the edition of 1610 states that some twenty more theses had been projected for the series.[2]

Most of the references will be to the American editions (*Writings*), although the *Examination of Gomarus' Theses* occurs only in the London edition (*WA*). Short titles will be used as needed to indicate which of Arminius' writings is being cited.

The Church

It should be apparent by now that Arminius worked within both the ecclesiastical and intellectual structure of the Reformed Church. To put it in most general terms, he had no rootage in Lutheranism, none in Anabaptism, none in spiritualism. He was not categorically opposed to bishops, for he admitted the validity of the office in the early church, but he was not an episcopalian. He represented a kind of Reformed churchmanship which did not finally prevail among the Reformed in his doctrine of the magistrate, but to call it non-Reformed or even a deviant form of Reformed religion is anachronistic and unhistorical. The church for him is neither an objective institution of grace nor a voluntary association. Certainly it is not a pietist *ecclesiola*. It is defined, rather, in terms of its vocation. It is "a company of persons called out from a state of natural life and of sin, by God and Christ, through the Spirit of both, to a supernatural life to be spent according to God and Christ in the knowledge and worship of both." [3] The church is one and catholic, but the catholicity refers merely to the amplitude of the church, not to its essence. The catholic church "is the company of all believers . . . who have been, are now, and will be, called by the saving vocation of God from a state of corruption to the dignity of the children of God." [4] Each congregation, however, possesses the essence of the whole.

The church both as catholic and as particular or local is both visible and invisible. This point has been made in the report on his Public Disputation on vocation. He repeats it also in Private Disputation 54. Vocation is also the clue to the relation of the church to Scripture. The Roman Catholic claim that the church produces the Scripture is rejected. The true church is that church which is called into existence by the word of God which precedes both Scripture and church. The

---

[2] *Iacobi Arminii Veteraquinatis Batavi . . . Disputationes . . . Publicae & Privatae.*
[3] Priv. Disp. 50; *Writings,* II, 123.
[4] Priv. Disp. 54; *ibid.,* p. 132.

church is that community which recognizes the word of God in Scripture; to reverse the matter is to fail to be the church.[5]

Arminius' anti-Catholicism has been discussed. When the question of secession arose, Arminius spoke in defense of the Reformed churches, although at this point he appears to broaden the term to include Lutherans. The secession which has occurred in the church is not that associated with the names of "Wyclif, Huss, Luther, Melanchthon, Zwingli, Oecolampadius, Bucer, and Calvin," but is to be identified with "the time nearest the apostles, when the mystery . . . of iniquity, or . . . of lawlessness, began to work, which mystery was subsequently revealed." [6] The lawlessness has culminated in "the man of sin," who is to be identified as the Pope. Thus it is the Roman Church which is in secession. While in a certain sense all churches (in the West) have been guilty of this secession, the Reformed churches are those who have returned to the true faith.[7]

The Reformed churches are defined positively:

Those congregations professing the Christian faith which disavow every species of presidency whatever assumed by the Roman Pontiff, and profess to believe in and perform acts of worship to God and Christ according to the canons which each of them has comprised in its own confession or catechism; and they approve of such canons, therefore, only because they consider them to be agreeable to the Holy Scriptures.[8]

The question is narrowed down when it comes to the sacraments. Arminius defines a sacrament following Calvin precisely:

A sacrament . . . is a sacred and visible sign or token and seal [signum ac sigillum] instituted by God, by which he ratifies to his covenant people the gracious promise proposed in his word and binds them, on the other hand, to the performance of their duty. . . . These tokens, beside the external appearance which they present to our senses, cause something else to occur to the thoughts. Neither are they only naked significant tokens, but seals and pledges, which affect not only the mind, but likewise the heart itself.[9]

That is neither Lutheran nor Anabaptist, and certainly not spiritualist.

The same is true specifically for baptism. Arminius rejects baptismal regeneration but affirms the propriety of the baptism of the infants of one or more parents who are in the covenant. The mode is sprinkling, which is an analogy to the inward sprinkling of the blood of Christ.[10]

---

[5] Cf. Priv. Disp. 6; ibid., pp. 16 ff.
[6] Publ. Disp. 22; ibid., I, 628.
[7] Ibid., p. 621.
[8] Ibid., p. 628.
[9] Priv. Disp. 60; ibid., II, 152-53. Cf. Calvin, Institutes, 4.14.4-6.
[10] Priv. Disp. 63; Writings, II, 160-61.

The Lord's Supper is also seen in terms of sign and seal. It is a sacrament

in which, by the legitimate external distribution, taking, and enjoyment of bread and wine, the Lord's death is announced and the inward receiving and enjoyment of the body and blood of Christ are signified, and that most intimate and close union by which we are joined to Christ our Head is sealed and confirmed on account of the institution of Christ and the analogical relation of the sign to the thing signified.

Both transubstantiation and consubstantiation are rejected. "The matter," he says, "is bread and wine, which, with regard to their essence, are not changed but remain what they previously were; neither are they with regard to place joined together with the body or blood so that the body is either in, under, or with the bread." [11] This should set at ease the minds of those who come to Arminius with the prejudice that he is a rationalist, a humanist, an Anabaptist, or even a Zwinglian.

When it comes to the church and the magistrate, Arminius is harder to understand. The problem has been discussed in its historical development earlier, but some of his systematic propositions will be presented. Arminius deals with the magistracy in at least four writings. In his rectoral address, previously discussed, he charges the magistracy with the calling of synods and of presiding over them. In his Public Disputation "On Magistracy" he deals more with the office itself than with its relation to the church. It is an administrative office of divine origin which would have been ordained even had there been no fall. It is for both the natural and spiritual good of man, although at such a time that spiritual life only prevails, the magistracy will no longer be necessary. Because it is for the good of the whole of mankind, "every member of the state is bound to defend with all his powers, yet in a lawful manner, the life, safety, and dignity of the prince, as the father of his country." [12] There are grounds for revolution, although Arminius does not use the term. If the magistrate enacts laws contrary to the divine laws, the people are bound to obey God rather than him. The problem is in the man in the office, however, and not with the office. Hence the Anabaptist rejection of magistracy is in error. "A Christian man can, with a good conscience, accept of the office and perform the duties of magistracy." Not only that, "no person can legitimately and perfectly fulfill all its duties except a Christian." Yet this is not to mean that there is no legitimate magistracy in non-Christian lands. [13]

The question of church and magistrate comes up in his Private Dis-

[11] Priv. Disp. 64; *ibid.*, p. 161.
[12] Publ. Disp. 25; *ibid.*, I, 667-68.
[13] *Ibid.*, p. 669.

putation "On Councils." The power of appointing a council resides in the church herself, but where there is a Christian magistrate, the power is transferred. "If she is under the sway of a Christian magistrate who makes an open profession of faith, or who publicly tolerates it, then we transfer this power to such a magistrate, without whose convocation those persons that protested to the Church concerning the nullity of the Council of Trent have maintained that a council is illegitimate." [14]

The mention of the Council of Trent may do much to explain the historical background of Arminius' doctrine of the magistracy. The Protestants had complained about the illegitimacy of Trent; their own councils had been called by princes. Arminius was adhering to an older Protestantism of the "magisterial" type when he rejected what Uitenbogaert called the "collaterality" of church and state.

But what if the magistrate is not a Christian (or tolerant to Christianity)? "Then those who preside in the church" will call and preside over councils.

It is in the "Certain Articles" that the most extreme Erastianism is to be found. God has given the magistrate the power of caring and providing for, and governing, both the natural and spiritual life of his subjects. He has the power of enacting laws concerning ecclesiastical polity, of appointing ministers, of taking care that they perform their ministry, and of admonishing and rewarding ministers. He can appoint only ministers who have been lawfully examined by the classis. For the discharge of all this oversight of the church "the magistrate must understand those mysteries of religion which are absolutely necessary for the salvation of men, for in this part he cannot depend upon and confide in the conscience of another person." [15]

It is hard to know whether these ideas are put forth tentatively or with utmost seriousness. Probably the latter, for Arminius represents a type of Reformed thought which had not yet made a decisive break with the earlier Erastianism of the magisterial Reformation. From a modern perspective we reject it. We know no such "magistracy" which can exercise a Christian governance of the church. In Arminius' defense, however, at least two things can be said. First, he had a high view of the spiritual nature of magistracy. Second, his opponents by no means disposed of the magistracy. While they put the church's supreme control over herself in her own hands, they freely relied upon the magistrate to provide funds for the church and to enforce the church's discipline.

On questions of church discipline Arminius was in general accord with the Reformed theory and practice of the time. There can be no

---

[14] Priv. Disp. 58; *ibid.*, II, 144-45.
[15] "Certain Articles," 28, "On Magistracy"; *ibid.*, pp. 508-9.

society without discipline. The church's discipline has to do with spiritual matters. Its purpose is "for edifying, confirming, amplifying and adorning the church . . . and for directing consciences." It does not use physical force, "unless, perhaps, it be the pleasure of the magistrate in virtue of the power granted to him by God to force an offender to repentance by some other method." [16] If Arminius offends the modern mind with this point, he at least was not at odds with his enemies on it.

Church discipline applies only to external sins. Only God can judge internal sins. External sins differ in degree of heinousness and in degree of privacy and publicity. The church must take these differences into account. Some repentance will be private; some will be before the whole congregation. There must be admonitions first, with excommunication exercised as the last resort. This ultimate "public exclusion" will be accompanied by a degree of avoidance, "so far as is permitted by the necessary relative duties" which are mutually owed. Thus there will be no avoidance within the family and in other similar instances.[17]

Arminius deals in his Private Disputations with the question of synods or councils (they were on his mind), but he does not deal with the structure of the local *gemeente,* the deacons and elders, the consistory, the classis, the question of music, and such matters. He seems to fit into existing practices of Dutch Reformed life, so far as is evident from his writings.

It may be concluded that on the doctrine of the church Arminius stood within the broad Reformed tradition. If he is to be distinguished from later Reformed thought, it is on the doctrine of the magistrate, but it would be wrong to regard him as "deviant" for retaining a position which had as yet not been rejected officially in his church. He taught nothing which was not consonant with the thirty-sixth article of the Belgic Confession; in fact, he was teaching precisely what that article contained before it was revised at the Synod of Dort ten years after his death. Even the Dort version, as A. C. Cochrane points out, "is framed on the theory of a union of church and state, and is applicable to Free Churches only so far as they may justly claim from the civil government legal protection in all their rights." [18]

Sin

The other broad area to be studied is the doctrine of salvation. Arminius never departed from the foundations laid in his *Examination of*

[16] Priv. Disp. 57; *ibid.,* p. 140.
[17] *Ibid.,* p. 143.
[18] Cochrane, p. 217.

Perkins' Pamphlet, but he did rephrase his views, elaborate them, and branch out to deal with new issues.

The keystone remains the same: grace is God's affection to man as sinner. His opponents had to deny that premise. Arminius did not mean to exclude a general love of God to all men apart from consideration of man's sin, nor did he mean that the biblical term "grace" is always used to refer to the salvation of sinners. What he meant was that the theological concept of "evangelical grace" presupposes sin. In his *Declaration of Sentiments* he put it again: "In reference to divine grace, I believe . . . it is a gratuitous affection by which God is kindly affected towards a miserable sinner, and according to which he, in the first place, gives his Son, 'that whosoever believeth in him might have eternal life.' " [19]

This implies a doctrine of sin, and since Arminius was so often accused of Pelagianism, his teaching should be examined closely. He describes the fall of Adam as "a transgression of the law which was delivered by God to the first human beings, about not eating the fruit of the tree of the knowledge of good and evil, perpetrated by the free will of man from a desire to be like God and through the persuasion of Satan who assumed the shape of a serpent." [20] The result is that "man fell under the displeasure and wrath of God, rendered himself subject to a double death, and deserved to be deprived of the primeval righteousness and holiness in which a great part of the image of God consisted." [21] The sin of Adam entailed "a liability [*reatus*] to two deaths" and "the withdrawing [*privatio*] of that primitive righteousness and holiness which, because they are the effects of the Holy Spirit dwelling in man, ought to have remained in him after he had fallen from the favor of God and had incurred the divine displeasure." [22]

The sin of Adam, both in the act and in its effects, is common to the whole race which was in the loins of our first parents. Even the punishment incurred by Adam "has likewise pervaded and yet pursues all their posterity, so that all men 'are by nature the children of wrath' (Eph. 11:3), obnoxious to condemnation, and to temporal as well as to eternal death. They are also devoid of that original righteousness and holiness (Rom. 5:12, 18-19) ." [23]

Original sin, then, is an act entailing guilt and penalty, and no man is exempt. But what about actual sins? Must they not be added to original sin before guilt can be ascribed to an individual? When the

[19] *Writings,* I, 253.
[20] Publ. Disp. 7; *ibid.,* p. 480.
[21] *Ibid.*
[22] *Ibid.,* p. 485.
[23] *Ibid.,* p. 486.

synodical deputies posed their nine questions to the Leiden theological faculty in 1605, they set up this question: "Does original sin, of itself, render man obnoxious [*reum*] to eternal death, even without the addition of actual sin? Or is the guilt of original sin taken away from all and every one by the benefits of Christ the Mediator?" [24]

Arminius counters with an opposite question: "If some men are condemned solely on account of the sin committed by Adam, and others on account of their rejection of the Gospel, are there not two peremptory decrees concerning the damnation of men, and two judgments, one legal, the other evangelical?" The problem is in the wording of the deputies' question, he says. It is wrong to say that original sin renders a man obnoxious to death, since "that [original] sin is the punishment of Adam's actual sin, which punishment is preceded by guilt." Original sin is itself the *poena*. As for the universal removal of the guilt of original sin, Arminius says that there *could be* such but there *is* not. Participation in Christ's benefits is by faith alone, hence only believers are delivered from the guilt. [25]

What, then, is the relationship between actual sin and original sin? Strictly speaking, Arminius says, actual sin is the sin of Adam, but in a more common usage it is the sins which men commit by reason of the corruption of their nature, a result of the privation [*privatio*] resulting from original sin. It is *anomia,* transgression, disobedience, or the idolatry of preferring a good which is less than God. "The object of it," Arminius says, "is a variable good to which, when man is inclined, after having deserted the unchangeable good, he commits an offence." [26]

It should be noted that Arminius sees the result of Adam's sin more in privation than in depravation. Linked with this is his avoidance of the term "original sin" (much as he avoided the term "Trinity"). This avoidance is made explicit in Private Disputation 31. If our first parents had continued in the covenant God had made with them, the gifts he conferred on them (eternal life, etc.) would have passed on to their posterity. Due to the fall, "all men who were to be propagated from them in a natural way became liable to temporal death and became devoid of this gift of the Holy Spirit or original righteousness. This punishment is usually called 'a privation of the image of God' and 'original sin.' " [27]

But does not original sin consist of something more than the absence of original righteousness, some depravity which is more than an absence

---

[24] *Nine Questions; ibid.,* p. 381.
[25] *Ibid.,* pp. 381-82.
[26] Publ. Disp. 8; *ibid.,* p. 492.
[27] Priv. Disp. 31; *ibid.,* II, 78-79.

of good? Arminius replies, "We think it much more probable that this absence of original righteousness, only, is original sin itself, as being that which alone is sufficient to commit and produce any actual sins whatsoever." [28]

This is one of the few passages where Arminius uses the term "original sin," and he uses it reluctantly. His view is not explicitly contrary to the received Lutheran and Reformed confessions of the time, as, for instance, the Formula of Concord, Article 1, and the Belgic Confession, Article 15, which speak of original sin in terms of corruption but do not distinguish between the negative and positive aspects of this corruption. It was later dogmaticians who spelled this out explicitly, such as J. A. Quenstedt, who says, "Original sin, formally considered, consists not in a mere want of . . . concreated righteousness, but also in a state of illegality . . . which, in one word, is called a depraved concupiscence." [29]

Heinrich Heppe, for the Reformed, says, "Concupiscence is then the faulty condition of human nature, and is first of all a *privatio justitiae originalis*. But it is not a mere *privatio;* it is simultaneously a positive evil, since it evokes definite effects in man's inner and outer life, to wit, obscuration of the capacity for knowledge, alienation from God and weakness in the will, the enslavement of man by selfishness, generally speaking his spiritual death." [30]

Arminius should not be judged by these later dogmatic developments, especially since he felt that the effect of the *depravity* language could be gained in terms of a simple *deprivation*. The main point for him is that the recipient of evangelical grace is a sinner in desperate straits, involved and caught in the consequences of Adam's sin. His acts of sin are not mere free choices in imitation of bad example but the result of the predicament of man in the fall.

Free Will and Grace

The question of human ability follows, and of free will. What liberty does the will have in a sinful man? Arminius distinguishes five kinds of liberty as applied to the will: freedom from control of one who commands, freedom from the government of a superior, freedom from necessity, freedom from sin and its dominion, and freedom from misery. The first two apply only to God; the last, only to man before the fall.

[28] *Ibid.,* p. 79.
[29] Quoted in Heinrich Schmid, *The Doctrinal Theology of the Evangelical Church,* p. 244.
[30] Heppe, *Reformed Dogmatics,* p. 340.

As for freedom from necessity, it is the very essence of the will. Without it, the will would not be the will. This may sound like Pelagianism, but Arminius goes on to say that the will which is free from necessity may not be free from sin. That is the point in question. "Is there within man a freedom of will from sin and its dominion, and how far does it extend? Or rather, what are the powers of the whole man to understand, to will, and to do that which is good?" [31] The question must be further restricted to spiritual good. The question, then, is briefly: What is the power of free will in fallen man to perform spiritual good? Arminius answers:

In this state, the free will of man towards the true good is not only wounded, maimed, infirm, bent, and weakened; but it is also imprisoned, destroyed, and lost. And its powers are not only debilitated and useless unless they be assisted by grace, but it has no powers whatsoever except such as are excited by divine grace. For Christ has said, "Without me ye can do nothing." [32]

Sinful man, then, has "free will," but not a will that is capable of accomplishing spiritual good, i.e., of doing a meritorious work. His free will is in bondage to sin and needs salvation from outside. Arminius quotes with approval from Bernard of Clairvaux:

Take away free will, and nothing will be left to be saved. Take away grace, and nothing will be left as the source of salvation. This work cannot be effected without two parties—one, from whom it may come: the other, to whom or in whom it may be wrought. God is the author of salvation. Free will only is capable of being saved. [33]

There is nothing here of grace as an *assistance* given to a man who is only weakened by sin.

All response of man to the divine vocation is the work of grace. The entire process of believing—from "initial fear" to "illumination, regeneration, renovation, and confirmation"—is of grace. But one result of gracious renewal is the *cooperating* which man does in believing. When grace has kindled new light and love, etc., man "loves and embraces that which is good, just, and holy, and . . . being made capable in Christ, cooperating [*cooperans*] now with God, he prosecutes the good which he knows and loves, and he begins himself to perform it in deed." [34] The cooperation is not the means to renewal; it is the result of renewal.

[31] Publ. Disp. 11; *Writings*, I, 524.
[32] *Ibid.*, p. 526.
[33] Quoted *ibid.*, p. 531, from Bernard's *De libero arbitrio et gratia*.
[34] *Ibid.*, p. 530.

It is not a meritorious work. Arminius explicitly disavows Pelagianism.

That I may not be said, like Pelagius, to practice delusion with regard to the word "grace," I mean by it that which . . . is simply necessary for the illumination of the mind, the due ordering of the affections, and the inclination of the will to that which is good. . . . I confess that the mind of a natural and carnal man is obscure and dark, that his affections are corrupt and inordinate, that his will is stubborn and disobedient, and that the man himself is dead in sins.[35]

And the saving faith that is exercised in response to grace is peculiarly the act of a sinner. "It is unnecessary to one who is not a sinner, and, therefore, no one except a sinner can know or acknowledge Christ for his Savior, for he is the Savior of sinners." [36]

Synergism

This raises the question of monergism and synergism. Arminianism has usually been described, by its friends as well as its foes, as a synergism. The foes have interpreted this to mean some kind of "co-earning." The self-avowed synergists have sought to avoid that meaning. H. Orton Wiley, for example, who numbers himself among the Wesleyan Arminians, speaks of synergism as a "basic truth of the Arminian system," and defines it as "the co-operation of divine grace and the human will." He is careful, however, to refer the ability to cooperate to the effect of grace, but he ties that effect closely to a general human capacity. "The capacity for religion lies deep in the nature and constitution of man. The so-called 'natural conscience' is due to the universal influence of the Spirit." [37] A similar use of the term "synergism" is found in the nineteenth-century Wesleyan Arminians Miner Raymond and John Miley.[38] Another Wesleyan theologian of the nineteenth century, William Burt Pope, distinguishes between synergism and Arminianism. He feels that the word as used by the Lutheran synergists implies the cooperation of man by virtue of a good nature in him not entirely affected by the fall, and this he does not regard as true Arminianism.[39] Arminius would agree. If the *ergo* (I work) of the synergism is a meritorious work, God does all of that.

---

[35] Letter to H. à Collibus; *ibid.,* II, 472-73.
[36] Priv. Disp. 44; *ibid.,* pp. 110-11.
[37] Wiley, *Christian Theology,* II, 355.
[38] Raymond, *Systematic Theology,* II, 346-47; Miley, *Systematic Theology,* II, 336-37.
[39] Pope, *Christian Theology,* II, 77-78, 389-90, and III, 24-25, 74.

Arminius has affirmed grace to be essential for the beginning, continuation, and consummation of faith. But can it be resisted? It is the question again of a universal call and a special call. Is there a universal call which may be, indeed must be, resisted, and a special call which may be, indeed must be, heeded? Arminius denies the distinction.

Whomsoever God calls, he calls them seriously, with a will desirous of their repentance and salvation. Neither is there any volition of God about or concerning those whom he calls as being uniformly considered, that is, either affirmatively or negatively contrary to his will.[40]

He warns against pleading the cause of grace to such an extent that one takes away the free will to do that which is evil. In the *Declaration of Sentiments* he attacks this point forthrightly, pointing out that injustice is done to grace by ascribing too much to free will. "The whole controversy reduces itself to this question, 'Is the grace of God a certain irresistible force?'" It is not a question of the extent of grace but rather of the mode of its operation. "I believe," he says, "that many persons resist the Holy Spirit and reject the grace that is offered." [41]

There is the point: grace is not a force; it is a Person, the Holy Spirit, and in personal relationships there cannot be the sheer overpowering of one person by another.

Who, then, can believe? It is too simple to say for Arminius that everyone can believe. Only he who does believe can believe. One is reminded of Karl Barth's statement: "The possibility of faith becomes manifest in its actuality." [42] The possibility and the act cannot be separated. Whatever is said about the possibility, however, it is a possibility of grace. Then, in the act of believing, man's will is liberated, and his liberated will concurs in its gracious liberation.

All of this may seem now to be a very crabbed, formal, and stultifying way of talking about God and man. It is indeed a language from another age that we see here. Can its intention still shine through? The intention was both simple and magnificent: that the gospel be truly good news. If man is not in a truly desperate condition, he does not need good news; he can get by with good advice. If the good news is only for a few, he has no hope to match his desperation. Arminius is fighting for the right to proclaim that where sin abounds, grace does

[40] "Certain Articles"; *Writings*, II, 497.
[41] *Ibid.*, I, 253-54.
[42] Barth, *The Knowledge of God and the Service of God according to the Teaching of the Reformation*, p. 109.

much more abound, for every man. That is simple, and that is magnificent.

Justification

Arminius is concerned that the salvation of sinful man not be a fiction. That raises the question of justification. Of what nature is the righteousness in the justified man?

The justification of man before God, for Arminius, is a forensic act whereby God the judge pronounces man righteous and worthy of the reward of righteousness. Since man is a sinner, however, this judgment must be according to the law of faith, not of works. Sinful man is justified by faith, then, but not because faith is the righteousness which man opposes to the rigid and severe judgment of God, but "because it obtains absolution from sins and is graciously imputed for righteousness." [43] Evangelical justification, then, "is a justification by which a man, who is a sinner, yet a believer, being placed before the throne of grace which is erected in Christ Jesus the Propitiation, is accounted and pronounced by God, the just and merciful Judge, righteous and worthy of the reward of righteousness, not in himself but in Christ, of grace, according to the gospel." [44] No matter what endowments of faith, hope, and charity (as virtues) the believer may have, his only hope of justification is that God the Judge "quit the tribunal of his severe justice and ascend the throne of grace."

But is there then any righteousness in the justified sinner? Bellarmine, who was always in the mind of Reformed theologians of this period, had tried to avoid the Pauline term "imputation." Arminius uses it. The righteousness by which we are justified is not inherent. It is imputed, either as that which is righteous "in God's gracious account" (reckoning) or as "the righteousness of another, that is, of Christ, which is made ours by God's gracious imputation." [45]

Arminius' enemies charged him with denying the doctrine of imputation. In the *Thirty-one Defamatory Articles* they accused him of saying: "The righteousness of Christ is not imputed to us for righteousness, but to believe or the act of believing justifies us." [46]

Arminius replies that he has taught that the righteousness of Christ is imputed to the sinner. On the grounds of II Corinthians 5:21 he points out that it is correct to say that the righteousness of Christ is imputed to us, but not that it is imputed to us *for righteousness*.

[43] Publ. Disp. 19; *Writings,* I, 598.
[44] *Ibid.,* pp. 598-99.
[45] *Ibid.,* p. 600.
[46] *Apology against 31 Articles; ibid.,* p. 355.

Rather, the righteousness of Christ is imputed to us, and faith is imputed to us for righteousness. This, he says, is in agreement with both II Corinthians 5:21 and Romans 4.[47] He sums it up in the *Declaration of Sentiments*: "To a man who believes, faith is imputed for righteousness through grace, because God hath set forth his Son, Jesus Christ, to be a propitiation, a throne of grace, through faith in his blood." [48] There, as mentioned earlier, he offers to subscribe to what Calvin had said in his *Institutes*. Calvin says:

We are justified before God solely by the intercession of Christ's righteousness. This is equivalent to saying that man is not righteous in himself but because the righteousness of Christ is communicated to him by imputation. . . . You see that our righteousness is not in us but in Christ, that we possess it only because we are partakers in Christ; indeed, with him we possess all its riches.[49]

Arminius could indeed concur. He was simply trying to guard against two aberrations. On one side, our righteousness contributes to our justification. This Arminius rejected. On the other side, Christ's righteousness is a cloak over our unrighteousness. That Arminius rejected, preferring Calvin's understanding that in the imputation of Christ's righteousness we are partakers in Christ, possessing his riches.

Arminius had to deal also with a subtlety introduced by Johannes Piscator, the Reformed theologian at Herborn. Piscator argued that only the "passive obedience" of Christ is imputed to believers, while his opponents (in the French churches) wanted to include also Christ's "original holiness" and "active obedience." Arminius refused to take sides, and his enemies used this against him.

Sanctification

Justification has to do with a relative change—that is, the change in relation between the believer and God—and as such it deals with the objective side of salvation. What about the real change, the subjective side, commonly comprehended in the terms "regeneration" and "sanctification"? Arminius does not often deal specifically with regeneration; he has no public or private disputation on the topic. He does have some theses on it in his "Certain Articles," but these turn out to cover the same ground as his theses on sanctification and on the perfection of believers. It is under the latter two topics, then, that the real and subjective side of salvation will be discussed.

[47] *Ibid.*, pp. 355-56.
[48] *Ibid.*, p. 264.
[49] *Institutes*, 3.11.23.

Arminius adheres closely to Reformed theology generally in speaking of sanctification, although within that tradition he makes some points more emphatically than others. Sanctification, applied to man as sinner, is

a gracious act of God by which he purifies man who is a sinner and yet a believer from the darkness of ignorance, from indwelling sin [*peccatum inhabitante*] and from its lusts or desires and imbues him with the Spirit of knowledge, righteousness, and holiness, that, being separated from the life of the world and made conformable to God, man may live the life of God, to the praise of the righteousness and glorious grace of God and to his own salvation.[50]

It consists of the death of the "old man" and the quickening of the "new man." This sinner-yet-believer is both contaminated by sin and united to Christ through faith in him. The line between the unregenerate and the regenerate, drawn so sharply in Arminius' earlier *Dissertation on Romans 7*, is here softened. He no longer denies the presence of "indwelling sin" in the believer, or else he has forgotten his youthful distinction between sin as *inhabitans* and *inexistens*. Now he stands squarely with Luther and Calvin in holding to man as simultaneously justified and sinful.

Sanctification, then, is a process of dying to sin and rising to new life, and it is coextensive with the life of faith. "This sanctification is not completed in a single moment, but sin, from whose dominion we have been delivered through the cross and the death of Christ, is weakened more and more by daily losses, and the inner man is day by day renewed more and more, while we carry about with us in our bodies the death of Christ, and the outward man is perishing." [51]

Arminius is obviously not talking about what some later Arminians, the Wesleys and their followers, have called "entire sanctification." He does raise the question, however, and that marks him off from his contemporaries. In a corollary appended to his Private Disputation on sanctification he sets out the question to be discussed: "We permit this question to be made the subject of discussion: Does the death of the body bring the perfection and completion of sanctification—and how is this effect produced?" [52] It is a leading question. If sanctification is a gracious work, how can the enemy death complete it?

Arminius did not answer the question in the context of sanctification itself, but in dealing with another question he incurred the wrath of his theological opponents. The question was: Can believers under the

[50] Priv. Disp. 49; *Writings*, II, 120.
[51] *Ibid.*, p. 121.
[52] *Ibid.*

grace of the New Covenant perfectly observe the law of God in this life? That question was one the synodical deputies wanted to put to the Leiden professors in 1605.

Arminius answers the question at two levels. If it refers to God's requiring obedience "according to rigor," which would involve "the highest degree of perfection," the answer is no. If it refers to God's requiring obedience according to clemency [ἐπιείκειαυ], "and if the strength or power which he confers be proportionate to the demand," the answer is yes.[53]

Arminius knows that this will bring upon him the charge of Pelagianism. He says that he cannot be called a Pelagian so long as he specifies that believers "could do this by the grace of Christ, and by no means without it."[54] He quotes Augustine for support: "provided a man confesses that it is possible to be done by the grace of Christ."[55] In the *Declaration of Sentiments* he quotes Augustine more extensively in his support,[56] and he declares, "But while I never asserted that a believer could perfectly keep the precepts of Christ in this life, I never denied it, but always left it as a matter which has still to be decided."[57]

Arminius is not a perfectionist, preoccupied with the problem. He does not belabor it. "I think the time may be far more happily and usefully employed in prayers to obtain what is lacking in each of us, and in serious admonitions that every one endeavor to proceed and press forward towards the mark of perfection, than when spent in such disputations."[58] His interest in the question came from his controversy with the supralapsarians. This link between predestination and perfection is spelled out in a letter to Uitenbogaert. It is one of his most crabbed arguments, but cogent nonetheless. It defies condensation, and the reader is referred to the source.[59]

Assurance

Arminius felt that supralapsarianism led to either unwarranted security or unwarranted despair. He tried to construct a doctrine of assurance that would avoid these twin errors. One point he wished to establish is that believers may have *present* assurance of *present* salvation. "It is possible for him who believes in Jesus Christ to be certain and

[53] *Nine Questions; ibid.,* I, 385-86.
[54] *Declaration of Sentiments; ibid.,* p. 256.
[55] *On Nature and Grace,* chap. 69 [lix].
[56] *A Treatise on the Merits and Forgiveness of Sins, and on the Baptism of Infants,* Bk. II, chaps. 7 [vi], 8 [vii], 26 [xvii], 34 [xx].
[57] *Writings,* I, 256.
[58] *Apology against 31 Articles; ibid.,* p. 371.
[59] January 31, 1606; *Ep. Ecc.,* no. 81; *Writings,* I, 387-89.

persuaded, and, if his heart condemn him not, he is now in reality assured, that he is a son of God and stands in the grace of Jesus Christ." [60] The absence of such assurance is, in fact, an impossibility. "Since God promises eternal life to all who believe in Christ, it is impossible for him who believes, and who knows that he believes, to doubt of his own salvation, unless he doubts of this willingness of God." [61]

He supports this in his earlier writings with an enthymeme: "I believe in Christ,—therefore I shall be saved." [62] But in the later and more mature *Declaration of Sentiments* there is a more personal and evangelical answer: "Such a certainty is wrought in the mind, as well by the action of the Holy Spirit inwardly actuating the believer and by the fruits of faith, as from his own conscience, and the testimony of God's Spirit witnessing together with his conscience." [63] In pastoral application, such a person should be able "with an assured confidence in the grace of God and his mercy in Christ, to depart out of this life and to appear before the throne of grace without any anxious fear or terrific dread." [64]

There is one important limit to this assurance, however. Arminius sets up two questions:

1. Is it possible for any believer, without a special revelation, to be certain or assured that he will not decline or fall away from the faith?
2. Are those who have faith bound to believe that they will not decline from the faith?

The affirmative, he says, has never been accounted a catholic doctrine in the church, and the negative has never been adjudged by the church universal a heresy.[65] In other words, there is no *present* assurance of *final* salvation.

Perseverance

If there is no present assurance of final salvation, it is because there is the possibility of falling from grace. Arminius' extensive treatment of this in his *Examination of Perkins' Pamphlet* has been discussed earlier. He does not depart from that position in his later writings, but he refines some of his language about it. In the *Declaration of Sentiments* he said that he had never affirmed "that a true believer can either

[60] *Declaration of Sentiments; Writings,* I, 255.
[61] *Nine Questions; ibid.,* pp. 384-85.
[62] *Analysis of Romans 9; ibid.,* III, 540.
[63] *Ibid.,* I, 255.
[64] *Ibid.*
[65] "Certain Articles"; *ibid.,* II, 503.

totally or finally fall away from the faith and perish." [66] Is this a reversal of his position in *Perkins?* He puts the matter cautiously elsewhere: "Believers are sometimes so circumstanced as not to produce, for a season, any effect of true faith, not even the actual apprehension of grace and the promises of God, nor confidence or trust in God and Christ; yet this is the very thing which is necessary to obtain salvation." [67]

This is in line with what he had said in *Perkins,* but has he departed from it in the *Declaration?* The answer is that for Arminius a believer who ceases to trust God is no longer a believer. When asked if believers can decline from salvation, Arminius replied that the possibility, "when rigidly and accurately examined, can scarcely be admitted; it being impossible for believers, as long as they remain believers, to decline from salvation." [68]

But does that mean that the elect become the nonelect? Arminius denies it, for the term "believer" is not exactly equivalent to the term "elect." "Since election to salvation comprehends within its limits not only faith but likewise perseverance in faith, . . . *believers* and *the elect* are not taken for the same person." [69]

In both these questions, assurance and perseverance, Arminius develops Reformed theology in a manner somewhat apart from the later "mainstream," but it is a development of Reformed theology, not an intrusion of Pelagianism or humanism from the outside. And there were many in the Reformed church of his day who agreed with him.

[66] *Ibid.,* I, 254.
[67] *Nine Questions; ibid.,* p. 385.
[68] *Apology against 31 Articles; ibid.,* p. 281.
[69] *Nine Questions; ibid.,* p. 385.

26

PREDESTINATION

PREDESTINATION has been the recurring theme of this entire story. What remains to be done is to look more closely at Arminius' own doctrine of predestination.

His most terse, systematic, and mature statement of his position is that of the *Declaration of Sentiments,* where he defines the doctrine in terms of four divine decrees. These decrees are not intended to be in historical succession but are the *logical order* held to be in the very structure of God's determination concerning sinful man. In the earlier part of his *Declaration* Arminius had criticized his opponents at length. From that criticism there emerge implicitly some parameters within which the four decrees must be defined. Predestination must be understood Christologically; it must be evangelical; it must not make God the author of sin; it must not make man the author of salvation; it must be scriptural, not speculative; and it must not depart from the historic teaching of the church, by which Arminius means the faith of the first six centuries, the confessions of the Reformation, and particularly the Belgic Confession and the Heidelberg Catechism. That is a big order, and here is how he sets about it.

1. *The election of Jesus Christ.* "The first precise and absolute decree of God for effecting the salvation of sinful man is that he has determined to appoint his Son, Jesus Christ, as a Mediator, Redeemer, Savior, Priest, and King, to nullify sin by his death, to obtain the lost salvation through his obedience, and to communicate it by his power." [1] Here is the Christological setting; the object of the first decree is not man, be it *in puris naturalibus,* as uncreated, or even as sinful, but Jesus Christ. He is the one who "obtains the lost salvation." Elsewhere Arminius says,

The love with which God loves men absolutely to salvation [a worthy idiom], and according to which he absolutely intends to bestow on them eternal life,

---

[1] The translation of the four decrees is my own, made from the Dutch text. Cf. *Writings,* I, 247-48.

this love has no existence except in Jesus Christ, the Son of his love, who, both by his efficacious communication and by his most worthy merits, is the cause of salvation, and not only the dispenser of recovered salvation, but likewise the solicitor, obtainer, and restorer of that salvation which was lost." [2]

Jesus Christ, then, is more than a means for carrying out a prior, non-Christological decree. He is more than the executor of the decree. He is the foundation of the decree, so that all election is "in Christ." [3]

It is noteworthy that the first decree is an abolute decree, and, taken in itself, is a single predestination. Thus Arminius can be said to believe in absolute predestination—of Christ. It is a point that Karl Barth rediscovered in the twentieth century.

2. *The election of the church.* "The second precise and absolute decree of God is that he has determined graciously to receive in favor those who repent and believe, and, the same persevering, to effect their salvation in Christ, for Christ's sake, and through Christ, and to leave the unrepentant and unbelieving in sin and under wrath, and to damn them as strangers to Christ." As Christ is the object of the first decree, so those who are "in Christ" are the object of the second. But no one is in Christ except by faith.

This is the predestination of the class of believers, which Arminius had expounded in his exposition of Romans 9. But the class is not a mere aggregate; it is the body of those who are in Christ. The church "is collected through the decree of the gracious mercy of God." [4]

Is the second decree then conditional? Does Arminius make repentance and faith the conditions of salvation? He is aware of the question. There is indeed repentance, but it is not a meritorious work. Man is only the "proximate yet less principal cause" of repentance, who acts as "converted and converting himself by the power and efficacy of the grace of God and the Spirit of Christ." [5] Repentance is a characteristic of the elect without being a meritorious condition of election. The same is true of faith. "We give the name of 'believers' not to those who would be such by their own merits or strength, but to those who by the gratuitous and peculiar kindness of God would believe in Christ." [6]

The first two decrees, then, lay down a doctrine of absolute predestination that has as its object Jesus Christ, and through him, the church. Nothing is said, however, about a decree that certain persons shall be in Christ by faith.

3. *The appointment of means.* "The third decree of God is that

[2] Priv. Disp. 40; *Writings*, II, 100.
[3] *Ibid.*; cf. Publ. Disp. 15, *Writings*, I, 566.
[4] Publ. Disp. 18; *ibid.*, I, 585.
[5] Publ. Disp. 17; *ibid.*, p. 579.
[6] Publ. Disp. 15; *ibid.*, p. 567.

by which he has predetermined to administer the necessary, sufficient, and powerful means of repentance and faith, which administration occurs according to the wisdom of God, by which he knows what becomes his mercy and his severity, and according to his justice, by which he is prepared to follow what his wisdom has carried out." This is a subjoined decree, carrying out what was laid down in the first two. It does not stand in the first place. If it did, the objects of election would be individuals *per se* rather than believers in Christ. Election would be not only absolute but arbitrary, related to no saving purpose, with Jesus Christ the mere means to a predetermined end.

The means are "'sufficient and powerful." The preaching of the gospel is a serious call. Divine mercy and justice are involved. If God is to be both merciful and just, the reprobate must not be denied access to sufficient, powerful means to repentance and faith. The reprobate cannot be damned for disobedience to a call not made to them.

4. *The election of individuals.* "From this follows the fourth decree to save certain particular persons and to damn others, which decree rests upon the foreknowledge of God, by which he has known from eternity which persons should believe according to such an administration of the means serving to repentance and faith through his preceding grace and which should persevere through subsequent grace, and also who should not believe and persevere." Now why did Arminius have to say *that?* This is where all the trouble arises, and from every side. The supralapsarian objections have already been presented: Arminius has reversed the relationship of foreknowledge to predestination. But the objections come in from the other side, too: if God *knows* who will believe, is not the belief or lack of it inevitable, if not predetermined?

Several things can be said in Arminius' defense. First, to omit this article would be to evade the big problem, the predestination of individuals. The predestination of classes is not enough. He has never denied the doctrine of predestination; he has always sought a constructive statement of it. So here, too, he must have a constructive statement. Second, Arminius does not begin with the decree to save or damn particular individuals. He subordinates it to the Christological basis of election; it comes in fourth place, not first. Third, he sets it in a soteriological, not a metaphysical framework. He wants to stay within the limits of biblical language and thought. He is not trying to speculate. Nevertheless, there are problems.

For the modern mind the foreknowledge itself is the problem, a problem that cannot be divorced from metaphysical or ontological questions. This was not a problem for Arminius' opponents; they did not deny foreknowledge. Their only quarrel was over its place in the scheme. Our quarrel is with the concept.

The matter can be approached by going back to Arminius' *Examination of Gomarus' Theses,* and a bit of a digression will be made. Gomarus, in his last (thirty-second) thesis, was struggling with the difficult question (from his point of view) of the human knowledge of divine election, and he had the same problem that Beza had had on the same point. It is intolerable that there should be no knowledge at all in this life of one's election. He proposes an answer:

The particular election becomes known ordinarily to the elect when grown up, in these lands, from a twofold revelation of God: partly external, by the gospel; partly internal, by faith and the Holy Spirit. For the gospel teaches, from the proper effects, *what kind of men God has chosen to life* [italics mine], to wit, believers. . . . And the consent of the Spirit, . . . sealing our hearts with his witness, confirm[s] us that we are believers and penitents.[7]

Arminius was gleeful; for once Gomarus was right. Gomarus had curiously conceded the very basic premise for which Arminius had contended, that election is of believers. This startling capitulation of Gomarus to Arminius seems to have escaped notice at the time and in all subsequent reports of the controversy.

The problem, however, is that Arminius, in the same *Examination of Gomarus' Theses* gives *his* case away! Gomarus, defending his supralapsarianism, had taught that God predestines man to salvation apart from a consideration of man as created. This, said Arminius, is to speak of God's power over a nonentity, which could mean nothing.

God's right over a non-entity, or over what is only possible, is an expression which cannot be used except metaphorically and in a borrowed meaning. For the right or power is the relation between two existences properly, and indeed one that derives its origin from some communication of one to the other. But there is no communication between God and the possible.[8]

Now Arminius rejects the notion of a power relationship between God and a possibility, which is to say a nonentity. But he accepts the notion of a knowledge relationship between God and a possibility, a nonentity, that is, a "future event." He tries to escape:

Since foreknowledge is of future things, strictly speaking, there is no indefinite foreknowledge: for it is knowledge that is indefinite, not foreknowledge: for the particle "fore" restricts the knowledge of *possible* things to the foreknowledge of *future* things, things that shall be.[9]

[7] Quoted in *Examination of Gomarus' Theses; WA,* III, 649.
[8] *Ibid.,* p. 536.
[9] *Ibid.,* p. 535.

He has it quite backward. *Knowledge* is of *entities; foreknowledge* is of *possibilities.* The first is certain; the latter, contingent. And to speak of future things *that shall be* is either a contradiction in terms or a statement of the divine predestination of those things, which would be another kind of contradiction in terms. So while Gomarus, curiously, threw over his whole case in his concession about the *kind of person* who is elected, Arminius threw over his whole case in adding a predestination of individuals on the basis of a necessary foreknowledge of future things *that shall be.*

Most Arminians who have struggled with this problem have followed Arminius in asserting an absolute divine foreknowledge of future contingent events. Daniel Whitby, a fractious but earnest self-styled Arminian of the seventeenth century, had taken the position that divine foreknowledge, which he affirmed, did not cause an event to happen. The event happened freely, that is, contingently. The divine foreknowledge was only of what the free decision would be. Jonathan Edwards, also affirming divine foreknowledge, admitted that foreknowledge is not causal, but he held that if there is foreknowledge, *that* event *would occur.* Hence it could not be said to be contingent.[10]

In other words, to make the assertion is not to solve the contradiction. It only represses the problem of divine predestination into a metaphysical contradiction of necessity and contingency.

Suffice it to say that Arminius is not exactly to be blamed for working within the presuppositions about God and creation, time and eternity, which he held. He shared them with almost all his contemporaries. Only the despised Socinians dared to think in new ways, and he had trouble enough without taking them on.

What must be said is that Arminius had a high degree of success in meeting the criteria which he had established for an evangelical doctrine of predestination. It is Christological—based on Jesus Christ. It is evangelical—the good news of free salvation, God is not the author of sin, and man is not the author of salvation; the Reformation principle of *sola gratia, sola fidei* is maintained. The intent to be scriptural and practical, not speculative, must be honored, conceding that a highly speculative element intrudes into the fourth decree. But at this point he is not to be faulted by his contemporaries. He has defended well his contention that his views had never been condemned by the catholic church and that they were consonant with the Reformation confessions and the Confession and Catechism used in his own church.

He has also, throughout his theology, remembered that theology is practical, not speculative; that it must result in true piety marred

---

[10] Cf. Jonathan Edwards, *Inquiry concerning the Freedom of the Will,* II, sec. 12.

by neither despair nor complacency, contributing to the conversion of sinners, the edification of believers, and the health and peace of the church, and, above all, to the worship of God our Father, who "destined us in love to be his sons through Jesus Christ, according to the purpose of his will, to the praise of his glorious grace which he freely bestowed on us in the Beloved" (Ephesians 1:5-6) .

EPILOGUE

THE STORY that has unfolded here did not end with the death of Arminius, but what followed is beyond the proper scope of this book. It may be of interest to the reader, however, to learn in very brief fashion some sequels to these events. Some of these have been told before; others are told here for the first time.

The year after his death the ministers who felt as Arminius did responded to the invitation of the States of Holland of November 23, 1608, to present their thinking about the Confession and Catechism. Their document, known as the Remonstrance of 1610, was signed by Borrius, Uitenbogaert, Bertius, Grevinchovius, Episcopius, Theophilus Rickwaert, Daniel Wittius, and thirty-seven other ministers not mentioned in this book. From this document they and their supporters became known as Remonstrants, and their (Gomarist) opponents as Contra-Remonstrants. The following years were stormy, marked by theological controversy, political intrigue, and violence. A mob stirred up by Contra-Remonstrant fervor sacked the home of Rem Bisschop in Amsterdam and burned his books (one of the mob thought that he had done it because Bisschop believed in predestination!). With the aid of the magistrates the Remonstrants remained in power in many Dutch cities, but political retribution fell upon them. In 1618 Maurice used the militia to occupy the principal towns of Holland and replace Arminian magistrates with supporters of the Contra-Remonstrants. After the magistracy of the country was purged of its Arminian influence, it proceeded to call the long-awaited national synod. It was held at Dordrecht in 1618-19, under the presidency of the Leeuwarden minister Johannes Bogerman. The Remonstrants were not seated but appeared only as the accused. Their doctrines were condemned; they were forbidden to preach or worship on pain of banishment and confiscation; many of the ministers had to flee the country. Some of them were imprisoned in the Loevestein castle. Hugo Grotius was imprisoned there too, but his wife enabled him to escape by smuggling him out in a book chest.

Oldenbarnevelt was arrested, tried, and convicted of treason, and beheaded publicly in the Binnenhof in The Hague. He was seventy-one years old. He had served his country in the office of grand pensionary for thirty-three years. His story has been told eloquently by John L. Motley.

The Remonstrant exiles, many of whom had gone to Antwerp, constituted themselves as a body under the leadership of Uitenbogaert, Episcopius, and Grevinchovius, among others. Maurice died in 1625 and was succeeded by his brother Frederick Henry, who favored the Remonstrants. They were able to return to the country and formed a religious denomination known as the Remonstrant Brotherhood or the Remonstrant-Reformed Church. It exists to the present time and is notable for its dedication to tolerance and to scholarship. It is unique among religious bodies in that it traces, unofficially but effectively, its "line of succession" through its professor of theology, from Simon Episcopius to the present. His successors include Stephanus Curcellaeus, Philip van Limborch, Abraham des Amorie van der Hoeven, J. J. Wettstein, C. P. Tiele, and more recently, G. J. Heering and G. J. Hoenderdaal, to mention a few.

Arminius' close friend Uitenbogaert died in 1644 at age eighty-eight. There is a fine etching of him by Rembrandt done in 1635. Episcopius died in 1643, Borrius in 1630. The last history of Bertius is not pleasant. He had long been a troublemaker, from his earliest years in the Theological College, where his severity provoked a student riot in which a student was killed in 1594. He became a troublemaker within Remonstrant circles, too, drawing the censure of Uitenbogaert. He then went over to the Contra-Remonstrants, who did not receive him warmly. Finally he went to Paris, returned to the Roman Catholic fold, and died in 1629.

Gomarus left Leiden for Middelburg in 1611, and in 1614 he became professor of theology at Saumur, and then at Groningen in 1618. He attended the Synod of Dort, where his extreme Calvinism was too much even for that body. He taught at Groningen for twenty-two years more, out of the public eye. Hommius was a vigorous Contra-Remonstrant until his death in 1642. Plancius continued to make maps, money, and trouble for the Arminians until his death in 1622. Lubbertus, at Franeker, died three years after Plancius.

Finally, Arminius' family. The curators drew up a resolution of appreciation for the work of Arminius and presented it to Lijsbet. It was signed by Daniel Heinsius. They also provided a grant of 300 guilders to cover the costs of Arminius' burial and to help the family with its financial problems. Lijsbet was permitted to remain in the *pastorie* of the Begijnhof Church, this due to the unwillingness of the designated new tenant, Antonius Walaeus, to evict her, according to one account. Her husband's books, more than 1,200 in number, were

Lijsbet Reael. Oil painting from life, after the death of Arminius.
By permission of the Remonstrant Church, Rotterdam

sold at an auction held in the home beginning on May 26, 1610. Thomas Basson printed the auction catalog. The family lived in the house at least into 1619. Later they appear in a house on the Steenschuur.

Lijsbet was to know a long life but much sorrow, for she outlived most of her loved ones. Pieter died in 1619 at age twenty-two, drowned while swimming in the Vliet, and was buried in the Pieterskerk on June 23. In about the same year Willem, age fourteen, died of tuberculosis. Engeltje married Frans van Noordwijk, of Utrecht, but she died childless in 1625. According to one report, Harmen, Jan, and Jacob all sailed to the East Indies, never to return, for they died there, unmarried, presumably as young men. There is a possibility, however, that Jacob returned and died in Amsterdam in 1636.

Laurens married a girl from a prominent Oudewater family, Cornelia Cuypers, in 1627, and they had five children. A son died unmarried. Their daughter Margarita married the secretary of Oudewater, Dirck Willemsz. Tromper. Their gravestone may be seen in the floor of the choir of the church there. The Trompers' daughter Maria married Dr. Egbert van Veen, of Amsterdam. The van Veens' daughter, Hermina, married the prominent Jacob de Wilde (not the one mentioned early in this book). Laurens' son Jacob married Anna Barlaeus, and his daughter Elizabeth married a cousin, Johannes Rombouts, also a grandson of Arminius. The name Arminius, now a surname for male children and grandchildren, survived only one more generation, although the female line descending from Laurens may have survived for a time under the name Guenellon. Laurens became a merchant in Amsterdam. He died in 1646.

Daniel became a medical doctor in Amsterdam. He married Maria Antonisdr. Regt. They had no children. He died in 1649.

That leaves Geertruyd, who could not remember her father but who became the matriarch of the vast clan of Arminius' descendants. In 1626 she married Jacob Rombouts, later an Amsterdam merchant, and they had five children. From this line Arminius and Lijsbet had twenty-eight great-grandchildren (there were thirty-six in all). The Rombouts' daughter Elisabeth married twice; her second husband was Marten Sorgh, the son of the famous painter Henrick Maertensz. Sorgh (died 1670). Many families come from this line, including the names Beyerman and van der Wallen. The great eighteenth-century Remonstrant professor, Abraham des Amorie van der Hoeven, was descended from the latter line (he was a great-great-great-great-great-great-grandson of Arminius!). There are many descendants today from this and other lines, probably several hundred who can be traced, and countless others.

Some of Arminius' descendants are Dutch, some English, some French, some Spanish, some Indonesian, and some American.

Lijsbet outlived all but two of her children, Daniel and Geertruyd. It is not known when she left Leiden. She may have lived in Utrecht for a time, because Engeltje married a Utrecht man, Geertruyd was married there in 1626, and Lijsbet signed a legal document there in 1627 (it is extant: a transfer of 2,100 guilders to Geertruyd and Jacob Rombouts). Nothing is known of her movements from 1627 until her death in Amsterdam in 1648. At that time she had been living on the Reguliers Breestraat. The modern visitor to Amsterdam will remember it as the short street connecting the Munt Plein with the Rembrandt Plein. Geertruyd also lived on that street, and it may be assumed that Lijsbet was living with her daughter. She thus lived to see Amsterdam at the height of its Golden Age, when the building of the great Town Hall had commenced, and when Rembrandt was flourishing.

She died on March 25, 1648, at the age of seventy-nine, and she was buried on March 28 in the New Church, where her husband had done some of his first preaching sixty years earlier.[1] There is a fine oil portrait of Lijsbet, done from life, in the Remonstrant Church in Rotterdam.

---

[1] DTB 1055/44. Documentation for the other information in this epilogue is in the author's files. It would require another chapter to present it all.

BIBLIOGRAPHY

This bibliography is designed to facilitate reference from footnotes. A key to abbreviations is provided on page 11.

1. *Writings of Arminius Cited in This Book or Used in Its Preparation*

Album amicorum. Manuscript book of poems from Arminius' student days, *c.* 1585. Collection of the Remonstrantse-Gereformeerde Gemeente Rotterdam, in Bibliotheek en Leeszalen der Gemeente Rotterdam.

Verclaringhe. Manuscript of the *Declaration of Sentiments,* 1608. Collection of the Remonstrantse-Gereformeerde Gemeente Rotterdam, in Bibliotheek en Leeszalen der Gemeente Rotterdam.

Iacobi Arminii Veteraquinatis Batavi . . . Disputationes . . . Publicae & Privatae. Leiden: Thomas Basson, 1610.

Verclaringhe Iacobi Arminii . . . Leiden, 1610.

Opera theologica. 2nd edition. Frankfurt: *Prostant apud Guilielmum Fitzerum Anglum,* 1631.

The Just Man's Defence . . . [and *Answers to Nine Questions*]. London, 1657.

Quelques Poésies de Jacques Arminius, Composées pendant son Séjour en Suisse (Carmine Arminii). The Hague: M. Nijhoff, 1925. Ed. by Herman de Vries [de Heekelingen].

The Works of James Arminius, D.D. 3 vols. Vols. 1 and 2, London: Longman, Hurst, Rees, Orme, Brown, and Green, 1825-1828; trans. by James Nichols. Vol. 3, London: Thomas Baker, 1875; trans. by William Nichols.

The Works of James Arminius, D.D. 3 vols. Auburn and Buffalo: Derby, Miller and Orton, 1853. Vols. 1 and 2 contain the translations by James Nichols of vols. 1 and 2 of the London edition, with slight revisions by W. R. Bagnall. Vol. 3 is translated by Bagnall.

The Writings of James Arminius, D.D. 3 vols. Photolithographic reprint of the 1853 edition of the *Works.* Grand Rapids: Baker Book House, 1956.

Verklaring van Jacobus Arminius. Lochem: De Tijdstroom, 1960. Ed. with introduction by G. J. Hoenderdaal.

2. *General Bibliography*

Acta Classis Amsterdam. Manuscript minutes of the Classis of Amsterdam. Archief Nederlands Hervormde Gemeente, Gemeente Archief Amsterdam.

van Aelst, A. C. *Schets der Staatkundige en Kerkelijke Geschiedenis en van den Maatschappenlijken Toestand der Stad Oudewater.* Gouda, 1893.

d'Ailly, A. E. *Historische Gids van Amsterdam.* Amsterdam: Allert de Lange, 1963. Rev. by H. F. Wijnman.

Album Studiosorum Academiae Lugduno Batavae. The Hague: M. Nijhoff, 1875.

Baker, Herschel. *The Wars of Truth*. Cambridge, Mass.: Harvard University Press, 1952.

Bakhuizen van den Brink, J. N. *De Nederlandsche Belijdenisgeschriften*. Amsterdam: Uitgeversmaatschappij Holland, 1940.

———. "Arminius te Leiden." *Nederlands Theologisch Tijdschrift*, XV (1960), 2.

Barbour, Violet. *Capitalism in Amsterdam in the 17th Century*. Baltimore: Johns Hopkins Press, 1950; Ann Arbor: University of Michigan Press, 1963.

Barth, Karl. *The Knowledge of God and the Service of God according to the Teaching of the Reformation*. London: Hodder and Stoughton, 1938. Trans. by J. L. M. Haire and Ian Henderson.

Bertius, Petrus (the younger). *Petri Bertii oratio in obitum reverendi & clarissimi viri d. Iacobi Arminii*. Leiden, 1609.

———. *Petri Bertii Liick Oratie over de Dood vanden Heere Iacobus Arminius . . .* Leiden, 1609.

Beza, Theodore. *A Briefe Declaration of the Chiefe Poyntes of the Christian Religion*. Other data missing from title page; see University Microfilm No. 10, 950.

———. *A Briefe and Pithie Summe of the Christian Faith*. London, n. d. [1565]. Trans. by R. F. [Robert Fyll].

———. *A Booke of Christian Questions and Answers*. London, 1574. Trans. by Arthur Golding.

———. *The Treasure of Trueth*. [1576]. Trans. by John Stockwood.

Biographisch Woordenboek van Protestantsche Godgeleerden in Nederland. 6 vols. The Hague: M. Nijhoff, n. d. [1911 ff.]. Ed. by J. P. de Bie and J. Loosjes.

Blok, P. J. *Geschiedenis van het Nederlandsche Volk*. 8 vols. Vols. 1-6, Groningen: J. B. Wolters, 1892-1904. Vols. 7-8, Leiden: A. W. Sijthoff, 1907-1908.

———. *Geschiedenis eener Hollandsche Stad*. 4 vols. The Hague: M. Nijhoff, 1910-1918.

den Boer, A. W., and Johan Schouten. *Oud-Oudewater*. Oudewater: Stichting Waagebouw, n. d. [c. 1966].

Bonboek. Manuscript, water-color plats. Gemeente Archief Leiden.

Bor, Pieter. *Oorsprongk, Begin en Vervolgh der Nederlandsche Oorlogen, 1555-1600*. 4 vols. Amsterdam, 1679, 1684.

Borgeaud, Charles. *Histoire de l'Université de Genève*. Vol. 1, Geneva: Georg & Co., 1900.

Boxer, C. R. *The Dutch Seaborne Empire: 1600-1800* New York: Alfred A. Knopf, 1965.

Brandt, Caspar. *Historia vitae Jacobi Arminii*. Amsterdam: Martin Schagen, 1724.

———. *Historia vita Jacobi Arminii*. Brunswick, 1725. Ed. by J. L. Mosheim.

———. *The Life of James Arminius, D.D.* London: Ward and Co., 1854. Trans. by John Guthrie.

———. *The Life of James Arminius, D.D.* Nashville: E. Stevenson and F. A. Owen, 1857. Trans. by John Guthrie with introduction by T. O. Summers.

Brandt, Gerard. *Historie der Reformatie en andre Kerkelyke Geschiedenissen, in en ontrent de Nederlanden*. 4 vols. Amsterdam: Jan Rieuwertsz., Hendrik en Dirk Boom, 1671-1704.

Breen, J. C. "Uittreksel uit de Amsterdamsche Gedenkschriften van Laurens Jacobsz. Reael, 1542-1567." *Bijdragen en Mededeelingen van het Historisch Genootschap Gevestigd te Utrecht,* XVII, 1-60.

————. "De 'Kinderlere' van Laurens Jacobszoon Reael." *Nederlandsch Archief voor Kerkgeschiedenis,* VI (1897), 130-57.

————. "Amsterdams Geschiedenis in 1601." *Amsterdamsch Jaarboekje voor 1901,* pp. 25-75.

Breward, I. "The Life and Theology of William Perkins, 1558-1602." Unpublished Ph.D. thesis, University of Manchester, 1963.

Brugmans, H. "De Pest te Amsterdam." *Maandblad Amstelodamum,* IX (1922), 1-3.

————. *Opkomst en Bloei van Amsterdam.* Amsterdam: Meulenhoff, 1944.

Calder, Frederick. *Memoirs of Simon Episcopius.* London: Simkin and Marshall and John Mason, 1835.

Calvin, John. *Commentaries on the Epistle of Paul the Apostle to the Romans.* Grand Rapids: Eerdmans, 1955. Tr. by John Owen.

Calvin, John. *The Epistle of Paul the Apostle to the Romans and to the Thessalonians.* Grand Rapids: Eerdmans Publishing Co., 1961. Trans. by Ross Mackenzie.

————. *Institutes of the Christian Religion.* 2 vols. Philadelphia: Westminster Press, 1960. Trans. by F. L. Battles; ed. by J. T. McNeill.

Catalogus librorum clarissimi viri D. D. Iacobi Arminii . . . . Leiden: Thomas Basson, 1610.

Cellerier, J. J. "Charles Perrot, Pasteur Genevois au XVIᵉ Siècle." *Mémoires et Documents Publiées par la Société d' Histoire et d'Archéologie de Genève,* XI (1859), 32 ff.

Cochrane, A. C., ed. *Reformed Confessions of the 16th Century.* Philadelphia: Westminster Press, 1966.

Crespin, Jean. *Le Livre des Martyrs depuis Jean Husz jusqu'en 1554.* Geneva, 1554, 1555. Latin translation, 1556, 1560. French editions with enlargements, 1570, 1597.

van Dam van Hekendorp, D. W., "Familie-aanteekeningen Rombouts, Arminius, Reael, e. a.," *De Nederlandsche Leeuw,* XLII (1924), 211 ff., 239 ff., 275 ff., 308 ff.

Daniélou, Jean. *Origen.* New York: Sheed and Ward, 1955.

Dickens, A. G. *The English Reformation.* New York: Schocken Books, 1964.

van Dillen, J. G. *Bronnen tot de Geschiedenis van het Bedrijfsleven en het Gildewezen van Amsterdam, 1512-1611.* 2 vols. The Hague: M. Nijhoff, 1929.

————. *Het Oudste Aandeelhoudersregister van de Kamer Amsterdam der Oost-Indische Compagnie.* The Hague: M. Nijhoff, 1958.

van Dis, L. M. *Reformatorische Rederijkersspelen uit de Eerste Helfte der Zestiende Eeuw.* Haarlem, 1937.

Donteklok, Reyner, and Arnold Cornelis. *Responsio ad argumenta quadam Bezae et Calvini ex Tractatu de praedestinatione, in caput IX. ad Romanus.* 1589.

Doop-, Trouw- en Begraafregisters [Baptism, marriage, and burial registers], Gemeente Archief Amsterdam.

van Dorsten, J. A. *Thomas Basson, 1555-1613, English Printer at Leiden.* Leiden: Sir Thomas Browne Institute, 1961.

van Duyn, Arnoldus. *Oudewaterse Moord.* Amsterdam, n. d.; reprinted 1725.

Dyck, Cornelius J. "The First Waterlander Confession of Faith." *The Mennonite Quarterly Review,* XXXVI (1962) , 5-13.

——. 'The Middelburg Confession." *The Mennonite Quarterly Review,* XXXVI (1962) , 147-54.

Edwards, Jonathan. *Inquiry concerning the Freedom of the Will.* New York, 1851.

van Eeghen, I. H. *Inventarissen der Archieven van de Gilden en van het Brouwerscollege.* Amsterdam, 1951.

——. "De Zandhoek." *Maandblad Amstelodamum,* XLII (1955) , 3.

——. "De Operatie en de Restauratie van Damrak 6." *Maandblad Amstelodamum,* LV (Feb., 1968) , 116-18.

Ekker, A. *Berigt omtrent de Latijnsche Scholen te Utrecht over den Cursus van 1863-1864.* Utrecht, 1864.

——. "Theodorus Cornelius Berg, Rector der Hieronymus School te Utrecht van 1573-1575," in *Lijsten van Leerlingen der Hieronymusschool te Utrecht Gedurende de Jaren 1631, 1632, 1658, en 1659.* Utrecht, 1877.

Elias, J. E. *De Vroedschap van Amsterdam.* 2 vols. Haarlem: Vincent Loosjes, 1903-1905.

——. *Geschiedenis van het Amsterdamsche Regentenpatriciaat.* The Hague: M. Nijhoff, 1923.

Enschedé, J. W. "Jan Pietersz. Sweelinck." *Maandblad Amstelodamum,* VIII (1921) , 57-59.

Evenhuis, R. D. *Ook Dat Was Amsterdam.* 2 vols. Amsterdam: W. ten Have, 1965, 1967.

Familie Archief Backer. Manuscript archives of the Backer family. Gemeente Archief Amsterdam.

de la Fontaine Verwey, H. "De Geschiedenis van een Drukkersmerk." *Maandblad Amstelodamum,* XXXV (1948) , 87-89.

Foster, H. D. "Liberal Calvinism; the Remonstrants at the Synod of Dort in 1618." *Harvard Theological Review,* XVI (1923) , 14.

Fruin, R. *Tien Jaren uit den Tachtigjaren Oorlog, 1588-1598.* No publishing data given.

van Gelder, H. E., and J. Duverger, eds. *Kunstgeschiedenis der Nederlanden.* Utrecht, 1954.

Gerlach, H. *Het Proces tegen Oldenbarneveldt en de "Maximen in den Staet."* Haarlem: H. D. Tjeenk Willink en Zoon, 1965.

Geyl, Pieter. *The Revolt of the Netherlands.* 2nd ed.; London: Ernest Benn, 1962.

Glasius, B., ed. *Godgeleerd Nederland. Biographisch Woordenboek van Nederlandsche Godgeleerden.* 3 vols. in 8. 's Hertogenbosch, 1851-1856.

Gomarus, F. *Francisci Gomari VVaerschouwinghe Over de Vermaninghe aen R. Donteclock.* Leiden: J. J. Orlers, 1609.

ter Gouw, J. *Geschiedenis van Amsterdam tot 1578.* 8 vols. plus the printed map of Cornelis Anthonijsz. to accompany vol. 5. Amsterdam: Tj. van Holkema, 1879-1893.

Graves, F. P. *Peter Ramus and the Educational Reformation of the Sixteenth Century.* New York: The Macmillan Co., 1912.

ter Haar, H. W. *Jacobus Trigland.* The Hague: M. Nijhoff, 1891.

Handvesten; ofte Priviligien ende Octroyen; mitsgaders Willekeuren, Costuimen, Ordonnantiën en Handelingen der Stad Amsterdam. Amsterdam, 1748.

Hania, J. *Wernerus Helmichius.* Utrecht: H. Honig, 1895.

Hannay, David. *The Great Chartered Companies.* London: Williams and Norgate, 1926.

Hargrave, O. T. "The Freewillers in the English Reformation." *Church History,* XXXVII (1968), 271-80.

Harrison, A. H. W. *The Beginnings of Arminianism to the Synod of Dort.* London: University of London Press, 1926.

Hemingius, Nicholas. *Tractatus.* Copenhagen, 1591.

Heppe, Heinrich. *Reformed Dogmatics.* London: Allen and Unwin, 1950. Trans. by G. T. Thomson.

Hodgson, L. *The Doctrine of the Trinity.* London: Nisbet, 1943.

van den Hoek Ostende, J. H. *Amsterdam Vroeger en Nu.* Bussum: Fibula-van Dishoeck, 1969.

Hoenderdaal, G. J. "De Kerkordelijke Kant van de Dordtse Synode." *Nederlands Theologisch Tijdschrift,* XXIII (1969), 349-63.

Hooft, P. C. *Neederlandsche Histoorien.* Amsterdam: Louis Elzevier, 1642.

Hooykaas, R. *Humanisme, Science et Réforme, Pierre de la Ramée (1515-1572).* Leiden: E. J. Brill, 1958.

Huwelijksaantekeningen. Manuscript marriage records. Gemeente Archief Leiden.

Index of coats of arms. Centraal Bureau voor Genealogie. The Hague.

Van Itterzon, G. P. *Franciscus Gomarus.* The Hague: M. Nijhoff, 1930.

Kam, J. G. *Waar Was dat Huis in de Warmoesstraat.* Amsterdam: published by the author, 1968.

Kernkamp, J. H. *De Handel op den Vijand, 1572-1609.* 2 vols. Utrecht: Kemink, 1931.

Keuning, J. *Petrus Plancius: Theoloog en Geograaf, 1552-1622.* Amsterdam: P. N. van Kampen & Zoon, 1946.

Knuttel. W. P. C. *Nederlandsche Bibliographie van Kerkgeschiedenis.* Amsterdam: Frederik Muller en Comp., 1889.

————. *Catalogus van de Pamfletten-verzameling Berustende in de Koninklijke Bibliotheek.* 8 vols. in 10. The Hague, 1889-1926.

Kouwenaar, D. "Het Laatste Heerenhuis op het Damrak Verdwijnt." *Maandblad Amstelodamum,* XXIII (1936), 80-81.

Kruimel, H. L. "Het Gebruik van Doopnamen in Vroegere Eeuwen." *Jaarboek, Centraal Bureau voor Genealogie,* XVIII (1964), 131 ff.

Kühler, W. J. *Geschiedenis der Nederlandsche Doopsgezinden in de Zestiende Eeuw.* Haarlem: H. D. Tjeenk Willink & Zoon, 1932.

Lobstein, Paul. *Petrus Ramus als Theologe: ein Beitrag zur Geschichte der Protestantischen Theologie.* Strasbourg: C. F. Schmidt's Universitäts-Buchhandlung, 1878.

Los, F. J. *Grepen uit de Geschiedenis van Hervormd Amsterdam.* Amsterdam, 1929.

Manschreck, Clyde L. *Melanchthon, the Quiet Reformer.* Nashville: Abingdon Press, 1958.

Maronier, J. H. *Jacobus Arminius: een Biographie.* Amsterdam: Y. Rogge, 1905.

Masselman, George. *The Cradle of Colonialism.* New Haven: Yale University Press, 1963.

van Meteren, Emanuël. *Historie van de Oorlogen en Geschiedenissen der Nederlanden.* 10 vols. Rev. ed.; Gorinchem: N. Goetzee *et al.,* 1748-1763.

Meursius, Joannes. *Icones, elogia ac vitae*. Leiden, 1613.

————. *Athenae Batavae, sive de urbe Leidensi et Academia virisque claris* . . . . Leiden, 1625.

Migne, Jacques. *Patrologiae Cursus Completus. Series Latina*. 221 vols. Paris, 1841-1842.

Miley, John. *Systematic Theology*. 2 vols. New York: Hunt and Eaton, 1892.

Miller, Perry. *The New England Mind*. New York: The Macmillan Co., 1939.

Molhuysen, P. C. *Bronnen tot de Geschiedenis der Leidsche Universiteit*. Vol. 1, 1574–Feb. 7, 1610. The Hague: M. Nijhoff, 1913.

Moll, W. "Johannes Anastasius Veluanus en 'Der Leken Wechwyser.'" *Kerkhistorisch Archief*, I (1857), 1-134.

Nichols, James. *Calvinism and Arminianism Compared in their Principles and Tendency: or the Doctrines of General Redemption, &c*. London: Longman, Hurst, Rees, Orme, Brown and Green, 1824.

van Nierop, Leonie. "De Bruidegoms van Amsterdam van 1578 tot 1601." *Tijdschrift voor Geschiedenis*, XLVIII (1933), 337-359; XLIX (1934), 136-160; and following.

Nobbs, Douglas. *Theocracy and Toleration, a Study of the Disputes in Dutch Calvinism from 1600 to 1650*. Cambridge: Cambridge University Press, 1938.

Notariale Archief. Manuscript notarial records. Gemeente Archief Amsterdam.

Ong, Walter J. *Ramus: Method, and the Decay of Dialogue*. Cambridge, Mass.: Harvard University Press, 1958.

Oorthuys, G. *Anastasius' "Wechwyser," Bullingers "Huysboeck" en Calvyns "Institutie" Vergeleken in hun Leer van God en Mensch*. Leiden: E. J. Brill, 1919.

Orlers, J. J. *Beschrijvinghe der Stad Leyden*. Leiden: Henrick Haestens, Jan Orlers, ende Jan Maire, 1614.

Ottley, R. L. *The Doctrine of the Incarnation*. 8th ed.; London: Methuen, 1946.

Oudewater manuscripts from the Gemeente Archief Oudewater.

Oudewater tax records, Staatsarchief, The Hague.

Outler, A. C., ed. *John Wesley*. New York: Oxford University Press, 1964.

Perkins, William. *A Christian and Plaine Treatise of the Manner and Order of Predestination, and of the Largenesse of God's Grace*. London, 1631. Trans. by Francis Cacot and Thomas Tuke.

————. *De praedestinationis modo et ordine et de amplificatione gratiae divinae*. London, 1598.

————. *Works*. London, 1626-1631.

Pers, Dirck Pietersz. *d'Ontstelde Leeuw, of Springhader der Nederlandscher Beroerten*. Amsterdam, 1641.

Petit, L. D. *Bibliographische Lijst der Werken van de Leidsche Hoogleeraren van de Oprichting der Hoogeschool tot op Onze Dagen*. Leiden: S. C. van Doesburgh, 1894.

Pope, William Burt. *Christian Theology*. 3 vols. New York: Phillips and Hunt, 1880.

Praestantium ac eruditorum virorum epistolae ecclesiasticae et theologicae. 3rd ed.; Amsterdam, 1704. Ed. by Philip van Limborch and Christian Hartsoeker.

Protocollen der Kerkeraad Amsterdam. Manuscript minutes of the Consistory of Amsterdam. Archief Nederlands Hervormde Gemeente Amsterdam, Gemeente Archief Amsterdam.

Ramus, Petrus. *Petri Rami Veromandvi, philosophiae et eloqventiae Regii professoris celeberrimi, Commentariorum de Religione Christiani, Libri quatuor, Eivsdem Vita.* Frankfurt, 1577.

———. *The Logike of the Most Excellent Philosopher P. Ramus Martyr.* London, 1581. Trans. by M. Roll.

Raymond, Miner. *Systematic Theology.* 3 vols. Cincinnati: Walden and Stowe, 1880.

Regt, W. M. C. "De Nakomelingschap van Jacobus Arminius." *De Navorscher,* 1919, pp. 193-206.

Reitsma, J., and S. D. van Veen, eds. *Acta der Provinciale en Particuliere Synoden.* 8 vols. Groningen: J. B. Wolters, 1892-1899.

Rogge, H. C. *Caspar Janszoon Coolhaes, de Voorlooper van Arminius en der Remonstranten.* 2 vols. Amsterdam: Y. Rogge, 1865.

———. *Brieven en Onuitgegeven Stukken van Johannes Wtenbogaert.* 3 vols. in 7. Utrecht: Kemink en Zoon, 1868-1875.

———. *Johannes Wtenbogaert en Zijn Tijd.* 3 vols. Amsterdam: Y. Rogge, 1874-1876.

Römer, R. C. H. "Aanbevelingsbrief van Jac. Arminius aan de Stedelijke Regering van Oudewater, voor de Weduwe van Petrus Bertius, Predikant te Rotterdam." *Nieuw Archief voor Kerkelijke Geschiedenis,* I (1852), 174-76.

Rooyboek. Manuscript plat-book of Amsterdam. Gemeente Archief Amsterdam.

Rupp, Gordon. *The Righteousness of God.* New York: Philosophical Library, 1953.

Rutgers, F. L. *Acta van de Nederlandsche Synoden der Zestiende Eeuw.* The Hague: M. Nijhoff, 1889.

Salnar [Francesco Salluardo]. *Harmonia confessionum fidei orthodoxarum et reformatorum ecclesiarum.* Geneva, 1581.

Schaff, Philip. *The Creeds of Christendom.* 3 vols. New York: Harper and Bros., 1877.

Schmid, Heinrich. *The Doctrinal Theology of the Evangelical Church.* 3rd ed.; Minneapolis, 1875. Trans. by C. A. Hay and H. E. Jacobs.

Schotel, G. D. J. *De Invloed der Rederijkers op de Hervorming.* Harderwijk, 1869.

Seeberg, Reinhold. *Text-book of the History of Doctrines.* 2 vols. in 1. Grand Rapids: Eerdmans Publishing Co., 1961.

Selijns, Henricus. "'t Kerck'lijck Amsterdam ofte 't verhael der Roomsche Mysterien ende Ceremoniën, die t' Amsterdam gepleegt sijn voor de Reformatie . . . ." Manuscript from *c.* 1669. Gemeente Archief Amsterdam.

Sepp, Christiaan. *Het Godgeleerd Onderwijs in Nederland Gedurende de 16ᵉ en 17ᵉ Eeuw.* 2 vols. in 1. Leiden: de Breuk en Smits, 1873, 1874.

———. *Bibliotheek van Nederlandsche Kerkgeschiedschrijvers.* Leiden: E. J. Brill, 1886.

———. *Het Staatstoezicht op de Godsdienstige Letterkunde in de Noordelijke Nederlanden.* Leiden: E. J. Brill, 1891.

van Slee, J. C. *De Geschiedenis van het Socinianisme in de Nederlanden.* Haarlem: De Erven F. Bohn, 1914.

Snapper, Frits. *Oorlogsinvloeden op de Overzeese Handel van Holland 1551-1719.* Amsterdam: Ellerman Harms, 1959.

Soermans, Martinus. *Kerkelyk Register van de Plaatsen en Namen der Predikanten . . . van Zuyd-Holland.* Haarlem: Wilhelmus van Kessel, 1702.

————. *Academisch Register . . . der Universiteyt tot Leyden.* Leiden: Hendrik Teering, 1704. Bound with his *Kerkelyk Register.*

Stadsrekeningen 1594-5. Manuscript treasury records. Gemeente Archief Amsterdam.

Strype, John. *The Memorials of Thomas Cranmer.* Oxford, 1812.

Thesaurie Ordinaris, Bagijnen Rapiamus. Manuscript treasury records. Gemeente Archief Amsterdam.

Thommen, Rudolf. *Geschichte der Universität Basel, 1532-1632.* Basel, 1889.

Tideman, Joannes. "Twee Brieven over den Student Jacobus Arminius." *Kerkhistorisch Archief,* III (1862) , 290.

————. "Remonstrantisme en Ramisme." *Studiën en Bijdragen op 't Gebied der Historische Theologie,* III (1876) , 389-429.

————. *De Remonstrantsche Broederschap: Biographische Naamlijst van hare Professoren, Predikanten en Proponenten.* Amsterdam: Y. Rogge, 1905.

van Toorenenbergen, J. J. *Een Bladzijde uit de Geschiedenis der Nederlandsche Geloofsbelijdenis.* The Hague: M. Nijhoff, 1861.

————. *Stukken Betreffende de Diaconie der Vreemdelingen te Emden, 1560-1576.* Werken der Marnix-Vereeniging, Series I, Part II. Utrecht: Kemink en Zoon, 1876.

Trelcatius, L. (the younger). *Scholastica, et methodica, locorum communium S. Theologiae institutio.* Leiden, 1604. English trans., London, 1610.

Triglandius, Jacobus. *Kerckelycke Geschiedenissen.* Leiden: Adriaen Wyngaerden, 1651.

Uitenbogaert, Johannes. *Tractaet van 't Ampt ende Authoriteyt eener Hoogher Christlicker Overheyt in Kerkelike Saecken.* 1610.

————. *Johannis VVtenbogaerts Leven, Kerckelijcke Bedieninghe ende Zedighe Verantwoordingh.* 3rd ed., 1647. Bound with Uitenbogaert's *De Kerck. Hist.,* 2nd ed.

————. *De Kerckelicke Historie.* 2nd ed. [Rotterdam], 1647.

Veluanus, Joannes Anastasius. *Der Leken Wechwyser.* In vol. 4 of *Bibliotheca Reformatoria Neerlandica,* ed. F. Pijper. The Hague: M. Nijhoff, 1906.

Vos Az., G. J. *Voor den Spiegel der Historie, Amstels Kerkelijk Leven van de Eerste Zestig Jaren der Vrijheid.* Amsterdam: G. D. Bom H. Gz., 1903.

de Vries [de Heekelingen], Herman. *Genève: Pépinière du Calvinisme Hollandaise.* Vol. 1, *Les Etudiants des Pays-Bas à Genève au Temps de Théodore de Bèze.* Fribourg: Fragnière Frères, 1918. Vol. 2, *Correspondance des Elèves de Théodore de Bèze après leur Départ de Genève.* The Hague: M. Nijhoff, 1924.

Waddington, Charles. *Ramus, sa Vie, ses Ecrits et ses Opinions.* Paris: Librairie de Ch. Meyruels et Cᵉ, Editeurs, 1855.

Wagenaar, J. *Amsterdam, in zyne Opkomst, Aanwas, Geschiedenissen, Voorrechten, Koophandel, enz.* 4 vols. Amsterdam, 1760-1788.

Walvis, J. *Beschrijving van Gouda.* Gouda, n. d.

Weeskamer Inbrengregister. Manuscript records of finances of the Amsterdam orphanage. Gemeente Archief Amsterdam.

Wiley, H. Orton. *Christian Theology.* 3 vols. Kansas City: Beacon Hill Press, 1940 ff.

Wingren, Gustaf. *Luther on Vocation.* Philadelphia: Muhlenberg Press, 1957. Trans. by Carl C. Rasmussen.

van der Woude, C. *Sibrandus Lubbertus.* Kampen: J. H. Kok, 1963.

INDEX OF PERSONS

INDEX OF PLACES (and EVENTS)

INDEX OF SUBJECTS